Contents at a Glance

W9-DED-787

SAMS
Teach Yourself
CSS
in 24 Hours

Kynn Bartlett

SAMS   800 East 96th St., Indianapolis, Indiana, 46240 USA

Sams Teach Yourself CSS in 24 Hours

Copyright © 2002 by Sams Publishing

International Standard Book Number: 0-672-32409-1

Library of Congress Catalog Card Number: 2002100942

Printed in the United States of America

First Printing: July 2002
Second printing with corrections: December 2002

06   05   04   7   6   5   4

Trademarks

Warning and Disclaimer

Bulk Sales

Sams Publishing offers excellent discounts on this book when ordered in quantity for bulk purchases or special sales. For more information, please contact

U.S. Corporate and Government Sales
1-800-382-3419
corpsales@pearsontechgroup.com

For sales outside of the U.S., please contact

International Sales
1-317-428-3341
international@pearsontechgroup.com

ACQUISITIONS EDITOR
Jill Hayden

DEVELOPMENT EDITOR
Susan Hobbs

MANAGING EDITOR
Charlotte Clapp

PROJECT EDITOR
Matthew Purcell

COPY EDITOR
Michael Kopp
(Publication Services, Inc.)

INDEXER
Jessica Matthews
(Publication Services, Inc.)

PRODUCTION EDITOR
Theodore Young, Jr.
(Publication Services, Inc.)

PROOFREADER
Phil Hamer
(Publication Services, Inc.)

TECHNICAL EDITOR
Marshall Jansen

TEAM COORDINATOR
Amy Patton

MULTIMEDIA DEVELOPER
Dan Scherf

INTERIOR DESIGNER
Gary Adair

COVER DESIGNER
Aren Howell

PAGE LAYOUT
Jennifer Faaborg
Michael Tarleton
James Torbit
(Publication Services, Inc.)

Contents

Part II Core Principles of CSS   79

Hour 5 Selectors   81

Hour 6 The CSS Box Model   103

About the Author

KYNN BARTLETT has been working on the Web since 1994 and is especially interested in universal accessibility. As president of the HTML Writers Guild, Kynn founded the AWARE Center in 1999 to promote accessible Web design, and he teaches online courses in Web accessibility. In addition to writing, speaking at conferences, and teaching online courses, Kynn is the cofounder of Idyll Mountain Internet (`http://www.idyllmtn.com/`), a Web development company. In his free time, he has an assortment of geek hobbies, documented in detail at `http://kynn.com/`. Kynn lives somewhere in southern California with his wife Liz and three large black dogs. You can write to him at `kynn@cssin24hours.com`.

Dedication

For my father, Bud Bartlett, who taught me how to teach.

Acknowledgments

A book isn't really created by the person whose name is on the cover. It's actually the result of a lot of help, encouragement, and support from a sizeable group, and I'm going to take this space to thank them.

First, of course, is my wife and partner Liz, without whose assistance you wouldn't be reading this. The rest of the family—my mom, Vicky; my dad, Bud; my grandmothers, Dot and Dolly; my mother-in-law, PK; my "sister," Eve Shaffer—were very supportive, even if most of them didn't quite understand what I was writing about. Kim, Angie, and Nying, our Tibetan Mastiffs, provided constant encouragement.

As for people who worked on this book, I want to thank Jill Hayden, Suz Hobbs, Marshall Jansen, Molly Redenbaugh, and the whole Sams team. Special thanks to Vicki Harding and everyone at Studio B agency.

The support of my friends has meant much to me. Thanks to my fellow writers Nick Mamatas, Russ Smith, and James Kiley; thanks to Erin Flachsbart, Vernon Lee, Andrew Boardman, Julius Yang, and the rest of the Surly Dinos. Thanks to Sam McLaughlin, Angelo Bongino, Mary Jo Mathews, Darryl Varner, and the rest of the Temecula Writers Group. Thanks to my trainer, Ryan Cisneros. Thanks to the WCAG Working Group, WebAIM, and ICDRI.

Also, in no particular order, thank you to Vadim Plessky, Richard Brinegar, Robin Mueller, Michael Dayah and Halle Berry, Eric Meyer, Joe Crawford, David Poehlman, Dwayne McDuffie, and everyone on my LiveJournal friends list.

Most of this book was written in Temecula, California; thank you to everyone at the TGI Fridays, Barnes and Noble, and Red Robin who provided me with working space, power outlets, and cherry Coke.

Thank you to everyone who chooses peace over violence in a troubled world.

We Want to Hear from You!

As the reader of this book, *you* are our most important critic and commentator. We value your opinion and want to know what we're doing right, what we could do better, what areas you'd like to see us publish in, and any other words of wisdom you're willing to pass our way.

You can e-mail or write me directly to let me know what you did or didn't like about this book, as well as what we can do to make our books better.

Please note that I cannot help you with technical problems related to the topic of this book, and that due to the high volume of mail I receive, I might not be able to reply to every message.

When you write, please be sure to include this book's title and author as well as your name, e-mail address, and phone number. I will carefully review your comments and share them with the author and editors who worked on the book.

E-mail: webdev@samspublishing.com

Mail: Mark Taber
            Associate Publisher
            Sams Publishing
            800 East 96th Street
            Indianapolis, IN 46240 USA

Reader Services

For more information about this book or any other Sams Publishing title, visit our Web site at www.samspublishing.com. Type either the ISBN (excluding hyphens) or the title of a book into the Search field to find the page you're looking for.

Introduction

Way back in 1998, I was all set to teach a course in Cascading Style Sheets through the HTML Writers Guild's online education program; I only needed a textbook—a good guide to learning CSS that I could supplement with learning exercises—and personal advice.

But there simply weren't any such CSS textbooks available at the time.

Eventually I managed to find a book that partially met my needs and the needs of my students—a book that has since become obsolete due to ongoing changes in Web standards and browser evolution—and managed to teach the class. But it left me wondering why there were so few CSS books available. I asked around, and the answer I got was that "CSS isn't ready yet"—browsers didn't support it, Web designers hadn't heard of it, and book publishers weren't interested in it.

Times have changed, thankfully, since those Dark Ages of CSS. All major browsers as well as some minor ones have increased support for Cascading Style Sheets in the latest versions. Web developers are aware of CSS and the vital role they play in designing great Web pages, and presumably you've got some idea of how important they are if you've bought this book. A number of excellent CSS books have been produced over the years, and I hope this book is a notable addition to that collection of worthy works.

The goal of this book is to give you a solid, practical foundation in Cascading Style Sheets. You'll not only learn what the CSS specifications tell you, but you'll also learn how those specs have been implemented in the browsers. In each hour, your knowledge of CSS will increase, and by the time you're done with the book, you'll be quite proud of how much you've learned. More than a reference book, this is a tutorial that will guide you to an understanding of what CSS can do for your Web designs.

How to Read This Book

The title of this book, *Sams Teach Yourself CSS in 24 Hours*, comes with a promise to you, the reader. The promise is that in 24 hours—or less—I'll have you up and running with CSS, producing your own style sheets that rival those of Web grandmasters. To do this, I've broken down that 24-hour period into 24 lessons of one hour or less.

Now, let's be honest—you really should not try to do everything in the book in 24 hours straight. I suppose if you have the stamina, and your loved ones don't mind too much, you *could* try, but really I suggest learning at a pace that's healthy for you and appropriate for your life's schedule. Don't let the title make you think that if you open this book at 10:41 a.m. today, you've got to force yourself to know everything by 10:41 a.m. tomorrow!

This book is divided into four parts. Part I is an introduction to Cascading Style Sheets where you'll learn the basic knowledge you need to understand CSS. Part II covers some of the most important core concepts of CSS, which will help you understand the rest of the book. Part III is the meat of the book (or the tofu patty, for my vegetarian readers)— it goes through every type of style you'd want to set and lays out clearly how to do it. Part IV covers advanced topics in CSS; once you finish this section, you'll know as much as anyone does about Cascading Style Sheets and how to use them.

Other Ways to Use This Book

You don't necessarily have to read through this book in sequential order. Each lesson is designed to stand alone, and you can skip over entire Hours, jump ahead to things that interest you, or go back to pick up something that catches your interest. Naturally, you'll get the most out of the book if you eventually read the whole thing, but often you only have time for the answers, so I've written this book with your needs in mind.

Here are some different ways to use this book:

- To get started quickly, read all of Part I, "Introduction to Cascading Style Sheets," and begin adding styles to your Web pages. Total time commitment: 2 to 4 hours.

- If you've worked with CSS informally before and want to sharpen your skills, jump directly to Part II, "Core Principles of CSS," and Part III, "Styling with CSS." Total time commitment: 7 to 14 hours.

- If you're primarily learning CSS to increase your site's accessibility for people with disabilities—perhaps because of the U.S. government's Section 508 regulations or similar policies—start with Part I, "Introduction to Cascading Style Sheets," skip ahead to Hour 21, "Accessibility and Internationalization," and then jump back to Hour 6, "The CSS Box Model," and Hour 16, "Page Layout in CSS," to learn how to replace HTML <table> code with CSS. Review Appendix B, "Replacing Presentational HTML with CSS." Total time commitment: 4 to 8 hours.

- If you're going to use CSS with XML instead of HTML, read Hour 2, "Getting Started with CSS," and then jump ahead to Hour 24, "CSS and XML." Read all of Part II, "Core Principles of CSS," as well as Hour 19, "Advanced Selectors." Hour 16 and Hour 17, "Advanced CSS Layout," will prove most useful from Part III. Read Appendix A, "How to Read W3C Recommendations." Total time commitment: 5 to 8 hours.

- To become a true expert on CSS, read the whole book! It's not that difficult, and you'll soon be the envy of your fellow Web designers who are not as well read. Total time commitment: 12 to 24 hours.

What's in Each Hour

To make it easy for you to learn exactly what you need to learn, each Hour is structured along the same basic outline.

At the start of each Hour, I'll tell you exactly what you'll learn in the next 60 minutes. Then we launch into the body of the lesson with plenty of examples and illustrative screenshots. At the end, I'll summarize the material to help put everything in perspective.

Starting with Hour 3, "Browser Support for CSS," I'll provide you with a "report card" on the CSS features covered in that chapter. This will let you see at a glance which CSS properties are safe to use across all browsers and which you'll want to be careful about.

The Q&A section at the end of each Hour is a mini-FAQ, answering Frequently Asked Questions you may have.

The Workshop is designed to be completed within the hour of time you've set aside for each lesson and is a way to test and apply the knowledge you've gained. The Activities section suggests step-by-step exercises to learn more about the topic, and Quizzes enable you to self-test your mastery of the subject.

Who Should Read This Book

I'm going to assume that you know the basics of HTML and have created Web pages before; that you know how to run a text editor, save files and publish them on the Web, and do all the normal tasks related to making a Web site. If the concept of Web design is completely new to you, Sams publishes some excellent introductory books, including *Sams Teach Yourself HTML and XHTML in 24 Hours*.

As you go through the 24 lessons of this book, you'll learn practical CSS that you can immediately put into practice. By the time you finish the whole book, you'll know everything you need to know about Cascading Style Sheets, from browser support to the most effective ways to integrate CSS into your Web development process. We'll make an expert out of you, in 24 hours or less!

What You Need

To display your CSS-based Web designs, you'll need a Web browser that has a reasonably good implementation of the Cascading Style Sheets specifications. The following browsers are recommended; you should have at least one of the following browsers installed on your system:

- Internet Explorer 6.0 (or higher) for Windows (`http://www.microsoft.com/windows/ie/`)
- Internet Explorer 5.1 (or higher) for Macintosh (`http://www.microsoft.com/mac/`)
- Netscape 6.2.1 (or higher) for Windows, Macintosh, or Linux (`http://www.netscape.com/`)
- Opera 6.0 (or higher) for Windows (`http://www.opera.com/`)
- Opera 5.0 (or higher) for Macintosh or Linux (`http://www.opera.com/`)
- Mozilla 0.9.7 (or higher) for Windows, Macintosh, or Linux (`http://www.mozilla.org/`)

These are most recent versions of each browser at the time this book is being written, and offer the highest level of support for CSS to date. Check the appropriate Web sites for newer updates of these browsers.

You will probably want to maintain a suite of additional browsers for testing purposes; older browsers have varying degrees of support for CSS. You'll learn more about browsers and their CSS implementations in Hour 3 of this book.

In addition, you'll need some kind of editing software that allows you to create text files. This could be something as simple as TextEdit or NotePad or as complex as an integrated Web development suite. Any HTML editor that enables you to edit the source code will work as a CSS editor; as I'm assuming you can create HTML files, anyone reading this book should have access to a text editor. In Hour 2, I'll give you some specific pointers to CSS editors.

The CSSin24hours.com Web Site

This book has a companion site maintained by the author—that's me—at `http://www.CSSin24hours.com/`. At that site, you'll find

- Downloadable copies of all code samples in the book
- Live links to URLs quoted in each Hour
- News on CSS standards and browser support
- Style sheets you can download and use
- Extra tips and advice from CSS experts
- Updates and additions to book material

Conventions Used in This Book

To make this book easier to understand, different typefaces are used in each Hour to identify specific types of information.

New terms are set off in *italics* when they're first defined.

CSS rules, properties, and values; HTML elements, attributes, and values; and other snippets of code are presented in a monospace font, `like this`. Placeholder values are shown in `italic monospace`. Longer code appears in a formal listing, which is also available on the Web site. For example:

LISTING 0.1   Code Listing Example

```
body
{
    color: white;
    background-color: maroon;
}
```

In addition, there are several boxed elements that appear throughout the book: Notes, Tips, and Cautions.

A *Note* is a short side comment from me that provides additional information or calls attention to something important. I'm usually chattier in a note than I am in the body of each Hour.

A *Tip* is a useful bit of advice that may not be immediately obvious. The most common types of tips you'll find in this book will be *workarounds*. A workaround is a tip that tells how to change your CSS or HTML to account for browser deficiencies. Each workaround begins with a short statement of which browsers the tip accounts for.

A *Caution* is exactly what it sounds like—it's a classic "Danger, Will Robinson!" warning alarm. If there's a possibility of you turning down the wrong path, I'll be there to steer you clear of it.

Ready, Set, Go!

Are you eager to start? Ready your browser, sit yourself in front of your computer in a comfortable position, and go on to the first hour!

Let me know how well you've done at teaching yourself Cascading Style Sheets; drop me an e-mail at kynn@CSSin24hours.com. I'll try to respond to each letter, although I can't guarantee I'll be able to give personal advice to everyone. By the time you finish this book, you'll know as much about CSS as I do!

Good luck, and have fun styling!

—Kynn Bartlett

PART I

Introduction to Cascading Style Sheets

Hour

Hour 1

Understanding Cascading Style Sheets

Cascading Style Sheets (CSS) can open up a whole new dimension to your Web designs, delivering power and flexibility beyond what's available in plain HTML.

In this introductory hour, you'll learn

- What style sheets are and what the term "cascading" refers to
- How the Cascading Style Sheets standard was written and what the two levels of CSS refer to
- How CSS is used with HTML and XML and when to use it
- The types of style effects you can produce with CSS and what you can't do
- How browser support for CSS affects what you can do with style sheets

What Are Cascading Style Sheets?

Cascading Style Sheets is the name of a simple language that allows you to declare how documents are displayed by Web browsers. This language is used extensively on the Web and can be applied to HTML as well as newer XML-based languages.

Through the application of CSS, you're able to change many aspects of how a Web page is displayed—the fonts, the colors, the layout, the graphics, the links, and more. Cascading Style Sheets allow for separation of content—your HTML markup, text, graphics, and multimedia—from presentation.

Defining Style Sheets

The concept of style sheets did not originate on the Web; it has been used extensively in computing for years now. The most familiar application of style sheets off the Web is the formatting styles used in word processors, such as Microsoft Word.

Microsoft Word allows you to assign parts of your file to specific styles, such as "Heading" or "Note," and then decide what sort of formatting should be applied to each style. For example, a Heading style should be larger and bold, with extra line spacing after the heading and in a specific heading font. This book, in fact, was composed in exactly that way; each part of the book, from headings to text paragraphs to tips and notes, has a specific style that I've set as I composed the manuscript, and those styles eventually determined how you see the printed page today.

In the same way, Cascading Style Sheets let you, the Web designer, assign specific styles to different types of HTML elements. You might want to make all of your text one color, to make all of your headings a specific font, and to specify that all notes should be centered in a box with a thin outline. You can do some of this in HTML using `<font>` tags and various attributes, but that can get cumbersome and difficult to maintain. When you define your presentation styles in CSS, it becomes quick and easy to apply new styles that can affect all styles on a page or even the whole site—without having to edit the source HTML at all!

Defining Cascading

The term "*Cascading*" in Cascading Style Sheets refers to a specific way in which browsers determine which styles to apply to a specific part of the page. This method is called "the cascade," and it's from the cascade that CSS takes its name.

When I'm designing something that I know is going to be used in a fixed medium, such as the printed page or this book, I can be pretty confident that the styles that I choose will show up exactly like I expect them to. All copies of this book will look exactly the same; the page layout won't vary from reader to reader, and the same fonts will appear in each copy. Page 57 of your copy of this book is identical to every other page 57 in existence.

When you're designing for a variable medium such as the Web, however, you don't have that certainty. The appearance of a Web page (designed with CSS or not) depends on a number of factors, including the characteristics of the user's display device, their computer's color resolution, the version of the browser they're using, and even their preferred font size.

> Some users might not even be using monitors at all! People with visual disabilities routinely use the Web as a primary source of information, relying on software known as screenreaders, which vocalize the content of a page. You'll learn more about how CSS benefits users with disabilities in Hour 21, "Accessibility and Internationalization;" you can also read more at the International Center for Disability Resources on the Internet Web site at `http://www.icdri.org/`.

This lack of absolute control over the final presentation can be somewhat disconcerting for designers who are used to fixed mediums; how can you fine-tune your design if you don't know how it will eventually look? It's important to keep in mind that this isn't a design flaw in CSS—it's a deliberate feature. Creating designs that adapt to the user's environment and preferences widens your audience and enables more people to access your content.

The *cascade* is the set of principles that tells browsers how to merge together a number of presentation choices: the Web developer's designs for the site, the Web browser's capabilities and default settings, and the Web user's preferences or requirements for display. In the cascade, items that are higher up in priority affect other properties with lower priorities, with the values "cascading" down like a waterfall. You'll learn more about this in Hour 7, "Cascading and Inheritance," but for now it's enough to understand that in CSS, the final presentation is an active collaboration between designer, browser, and user.

The Origin of Cascading Style Sheets

The Cascading Style Sheets language was created through a collaborative effort between Web developers and browser programmers under the auspices of the World Wide Web Consortium (W3C for short).

The W3C is an international industry group that comprises over 500 companies, research institutions, and Web development organizations that issues technical specifications for Web languages and protocols.

W3C specifications are called "recommendations" because the W3C is technically not a standards-issuing organization, but in practice this is usually an issue of semantics. W3C recommendations are taken as defining a standard form of a Web language, and they are used by Web developers, software tool creators, browser programmers, and others as a blueprint for computer communication over the Web. Examples of W3C recommendations include Hypertext Markup Language (HTML), Extensible Markup Language (XML), Extensible Style Language (XSL), and Scalable Vector Graphics (SVG).

The CSS Specifications

The W3C Recommendations issued by the Cascading Style Sheet working group compose the official specification for the CSS language. The CSS working group consists of a number of experts in Web development, graphic design, and software programming, representing a number of companies, who all work together to establish a common styling language for the Web.

Two full Recommendations have been issued for Cascading Style Sheets so far; these are called Cascading Style Sheets Level 1 and Cascading Style Sheets Level 2. Work is under way currently on Cascading Style Sheets Level 3, but these are only draft proposals at the time of writing.

CSS Level 1

The Cascading Style Sheets Level 1 (sometimes called CSS1 for short) was officially issued as a W3C Recommendation in December 1996. The URL for this specification is `http://www.w3.org/TR/REC-CSS1`.

> If you try to read the W3C Recommendation for CSS1, you may end up confused. That's because W3C documents aren't written as a general introduction to a subject but rather as precise language definitions for software developers. Most W3C Recommendations are quite opaque to most normal people, although the CSS1 specification isn't too bad compared with some. Being able to refer to the official specification is quite useful, though, so in Appendix A, "How to Read W3C Recommendations," I've given some useful advice about how to understand "W3Cese" and read a W3C Recommendation.

CSS Level 1 defines a number of simple text formatting properties, along with properties for colors, fonts and boxes, principles of the cascade, and the linking mechanism between CSS and HTML. CSS1 may be used to create some impressive results, but it doesn't deliver the full range of function found in CSS Level 2.

CSS Level 2

CSS Level 2 was published in May 1998 (at http://www.w3.org/TR/REC-CSS2) and extends the power of CSS considerably. CSS Level 2 provides the Web developer with the ability to use CSS to lay out a page, replacing HTML tables; to create style sheets for specific output devices, such as printers or even Braille devices; to have fine control over which parts of the page receive styling; and to designate a wider range of effects, such as text shadows or downloadable fonts. CSS Level 2 includes and extends all properties and values defined in CSS Level 1.

In this book, I won't make a distinction between a property that originated in CSS Level 1 and CSS Level 2; Level 2 is the current standard and the definitions in CSS2 supercede those in CSS1.

Other Style Languages

CSS isn't the only style language, but it's the primary one used on the Web. Some other style languages include Document Style Semantics and Specification Language (DSSSL) and Extensible Style Sheets (XSL).

DSSSL is an older and more complex styling language developed for Standard Generalized Markup Language (SGML), an ancestor of XML and the basis for HTML syntax. DSSSL is rarely used on the Web, just as non-HTML SGML is quite uncommon.

XSL is a group of related languages intended for styling XML documents. *XSL Transformations (XSLT)* is a method to describe a transformation from one XML-based language to another. XSL Formatting Objects (XSL-FO) is one such language; an XML document can be converted to XSL-FO using XSLT. XSL-FO files contain XML formatting objects, which can be used by browsers or printing software to precisely lay out the appearance of a document, most commonly for print media.

CSS in Web Design

Because the Cascading Style Sheets language was designed to be used primarily with HTML, CSS is ideally suited for use in Web design. The language is simple and flexible enough to encompass all common Web presentation effects, and the concepts should be familiar to anyone who has used HTML before. To use the CSS language effectively, it's important to understand how it's used, what it can do, and what it can't do.

How CSS Is Used

In CSS, the term style sheet refers to a file consisting of a number of CSS rules. A *rule* is the smallest unit of CSS, defining one or more style effects. Each rule identifies which parts of the Web page it selects and what properties it applies to that section of the page. The Web document then links to that style sheet, which means the browser will download the style sheet and apply the rules when it displays the Web page. A single CSS file can be linked to by any number of documents, so one style sheet can control the look of the entire site or a portion thereof.

CSS can be used with several different markup languages, including HTML and XML-based languages.

CSS and HTML

The *Hypertext Markup Language* (*HTML*) consists of a series of tags that mark up specific elements within a document. Each of those elements has a default presentation style, which is provided by the browser, based on the formal specification for HTML. A style sheet can be applied to an HTML page by linking to it or even by including the style sheet within the HTML file, and the presentation style for each element could be redefined.

For example, a style sheet could be created that states that all <h1> tags should be presented on a green background with white text. This would change the appearance of any Web page that links to that style sheet.

For example, CSS is used extensively to define the color and look of the HTML Writers Guild's Web site (http://www.hwg.org), although the layout is done with traditional HTML tables instead of CSS positioning. We'll look at the HWG home page, both with and without style sheets, to see what kinds of effects are possible with CSS.

In Figure 1.1, no style sheet has been applied to the Guild's site, and so the appearance is quite plain. Few HTML attributes have been used for formatting, since the site relies on Cascading Style Sheets for presentation effects. The fonts are all browser defaults and the colors are very basic. Despite the somewhat boring appearance, all information is clearly visible and the page can be used easily. All that it needs is a style sheet to make it look better.

Figure 1.2 is the HWG site as it appears in a browser that understands Cascading Style Sheets. The Guild's style sheet not only specifies more attractive fonts for the page, but it also casts the entire site in the HWG's green and tan colors. The navigation bar on the left hand has been styled to look like a set of three-dimensional buttons, and important text on the right has been set aside in boxes to draw attention. The overall effect of the style sheet is to enhance the appearance considerably, making the site appear more friendly, identifiable, and usable.

FIGURE 1.1

The HTML Writers Guild's Web site without CSS.

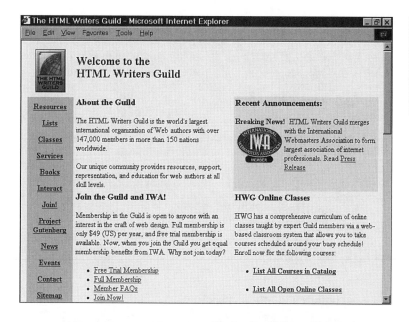

FIGURE 1.2

The HTML Writers Guild's Web site with the HWG style sheet applied.

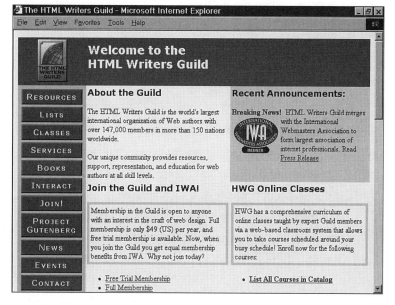

HTML pages can contain attributes and tags that set presentational styles, but their versatility and utility are limited compared with CSS. Style sheets can be used either in conjunction with HTML presentational markup, such as `<font>` or `color="red"` attributes, or can replace presentational tags and attributes entirely.

CSS and XML

Cascading Style Sheets are also designed to work with *Extensible Markup Language* (*XML*). XML languages often don't have an inherent presentation defined, and CSS files can be applied directly to XML files to add presentational styling.

 For most of this book, I'm going to assume you're using CSS with HTML. The techniques for using CSS with XML are pretty much the same as using CSS with HTML. Specific issues related to XML will be covered in Hour 24, "CSS and XML."

What CSS Can Do

As you see on the HTML Writers Guild site, the application of a style sheet can drastically change the appearance of an HTML page. CSS can be used to change anything from the styling of text to the layout of the page and can be combined with JavaScript to produce dynamic presentation effects.

Text Formatting and Colors

CSS can be used to produce a number of text effects, such as

- Choosing specific fonts and font sizes
- Setting bolds, italics, underlines, and text shadows
- Changing text color and background color
- Changing the colors of links or removing underlining
- Indenting or centering text
- Stretching and adjusting text size and line spacing
- Transforming sections of text to upper-, lower-, or mixed-case
- Adding drop-capitals and other special effects

These are all accomplished by creating CSS rules to set properties on text.

Graphical Appearance and Layout

CSS can also be used to change the look of the entire page. CSS properties for positioning—sometimes called CSS-P—were introduced in CSS Level 1 and allow you

1

to format a Web page without using tables. Some of the things you can do with CSS to affect the graphical layout of the page include

- Setting a background graphic and controlling its location, tiling, and scrolling
- Drawing borders and outlines around sections of a page
- Setting vertical and horizontal margins on all elements, as well as vertical and horizontal margins for the page
- Flowing text around images, or even around other text
- Positioning sections of the page in precise locations on the virtual canvas
- Redefining how HTML tables and lists are presented
- Layering page elements atop each other in a specified order

Dynamic Actions

Dynamic effects in Web design are those that are interactive, changing in response to being used. CSS lets you create interactive designs that respond to the user, such as

- Mouseover effects on links
- Dynamically inserted content before or after HTML tags
- Automatic numbering of page elements
- Fully interactive designs in Dynamic HTML (DHTML) using JavaScript

What CSS Can't Do

Although CSS is powerful, it does have certain limitations. The primary limitation of CSS is that it is restricted to mainly working with only what is present in the markup file being styled. The display order can be somewhat altered, and a small amount of text content can be inserted, but to produce major changes in the source HTML (or XML), you'll need to use another method—such as XSL Transformations.

Also, CSS is a younger language than HTML by about five years; this means that some of the oldest browsers won't understand styles written in CSS, or might not load a style sheet at all. CSS is also of limited use on simple text browsers, such as those written for cell phones or mobile devices.

The Cascading Style Sheets language was designed to be backwards compatible, which means older browsers won't refuse to show your Web page if they aren't able to display your styles. Instead, the default HTML presentation will be used, and if you've designed your CSS and HTML properly, the page content will be usable even if your CSS styles aren't shown. This allows older browsers to access even advanced CSS pages.

When to Use CSS

Once you start learning to create Cascading Style Sheets, you probably will never want to stop using them! You can start using CSS today, as a supplement to your presentational markup, and then gradually move toward purer CSS presentations as you learn more.

Browser Support

Unfortunately for those of us who want to reap the full benefits of using CSS, the browser manufacturers were slow in providing support for CSS in their software. This meant that people who programmed authoring software didn't bother to produce CSS (after all, which browsers could display it?) and Web developers didn't bother to learn CSS, since it was a pointless exercise.

Early browsers that understood Cascading Style Sheets, such as Internet Explorer 3 and Netscape 4, had only incomplete implementations, meaning that even simple style sheets using rules defined in CSS1 might not display consistently. This meant that CSS was considered unreliable for several years after the Recommendations were issued.

Thankfully, the Dark Age of CSS didn't last forever, and current browsers have decent support for the CSS standards. The newest versions of Netscape, Mozilla, Internet Explorer, and Opera all have good implementations of the Cascading Style Sheet specifications. We're on the cusp of a new age of CSS, one where you can design safely and confidently, knowing that your style sheet won't confuse some old browser with buggy CSS implementations.

Workarounds for Browser Limitations

However, those older browsers still exist and are used by a number of Web surfers, despite the poor support for CSS. Furthermore, not even the newest browsers adhere 100% to the specifications, although they come very close.

For these reasons, it may be necessary to employ workarounds in your CSS or HTML to ensure that your style effects come through as intended. In this book I've identified known problems with CSS implementations, and whenever possible, I've provided you with the tips and tricks you need to compensate for browser limitations.

Summary

Cascading Style Sheets are files that describe how to present specific effects when displaying a Web page. They're named because they follow a specific pattern, called

1

the cascade, which determines the order in which style effects are applied. The CSS language is a Web standard, defined by the World Wide Web Consortium; the current version is CSS Level 2.

A style sheet consists of CSS rules that define styles to apply to specific parts of the page. Style rules can change the color, font, and other qualities of the text of a page; they can define the layout and graphical appearance; and they can add interactivity to a site.

Although Cascading Style Sheets are quite powerful and useful, care needs to be taken to apply them in ways consistent with current browser implementations. Not all browsers have good CSS support, and using CSS without understanding the support issues can lead to problems. This book provides workarounds and warnings related to known browser problems.

Q&A

Q Which version of CSS should I use, CSS1 or CSS2?

A Cascading Style Sheets Level 2 is the most current W3C recommendation; it contains all of the CSS1 properties and gives more complete definitions for them, in addition to defining new properties that weren't included in CSS1. Very few browsers (if any) supported only CSS1; most of them either supported a subset of CSS1 or a set chosen from CSS1 and CSS2 properties, so the division between the two is not really meaningful when looking at browser support. For these reasons it's best to simply treat the CSS2 specification as a replacement for CSS1. This book will teach you CSS Level 2.

Q So what's so cool about CSS anyway?

A Because Cascading Style Sheets let you encode your style effects separately from your HTML, this promotes separation of presentation and content. This means that the look of the page can be created independently from the information on the page, and that's cool for a number of reasons. You can create a single style sheet that styles the entire site at once. You can develop alternate style sheets for specific output devices, such as printers. You can ensure greater accessibility for people with disabilities. In addition, Cascading Style Sheets also afford a measure of control over the presentation, which simply is not available in traditional HTML Web design.

Q What's the most important thing to know about Cascading Style Sheets?

A Browser support is the critical issue in CSS design. You will see this theme repeated throughout the book. Lack of browser support has seriously hindered the use of CSS, and many of the really great things you can do with style sheets continue to be limited in many browsers. That's why I spend so much time on workarounds and warnings; I'll tell you exactly which CSS rules you can count on, and which ones you need to avoid using.

Workshop

The workshop contains quiz questions and activities to help reinforce what you've learned in this hour. If you get stuck, the answers to the quiz can be found after the questions.

Quiz

1. What is the cascade in CSS?
2. Which markup languages can be used with CSS?
3. What's the current version of Cascading Style Sheets?

Answers

1. The cascade is the set of rules that order how style preferences are combined together. The effects of higher priority rules cascade down like a waterfall.
2. CSS was designed to work with HTML as well as with any XML-based markup language.
3. The current version of Cascading Style Sheets is CSS Level 2, although Level 3 is under development.

HOUR 2

Getting Started with CSS

Creating a style sheet is simply a matter of creating a file of CSS rules and then applying them to an HTML file.

In this hour, I'll take you through the whole process, and you'll learn

- What kinds of tools, from text editors to CSS software, you can use to write your style sheets
- How to create, name, and save a style sheet
- What the different parts of a CSS rule are and the function of each
- How and when to add comments to a style sheet
- Which simple rules you can use to create a basic style sheet
- How to apply your style sheet to a simple HTML file
- Which browsers to use to test your style sheet

Creating a Style Sheet

A Cascading Style Sheet, as you learned in Hour 1, "Understanding Cascading Style Sheets," is simply a file made up of style rules. CSS files are ordinary text files, just like HTML files are ordinary text files. This means that you can use a wide variety of programs to create a style sheet, from simple text editors to specialized software written just for creating and maintaining style sheets. Anything that can be used to create a text file can create a style sheet.

Because Cascading Style Sheets are pretty simple to write, you don't have to have use complex tools to create a basic style sheet. Many Web developers will write CSS by hand, meaning that they type out the text of each rule; however, authoring tools exist that can make this task easier.

Software Tools for CSS

Your editing environment is the program or set of programs that you use to create your style sheet. You'll want to choose the editing environment that works best for you, be that a text editor, a style sheet editor, or a Web development tool. I use a text editor myself, and I recommend starting simple, at least until you've learned enough about the basics of CSS to understand how editing tools can help you.

Text Editors

Every operating system comes with a basic text editor, and because CSS is just basic text, it's a good match for one of these programs. A text editor is a simple program that just produces plain text files, which means it can also be used to create HTML or CSS files. Unlike word processing software, text editors don't save formatting with the text; that's why they are said to produce plain text. Text editors are ubiquitous and won't get in the way of learning about CSS, so this is probably where you want to start. You probably already know how to use one of the text editors on your computer. Some basic text editors include

- Notepad or WordPad on Microsoft Windows
- SimpleText or TextEdit on Macintosh
- vi, vim, or emacs on Linux or Unix

Figure 2.1 shows a style sheet being edited in Notepad on Windows; this is the style sheet from the HTML Writers Guild's Web site, which was shown in Hour 1. Don't worry too much about reading and understanding the properties; the Guild's style sheet is rather complex and has a lot of properties from the middle or end of this book.

FIGURE 2.1

Editing a style sheet using Notepad.

```
hwg.css - Notepad                                         _ B X
File  Edit  Search  Help
   clear: both;
}

DT, .heading, H2, H3, H4, H5, H6 {
   font-family: Verdana, Arial, Geneva, Helvetica, Sans-Serif;
}

/* The following try to address a problem in IE 3.0, it seems to have worked */

.content A:link {
   color: #000099;
}

.content A:visited {
   color: #990099;
}

.content A:active {
   color: #990000;
}

/* end of test */

/* Location Bar */
.locbar {
   font-size: smaller;
   font-family: Verdana, Arial, Geneva, Helvetica, Sans-Serif;
   background-color: #006666;
   padding: 2px;
   color: white;
}

.locbar A:link, .locbar A {
   color: white;
   font-weight: bolder;
   text-decoration: none;
```

2

You can use a word processing program, such as Microsoft Word, to create text files, but you need to remember to save your files as plain text without any special formatting. It's probably easier to just use a text editor, although most of them lack the advanced features found in word processors, such as advanced find-and-replace and word counting. Fortunately, you'll rarely need those features when editing CSS.

Style Sheet Editors

Some software has been written specifically to create CSS style sheets; these have advanced features such as color-coding of rules and properties, syntax checking, and more. These are great tools, and I highly recommend them when you're doing serious CSS development; if you're just beginning, though, they may be more than you need right now and could overwhelm you with options. Once you understand the principles and language of CSS, however, a style sheet editor is invaluable. Some of the CSS editors available include

- TopStyle, from Bradbury Software; Windows; $49.95 (trial and free versions available); download from http://www.bradsoft.com/topstyle/

- Style Master, from WestCiv; Windows and Macintosh; $29.00 (free trial version available); download from http://www.westciv.com/style_master/

- JustStyle CSS Editor, from UCWare; Windows and Java-enabled computers; $20.00 (free trial version available); download from `http://www.ucware.com/juststyle/`

The screenshot in Figure 2.2 shows the HWG style sheet being edited in TopStyle. As you can see, the TopStyle program offers a lot more in the way of development features, but it's also more complex to use.

FIGURE 2.2

Editing a style sheet in TopStyle.

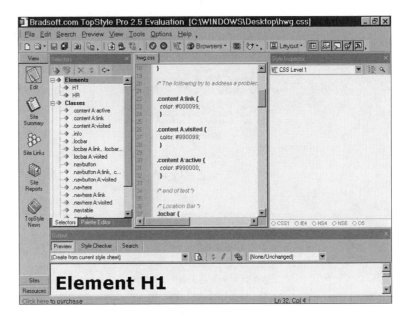

HTML Editors and Web Development Software

Because CSS is an integral part of Web design, Web design packages that let you create HTML will often support CSS editing. Visual editors will let you set styles and create the style sheet behind the scenes, whereas those with source editing modes allow you to directly edit the style sheet. As with CSS editors, I recommend using these once you've become familiar with the basics of CSS syntax. Your favorite Web editing environment may already include CSS support; some that do include

- Microsoft FrontPage; Windows; included with Microsoft Office (30 day demo available for $9.95); `http:/www.microsoft.com/frontpage/`
- Macromedia Dreamweaver; Windows and Macintosh; $299 (30 day free trial available); `http://www.macromedia.com/software/dreamweaver/`
- Adobe GoLive; Windows and Macintosh; $399; `http://www.adobe.com/products/golive/`

- CoffeeCup HTML Editor; Windows; $49 shareware (free download available); http://www.coffeecup.com/editor/

Naming and Saving a Style Sheet

However you edit your style sheet, the basic principle will be the same: You create a text file that contains the CSS rules, and you save that as a CSS file. Your style sheet's file-name shouldn't contain spaces, so that it will be easier to use on the Web.

The extension you should use is .css, so your files should be named something like test.css or sitedesign.css. While you're learning and practicing, you'll probably want to keep the .css file in the same directory as your HTML pages. Once you've got the hang of CSS, you'll probably want to store your style sheets in a designated directory on your Web site; I usually create a /styles/ directory for mine.

Writing CSS Rules

The building blocks of any style sheet are the CSS rules that compose it. Each rule is a single statement that identifies what should be styled and how those styles should be applied. Style sheets are then composed of lists of rules, which the browser uses to determine what a page should look like (or even sound like).

The Basic Structure of a CSS Rule

A *CSS rule* consists of two sections: the selector(s) and the declaration(s). A declaration is made up of a property and a value for that property. A simple CSS rule would therefore look something like this:

```
selector { property: value; }
```

One important thing to note is that CSS ignores extra whitespace, just like HTML usually does. This means that as far as CSS-enabled browsers are concerned, one space is equal to twenty spaces or even five spaces, four blank lines, and four more spaces. So the rule could be written like this and still mean the same thing:

```
selector
  {
    property:
      value;
  }
```

You should feel free to use whatever spaces and lines you need within your CSS to make it easy to read and maintain. For example, I usually indent the property and value pairs quite a bit by inserting spaces; this makes it easier for me to see at a glance where one rule ends and the next begins. By being consistent in how you use blank spaces in your style sheets, you can keep them easy to read and maintain. There is no one best way to write a style rule, and you may end up using different spacing in different situations. As long as it works for you, that's what matters.

The Selector

The *selector* part of the rule tells which section of the document the rule covers. The simplest type of selector is a type selector that indicates a specific markup element, such as the <p> tag in HTML. A type selector is written by just giving the name of the element without the <> brackets. It's written like the following:

```
p { property: value; }
```

Such a rule would select the styling of all <p> tags.

The Declaration

The next part of the rule is the *declaration*. Declarations are enclosed in {} braces. Within the braces, the property name is given first, followed by a colon, and then a property value. An ending semicolon is optional but recommended for reasons that will become apparent later this hour. The entire rule is concluded by the ending brace.

Properties

Properties are defined by the official CSS specifications; these are the list of specific style effects you can define and expect to be supported by CSS-compliant browsers. Most browsers will probably ignore properties that aren't part of the CSS specification, although some browsers recognize nonstandard properties that are not part of the formal language specification. It's best to not rely on these proprietary extensions, but browsers that don't recognize them will simply overlook them. In Hour 3, "Browser Support for CSS," you'll learn more about how browsers handle or don't handle CSS.

Values

The *value* of the declaration follows the property name, after the colon, and defines exactly how that property should be set. The range of values for each property is also defined in the CSS specifications. For example, the property named color can take values that consist of color names or codes, as in the following:

```
p { color: blue; }
```

This rule declares that the content of all paragraph tags should have their color properties set to the value blue. So all <p> text would turn blue.

What happens if you don't set the `color`? Well, you can probably guess from your work with HTML that a default will be chosen—one set by the browser or the user's preferences. The color might also be set by the text attribute on the `<body>` tag, or on a `<font>` tag. CSS adds additional ways to determine the color, including writing a rule with the `<body>` tag as the selector, which would then apply to all `<p>` tags within the `<body>`—that is to say, it would apply to all paragraphs on the page.

The specific process CSS uses to determine the color of the text or of any other property settings is called the *cascade*. You'll learn more about how the cascade works in Hour 7, "Cascading and Inheritance."

2

Combining CSS Rules

Two CSS rules that share the same selector can be combined by listing their declarations within the curly braces. The ending semicolon is no longer optional between two rules combined this way; it's a necessary separator between the two declarations. For ease of editing and combining, I suggest always including the semicolon even if your braces contain only one declaration.

Here's an example of two CSS rules with the same selector:

```
p { color: blue; }
p { font-size: large; }
```

These rules can be combined into one rule like the following:

```
p { color: blue; font-size: large; }
```

I could have also written the rule like this:

```
p
  {
    color:        blue;
    font-size:    large;
  }
```

That particular style of spacing makes it a little easier to cut and paste entire lines while writing or testing the CSS. The browsers don't care about the whitespace—it's there to help you organize your style sheet in whatever manner works best for you.

You can also combine rules if they have the same declarations and different selectors. Selectors are combined by putting them in a list, separated by commas. For example, the following rules have the same declarations:

```
p { color: blue; }
address { color: blue; }
```

You can write them as one rule, as follows:

```
p, address { color: blue; }
```

This rule says, "The content of <p> tags and of <address> tags should be colored as blue text."

You can use multiple selectors together with multiple declarations; that is perfectly legal and very common. You can also write additional rules to further style those selectors together or separately. Here's what that might look like:

```
p, address
  {
    color:        blue;
    font-size:    large;
  }
p
  {
    font-family:   Arial;
  }
```

CSS Comments

Like many other languages, including HTML, CSS allows you to embed *comments* in the source code. A comment is a special bit of code that you embed in your CSS that is completely ignored by the browser. Comments serve as a way of adding to the source notes that are meant for the author of the style sheet or someone maintaining it. The user won't ever see a comment, and they won't affect the style of the page; they are significant only when reading or editing the style sheet itself.

Comments can be used to describe what your style sheet is doing at a particular point, or perhaps why it's doing it, so that when you come back to the style sheet later, you can recall why you wrote it that particular way. Comments are also useful for hiding sections of code that you feel you don't need any more or that you want browsers to ignore; this is known as *commenting out* your code. Comments can also be used to identify the author and the creation date of the style sheet and to provide a copyright notice.

Comments in CSS begin with the characters /* and end with the characters */. Anything between the start of the comment and the end will be ignored. Here's an example of a comment:

```
/* Let's turn all the paragraph text blue */
p { color: blue; }
```

Your comments can appear anywhere you like, even inside of a rule:

```
p
  {
    color:        /* make it less blue */  purple;
    font-size:    large;
  }
```

You can comment out parts of a declaration if you decide you don't want that particular part of the style rule to be applied, but you don't want to delete it. This is useful for testing various options when developing your style sheet. For example, this comments out the font-size declaration:

```
p
  {
    color:        /* make it less blue */  purple;
/*  font-size:    large;      */
  }
```

However, you can't *nest* comments, meaning that if you try to enclose one comment within another, both comments will end when they hit the first */. For example, let's try to comment out the color purple instead; if we put our comment markers in the wrong place, as in the following, it won't work:

```
p
  {
/*  color:        /* make it less blue */  purple;    */
    font-size:    large;
  }
```

In this case, the comment ends after `blue`, not at the end of the declaration. This leaves the word `purple` floating there outside the comment. CSS browsers will probably ignore it because a `purple` by itself doesn't have any particular meaning in CSS, but that's just because we got lucky this time. You need to be careful when placing your comments so that you don't accidentally try to nest them.

Simple CSS Properties for Text Formatting

As you've probably surmised from the previous examples, there are CSS properties that can be used to set the text color, the size of the font, and the family of the font—`color`, `font-size`, and `font-family`, respectively. These are some of the simplest and yet most useful CSS properties; collectively, they perform the same function as the HTML `<font>` tag. Another very useful property is `background-color`, which naturally sets the color of the background.

The color Property

The color property is used to set the foreground color of the element, which is the property controlling the color of the text. For example,

```
h1 { color: lime; }
h2 { color: red; }
```

This makes all <h1> elements a bright, lime-green color and makes all <h2> elements red. As with HTML, you can use one of 16 standard color names, or you can give an RGB value, such as #FF0000. The color names and their corresponding RGB values are shown in Table 2.1.

TABLE 2.1 Color Names in CSS

Color Name	RGB Value	Color Name	RGB Value
aqua	#00FFFF	navy	#000080
black	#000000	olive	#808000
blue	#0000FF	purple	#800080
fuchsia	#FF00FF	red	#FF0000
gray	#808080	silver	#C0C0C0
green	#008000	teal	#008080
lime	#00FF00	white	#FFFFFF
maroon	#800000	yellow	#FFFF00

The background-color Property

You can use the background-color property to set the background color. The values are the same as for the color property—color names or RGB values. To set the background color for the whole page, use the <body> tag in your selector; you can set backgrounds on any other elements as well. For example,

```
body { background: silver; }
h1 { background: #FFFF00; }
```

> When you set the background color, make sure you've also set a foreground color that is visible against it! Otherwise your text may be very hard to read.

The `font-size` Property

The `font-size` property allows you to specify the size of the text that's displayed to the user. One of the easier ways to specify font sizes is to give a value relative to the user's default text size; this respects the user's preferences as set in the browser.

The default text size has a value of `normal`; larger sizes go up in increments of about 20% to values of `large`, `x-large`, and `xx-large`. Smaller sizes decrease by 20% to `small`, `x-small`, and `xx-small`. You can also use the relative values `larger` and `smaller` to indicate one step up or down the scale from the current size. Here are some examples:

```
dl { font-size: large; }
caption { font-size: small; }
em { font-size: larger; }
```

In Hour 8, "Fonts and Font Families," you'll learn more about sizing fonts, including other types of values you can use for font sizes.

The `font-family` Property

You can use the `font-family` property to set the font face of the text. So why is it called `font-family` and not `font-face`? When you designate a font, you're really designating a whole family of related variants within the same font family. So when choosing Arial font, you're actually choosing the Arial family of fonts, each one slightly different in size.

CSS also uses *generic font families*. The generic font families are `sans-serif`, `serif`, `monospace`, `cursive`, and `fantasy`. These aren't names of specific fonts but rather a broad class that can be used as defaults if the browser doesn't know what a font name represents. If you choose a font that isn't installed on the user's machine, the browser will just use the normal font, so you'll want to make sure you designate a generic font family as well as a specific one. You indicate the generic font by listing it after the specific font, separated by a comma.

Common Web fonts and their generic families are shown on Table 2.2.

TABLE 2.2 Common Font Families

Font	Generic Font Family
Arial	sans-serif
Times New Roman	serif
Courier New	monospace
Verdana	sans-serif

If the name of the font family has more than one word, enclose it in quotes. Here are some examples of CSS rules using font-family:

```
body { font-family: Arial, sans-serif; }
h1 { font-family: "Courier New", monospace; }
h2 { font-family: "Times New Roman", serif; }
```

You'll learn more about font families and how to use them in Hour 8.

A Simple Style Sheet

Using just the simple properties and values you've learned so far this hour, you already can create a basic style sheet; an example of a complete style sheet is shown in Listing 2.1.

LISTING 2.1 A Basic Style Sheet with Color, Size, and Font Declarations

```
/* basic-2.1.css                                        */
/* Written by Kynn Bartlett <kynn@kynn.com>             */

body { font-family: Arial;
       color: black;
       background-color: white; }

/* I think Verdana looks nice for headlines */
h1, h2, h3, h4, h5, h6 { font-family: Verdana, sans-serif; }

/* This puts the second level heading in red */
h2 { color: red; }

address { font-family: Verdana, sans-serif;
          font-size: smaller; }
```

You can find a copy of this style sheet on the Web at http://CSSin24hours.com/02/basic-2.1.css.

Linking a Style Sheet to an HTML Page

A style sheet by itself doesn't really do anything except sit there on your hard drive or Web server. If you try to load it in your browser, it will just display as plain text. To actually use the CSS rules, you need to have a file with markup, such as an HTML page, and you need to add an HTML tag to link the CSS file to the Web page.

A Simple HTML Page for Styling

Listing 2.2 shows the structure of a basic HTML page like one you might find on the Web; it has headlines, paragraphs, horizontal rules, and even a little table on the side. You can download a copy of this file from `http://CSSin24hours.com/02/basic-2.2.html` because that's easier than typing in the whole thing.

LISTING 2.2 A Simple HTML File That Needs Styling

```
<!-- basic-2.2.html                                         -->
<html>
  <head>
    <title>
      Review - The Lord of the Rings: Fellowship of the Ring
    </title>
  </head>
  <body>

    <h1>Movie Review</h1>
    <table border="1" align="right">
      <tr> <th colspan="2">Rating Scale</th>            </tr>
      <tr> <td>One *</td>         <td>Not recommended</td>   </tr>
      <tr> <td>Two **</td>        <td>Mediocre</td>          </tr>
      <tr> <td>Three ***</td>     <td>Above Average</td>     </tr>
      <tr> <td>Four ****</td>     <td>Highly Recommended</td></tr>
      <tr> <td>Five *****</td> <td>A Must-See!</td>          </tr>
    </table>

    <h2>
      The Lord of the Rings:
      <br>
      Fellowship of the Ring
    </h2>

    <h3>Rating: Four ****</h3>

    <p>
      This movie perfectly captures the feelings of reading
      <cite>The Lord of the Rings</cite> books by J.R.R. Tolkien
      — large, impressive, fantastic, and mythic, but also
      large, ponderous, slow, and meandering.
    </p>
    <p>
      Now, I like the original books as much as any other
      Science-fiction and fantasy fan, despite getting only
      halfway through the second of three books before giving
      up. Nevertheless, I gaped in awe at the majestic
      landscapes of Middle Earth depicted on the big screen rather
      than only in my imagination. I saw elves, hobbits, wizards,
      dwarves, orcs, and even a few humans come to life, and it
      all <em>felt right</em> — but it also felt very long,
      nearly 3 hours in length, even with the plot pared
      down for the movie.
```

continues

LISTING 2.2   Continued

```
  </p>
  <p>
    Some story points were inexplicably confusing; bit
    characters wander off and onto the screen, and none ever
    stop to really explain what the big deal is about the
    ring. If I hadn't read the first book already, I might
    have been scratching my head in confusion. But
    ultimately, <cite>Fellowship of the Ring</cite> is a treat
    designed especially for anyone who loves Tolkien's epic
    work of mythic fantasy; it's a faithful, if exhausting,
    adaptation of this 20th-century classic.
  </p>

  <hr>
  <address>
    Reviewed by
    <a href="mailto:kynn@kynn.com">Kynn Bartlett</a>
  </address>
</body>
</html>
```

As seen in the screenshot in Figure 2.3, this displays as a rather plain page without CSS. This is our "before" picture.

FIGURE 2.3

Internet Explorer 5's default rendering of basic-2.2.html.

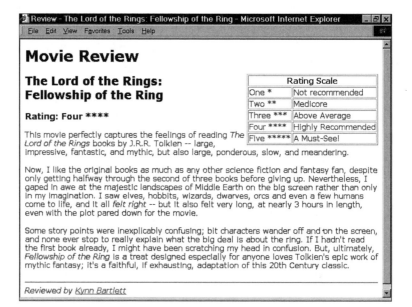

Linked Style Sheets in HTML

To apply the style sheet to our HTML page, we'll need to tell the browser which style sheet to use. We do this by using the `<link>` element of HTML, and we'll use the `basic-2.1.css` file from Listing 2.1.

The `<link>` tag can appear only within the `<head>` section of our HTML page. To link the style sheet, I open the HTML file and add the following line (shown in bold):

```
<head>
  <title>
    Review - The Lord of the Rings: Fellowship of the Ring
  </title>
  <link type="text/css" rel="stylesheet" href="basic-2.1.css">
</head>
```

The effect of applying the style sheet can be seen in Figure 2.4; compare this with Figure 2.1 to see the difference some styles make.

FIGURE **2.4**

Styles change the appearance of the plain HTML page.

Adding More Styles

If we want to add more to our page, we can just fire up the text editor and change the CSS file. Alternately, we could create a different style sheet and change the `<link>` tag's `href` attribute.

Listing 2.3 shows a longer style sheet, and Figure 2.4 is our "after" shot, applying the new style sheet (which can be downloaded from `http://CSSin24hours/02/basic-2.3.css`).

LISTING 2.3   More Styles to Make Our HTML Page Interesting

```
/* basic-2.3.css                                    */
/* Written by Kynn Bartlett <kynn@kynn.com>          */

body { font-family: Arial;
       color: navy;
       background-color: white; }
h1, h2, h3, h4, h5, h6 { font-family: Verdana, sans-serif; }
h1 { color: maroon; }
h2 { color: red; }
h3 { color: green; }

p { color: black; }
th, td { font-size: smaller; }
th { color: navy;
     font-family: Verdana, sans-serif; }
td { color: green;
     font-family: Times, sans-serif; }

em { color: red; }
cite { color: teal; }

address { font-family: Verdana, sans-serif;
          font-size: smaller; }

a { color: fuchsia; }
```

FIGURE 2.5

A few simple CSS rules spice up the appearance of the page.

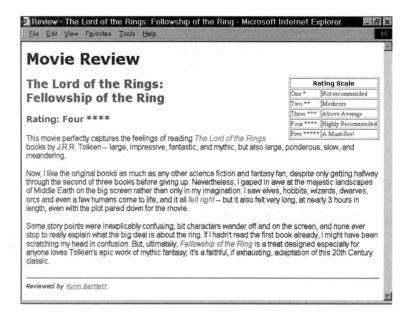

Viewing Your Style Sheet

Once you've created a style sheet, you'll want to take a look at it to ensure that it works. Uneven browser support for CSS means that it's important to check how it appears in various browsers, as well as to make sure you got the syntax correct.

To view the style sheet, simply view the HTML file that links to your CSS file. Don't try viewing the CSS file directly; it will just look like source code in many browsers. The way to know if it worked is to look at the HTML page that's being styled.

Recommended Browsers

You'll want to verify your style sheet in at least the major browsers because they represent the greatest number of users who may access your page. You'll also want to test in browsers that have good support for the CSS standard. Browsers can vary between operating systems; Internet Explorer on Microsoft Windows handles CSS quite differently from Internet Explorer on a Macintosh.

Naturally, it's difficult for one person to have access to every different browser combination available, but the more you're able to use, the better your results will be. I recommend a standard testing suite consisting of four browsers:

- Internet Explorer (5.0, 5.5, or 6.0 on Windows; 5.0 or 5.1 on Macintosh)
- Netscape (4.7 or higher; Windows, Macintosh, or Linux)
- Mozilla (0.9 or higher; Windows, Macintosh, or Linux) or Opera (5.0 or 6.0; Windows, Macintosh, or Linux)
- Lynx (2.7 or higher; Windows, Macintosh, or Linux)

These browsers represent a good cross-section for testing, and are generally widely available on most popular operating systems. In Hour 3 and Hour 18, "Web Design with CSS," you'll learn more about testing strategies.

Summary

In this hour, you learned about using text editors and specialized software to create and edit style sheets, which are just ordinary text files of CSS rules. You learned the general structure of a CSS rule and its component parts, including the selector, the declaration, the property name, and the property value. You learned how and why to include comments in your CSS files. You got to see a few simple styles change an HTML page, setting the text color, size, and font, and you learned how the HTML `<link>` tag associates a style sheet with a Web page. Finally, you learned how to display your page in your browser and see your CSS in action.

Q&A

Q I'm not sure what the "RGB" values used for colors are. Can you explain?

A Sure! RGB triples are one of the most common ways to specify color on the Web, in both HTML and CSS. RGB stands for Red-Green-Blue and is a standard way for specifying a color as a composite of three values: the amount of red, the amount of green, and the amount of blue. In HTML and CSS these are written in hexadecimal numbers (base 16), which start with 0, go up to 9, and then continue on to A, B, C, D, E, and F. If you don't know how to use RGB hexadecimal values, you can use the rgb() function to specify colors, like this:

```
h1 { color: rgb(100%, 50%, 25%); }
```

Q Can I set the font-size to a specific value, such as 12 point?

A Yes, you can; 12 point is written as 12pt (no space). This is what's known as an absolute font size, though, and it can cause problems for users who need to adjust their preferences to account for visual impairments. For now I recommend sticking with the relative values given earlier in this hour, like larger and x-small, but if you want you can read ahead to Hour 8 for more font size units.

Workshop

The workshop contains quiz questions and activities to help reinforce what you've learned in this hour. If you get stuck, the answers to the quiz can be found after the questions.

Quiz

1. What kind of software is needed to create a CSS file?

2. What is the name of the part of a CSS rule that goes within the curly braces?

   (a.) The selector

   (b.) The declaration

   (c.) The property name

   (d.) The property value

3. You want to make all of your HTML headings (<h1>, and so on) blue and in Arial font. What CSS rule(s) do you write?

Answers

1. Because CSS files are just ordinary text files, anything that can create or edit text files can make a style sheet. This includes text editors, style sheet editors, Web development tools, and word processors. The important thing is to save the files as plain text, usually with a .css file extension suffix.

2. The declaration, which consists of the one or more pairs of property names and values, is the part of the CSS rule between curly braces.

3. Here's the easiest way to make headings blue and Arial:

```
h1, h2, h3, h4, h5, h6
  {
    color:        blue;
    font-family:  Arial;
  }
```

You could also write this as several rules—as many as 12—but this combined form is the easiest way to do it.

Activity: Create Your First Style Sheet

Learning by doing is the key to understanding Cascading Style Sheets, and building your own style sheet is the first step in the process. Follow these instructions to create and test your own CSS:

1. Select an HTML page to style. This could be one you've created before, a brand new one, or perhaps the basic-2.2.html file used earlier this hour.

2. Create a new CSS file using the text editor of your choice. Using the style properties you learned this hour, add style rules to apply to your HTML page. Change the color of the text, the background color, the font sizes, and the text font. Save this file with a .css extension.

3. Use the <link> tag in your HTML to associate the style sheet with the HTML page. Be sure the HTML and CSS files are in the same directory, or else the browser might not be able to find the CSS file. (You can use full URL paths if you want, but for now, it's easiest to have HTML and CSS in the same location.)

4. Open your page in your primary Web browser and view the results of your work. You may want to go back and tweak the CSS to see what effect additional styles have; go right ahead!

5. If you have any of the other recommended browsers, try the page with those. You probably won't see much difference because the CSS properties introduced are relatively safe and reasonably well supported.

HOUR 3

Browser Support for CSS

To be able to master the full power of Cascading Style Sheets, you need to understand the biggest issue related to using CSS—browser support. No other Web-related technology has been more limited by poor browser implementation than Cascading Style Sheets. However, the situation continues to improve, as recent browsers are getting closer and closer to full support for CSS.

In this hour, you'll learn

- What the browser problem is and why it's a problem
- The general categories of browsers and how each type affects your CSS Web designs
- The essential need for workarounds and how to measure the cost of failure
- How the current browsers use Cascading Style Sheets
- How to read the Browser Support Report Card found in each subsequent hour of this book

The Browser Problem

A Web browser is the essential Internet access tool of the early twenty-first century. Browsers are becoming indispensable to business, education, and personal communication. They create a common platform upon which Web-based applications can be built, with an HTML framework driving e-commerce, business-to-business transactions, Web-based learning, and online communities. Hundreds of thousands of pages of new information are added to the Web each day. Cascading Style Sheets play a crucial role in this adolescent communications medium not only by providing a pleasant visual layer on the surface of these Web applications, but also by potentially reshaping the entire user experience.

So what's the problem? In short: Web browsers are terrible at CSS.

There are a variety of reasons for this. Some browsers, such as Netscape 3, were created before the CSS specification was published. Other browsers are limited in what they're meant to do: Lynx is a text-only browser and doesn't do CSS at all, whereas WebTV terminals understand only a subset of CSS. Some browsers jumped the gun; Microsoft is notorious for jumping the gun and using draft specifications of standards in their browsers. And sadly, some browsers are just plain bad. They may seem to function normally, but when it comes to consistent and standardized support for CSS, they fall very short.

The good news is that the problem is being solved. Slowly but surely, each new major browser release is better than the last, and you can get pretty decent, though not perfect, CSS implementations from Mozilla, Netscape 6, Opera, and certain versions of Internet Explorer.

How Browsers Deal with CSS

When a browser encounters anything—from CSS rules to HTML, JavaScript to Flash multimedia—it has three choices as to what it can do. If the browser has been programmed to understand the thing it has encountered, it will attempt to display it according to the specification. If it has no idea what it has come across, it can ignore it. Both of these options can be considered "doing the right thing." Or, the browser can do the wrong thing. It can get confused; it can display in some nonstandard way; it can crash. This third option is the least desirable and is the primary root of our problem.

Cascading Style Sheets were designed from the start to degrade gracefully. This means that if your CSS rules aren't recognized for some reason, your page will still be usable and the content accessible. Because we've separated presentation from content, our content should be able to stand on its own, albeit not as beautifully, once our presentation is removed. At least, that's the theory.

In practice it's not nearly as easy as that. To be an effective CSS author, you'll need to know not only what works in any given browser—or in most or all of them—but also what happens when it doesn't work. Is it as simple as your style not being applied correctly and you losing a bit of decoration, or is it as serious as your entire layout being disrupted and content being lost?

To understand how browsers deal with CSS, I've divided them up into four categories: older browsers, which pre-date the CSS specification and thus ignore it completely; limited browsers, which don't even attempt to support all of CSS; broken browsers, which try to provide CSS functionality but fail horribly in some manner; and compliant browsers, of which there are sadly few to none. Each category of browsers will treat Cascading Style Sheets differently, and it's important to understand what those differences are.

Older Browsers

Older browsers are those that existed before Cascading Style Sheets were even a glimmer in the W3C's collective eye. Netscape 3 is the classic example of an older browser, and it does exactly what it's supposed to do: it ignores CSS entirely. If you try to visit a Web page styled with CSS, Netscape 3 won't notice a single rule you've written. The style sheet won't even load.

This is actually ideal behavior for older browsers; with CSS designed for backwards compatibility, most CSS-based Web sites should still work, although they may be somewhat boring in appearance. Because Netscape 3 is ignoring all CSS rules, we know exactly what it will do with them; there's no guesswork necessary on the part of the author. You won't have to do anything special to support these types of browsers, except for testing your designs to see if they still function without CSS.

> You can simulate an older browser by configuring a newer browser to deliberately ignore CSS in the preferences settings for each browser. By doing so, you can check to see if your designs work in browsers that don't understand CSS; a properly designed style sheet should be perfectly understandable in an ancient browser, such as Netscape 3.

Limited Browsers

Limited browsers are those that are not intended to be full-fledged general-use multimedia Web browsers; instead, they serve a very specific function and thus don't have a need for all the capabilities found in CSS.

A limited browser is troubling because it supports only a subset of Cascading Style Sheets—and not one that's broken cleanly along the lines of the CSS Level 1 and CSS

Level 2 specifications. Microsoft's WebTV is an example of this type of browser; it supports only a small number of CSS properties, and not all of them. Another example is EmacSpeak, a screenreader for the visually impaired that supports aural CSS but not most visual formatting properties.

Supporting these browsers can be difficult, but they tend to be uncommon in practice, and usually the subsets of CSS they support are intelligently chosen, such as how EmacSpeak doesn't support visual properties but has a good reason for not doing so. Testing your design in an older browser (or one with CSS purposely disabled) is usually enough to cover limited browsers, although if you're designing specifically for audiences using these types of browsers, you may want to have a copy for your own testing purposes.

Broken Browsers

The worst kind of browser is one that is simply broken when it comes to CSS, despite whatever claims the provider makes to standards compliance. A broken browser is one that, when given perfectly legitimate Cascading Style Sheets rules, doesn't present a Web surfer with anything she can use, but instead displays a mishmash of styles where information gets lost. The difference between an older browser and a broken browser is that older browsers don't try to display CSS, and broken browsers try and fail horribly.

Internet Explorer 3 was the first browser to implement any CSS, but it did an overall bad job at it, based in part on the fact that they coded to a specification that was still being written at the time. When the final version of CSS Level 1 came out, it was quite different from Internet Explorer 3's attempt to implement CSS support.

Fortunately, Internet Explorer 3 has almost passed into memory, replaced by newer versions of Internet Explorer that are closer to the CSS specification, meaning that the buggy CSS implementation in Internet Explorer 3 really isn't a factor in current CSS usage.

The current front-runner in broken browsers—causing the most headaches for CSS developers around the world—is Netscape 4. Unlike Netscape 3, Netscape 4 does indeed attempt to support Cascading Style Sheets but fails miserably in many ways. For example, Netscape 4 doesn't understand many of the key CSS properties needed to lay out a page, set font styles, or align text.

To account for the broken browsers out there, it's necessary to understand how they're broken and what happens when you give each browser some CSS rules that it doesn't understand. In some cases, the broken browser will just ignore your CSS, as is the case with a limited or older browser; in others, it may do something horribly wrong. In this book we'll point out those problems and help you design CSS that will work on as wide a selection of browsers as possible.

Compliant Browsers

Working with a completely CSS-compliant browser is a joy—or it would be, if such a creature existed. At the moment there are no browsers that completely support all of the Cascading Style Sheets Level 2 specification, and only a handful that can legitimately claim full CSS Level One support.

Luckily, there's plenty of motion in the direction of full support, which means things are only getting better with each released browser version. Browsers that are very close to being compliant with the standard include—starting with the most compliant—Mozilla, Netscape 6, Opera 5 and 6, and recent versions of Internet Explorer, especially for Macintosh.

Coding CSS for a compliant browser is simply a matter of following the standard and reaping the benefit of your work. Unfortunately, this idyllic vision is still not yet a reality, as near-compliant browsers constitute only a small fraction of the browsers in use. For the foreseeable future, you'll need to keep in mind the needs of users without fully CSS-compliant browsers, and that means using workarounds when necessary.

The Importance of Workarounds

Because there are so many broken browsers out there, it's often necessary to use a *workaround* to effect the same functionality you would get on a compliant browser. A workaround is a *hack*—a nonstandard way of getting a certain result that bends and tweaks the syntax of CSS or HTML in order to produce the type of style effects you're trying to achieve.

A good workaround is one that stays within the published standards—CSS and HTML primarily—so that it doesn't break on browsers that are compliant with the standards. A partial workaround is one that gives a similar effect but doesn't fully measure up to the kind of styling you could do if the browser were standards-compliant.

Workarounds in This Book

Whenever possible, I've identified useful workarounds to compensate for browser limitations. These are formatted like this, as a tip, with the titles of the affected browsers in the heading of the tip.

For some browser limitations and bugs, there are simply no viable workarounds that give the same functionality; in those cases you will have to make a difficult choice—include the CSS despite browser limitations or leave it out entirely. The basis for this decision is the cost of failure.

The Cost of Failure

The *cost of failure* is simply an understanding of what will happen if you use specific CSS rules or properties that aren't understood by the browser.

In some cases, you'll want to use CSS properties that aren't well supported; you may figure that the cost of failure is low enough that you don't mind some users missing out on a special styling if it improves the site for those users with more advanced browsers. In other cases, you may decide you can't take that chance, and you'll have to make a choice whether to support the broken browsers with workarounds or ignore that audience.

For example, consider a CSS rule that makes the first letter of each section stand out large in a stylized font. This may just be simple decoration, and if the font is normal sized in some browsers, so be it; it may not affect at all the way your page functions.

Browser Compatibility Charts

A *browser compatibility chart* is an invaluable resource for anyone doing serious CSS work. What is it? A compatibility chart lists every CSS property in a matrix, cross-referenced with a number of different browsers (including various version numbers and platforms). For example, if you want to know if the Netscape 4 browser supports the `color` property, you can consult a compatibility chart. For each property you look up, you'll see whether or not it's supported by the browser, and if there are any special notes or known bugs in the implementation.

The best-known CSS browser compatibility chart is maintained by Eric Meyer as part of the WebReview site and is located at `http://www.webreview.com/style/`; I highly recommend bookmarking that site and referring to it as you test your CSS-based designs. Another good browser compatibility chart is from WestCiv, the makers of the Style Master CSS editor; their charts are at `http://www.westciv.com/style_master/ academy/browser_support`.

In this book, I take a complementary approach to reporting compatibility; instead of rating the browsers, I give each CSS feature or property a grade at the end of each hour. This grade reflects not only the browser support but also the cost of failure in nonsupporting browsers. This will let you make an informed choice when creating your cross-browser CSS, and avoid those properties or features that are not safe yet for general use.

Web Standards and You

As you know, CSS is defined by the Cascading Style Sheets Level 1 and Level 2 recommendations from the World Wide Web Consortium. These recommendations function as standards for the CSS language.

Standards are a good thing for developers; the more the browsers support the standards, the easier it is for us to create expressive and attractive designs in CSS and know they'll work reliably. Increased support from standards, the browser makers, the Web developer community, and the Web software manufacturers will only make our jobs easier.

One group of Web designers decided to take their support for standards public and founded the Web Standards Project to encourage browser makers to adhere closely to the CSS recommendations and other Web standards. In addition to their advocacy work, the Web Standards Project site contains useful FAQs and links on standards support. Their URL is `http://www.webstandards.org/`.

CSS Support in Current Browsers

The rest of this hour represents a snapshot of the browser world as of the first half of 2002. Newer versions of these browsers may be out by the time you read this and could offer even greater support for the CSS standards, so be sure to check the Web sites for the latest versions.

For the major browser types I've provided screen shots of the browsers in action, displaying a page with some high-powered CSS—part of the css/edge, a CSS site by Eric Meyer that pushes the boundaries of what you can do with standards-compliant CSS.

The URL for each of these examples is the *css/edge spiral*, from `http://www.meyerweb.com/eric/css/edge/complexspiral/demo.html`. Figure 3.1 illustrates how the spiral is supposed to appear, as shown by Netscape 6.

FIGURE 3.1

The css/edge spiral demo as it should look (Netscape 6).

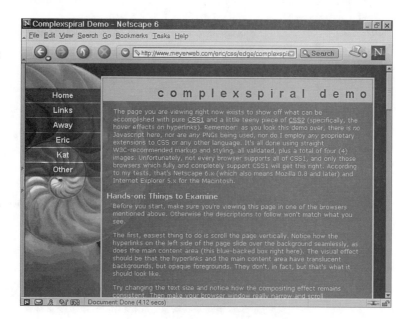

Internet Explorer

Microsoft's Internet Explorer has been declared by many to be the winner of the 1990s browser wars. Internet Explorer 3 had the first support for Cascading Style Sheets, but unfortunately it was quite disastrous and unusable. Subsequent versions have improved a lot.

Internet Explorer is available on two primary platforms—Windows and Macintosh. (A "pocket" version exists for Pocket PCs running Windows CE.) An important point to keep in mind is that the Windows and Macintosh versions of Internet Explorer are effectively completely different browsers. They share some common functionality, but the core code for each is different, and they have vastly divergent support for Cascading Style Sheets and other Web standards.

IE 5, 5.5, and 6 for Windows

CSS support in Internet Explorer 5 for Windows is what one would call "almost compliant and just somewhat broken," and each subsequent version gets one step better. Internet Explorer 6 implements a standards compatibility mode that pretty much moves it into the category of compliant browsers.

You can download a copy of Internet Explorer for Windows from the Microsoft Web site at http://www.microsoft.com/windows/ie/default.asp.

The css/edge spiral as displayed by Internet Explorer 6 for Windows is shown in Figure 3.2.

FIGURE 3.2

Internet Explorer 6 (Windows) displays the css/edge spiral.

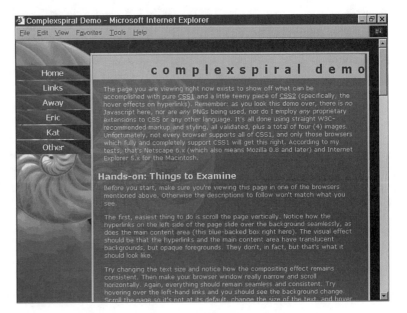

IE 5 and 5.1 for Macintosh

As mentioned before, Internet Explorer for Macintosh should be considered a completely
different species of browser than its Windows cousin. Internet Explorer 5 for Mac, at the
time it was first released, was the most standards-compliant browser available and was
far ahead of the Windows counterpart. Version 5.1 continued this strong support for CSS
and other standards.

 The Web site for Internet Explorer for Mac is http://www.microsoft.com/
mac/products/ie/.

You can see the css/edge spiral displayed as it's meant be shown in Figure 3.3.

3

FIGURE 3.3

*The css/edge spiral in
Internet Explorer 5.1
for Macintosh.*

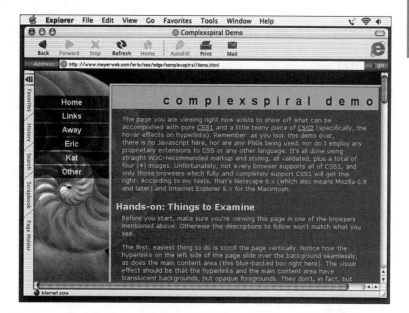

Older Versions of Internet Explorer

Internet Explorer 3 and 4—on either platform—have had serious problems with CSS and
fall into the category of broken browsers. Users with these older versions should be
encouraged to upgrade or to possibly just disable CSS.

Netscape

Like the brand name Internet Explorer, the Netscape brand name also applies to two vastly different browsers with the same name. Netscape 4 is the earlier version and is quite buggy, especially when it comes to browser support, whereas Netscape 6 is quite possibly one of the most CSS-compliant browsers available.

Netscape 6 and Mozilla

It's important to realize where Netscape 6 came from. In the middle of the fierce browser competition of the late 1990s, Netscape proposed a daring plan. The core browser engine code was made publicly available as part of an open source project—one in which anyone is welcome to volunteer and contribute programming code to the collective, public code base. This was known as the Mozilla project.

Admittedly, the results have been slow in coming—Netscape even had to skip browser version 5 entirely to maintain the illusion of keeping up—but there have also been impressive results. Netscape 6, based on the Mozilla project's work, is a browser that is very good at Cascading Style Sheets as well as one that offers excellent support for HTML standards.

Mozilla is available on a multitude of systems, including Windows, Macintosh, Linux, and others. As it is a work in progress, there are daily developer builds available for testing as well as regular milestone releases.

> You can download the most recent version of Mozilla from http://www.mozilla.org/.

Netscape 6.2.1 is the most current version of Netscape 6 as this book is being written. You've already seen an example of Netscape 6 displaying the css/edge spiral in Figure 3.1.

> The URL for downloading Netscape is http://home.netscape.com/computing/download/.

Netscape 4

Netscape 4.79 is the most recent version of Netscape 4, but as noted before, Netscape 4 has very poor support for Web standards, including CSS. However, as a CSS developer you'll probably want to have a version of Netscape 4 available for testing.

You can download a version of Netscape 4 from `http://home.netscape.com/download/`.

Figure 3.4 shows Netscape 4's attempts to display the css/edge spiral.

FIGURE 3.4

As you can see, Netscape 4 can't quite handle the complex CSS of the css/edge spiral.

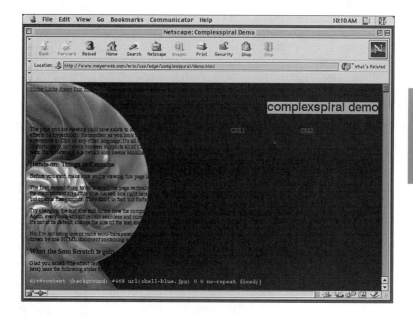

Older Versions of Netscape

Some older versions of Netscape 4 were even worse at CSS; for example, version 4.02 would routinely crash if you tried to apply certain styles to a table cell. Netscape 3 is useful for testing, however, as it is an excellent example of an older browser that completely ignores CSS.

Older versions of Netscape can be found at `http://home.netscape.com/download/archive.html`.

Opera

Opera is the perpetual third-runner of browsers; fast and small and standards-compliant, it still doesn't enjoy the same popularity as the big two browser names. The Chief Technology

Officer at Opera, Håkon Wium Lie, was one of the principal authors of the CSS Level 1 and Level 2 recommendations, so you know they know their stuff! Since version 3, Opera has consistently had great CSS support, improving incrementally with each release.

Opera 6

Opera 6 is the current version available for Windows, and I highly recommend getting a copy if you're a Windows user. In addition to the CSS support, it also features one-click buttons to turn off and on CSS rendering, user style sheets, and more, which combine to make this an excellent testing tool.

> You can download Opera 6 from http://www.opera.com/download/win.html.

The css/edge spiral is shown in Figure 3.5 on Opera 6.

FIGURE 3.5

Opera 6 is up to the task of displaying the css/edge spiral.

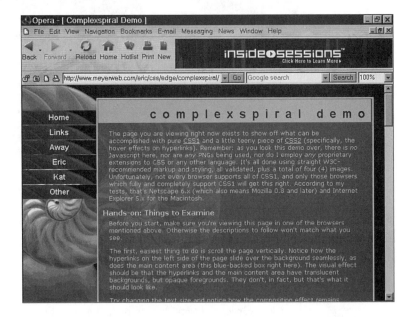

Opera 5

Opera 5 is the most recent version for Macintosh, Linux, and other platforms. Unlike Internet Explorer, Opera is consistent across various platforms and functions much the same no matter what it's running on, especially when it comes to rendering CSS.

The Opera 5 download page is `http://www.opera.com/download/`.

Other Browsers

The world of browsers definitely doesn't end with just Internet Explorer and Netscape, and not even with Opera. There are a number of other browsers that understand CSS to varying degrees, including iCab for Mac, WebTV on set-top boxes, Konqueror for Linux, and Lynx for nearly any system.

iCab

iCab is a Macintosh Web browser made by a company in Germany; you can run iCab in German or in English. iCab has limited CSS support, but they do take standards seriously; the iCab browser displays a sad face when it reaches a page with invalid HTML and a happy face when the page conforms to the HTML standards. Figure 3.6 shows iCab's attempt to display the css/edge spiral.

The iCab Web site is `http://www.icab.de/`.

FIGURE 3.6

iCab makes an attempt to display the css/edge spiral.

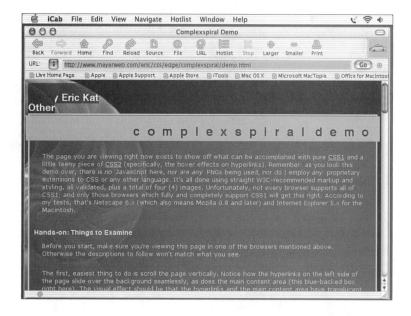

WebTV

The set-top WebTV boxes were an early attempt to make Internet appliances—devices that make Web access as easy as using your microwave. They're interesting to us as CSS developers because they supported a limited subset of CSS, mainly for simplicity's sake, but also because some properties (such as fonts) didn't make sense based on the type of browser built into a WebTV. A WebTV emulator is available for Windows and Macintosh and was used to view the css/edge spiral, as seen in Figure 3.7.

You can download the WebTV emulator from
http://developer.msntv.com/.

Figure 3.7
WebTV has limited CSS support, and so it can't quite handle the css/edge spiral.

KDE Konqueror

Konqueror is part of the K Desktop Environment, an open source project creating software for the Linux operating system. Konqueror functions as a Web browser (among other functions) and has generally good support for CSS.

You can learn more about Konqueror at http://www.konqueror.org/.

FIGURE 3.8

Konqueror takes the css/edge spiral challenge.

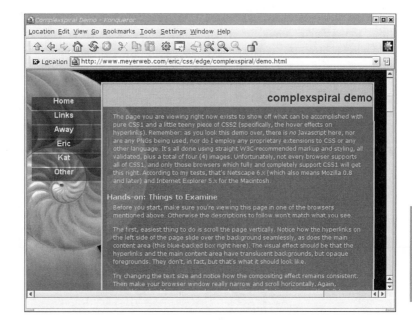

Lynx

The Lynx browser is one of the oldest browsers around; it's entirely text based. Lynx doesn't do JavaScript, doesn't do Java, doesn't do graphics, doesn't do sound, doesn't do Flash, and doesn't really do tables or frames particularly well (although those latter two it can deal with okay).

What about CSS? Lynx doesn't understand CSS at all. As such, it's a perfect example of the older browser category discussed earlier in this hour. Lynx is a good testing tool for CSS development because it lets you see what your Web design will look like if style sheets are turned off. Lynx is also a good approximation (although not an exact one) for how people with visual disabilities access the Web using screenreaders.

Lynx is available for Windows, Mac, Linux, and a number of other operating systems. You can download a copy of Lynx from `http://lynx.browser.org/`.

So how does Lynx handle the css/edge spiral? As you can see in Figure 3.9, all of the formatting and images are completely gone, but the page content is still understandable and usable. This is how CSS is backwards compatible; older browsers can still access and use the content even if the styling is lost.

FIGURE 3.9

Lynx doesn't display the css/edge spiral styles at all.

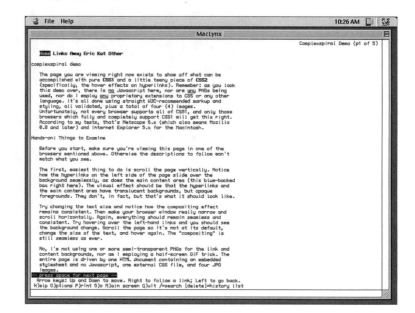

Summary

Browser support is the key issue to understanding how to use Cascading Style Sheets effectively. Older browsers ignore CSS, compliant browsers support CSS, and other browsers either provide limited or broken support for the standards. Knowing how to deal with the different types of browsers makes your style sheets more effective across a variety of platforms and browser versions.

Internet Explorer for Windows version 6, Internet Explorer for Macintosh version 5, Netscape 6, Opera for Windows 6, and Opera for Macintosh 5 are the latest available browser versions at the time of writing, and they all have impressive support for CSS standards that continues to increase with each new release. Other browsers, such as iCab, WebTV, Konqueror, and Lynx, offer varying support for the CSS specifications.

Browser Support Report Card

The Browser Support Record Card will appear in each subsequent hour, and provides a measure of browser support for each particular CSS feature mentioned earlier in the hour. The following report card is based on the CSS properties you've learned so far, in this and previous hours:

CSS Feature	Grade	Notes
Tag names as selectors	A	
The color property	A	
The background-color property	A	
The font-size property	A	
The font-family property	A	
Combining selectors	A	
Combining declarations	A	
The <link> tag in HTML	A	

How to Read the Grades

As you can see, all of the CSS features on this report card, which were introduced in Hour 2, "Getting Started with CSS," get a grade of A. (This was intentional; I didn't want to introduce problematic CSS until you'd learned more about the browsers, so Hour 2's properties were simple and safe.)

The grades are based on the American public school system's letter grades and can include plusses or minuses to indicate fractionally higher or lower rankings. The general meaning of each grade is as follows:

Grade	Meaning
A	You can safely use this feature as described in the hour without fear of browser errors.
B	A workaround is required for some browsers, but once applied, the feature works as described in the hour.
C	A partial workaround exists, but it's not possible to get the result described in the hour in all browsers, even using the workaround.
D	Browser support exists, but is so poor that you should never rely on this working, and there's no easy way to make this perform as desired.
F	The implementation of this feature is nonexistent or extremely poorly done, and you shouldn't even try to use it.

Browser support grades are based in part on the support of the browsers for the particular CSS feature, but they are also based on the subjective measure of the cost of failure for each property. The more browsers that don't support a feature, the lower the grade it receives.

Q&A

Q Which browsers should I use?

A For your own personal use, you're free to use any you prefer! I like Opera and IE for Windows, myself. For testing purposes, as described in Hour 2, a good minimal set of browsers consists of Internet Explorer, Netscape 4, Opera or Mozilla, and Lynx. If you have access to additional platforms, you'll want to get appropriate browsers for those. In short, testing on as many browsers and platforms as possible will always be to your advantage.

Q Are there more browsers out there than just those you've listed? What about older versions?

A It turns out there are dozens and dozens of browsers that run on a wide variety of operating systems and configurations. You can find these alternate browsers, as well as older versions of more popular browsers, at the evolt browser archive at `http://browsers.evolt.org/`.

Q What do I look for when testing a Web page with a browser?

A Well, the most obvious thing to check for is simple access to information. Are you able to read what's on the screen and get at the content of the HTML? Next, check for functionality. You may find that some browsers make it impossible to follow links or submit forms if your style sheet is not understood. Finally, check for aesthetics; does the page look like you want it to look, or a reasonable approximation? If so, you're in luck; if not, you may want to change your style sheet by adding or removing properties. The workarounds in subsequent hours of this book can help you figure out how to make effects work in specific browsers.

Q I don't have access to every browser ever created, and I certainly don't have multiple computers with a variety of operating systems. What can I do, short of spending a fortune on new hardware?

A A great resource for all Web developers is the HTML Writers Guild. The Guild has a mailing list especially devoted to site testing, including style sheet testing, called HWG-Critique. You simply send a polite message to the mailing list requesting a critique by your fellow list subscribers, and Guild members will review your site and provide helpful suggestions on how to improve it. For subscription information, see the HWG's Web site at `http://www.hwg.org/lists/hwg-critique/`.

Workshop

The workshop contains quiz questions and activities to help reinforce what you've learned in this hour. If you get stuck, the answers to the quiz can be found after the questions.

Quiz

1. What will an older browser do if it encounters Cascading Style Sheets? Is this a good thing or a bad thing?

2. Which browsers are the closest to being fully compliant with the CSS specifications?

3. Why is it important to test in Netscape 4?

Answers

1. An older browser—one written before the CSS recommendation was issued—won't understand anything about Cascading Style Sheets. This is not great, but it's not bad either because CSS is designed so that if you design your style sheets correctly, your Web pages will still function even with CSS unavailable. The presentation may look dull or even awful, but your message will still shine through.

2. The best browsers for CSS support currently are Netscape 6, Mozilla, Opera 6, Internet Explorer (Mac) 5, and Internet Explorer (Windows) 6.

3. It's important to test your designs in Netscape 4 because it's still used by a sizable minority of Web surfers, and because it contains serious problems that can render your content unintelligible for those users.

Activity: Browser Test-drive

The more browsers you use for testing, the better you'll be able to understand how your CSS works with those browsers. To get some hands-on experience with new browsers, follow these directions:

1. Choose one or more browsers from earlier in this hour that will work on your operating system. If you've already used them all, download an older version or an alternate browser from the evolt browser archive.

2. Install the browser and fire it up for surfing the Web.

3. Visit several Web sites that use CSS, including Eric Meyer's css/edge spiral and the site for this book, http://www.CSSin24hours.com.

4. How does your experience using these browsers differ from your experience using your normal browser-of-choice? Note whether the CSS support is better or worse, and rank the browser you're using as "older," "limited," "broken," or "compliant."

HOUR 4

Using CSS with HTML

In previous hours, you've used Cascading Style Sheets to style your HTML pages by linking in an external CSS file. The true power of CSS and HTML really shines through only when you understand both of these complementary languages, how they relate to each other, and how they can be used effectively.

HTML and CSS blend together well not by coincidence but by design; they were literally made for each other. Using that designed synergy is the key to creating effective presentations on your Web sites.

In this hour, you'll learn

- What the different types of HTML are and how to use them with Cascading Style Sheets
- The three ways to link CSS to styles and when to use each
- How to create an external style sheet for your entire Web site
- How to embed style sheets directly in your HTML
- How to create CSS rules based on the HTML attributes of class and id

Types of HTML

To fully understand how HTML and CSS work together, it's important to know what we're talking about when we talk about HTML. Hypertext Markup Language is defined by formal recommendations issued by the World Wide Web Consortium (W3C), just like the Cascading Style Sheets language.

HTML 4.01

The most recent version of HTML is HTML 4.01. HTML 4.01 is an updated version of HTML 4.0, which itself was an improvement over HTML 3.2 and 2.0. (There was no official version numbered 1.0; the first version of HTML was a quickly changing ad hoc language put together primarily by World Wide Web creator Tim Berners-Lee. When efforts began to standardize HTML, they started numbering with 2.0.)

HTML 4.01 comes in three "flavors"—Strict, Transitional, and Frameset. The type of HTML used on your page is indicated by the DOCTYPE statement you place as the first line of the page. Each flavor has a set of tags and attributes that are allowed and disallowed; they're like a variant of spoken human languages, in a way.

What's the difference between the three? HTML Strict relies entirely on CSS for presentational styling, HTML Transitional includes some HTML attributes and elements for presentation effects, and HTML Frameset is used to create frames.

Strict

HTML 4.01 Strict is a version of HTML that removes nearly all of the presentational markup—the <font> tags, the color and link attributes on <body>, the border attribute, and other old standbys that have been used for years to make pages more visually appealing. So what's a Web developer to do if she doesn't want boring pages?

The answer is hopefully clear to anyone reading this book: Use Cascading Style Sheets! The Strict variety relies heavily on CSS for presentation; that's why it's considered strict.

To declare your page as using HTML Strict, put the following at the very top of your HTML file as the first line:

```
<!DOCTYPE HTML PUBLIC "-//W3C//DTD HTML 4.01//EN"
    "http://www.w3.org/TR/html4/strict.dtd">
```

You'll want to use HTML Strict if you're designing primarily for newer browsers or if you don't mind giving unstyled pages to older browsers that will ignore CSS.

Several newer browsers have a special compatibility mode for HTML and CSS where they adhere more closely to the published standards. Mozilla, Netscape 6, and Internet Explorer 6 turn on this mode when they encounter a valid DOCTYPE for HTML Strict and a few other DOCTYPE declarations; other pages are shown in a "quirky" mode for backward-compatibility with older browsers. For more information, see the following URLs:

- http://www.mozilla.org/docs/web-developer/quirks/
- http://msdn.microsoft.com/library/default.asp?url=/library/
  en-us/dnie60/html/cssenhancements.asp

Transitional

HTML 4.01 Transitional adds back in those presentation markup tags and attributes, although some, such as the `<font>` tag, are considered deprecated. What's deprecated mean? That's W3C-talk that means "This is still within the formal specification, but you really should not use it, and it won't be in future versions of this language." Not all presentation markup in HTML 4.01 is deprecated, and you can freely use those nondeprecated elements and attributes as part of HTML 4.01 Transitional.

Transitional HTML is so named because at the time the HTML 4.0 specification was released, few browsers had particularly good CSS support, which meant Strict wasn't really usable on most Web sites, unless you wanted plain gray or white backgrounds, black text, and default fonts.

Transitional is intended as a temporary measure until browsers catch up. So far, the browsers have been slow in catching up; Transitional HTML is therefore what I suggest for most Web development. If you are concerned about delivering your design to the majority of browsers out there, you should use HTML Transitional.

You can use CSS and Transitional HTML together, and in fact that's highly recommended; CSS rules will be followed if the browser understands CSS, and if not, it will look at the HTML attributes or elements instead. This allows you to have "fallback" presentation in the HTML markup for non-CSS browsers, such as Netscape 3.

This is the DOCTYPE statement for HTML 4.01 Transitional; it should be the very first line of your document:

```
<!DOCTYPE HTML PUBLIC "-//W3C//DTD HTML 4.01 Transitional//EN"
    "http://www.w3.org/TR/html4/loose.dtd">
```

Frameset

The Frameset variety of HTML 4.01 is intended for use only in creating frameset pages—those that use the `<frameset>` element, along with `<frame>` and `<noframes>`, to lay out different windows within the page. It's otherwise identical to Transitional HTML; you need to use this only on the page that establishes the frames, not on the frames contained within that set (unless they define other `<frameset>` elements, of course).

You'll want to use HTML Frameset whenever you're creating a frame presentation and at no other time otherwise.

The DOCTYPE for HTML 4.01 Frameset is

```
<!DOCTYPE HTML PUBLIC "-//W3C//DTD HTML 4.01 Frameset//EN"
    "http://www.w3.org/TR/html4/frameset.dtd">
```

XHTML

XHTML 1.0 is a version of HTML 4.01 written as XML, which means it follows the very specific rules and structure imposed on XML documents. The tags are all the same as in HTML, but how you write them may be different. For example, all XHTML tags are lower case, and all attribute values have to be quoted. XHTML 1.0 comes in the same three varieties: Strict, Transitional, and Frameset. The next version, XHTML 1.1, is available only in a Strict flavor and thus relies entirely on CSS for presentation.

Using CSS with XHTML is pretty much the same as using CSS with HTML. As XHTML represents a move forward to an XML-based Web, you may end up migrating from HTML to XHTML sometime in the future. For this reason, I recommend writing all your CSS rules so that element names are written in lower case letters. It doesn't matter in HTML, but it will in XHTML, and making this a habit will save you time now if you choose to use XHTML in the future; you won't need to rewrite all your style sheets.

Validating HTML

Validating your HTML means that you run your page through an HTML validator, which is a program to analyze HTML code and ensure that the code you write is in compliance with the HTML specification. In this way, an HTML validator is like a spellchecker or grammar checker for HTML.

By validating your HTML, you can catch errors in your code, such as misspelled attributes (like `aling` or `scr`) or closing tags you've accidentally left out. Validation also improves your compatibility with browsers; valid HTML code is closer to what browsers—especially newer ones—are expecting. You can validate against your chosen variety of HTML (Strict, Transitional, or Frameset) to ensure that you're using only tags and attributes within that subset of the language.

From the standpoint of troubleshooting your style sheet, it's much easier to catch CSS errors if you know you don't have many HTML errors. I've spent hours chasing down what I thought were mistakes in my CSS when really I'd just written an HTML attribute or element incorrectly.

I recommend always making sure your HTML is valid. Valid code conforms to the appropriate HTML Document Type Definition, which is a formal specification of HTML syntax. You use the DOCTYPE statement as the first line of your HTML file to indicate the correct version of HTML.

To check your HTML, you can use one of the validation services listed here:

- W3C's HTML Validator (`http://validator.w3.org`)
- Web Design Group's HTML Validator (`http://www.htmlhelp.com/tools/validator`)

Style Sheets in HTML

Cascading Style Sheets were designed specifically to work with HTML and can be applied to Web pages in the following three different ways:

- Linked Style Sheets
- Embedded Style Sheets
- Inline Style Attributes

The CSS rules that you will write for each method are generally the same, but the way your HTML and your CSS work together depends on the method you used. So far, you've worked with linked external style sheets, as that's the most useful way of dealing with Cascading Style Sheets and offers the most flexibility.

4

Examples in this book, unless stated otherwise, assume you're using a linked style sheet, and complete listings will be shown as external CSS files. CSS rules (and declarations, for inline styles) are written the same regardless of how they're applied to HTML, so you'll get the same styling effects if you use linked, embedded, or inline style rules.

Linked Style Sheets

In Hour 2, "Getting Started with CSS," you learned about how to create external style sheets and link them with the `<link>` element in HTML. Linking style sheets in this manner gives you the greatest portability and ease of maintenance when designing your styles for your Web site.

Many sites use one or more global style sheets that are linked from every page on the site. Using a global style sheet lets you make changes to one file that will affect the appearance of every page on your site. With a simple change, you could switch the colors, fonts, sizes, and more across your whole Web site.

External style sheets let you separate your content fully from your styles, which means it's easy to replace those styles with something else. For example, you could easily change the appearance of a site by replacing the old style sheet with a new set of rules under the same name.

You can also link in specific style sheets for specific uses, such as one style sheet per company division, as well as a global style sheet for the whole company, on a corporate Web site. You can link style sheets for specific types of output devices as well, using styles written just for those types of devices. For example, you could create a style sheet specifically for handheld wireless devices, screenreaders, or printers. In Hour 21, "Accessibility and Internationalization," and Hour 22, "User Interface and Generated Content," you'll learn more about designing for alternate output devices.

As seen in Hour 2, linked style sheets are created by using the HTML `<link>` element in the `<head>` section of the page. A number of attributes can be used with the `<link>` element, but for our purposes only the following options are important:

```
<link rel="relationship" href="URL"
      type="content-type" media="media-type">
```

The `<link>` tag is actually an all-purpose linking element; it doesn't just define style sheets but also can be used to create any link between the entire document and some other URL location. To use it to identify a linked document as a style sheet, we need to specify what the relationship is. Other types of relationships include `contents` (specifying the location of a table of contents), `alternate` (an alternate version of the page for specific types of output devices or languages), and `glossary` (for a glossary of terms). To indicate a style sheet, however, we simply need `rel="stylesheet"`.

The `href` attribute indicates the location of our style sheet and is a normal Web URL. The location can be relative or absolute; without a directory path, it's assumed to be within the same directory, but you can use any URL path (and machine name), as with any other link in HTML.

Your style sheet can reside even on a different Web server than your HTML file; in fact, this is a good way to quickly and easily add style to a Web page. However, this isn't a license to merely steal someone else's work, any more than viewing the HTML source is an invitation to swipe source code. Use an offsite style sheet only if the site operator has explicitly given permission for it to be used in such a manner. Keep in mind that many

Web hosting services will charge for bandwidth usage, so you may be costing someone money each time you use their style sheet without permission. Also remember that since you don't control the style sheet, it could affect the look of your Web page if it's changed or removed.

> The World Wide Web Consortium offers a number of style sheets for public use at http://www.w3.org/StyleSheets/Core/. You can use these to test styles on your pages by applying them as linked style sheets.

The content-type attribute of the <link> tag indicates the styling language of the linked style sheet. For Cascading Style Sheets—Level 1 and Level 2 alike—this should be "text/css". This is also the MIME type that your server should return when serving up CSS files. All modern Web servers will recognize the file extension .css as being a CSS file and will send an appropriate MIME type. If you name your file something ending in .css, the server will send it as text/css. If you think your server doesn't do this properly for some reason, you should consult your Web server administrator or the documentation for your server software. Also, if you write a server-side script to create a CSS document, for example, in Perl, Java, or PHP, you should make sure you set the content-type HTTP header line to text/css.

4

The media attribute tells the browser which types of media or output device categories the style sheet should be used with. A browser will apply different style sheets depending on the media—for example, one style sheet for printing and another for on-screen display. Style sheets for other media will be ignored, and those rules won't be applied.

For the most part, we are concerned with the media-type screen, which means visual, on-screen display. As screen is assumed to be the default, you don't need specify this unless you're linking a style sheet for another type of output device. Other media types include printer (for printed documents), braille (for tactile Braille devices), aural (for speech synthesizers), and all, which covers all media types. You can list more than one media-type by separating them with commas, such as screen, printer.

> You'll learn more about media-type printer in Hour 20, "CSS for Printing," and about braille and aural display in Hour 21.

Workaround: Netscape 4

Netscape version 4 doesn't accept multiple medias, even when separated by commas or the media type `all`. If you specify something like media=`"screen, printer"`, Netscape 4 simply ignores it and doesn't apply the style sheet to your HTML. If you need to define more than one media type, use multiple `<link>` elements so that Netscape will understand it correctly. Avoid the use of `media="all"` and instead clearly indicate media types for all style sheets. Examples of this workaround include:

```
<!-- Netscape 4 won't understand the following -->
<link type="text/css" href="display.css"
      rel="stylesheet" media="screen, printer">
<link type="text/css" href="base.css"
      rel="stylesheet" media="all">
<!-- Netscape 4 (and everything else) will understand these -->
<link type="text/css" href="display.css"
      rel="stylesheet" media="screen">
<link type="text/css" href="display.css"
      rel="stylesheet" media="printer">
<link type="text/css" href="base.css"
      rel="stylesheet" media="screen">
<link type="text/css" href="base.css"
      rel="stylesheet" media="printer">
<link type="text/css" href="base.css"
      rel="stylesheet" media="aural">
<link type="text/css" href="base.css"
      rel="stylesheet" media="braille">
```

Embedded Style Sheets

Another way to apply CSS to HTML is by embedding the CSS directly within the HTML file using the `<style>` tag. Your CSS rules will then be part of the same file as the HTML, which makes editing easier, at least at first. An embedded style sheet also is useful for rules that apply only to a specific page and won't need to be used by other parts of the site, which helps keep the size of your global style sheet relatively small. For example, if you have a rule that applies only to the front page of the site, you don't need that in a site-wide style sheet that is accessed by every page, even those that don't use the rule.

On the other hand, it's also harder to maintain and update a site only with embedded style sheets; you'll have to edit every single page when you want to make a change in the appearance of the site.

For this reason, I prefer linking instead of embedding CSS, but in many situations it's easier or more appropriate to use an embedded style sheet. For example, when testing

CSS rules or developing a style sheet, it may be easiest to use an embedded style sheet and then convert it to an external style sheet for production use.

> How do you convert an embedded style sheet to an external one? Simple, you just cut-and-paste the content of the `<style>` tag and paste it into a new file with a name ending in `.css`. Here's the tricky part: if there are any URL references (such as background images) in your CSS, you'll need to make sure that they apply relative to the new style sheet and not the original document. To convert an external style sheet to an embedded one, just paste it into a `<style>` element and check the URLs again.

To embed a style sheet, use the `<style>` tag, which can be used only within the `<head>` of a Web page:

```
<style type="text/css" media="media-type">
 ... CSS rules go here ...
</style>
```

The `type` attribute is required. Theoretically, this is because a different style language could be used with HTML, although in practice only CSS is ever used. The media attribute is optional; the default is `screen`. As with the `<link>` element, multiple media types can be set by listing them with comma separators.

You can have more than one `<style>` element within the `<head>` section of the page if you like; for example, you could have one for `screen` and one for `printer`. (You could have two for `printer`, if you want, but it usually makes more sense to combine them together in a single `<style>` tag.)

Hiding CSS from Older Browsers

Browsers shouldn't ever reveal the contents of a `<style>` tag; even if a browser doesn't support CSS, it shouldn't display the rules to the user. However, some very old browsers were written before CSS was created, and because these browsers don't know what the `<style>` tag is, they just display it as HTML text. The best way to avoid this is by wrapping your CSS rules within HTML comments:

```
<style type="text/css" media="screen">
 <!--
 ... CSS rules go here ...
 -->
</style>
```

The older browsers will just interpret this as a normal comment, whereas the newer browsers will understand the CSS. As nearly every browser used these days understands the `<style>` tag, it's not particularly necessary, but it doesn't hurt anything to do it, either. The examples in this book don't include comments.

Inline Style Attributes

Inline styles are set on HTML tags using the `style` attribute. Such a style applies to that particular element, or possibly to that element's children, if the rule's properties can be inherited.

 In Hour 7, "Cascading and Inheritance," you'll learn more about inheritance and cascading.

The `style` attribute can be set on nearly any HTML tag that is displayed by a browser. The attribute contains the declaration of a CSS rule but not a selector; the tag itself (and its content) serves as the selector.

Here's an example of using inline styles to set some CSS properties:

```
<table style="font-family: Arial; font-size: large">
  <tr>
    <th style="color: blue">
      Writer's Name
    </th>
    <th style="color: green">
      Primary Genre
    </th>
  </tr>
  <tr><td>Kynn</td><td>Technical (Web Design)</td></tr>
  <tr><td>Sam</td><td>Non-Fiction (Travel)</td></tr>
  <tr style="color: red">
    <td>Mary Jo</td>
    <td>Non-Fiction (Newspapers, Cookbooks)</td>
  </tr>
</table>
```

As you can see, the selector is unnecessary; the style is applied to the tag on which the `style` attribute is set. Also, there are no ending semi-colons on the rules. Within `style` attributes, the ending semi-colon is optional. I usually write it myself because it makes it easier to add additional rules if I need them.

Style attributes are most useful for single-point changes, such as changing the color of an announcement to make it stand out, like this:

```
<h1 style="color: red;">
  Just Added: New book signing at City Lights on Feb. 5.
</h1>
```

Inline styles are easier to add into your page as you go along creating the HTML if you're doing it by hand; you won't have to go back to the `<style>` section or an external style sheet but can just type the declaration directly into an attribute. However, in the long run it's harder to maintain inline styles, as they'll be scattered throughout your HTML source.

Ultimately, the use of inline styles reduces the separation of content from presentation because it mixes the two together within the same markup. It makes more sense to use HTML for structure and content and CSS for presentation; in this regard, inline CSS is just a single step up from HTML presentation attributes.

In general, you should avoid using inline styles unless you have a very specific use in mind. If you have to style more than one part of your page the same way, it's better to use an embedded or external style sheet and define a class instead.

It's perfectly valid to use all of these within one document—for example, a global style sheet for the entire site applied with a `<link>` tag; an embedded style sheet inside a `<style>` tag; and styles set on individual elements using the `style` attribute.

Classes and IDs

In addition to setting styles based on HTML elements, CSS allows for rules based on two optional attributes in HTML: `class` and `id`. Each of these can serve as the selector part of a CSS rule and can be set on any visible HTML tag.

For even more selectors you can use with HTML and CSS, see Hour 5, "Selectors."

The `<div>` and `<span>` elements really come into their own with `class` and `id` selectors. Through the use of `class` and `id` attributes, `<div>` or `<span>` tags can be made to have nearly any effect and presentation, which is often good but sometimes bad. Care must be taken to avoid using `class` or `id` selectors that you're not ignoring more appropriate markup, which has understood semantics. In other words, a `<div>` with a class of `bldtxt` has no specific meaning in the context of HTML, but a `<strong>` tag definitely does. Before using `<div>` or `<span>`, consider if another tag would make more sense.

The `class` Attribute in HTML

The `class` attribute is used to define a related group of HTML elements on a page. It could be that they have the same function or role, but in a CSS context, it means they have the same style rules applied to them. (The `class` attribute could be used for more than just styling, but in practice it's rarely used for any other purpose.)

The elements within a class can be of any type; one might be a <p>, another a <span>, and a third an <img>. That's perfectly fine; they will have the same style rules applied to them, but the fact that each one has a default presentation (defined by the browser or the HTML specifications) means those styles will be applied relative to the way they're normally rendered.

To create a class, you simply have to give it a name. A class name may be nearly anything, but has to be one word; in practice, it's best to stick to letters and numbers. Avoid using underlines, periods, and other nonalphanumeric characters when naming your classes.

You can name a class anything you like; it's basically just an arbitrary word used to group these items together. A descriptive name is good, especially one that describes function instead of presentation. For example, `class="detail"` makes more sense than `class="bluetext"`; if I can't come up with a good descriptive name, I'll use something arbitrary instead, such as the names of planets or the seven dwarves. Class names are not inherently case-sensitive, but you should try to use the same case of characters when writing your HTML and your CSS rules.

Once you've chosen a name for your class, you just have to assign HTML elements to that class by setting the class attribute on each. A given HTML element can be part of one or more classes by separating them with spaces. Here are some examples:

```
<div class="p1">
  <h2 class="q2">Meeting Times</h2>
  <p class="r3">
    We will be meeting every other Wednesday, at
    <span class="q2 j4">7:30 p.m.</span>
  </p>
</div>
```

In this example, the <div> is part of the p1 class. The <h2> and the <span> are both part of the q2 class. The <p> is part of the "r3" class, and the <span> is also part of the j4 class.

Workaround for Netscape 4

Unfortunately, Netscape 4 does not properly understand space-separated multiple classes. In the previous example, Netscape would not consider the `<span>` to be part of either q2 or j4. For this reason, you'll want to avoid setting more than one class per tag. If you need to set multiple classes on one element, you can use the `<div>` or `<span>` elements to wrap the tag and set the additional class on the `<div>` or `<span>`. For example:

```
<p>
 We will be meeting every other Wednesday, at
 <span class="q2"><span class="j4">7:30 p.m.</span></span>
</p>
```

Class Selectors in CSS

Once you've defined a class in your HTML, you can use it as a class selector in CSS. Class selectors are indicated by a period (.) before the name of the class, like this:

```
.q2 { color: blue; }
.r3 { font-family: Arial; }
```

You can combine an element selector with a class selector; the result selects only those members of the class, which are of that particular element. (Or, it selects only those elements that are members of that particular class; six of one and half-dozen of the other.) Just put the name of the element directly in front of the period and then the class name. For example:

```
span.q2 { font-size: large; }
p.r3 { color: green; }
```

The first refers to all `<span>` elements with `class="q2"`; the latter to all `<p>` elements in the r3 class. You can combine together several classes within a rule to select only elements that have those classes listed (separated by spaces, as described before) by separating them with periods, as shown here:

```
.q2.j4 { font-family: Arial; }
```

This rule would select the `<span>`, which is part of both class q2 and class j4.

Workaround for Netscape 4, Internet Explorer 4, 5

Because Netscape 4 doesn't understand multiple classes, it won't understand this rule either. Also, Internet Explorer 4 and 5 has problems with combined class selectors; it seems to ignore the first class entirely. Use a contextual

continues

selector (from Hour 6, "The CSS Box Model"), combined with an enclosing `<span>` or `<div>`, for compatibility with those browsers, as in the following:

`.q2 .j4 { font-family: Arial; }`

Due to poor browser support, it's probably best to avoid selectors of multiple classes entirely.

A complete example of using class selectors is shown in Listings 4.1 and 4.2, and the result of displaying in a browser is presented in Figure 4.1.

LISTING 4.1 HTML Code Illustrating Class Selectors

```
<html>
  <!-- This is file 4-1.html -->
  <head>
    <title>
      Class Selectors in Action
    </title>
    <link type="text/css" rel="stylesheet" href="4-2.css">
  </head>
  <body>
    <h1 class="mercury">
      Welcome!
    </h1>
    <div class="mars">
      <p class="saturn">
        This is a short page to tell you about our writers
        group. We meet in the bookstore every other Wednesday;
        our meetings are at <span class="mercury">7:30 p.m.
        sharp.</span>
      </p>
    </div>
  </body>
</html>
```

LISTING 4.2 CSS Code Illustrating Class Selectors

```
/* This is file 4-2.css */
.mercury    { color: red; }
.mars       { font-family: Arial; }
.saturn     { color: blue; }
h1.mercury  { font-family: Verdana; }
```

FIGURE **4.1**

Opera displays the style rules defined with class selectors.

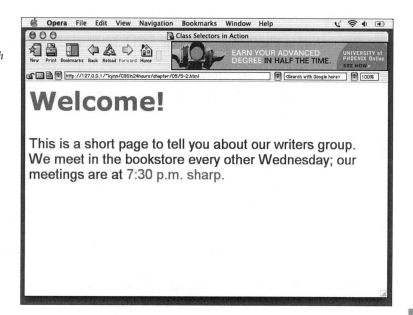

The `id` Attribute in HTML

The HTML attribute `id` is similar to the `class` attribute—it can be set on nearly any tag and can be used as a CSS selector—but is much more restricted. Only one tag on a page can have a given `id`; it must be unique within the page and is used to identify just that element. An `id` attribute's value has to begin with a letter and can be followed by letters, numbers, periods (.), underlines (_), hyphens (-) or colons (:); however, if you're using it as a selector in CSS, it's safest to stick to just letters and numbers. Case matters, so be consistent in the case of your `id` attributes. Here's an example:

```
<a href="next.html" id="next">The next page</a>
```

`id` Selectors in CSS

An `id` selector is indicated by a # (the hash, also called the pound sign) before the value of the `id`. For example:

```
#next { font-size: large; }
```

Why would you want to use `id` selectors and not class selectors? Good question. A class selector is more flexible; it can do anything an `id` selector can do and more. If you want to reuse the style, you can do it with a class selector by adding new elements to the class, but you can't do that with `id` selectors because an `id` value must be unique in a document, and only one element on the page can have that value.

An id selector is useful if you know that you have to identify one unique item within a page—for example, the "next" link, or maybe a common navigation or layout element that appears on each page. In general, id selectors are less useful than class selectors when using CSS with HTML. When using CSS with XML, however, id attributes play a larger role because XML uses id attributes more than HTML does.

Summary

In this hour, you learned about the three flavors of HTML 4.01 and how CSS is used in each, and you learned about the benefits of validating your HTML code. You learned that Cascading Style Sheets can be applied to HTML pages in three ways: external style sheets using the `<link>` tag, embedded style sheets defined inside a `<style>` tag, or specific styles set using the style attribute. You learned how to set class and id attributes in HTML and how to create rules using class and id attributes as selectors.

Browser Support Report Card

CSS Feature	Grade	Notes
`<link>`	A	
`<link media="media-type">`	B+	Requires workaround for Netscape 4
`<style>`	A	
`<style media="media-type">`	B+	Requires workaround for Netscape 4
style attribute	A	
class selectors	A	
Multiple class selectors	B-	Requires workaround for Netscape 4 and IE 5
id selectors	A	

Q&A

Q Will there be such a thing as HTML 5?

A No, and yes. The W3C has stopped work on developing HTML and is concentrating on XHTML instead. The next version of HTML will be XHTML 2.0, and in addition to being composed of distinct modules, it will have new elements and attributes that don't currently exist in HTML. You can track the progress of XHTML 2's development at http://www.w3.org/Markup/.

Q Can you use selectors with inline styles? For example, <div style=".dot { color: black; }">?

A No; a style attribute contains only the declaration part of a CSS rule, not the selector portion. The selector is the content of the element itself.

Q You said I could use style attributes, embedded style sheets, and linked style sheets on the same HTML page. What happens if they have different values for the same property?

A When two or more rules conflict, the method of resolving the conflict is known as the cascade. You'll learn more about this in Hour 7, but the general principle is that the more specific rule will usually win.

Workshop

The workshop contains quiz questions and activities to help reinforce what you've learned in this hour. If you get stuck, the answers to the quiz can be found after the questions.

Quiz

1. What HTML tag is used to insert an embedded style sheet? What are the primary attributes of that tag?

2. What HTML tag is used to associate an external style sheet with an HTML tag? What are the primary attributes of that tag?

3. What is the default value for the `media` attribute?

4. What is the difference between a class selector and an `id` selector? When would you use each?

5. What are the three "flavors" of HTML, and which one relies on CSS for nearly all presentation styling?

6. What does HTML validation check for?

Answers

1. The `<style>` tag is used to embed a style sheet in an HTML file. The main attributes are `type`, which should be `text/css`, and an optional `media` attribute.

2. The `<link>` tag can be set in the `<head>` of an HTML file to link to an external style sheet. The primary attributes used with CSS are `type`, `media`, `rel="stylesheet"`, and `href`.

3. The default value of the `media` attribute is `screen`.

4. An `id` selector applies to only one element within each document, whereas a `class` selector can be used to select any element within that class. You'd use class when you needed to select multiple elements and id if you wanted to select only a single, unique element.

5. The three types of HTML 4.01 are Strict, Transitional, and Frameset. HTML Strict has almost no presentational markup and depends on CSS to provide styling instructions.

6. HTML validation checks your HTML code against the formal specification and DTD for the HTML language.

Activity: Using HTML and CSS Together

To apply what you've learned this hour, you'll create an HTML page and validate it; create an external CSS file and link it to the HTML file; and add embedded and inline styles. This will make you familiar with the ways HTML and CSS are used together in Web design.

1. Create a basic HTML document with headers, paragraphs, `<div>` and `<span>` tags, and other markup. Be sure to set some class and id attributes on your tags. Save this HTML file.

2. Choose an appropriate flavor of HTML, and add the `DOCTYPE` statement at the top. Validate your HTML at one of the HTML validator sites; fix any errors that exist.

3. Create a CSS file with rules based on element selectors, `class` selectors, and `id` selectors. Save this CSS file.

4. Use `<link>` to apply the CSS style sheet to the HTML file. View the results in an HTML browser that supports CSS.

5. Add additional styles directly into the HTML file by creating a `<style>` element in the `<head>`; view the results.

6. Create some inline styles using the `style` attribute, and check your creation in a browser.

You'll have successfully completed the activity if you're able to use CSS with your HTML in each of the ways discussed this hour—external style sheets, embedded style sheets, and inline `style` attributes—and if you can utilize `class` and `id` attributes as selectors in your CSS rules.

PART II

Core Principles of CSS

Hour

HOUR 5

Selectors

As you learned in Hour 2, "Getting Started with CSS," selectors are the part of the CSS rule that identifies the target of the styling. Putting the power of selectors to use is vital for getting the most out of CSS.

In this hour, you'll learn

- More about simple selectors you've already been using
- How to use `class` and `id` selectors
- What the universal selector is and when to use it
- What pseudo-classes and pseudo-elements are and how they can be used
- How to specify styles that affect hypertext links

Simple Selectors

You've seen the simplest type of selectors already: type selectors, `class` selectors, and `id` selectors. In this hour, you'll look at how you can use them more effectively.

So far you have learned how to create CSS rules using simple selectors—type selectors based on the HTML tag and `class` or `id` selectors based on attributes in the HTML.

A type selector is simply the name of an HTML tag minus the <> angle brackets. For example:

```
h1 { color: blue; }
```

This selects all <h1> tags and specifies that they're the color `blue`. Type selectors are the easiest to use because they're so straightforward, but they're also very limited. What if you want only some of the <h1> tags to be `blue` and others to be `green`? That's when you'd use class and id selectors.

> Although I said type selectors had to be HTML tags, I must admit that's only half true. They actually have to be any sort of legitimate element for the language you're styling; this is how you can use CSS with XML, for example. And in fact, you don't have to have the actual tag present! HTML (but not XML or XHTML) lets you leave out certain tag declarations entirely, such as the <body> element. The opening and closing tags are implied. If you have a rule based on body, such as 'body { font-family: Arial; }', a CSS-compliant browser will still apply your font to the implied <body> even though no tags are present.

In Hour 4, "Using CSS with HTML," you learned how you can set `class` and `id` selectors in your rules based on HTML attributes of `class` and `id`, such as

```
#here      { font-size: large;      }
.there     { color: green;          }
```

An `id` selector uniquely identifies part of a page, whereas a `class` selector allows you to identify specific tags as being part of a certain set you've defined.

Using `class` and `id` Selectors

You can combine `class` selectors (or even `id` selectors) with <div> tags to designate specific sections of a page that should receive special styling. For example, consider the HTML page shown in Listing 5.1, which has a `class` attribute set on each <div> tag.

LISTING 5.1 HTML Sections Set via `<div>` and class

```
<!-- imgtip-5.1.html                  -->
<!-- Accessibility tips for images    -->
<!-- By Kynn Bartlett, kynn@kynn.com  -->
<html>
  <head>
    <title>Image Accessibility</title>
    <link type="text/css" rel="stylesheet"
          media="screen" href="tips-5.2.css">
  </head>
  <body>
    <div class="nav">
      <a href="http://access.idyllmtn.com">access.idyllmtn.com</a>
      &middot;
      <a href="http://access.idyllmtn.com/tips/">Tips</a>
      &middot;
      <!-- this page's short title -->
      Images
    </div>
    <div class="header">
      <h1>Image Accessibility</h1>
      <h2>Making your graphics accessible</h2>
    </div>
    <div class="tips">
      <p>
        Here's some helpful tips on making your graphical
        content accessible to users who can't see images:
      </p>
      <ul>
        <li>Always include an <tt>alt</tt> attribute on your
            <tt>&lt;img&gt;</tt> tag.</li>
        <li>The <tt>alt</tt> attribute should contain a short
            replacement for the graphic, in text. If the image
            itself has text, list that in <tt>alt</tt>.</li>
        <li>If the image is purely decorative and doesn't convey
            any additional information, use <tt>alt=""</tt>.</li>
        <li>If there is more information in the graphic than you
            can convey in a short <tt>alt</tt> attribute, such
            as the information in a graph or chart, then use
            the <tt>longdesc</tt> attribute to give the URL of
            a page which describes the graphic in text.</li>
      </ul>
    </div>
    <div class="footer">
      <hr>
      <address>
        Copyright &copy; 2002 by Kynn Bartlett
      </address>
```

continues

LISTING 5.1   Continued

```
    </div>
  </body>
</html>
```

As you can see, you linked in an external style sheet, `tips-5.2.css`, using a `<link>` tag. That style sheet defines a style for each section of the page; your sections are "nav," "header," "tips," and "footer." The style sheet is shown in Listing 5.2.

LISTING 5.2   Sectional Styles Using Classes

```
/* tips-5.2.css                   */
/* By Kynn Bartlett, kynn@kynn.com */

.nav            /* Navigation bar */
  {
    font-family: Verdana, sans-serif;
  }
.header        /* Top heading of the page */
  {
    color: white;
    background-color: maroon;
    font-family: Verdana, sans-serif;
  }
.tips          /* A list of tips for accessibility */
  {
    color: white;
    background-color: gray;
    font-family: Arial, sans-serif;
  }
.footer        /* Bottom of the page */
  {
    color: green;
    background-color: white;
    font-family: "Times New Roman", serif;
  }
```

The effect of applying these styles is shown in Figure 5.1. You'll notice that I've used background colors to make two of the `<div>` sections visible; in practice, this can be a somewhat unattractive effect; some of my examples are written simply to illustrate a principle rather than to be aesthetically appealing, especially in the limited black, white, and gray shades available in this book.

FIGURE 5.1

Netscape 6 displays sectional styles set by `<div>` *and* `class`.

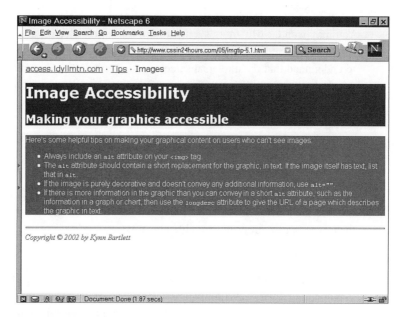

The Universal Selector

In addition to type, `class`, and `id` selectors, CSS also defines a *universal selector*. The universal selector applies to all tags and content within a page and is represented by an asterisk (*). Here's an example of a universal selector rule:

```
* { color: blue; }
```

Workaround for Netscape 4 and Internet Explorer

The 4.0 versions of both Netscape and Internet Explorer do not support the universal selector. For this reason, you'll probably want to write your universal selectors to also include the `<body>` tag, like this:

```
*, body { font-family: Arial; }
```

If you're writing a rule that uses the universal selector and there's something else to that rule, such as a class selector, you can leave out the asterisk. In fact, the general way of writing class selectors is just a special case of the universal selector with the asterisk omitted. The following two declarations are identical:

5

```
*.there    { color: green;              }
.there     { color: green;              }
```

You may wonder why there's a need for a universal selector; as you've seen before, you can affect the style of an entire page by using a selector of the `<body>` tag. It's important to understand that the universal selector sets the style on all elements and doesn't just set an inherited default. What do I mean? Consider the following style sheet:

```
* { color: green; }
h1 { color: blue; }
```

Let's assume you'll link that to an HTML file that includes this:

```
<h1>This is <em>very</em> important</h1>
```

What color will the word "very" be? It will be green and in the middle of a blue headline because the universal rule says everything has the color green explicitly set, just as if there were a rule for every possible element, reading

```
element { color: green; }
```

In practice, you'd probably want the color of the `<em>` to inherit from the `<h1>`'s style, so you need to be very careful about when and where you use a universal selector. You'll learn more about inheritance in Hour 7, "Cascading and Inheritance."

Combining Simple Selectors

To get the most utility out of your CSS rules, you'll want to write combined rules. You've already learned a little about grouping selectors together; now you'll see how you can use descendant selectors as well.

Grouping Selectors

As you learned in Hour 2, you can combine rules by listing the selectors together, separating them by commas. You can combine any sort of selectors in this way, such as in the following rule:

```
/* Anything that is sorta heading-like is in Arial;
   only odd headings are maroon and the rest are green */
h1, h2, h3, h4, h5, h6, .heading, .standout, #headline
  { font-family: Arial; }
h1, h3, h5, dt, .heading, .standout, #headline
  { font-color: maroon; }
h2, h4, h6
  { font-color: green; }
```

You could have written the same set of rules in this manner:

```
/* Anything that is sorta heading-like is in Arial;
   only odd headings are maroon, and the rest are green */
```

```
h1, h3, h5, dt, .heading, .standout, #headline
  { font-family: Arial;
    font-color: maroon; }
h2, h4, h6
  { font-family: Arial;
    font-color: green; }
```

Writing it the first way makes it easier to change the font color if you need to; the declaration font-family: Arial; appears only one place in your document. The way you group your rules can improve the ease with which you can modify them. Note, though, that there's a drawback to this approach, as well; to change how one type of selector is rendered (say, anything in the standout class), you'll need to edit several rules. There are no hard-and-fast guidelines, therefore, about how you can group your rules in modules; as you gain experience with CSS, you'll form your own methods for style rules grouping.

Descendant Selectors

One of the most useful ways to group selectors together is to use a *descendant selector.* A *descendant,* in HTML and XML, is an element that's completely contained within another element's content. As an example, the <h2> is a descendant of the <div>, and the <em> of the <h1>, in Listing 5.3. The <em> is also a descendant of the <div>, as it's contained by both the <div> and the <h1>.

LISTING 5.3   Descendants in HTML

```
<!-- babe-5.3.html              -->
<!-- By Kynn Bartlett kynn@kynn.com -->
<html>
  <head>
    <title>Best Family Movie Ever</title>
    <link type="text/css" rel="stylesheet"
          href="babe-5.4.css">
    <style type="text/css">
    </style>
  </head>
  <body>
    <div class="header">
      <h1>Movie Review: <cite>Babe</cite></h1>
      <p>
        Mini-Review by Joe Moviefan
      </p>
    </div>
    <div class="opinion">
      <h2>The Best Family Movie <em>Ever</em></h2>
      <p>
        The movie <cite>Babe</cite> was the best family
        movie ever produced!  This great movie featured
```

5

continues

LISTING 5.3 Continued

```
         talking animals, a cantankerous old man, and
         subtle-yet-Oscar-winning special effects -- who
         could ask for more?  The clever writing and
         humorous touches make this all-ages movie great
         for children while still very enjoyable by
         adults. Feel like a kid again -- see
         <cite>Babe</cite>!
      </p>
    </div>
    <hr>
    <div class="footer">
      <p>
        Copyright &copy; 2002 by
        <a href="mailto:joe@kynn.com">Joe Moviefan</a>
      </p>
    </div>
  </body>
</html>
```

Descendant selectors define rules based on where a given tag appears within the page by combining together simple selectors, separated by spaces. For example, here's a rule to change the color of all `<cite>` tags contained within paragraphs:

```
p cite { color: white; background-color: black; }
```

You'll notice that I listed the outside tag first and then the inside. If you did it the other way around, you wouldn't match anything because there are no cite tags that contain paragraph tags.

If you add this rule to the `<style>` element of your HTML page from Listing 5.3, you get the effect shown in Figure 5.2. Notice that the `<cite>` within the `<h1>` is not styled by this rule, just the `<cite>` inside the `<p>` element.

It's important to keep in mind that a descendant selector means any descendant, not just an immediate child. A descendant could be an element inside an element inside an element. This allows us to make rules that apply to any descendant element, no matter how deeply it's nested.

You can combine section styles (set via `class` and `<div>`) with element-based type selectors, as well; for example, the following code changes the font face of `<p>` tags within the `header` section but modifies no others:

```
.header p { font-family: "Courier New", monospace; }
```

The effects of this rule are shown in Figure 5.3.

FIGURE 5.2

Netscape 6 displays the second <cite> with your chosen style.

FIGURE 5.3

Changing the header paragraph font style, as shown in Netscape 6.

Header paragraph

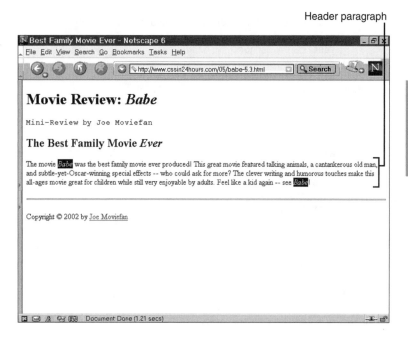

5

A more complete style sheet that demonstrates how to set a number of different combined selectors is listed in Listing 5.4. Figure 5.4 shows how Listing 5.3 looks with this style sheet applied.

LISTING 5.4   A Variety of Selectors in a Single Style Sheet

```
/* babe-5.4.css: Style sheet for Babe review       */
/* Written by Kynn Bartlett <kynn@kynn.com>         */

body
  {
    font-family: Arial, sans-serif;
    color: black;
    background-color: white;
  }

.header h1
  {
    font-family: Verdana, sans-serif;
    color: fuchsia;
  }

.header p
  {
    font-family: "Courier New", monospace;
    color: teal;
    font-size: larger;
  }

.header cite
  {
    color: purple;
  }

.opinion h2
  {
    color: white;
    background-color: navy;
    font-family: Arial, sans-serif;
  }

em
  {
    font-size: larger;
  }

p cite
  {
    color: white;
    background-color: black;
  }
```

LISTING 5.4   Continued

```
.footer
  {
    font-family: "Times New Roman", serif;
    font-size: small;
  }

.footer a
  {
    color: green;
  }
```

FIGURE 5.4

*Displaying various
selectors in Netscape 6.*

Pseudo-classes and Pseudo-elements

In addition to type selectors and class selectors, CSS also allows pseudo-class and pseudo-element selectors.

A *pseudo-class selector* is a selector based on a set of predefined qualities that an HTML element can possess. These qualities function in practice similar to a class attribute on the element, so in CSS terms, they are called pseudo-classes. No actual class attributes exist in the markup that correspond to these pseudo-classes; instead, they represent some aspect of the element to which they're applied, or even the state of the browser's user interface relative to that element.

A *pseudo-element selector* identifies a virtual element, one that doesn't exist in the markup but can be deduced by the browser and used to apply a style. Like pseudo-classes, there is no markup that corresponds to the pseudo-element.

Simple Pseudo-classes

The pseudo-classes in CSS are shown on Table 5.1. The `:active`, `:focus`, and `:hover` pseudo-classes are covered in Hour 11, "Styling Links;" the `:lang` pseudo-class is discussed in Hour 21, "Accessibility and Internationalization."

TABLE 5.1   CSS Pseudo-classes

Pseudo-class	Selects
`:active`	Elements that have been activated (such as active links)
`:first-child`	The first child of an element
`:focus`	Elements that have focus (such as form fields receiving input)
`:hover`	Elements that are pointed at (such as by a mouse)
`:lang()`	Styles for a specific language
`:link`	Unfollowed links
`:visited`	Previously visited links

Pseudo-classes can stand alone in a style rule, as classes can, but most commonly they're used with elements as a type selector, as follows:

```
:link      { color: red; }
a:link     { color: red; }
```

Both of these rules are valid; the former applies to any element that happens to be a link, whereas the latter rule covers only `<a>` tags. In practice, these are the same things in HTML, only the `<a>` elements are links, and so the rules mean the same thing.

You can combine pseudo-classes with real classes or even other pseudo-classes by putting them together with no spaces between, just the . and : indicators. For example, here's HTML with `class` attributes set on links:

```
<a href="search.html" class="nav">
  Search the Site
</a>
...
<a href="http://www.idyllmtn.com/" class="offsite">
  Idyll Mountain Internet
</a>
```

Here are rules to work with each of those links; note that the order of the class and the pseudo-class doesn't matter:

```
a:link.nav        { color: cyan; }
a.offsite:link    { color: green; }
```

The :link and :visited Pseudo-classes

In HTML, you can use attributes on the <body> tag to determine the colors of links:

```
<body link="red" visited="gray">
```

CSS gives the same functionality through pseudo-classes, and by combining pseudo-class selectors with class or id selectors, you can put different link colors on different parts of the page as you'll see later in this hour.

The :link pseudo-class is the equivalent of the <body> attribute link in HTML; it defines a style for links that have yet to be followed. You'll usually set these on the <a> tag because <a> is the only visible linking element in HTML. Here's an example CSS rule using :link:

```
a:link    { color: red; }
```

Visited links are those that the user has already been to; the browser keeps track of a list of visited URLs and colors them differently. The :visited pseudo-class is used to write rules applying to those types of links, as follows:

```
a:visited  { color: gray; }
```

The :link and :visited pseudo-selectors are mutually exclusive; a given link is either one or the other at any given time and can't be both at once. However, you can write a rule that applies to both, such as

```
a:link,
a:visited  { color: blue; }
```

> Note that changing the :link and :visited colors to the same value can cause problems for users! Most users expect links to change to some color—anything other than the original, although usually from blue to purple—after visiting links. Unless you've got a good reason for it, you'll probably want to supply different :link and :visited colors.

Unlike HTML, which lets you change only the colors of links, CSS allows you to apply nearly any style to unvisited or visited links by using the :link and :visited pseudo-selectors. For example:

```
a:link    { color:            black;
            background-color:  lime;
            font-family:       Arial, sans-serif; }
```

5

```
a:visited    { color:               gray;
               background-color:     yellow;
               font-family:          "Times New Roman", serif; }
```

This puts your unvisited links in black text on a lime green background and puts the visited links in gray on a yellow background. Unvisited links are in Arial font, and visited links are in Times New Roman. Now, apart from an illustrative example, you may never want to write rules like these; it doesn't make sense, for example, for the font face to change when you've clicked on a link, and some of my color choices are just plain ugly. Background colors on links do help them stand out from rest of the page, though, and that's not such a bad thing. You'll learn more about styling links in Hour 11.

To color links differently on different sections of the page, combine :link and :visited pseudo-selectors with section classes in a descendant selector, like this:

```
.nav               { background-color: black;
                     color: white; }
.nav a:link        { color: cyan; }
.nav a:visited     { color: fuchsia; }
```

This creates a black navigation bar with unvisited links in cyan (bright blue) and visited links in fuchsia (bright purple). If you add these styles to the style sheet in Listing 5.2, the accessibility tip page from Listing 5.1 will look like the page shown in Figure 5.5.

FIGURE 5.5

Netscape 6 demon-strates pseudo-class selectors coloring links on a page.

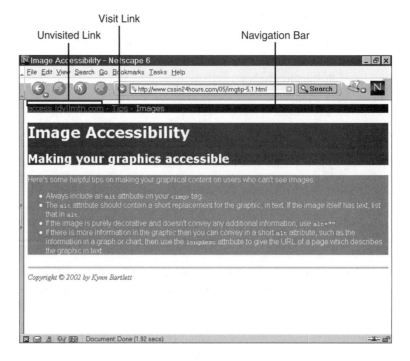

The `:first-child` Pseudo-class

The `:first-child` pseudo-class is used to select an element that's the first child of another element. The first child is the first tag within some other element; if the first child matches the base type of the selector—the part before the `:first-child` pseudo-class—then the rule applies to that element.

Listing 5.5 shows the start of a short story; you want to make the first paragraph larger, for effect. The style sheet to do this is shown in Listing 5.6, and the results are displayed in Figure 5.6.

LISTING 5.5   A Few Paragraphs in HTML

```
<!-- story-5.5.html                              -->
<!-- By Kynn Bartlett                            -->
<html>
  <head>
    <title>Fortune of Reversal</title>
    <link type="text/css" rel="stylesheet"
        href="story-5.7.css">
  </head>
  <body>
    <h1 class="storytitle">Fortune of Reversal</h1>

  <div class="storybody">
     <p>
        They dined on heaping platters of Szechuan chicken, of
        spicy beef, of shrimp and vegetables in some exotic dish
        without a name. Bits of food were passed from chopsticks
        to chopsticks, violating all known laws of Chinese
        cuisine etiquette. The tea flowed hot and fast that night,
        until the meal finally concluded itself.
     </p>

     <p>
        "Thank you for dining here tonight," said the badgeless,
        anonymous waitress. She placed a small tray containing the
        check and two wrapped fortune cookies on the edge of the
        table, and hefted the empty plates one by one, forming a
        stack on the crook of her elbow.
     </p>

     <p>
        "Absolutely delicious," declared Oliver as he pulled a card
        from his wallet and flicked it onto the bill. He picked up
        the two cookies, an afterthought. "Fortune cookie, my
        love?" he asked Amanda.
     </p>
```

5

continues

LISTING 5.5   Continued

```
    </div>
  </body>
</html>
```

LISTING 5.6   A Style Sheet Using `:first-child` Pseudo-class Selector

```css
/* story-5.6.css            */
/* By Kynn Bartlett kynn@kynn.com */

.storytitle
  { font-family: Verdana; }

.storybody p
  { font-family: Arial; }

.storybody p:first-child
  { font-size: large; }
```

FIGURE 5.6

Netscape 6 uses the `:first-child` selector to style the first paragraph.

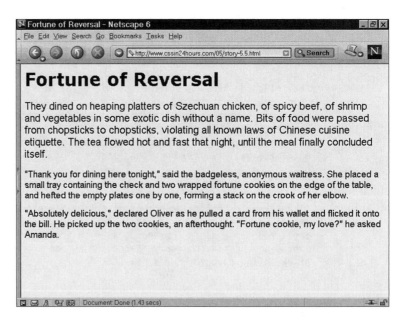

Fortune of Reversal – Netscape 6

File Edit View Search Go Bookmarks Tasks Help

http://www.cssin24hours.com/05/story-5.5.html

Fortune of Reversal

They dined on heaping platters of Szechuan chicken, of spicy beef, of shrimp and vegetables in some exotic dish without a name. Bits of food were passed from chopsticks to chopsticks, violating all known laws of Chinese cuisine etiquette. The tea flowed hot and fast that night, until the meal finally concluded itself.

"Thank you for dining here tonight," said the badgeless, anonymous waitress. She placed a small tray containing the check and two wrapped fortune cookies on the edge of the table, and hefted the empty plates one by one, forming a stack on the crook of her elbow.

"Absolutely delicious," declared Oliver as he pulled a card from his wallet and flicked it onto the bill. He picked up the two cookies, an afterthought. "Fortune cookie, my love?" he asked Amanda.

Document Done (1.43 secs)

Workaround for Netscape 4, Internet Explorer (Windows), and Opera

Only Netscape 6, Mozilla, and Internet Explorer 5 (Macintosh) support the `:first-child` pseudo-element; other browsers ignore it. For maximum compatibility, set a `class` attribute manually on your first child elements, such as `class="firstone"`, and then include that `class` as an additional selector in your rule. For example:

```
storybody p:first-child, .storybody p.firstone
 {
  font-size: large;
 }
```

Of course, by doing so you've made the first half of the selector redundant, as Netscape 6, Mozilla, and IE 5/Mac all understand the class-based workaround! So you may want to drop the use of `:first-child` if you're going to add the workaround.

Pseudo-elements in CSS

Cascading Style Sheets defines four *pseudo-elements*—virtual elements created from their content in the document in relationship to a base element. These are shown in Table 5.2. The pseudo-elements `:before` and `:after` are used to insert generated content and are discussed in Hour 22, "User Interface and Generated Content."

TABLE 5.2   The Pseudo-elements of CSS

Pseudo-element	Selects
`:before`	Inserts something before an element
`:after`	Inserts something after an element
`:first-letter`	The first letter of a block element
`:first-line`	The first line of a block element

The pseudo-elements `:first-line` and `:first-letter` select portions of another element, and these portions operate as if they were separate inline elements; however, only certain properties can be applied to these pseudo-elements, as shown in Table 5.3.

TABLE 5.3   Recognized Properties for `:first-line` and `:first-letter` Selectors

Property or Category	`:first-line`	`:first-letter`	Hour Covered
Background properties	yes	yes	Hour 10
Border properties		yes	Hour 13
Color properties	yes	yes	Hour 9
Font properties	yes	yes	Hour 8
Margin properties		yes	Hour 13

continues

TABLE 5.3   Continued

Property or Category	:first-line	:first-letter	Hour Covered
Padding properties		yes	Hour 13
clear	yes	yes	Hour 16
float		yes	Hour 16
letter-spacing	yes		Hour 12
line-height	yes	yes	Hour 12
text-decoration	yes	yes	Hour 9
text-shadow	yes	yes	Hour 9
text-transform	yes	yes	Hour 9
vertical-align	yes	yes	Hour 12
word-spacing	yes		Hour 12

The :first-line Pseudo-element

The :first-line pseudo-element is a virtual element used to identify the first line of an element for adding specific styles that apply only to the first line. For example, you might want to put the first line of a news story in larger print to make it stand out. Such a rule would look like this:

```
p:first-line    { font-size: large; }
```

A :first-line pseudo-element creates a fictional tag set that is similar to a <span> or another inline element but whose content is determined when the page is rendered. As much as will fit on one line is included in the fictional tag; as this will vary depending on the size of the user's browser window, the font size, and other factors, there's no way to calculate it beforehand. This means that there aren't any viable workarounds for browsers that don't support :first-line because there's no way to know what will fit on one line.

In fact, many browsers currently don't support :first-line; Netscape 4.0 and (Windows) Internet Explorer 4.0 and 5.0 will ignore it, whereas Mozilla, Netscape 6, Opera, and Internet Explorer 5.5 (Windows) or 5 (Mac) support it. Because of this and the lack of workarounds, :first-line should be considered an optional part of your design process; if it works in any given browser, it may enhance the appearance of the page for those users, but your design should not depend on it.

The :first-letter Pseudo-element

A :first-letter selector also references one of those imaginary, generated elements that doesn't appear in the source code but can be referenced by CSS rules. In this case, the imaginary tag is one surrounding the first letter of the element. The most common use for this is creating an initial capital letter that's larger than surrounding text.

Here's an example of a style sheet that uses both `:first-letter` and `:first-line`:

```
/* story-5.7.css               */
/* By Kynn Bartlett kynn@kynn.com */

.storytitle
  { font-family: Verdana; }

.storybody p
  { font-family: Arial; }

.storybody p:first-child
  { font-size: large; }

.storybody p:first-child:first-line
  { font-size: x-large; }

.storybody p:first-letter
  { font-size: larger; }
```

The result of applying this style sheet to the story sample from Listing 5.5 can be seen in Figure 5.7.

FIGURE 5.7

A large initial capital letter styled by a `:first-letter` rule, as shown in Netscape 6.

First letter   First line

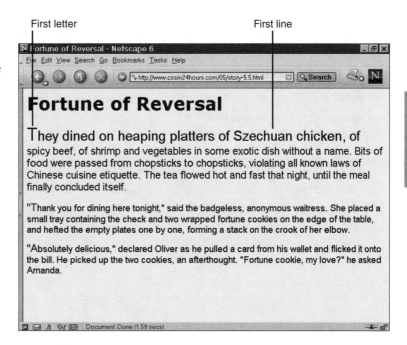

Naturally, `:first-letter` selectors work only in browsers that support them; once again, that's limited to Mozilla, Netscape 6, Opera, and Internet Explorer 5.5 and higher (Windows) or 5.0 and higher (Mac).

Workaround for Netscape 4, Internet Explorer 4

Unlike `:first-line`, the first letter can be easily determined at the time of HTML creation. Therefore, you can use a `<span>` element with a `class` attribute around the first letter, like this:

```
<p>
  <span class="firstletter">I</span>t was the best of times...
</p>
```

Then your CSS rule would look like this:

```
p:first-letter, p span.firstletter { font-size:x-large; }
```

Summary

The selector is the part of the CSS rule that designates the recipient of the styles defined in the style declaration. Type selectors can be used to style specific types of HTML elements, and `class` and `id` selectors choose them according to attribute values. The universal selector sets a style on all elements.

You create a descendant selector by combining two or more simple selectors together to show the hierarchy of the elements on the page. Using this technique, you can apply different styles to different sections of the page.

Pseudo-element and pseudo-class selectors let you select parts of the page that aren't otherwise distinguished in the HTML. Rules with `:link` and `:visited` pseudo-class selectors can be used to style hypertext links. The `:first-child`, `:first-letter`, and `:first-line` selectors are used for text formatting.

Browser Support Report Card

CSS Feature	Grade	Notes
The universal selector (*)	C	Partial workaround in Netscape 4 and Internet Explorer 4
Descendant selectors	A	
`:link` selectors	A	
`:visited` selectors	A	
`:first-child` selectors	B-	Requires workaround for Netscape 4, Internet Explorer (Windows), and Opera
`:first-line` selectors	C	No viable workarounds exist
`:first-letter` selectors	B+	Requires workaround for Netscape 4 and Internet Explorer 4

Q&A

Q Are there other selectors that aren't covered here?

A Yes, but unfortunately they're very poorly supported by the browsers. These advanced selectors are very powerful and useful, so you'll learn about them in Hour 19, "Advanced Selectors."

Q Can I string together as many selectors as I like?

A Certainly. You aren't limited to just two items in a descendant selector, for example. You could write a rule with a selector like the following, if you wanted:

```
body div #content p.special a:visited { color: green; }
```

Workshop

The workshop contains quiz questions and activities to help reinforce what you've learned in this hour. If you get stuck, the answers to the quiz can be found after the questions.

Quiz

1. Which of the following selectors means "select any `<em>` tag that's both part of the class `old` and within a `<p>` tag?"

   (a.) `em.old p`

   (b.) `em.old, p`

   (c.) `p.old em`

   (d.) `p em.old`

2. What rules would you write to make all visited links red and all unvisited links lime, and to make both kinds of link display in Arial font?

3. Which pseudo-element or pseudo-class can't be duplicated by using a `<span>` tag with an appropriate class set, and why?

   (a.) `:first-child`

   (b.) `:first-line`

   (c.) `:first-letter`

Answers

1. The correct answer is (d.), `p em.old`.

2. Here is one set of CSS rules to make unvisited links lime and visited links red, both in Arial font:

```
a:link { color: red; font-family: Arial, sans-serif; }
a:visited { color: lime; font-family: Arial, sans-serif; }
```

5

3. The :first-line cannot be duplicated by the <span> tag because the author of the Web page doesn't know where the first line will end when displayed on the user's browser.

Activity

In this hour, you saw several HTML pages and associated style sheets that used selectors to style the page. To further explore selectors, you can create additional style rules by selecting specific elements and styling them appropriately.

Hour 6

The CSS Box Model

This hour we are going to get into the core of Cascading Style Sheets—the part of the specification that defines how parts of a Web page are displayed, as stacks of boxes. The visual presentation of CSS is defined as a series of boxes based on the structure of the original document.

In this hour, you'll learn

- How Web content is displayed visually in CSS as boxes
- What categories of display elements are used and how you can affect an element's display type
- How CSS browsers interpret and display Web pages
- How to set margins, borders, and padding on a box

Displaying Content in CSS

The *content* of a Web page is the information encoded within the HTML page, found between the opening and closing tags of the HTML markup. These tags define the *structure* of the content, a framework that gives meaning to the content. For example, consider the following HTML:

```
<p>This is the <strong>tricky part</strong>,
    so pay attention!</p>
```

The content in this example is simply the sentence This is the tricky part, so pay attention! The tags embedded within (and surrounding) the content create the structure, which gives meaning to the content. Any browser that understands HTML will know that the whole thing is a paragraph (identified by the <p> tag) and that the phrase tricky part is strongly emphasized.

The presentation of the content, however, is not defined by the HTML; instead, it's determined by CSS rules. The browser has default rules for <p> and <strong> tags, which say that a <p> is shown visually as a paragraph on lines of its own, with leading and trailing space, and that the <strong> is shown as bold text within that paragraph.

Both the <p> and <strong> tags are shown as *display boxes,* which is how CSS browsers deal with HTML elements. Each HTML element corresponds to a display box, although not all elements are shown on the screen. A display box is a rectangular shape on the screen that can contain text content, images, form controls, or other display boxes.

The exact method by which HTML elements are shown as CSS display boxes is called the visual formatting method. The visual formatting method tells browsers how they should show HTML content on the screen.

Types of Elements

In the visual formatting model, markup elements are classified into two basic types—*block* and *inline*. The type of element determines how CSS browsers will display instances of that element.

The initial type of each HTML element is set by the HTML specification. For example, <p> tags are block elements, and <em> tags are inline elements. The full list is given in the HTML 4.01 Recommendation; each tag has an indication as to what type it is. You can change the type of a specific element using CSS, although often you won't need to.

Certain CSS properties can be set only on block or inline elements; for example, the text-indent property (which you'll learn about in Hour 12, "Alignment and Spacing") applies only to block elements.

Block

A block element is one that is intended to be displayed as a distinct block of content, starting and ending with a new line. Besides the <p> tag, other block elements in HTML include <div>, <blockquote>, <table>, <br>, <ol>, and the <h1> to <h6> tags.

Block elements are listed one after another, vertically down the page. They are as wide as they can be, which means that unless they're constrained in some way (by other block elements, by CSS properties, or by HTML markup), they'll stretch across the whole page.

> One thing you'll notice when you start using CSS is that your headers (`<h1>` and friends) go all the way across! Set the `background-color` property on an `<h1>` and you'll see how big it really is.

Inline

An inline element doesn't begin and end lines; instead, it is contained within the flow of the text. Examples of inline tags include `<em>`, `<span>`, `<b>`, `<img>`, `<input>`, and `<a>`.

Inline elements flow one after another in a line, with no line breaks, horizontally across the page until the end of the available space is used up; then they just continue where they left off on the next line down.

The `display` Property

You can change the type of an element by using the `display` property. This property can take several values; the ones we're primarily concerned with in this hour are `block` and `inline`. There's another important value for `display` that's called `none`; something that has the `display` property set to `none` will not display at all, nor will anything inside of it be displayed.

Setting the `display` property to `block` or `inline` will change the type of that element to the specified type. For example, let's say that we want to make a navigation menu, and we want all of our `<a>` elements within that menu to appear as block elements. Our HTML code may look like this:

```
...
<div class="navmenu">
  <a href="friends.html">My Friends</a>
  <a href="dogs.html">My Dogs</a>
  <a href="friendsdogs.html">My Friends' Dogs</a>
  <a href="dogsfriends.html">My Dogs' Friends</a>
</div>
...
```

To display these `<a>` tags as block tags, we use this rule:

```
.navmenu a { display: block; }
```

Figure 6.1 shows the effect of applying this rule; the first set of links is identical to the second, except that the previous rule and a silver background have been applied to it. The background illustrates that the block element goes all the way across the browser window

6

and doesn't stop at the end of the text within it. Also, the links are clickable even on the far right side of the screen, not just on the blue underlined words.

FIGURE **6.1**
Before and after, displayed in Internet Explorer 5.1 (Mac).

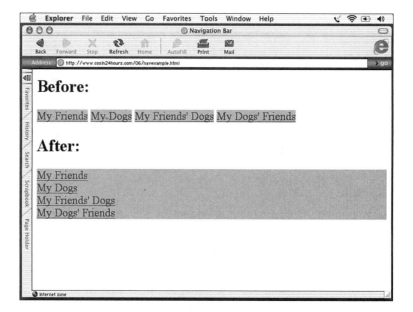

Understanding the Box Model

Within the visual formatting model, all elements generate specific types of boxes. The method for displaying these boxes is called the *box model,* and understanding the box model is crucial for understanding how Cascading Style Sheets will display Web pages.

The box model is defined in terms of elements, documents, trees, and of course, boxes. Many of us are not used to thinking about Web pages in terms of these elements unless we've done a lot with XML or SGML. So first we'll take a look at the assumptions that CSS makes about Web documents.

In formal W3C specifications, they rarely use terms such as *Web page;* instead they talk about *documents.* Likewise, they don't say much about *tags* and *browsers* but are always referring to *elements* and *user agents.* Although it may seem that this is just semantic snobbishness—and to some degree it is!—there are actually some valid reasons for drawing these distinctions when speaking formally. In this book, I try to avoid writing like a W3C Recommendation; if you want one of those, you can find it on the W3C site at http://www.w3.org/. However, terminology counts for this discussion, and my apologies if I sound formal.

Documents as Trees

Did you know that every Web page is actually a tree of tags and content? If you didn't, that's okay; these types of trees are the same kind of data structures used in computer science, and most Web developers aren't necessarily computer scientists.

A *tree* is a way of representing information in a hierarchy of elements. Think of it as somewhat similar to a family tree in genealogy—one that starts at a certain ancestor and goes down from there. Your great-grandmother may be at the top; her children (including your grandmother) in the second level down; your mother, her siblings, and her cousins in the third level down; and you and the other members of your generation in the fourth level.

In the same way, an HTML document can be thought of as a tree with the <html> element as the top. In this context, the <html> element is known as the *root element*.

The <html> element has two children: the <head> and the <body>. These are shown lower on the tree—the next levels down. The <head> has children too; <title> is one in every document, and <link> may be there to call in an external style sheet. The <body> element contains the content of the page; this could be anything from <h1> and <table> to <div> or <hr>. Some of those may have their own children, and some may not.

Each part of a tree is called a *node*. A node is either an element (possibly with children) or some text. *Text nodes* can't have children; they're just text.

Listing 6.1 shows a very simple Web page, and Figure 6.2 shows a representation of a tree based on that page.

LISTING 6.1   The First Two Lines of a Poem about Trees

```
<html>
  <head>
    <title>Trees</title>
  </head>
  <body>
    <h1>Trees, by <i>Joyce Kilmer</i></h1>
    <p>
      I think that I shall never see
      <br>
      A poem as lovely as a tree.
    </p>
  </body>
</html>
```

6

FIGURE 6.2
*Our poem
represented
as a tree.*

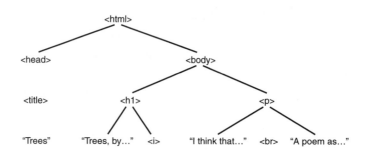

Documents as Boxes

Once an HTML document has been defined as a data tree, it can then be visually interpreted as a series of boxes. This is probably an easier way for Web developers to think of
a page, but it's important to reach that understanding by first visualizing a tree because
that's how a CSS browser considers the page.

You can think of these boxes as containers that hold other boxes or that hold text values.
Each box in the CSS box model is held within by another box, except for the box corresponding to the root node in our tree. The outer box is called the containing box. A
block-containing box can hold other block boxes or inline boxes; an inline-containing
box can hold only inline boxes.

In Figure 6.3, you can see the tree poem expressed as a series of nested boxes. You'll
notice that some of these boxes don't have labels; a box exists, but no HTML tag! Those
boxes are known as anonymous boxes. Anonymous boxes result whenever a tag contains
mixed content—both text and some HTML tags. The text parts become anonymous
boxes. An anonymous box is styled the same as its containing box.

Also notice that the <br> tag is an empty tag; it doesn't contain any content, but it still
generates a box. The <head> box appears in Figure 6.3, but in HTML the <head> tag is
defined as `display: none;`; this is why you never see the content of the <head> tag.

FIGURE 6.3

The tree poem as nested boxes.

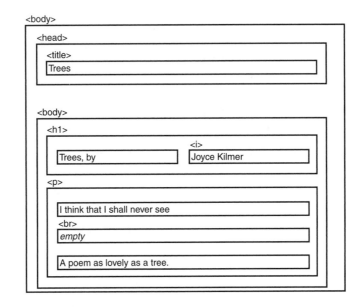

Box Display Properties

Once a browser has established that a box exists by building a tree as shown earlier and then by filling in the box model, it displays that box, either according to its own internal rules for displaying HTML or according to the style properties on that box.

In a way, all of the CSS properties are box-display properties; they control how a box is displayed. However, there are three properties that define the edges of that box: the margin, the border, and the padding.

The relationship between margin, border, padding, and the content itself is shown in Figure 6.4. In this example, the border color has been set to gray and the background-color to silver.

FIGURE 6.4

The margin, border, padding, *and content of a box.*

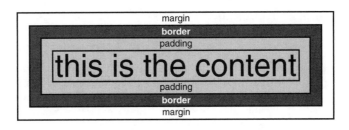

6

You'll learn more about the `margin`, `border`, and `padding` properties in Hour 13, "Borders and Boxes"; this hour is a general introduction to the box model, and we'll get into more detail about other property values later in the book.

The `margin` Property

The margin is an invisible property that surrounds all CSS boxes; it dictates how far that box is from other boxes. The margin is the outermost property of the box and defines the far edge of the box. Nearly all of the visible HTML elements have margins, although for many the default margin is 0 pixels.

Values for `margin` can be expressed in a variety of units; the most common values are pixels or ems. A pixel is the width of a single dot on the screen; pixel values are written as a number followed by `px`, such as `4px` or `12px`. An em is unit of measure that refers to the size of the current font; if the font is 12 pixels, an em is a unit of measure equal to 12 pixels. Ems are written by putting the word `em` after a number, such as `3em` or `0.5em`.

Pixels are absolute units; they do not scale with the user's preferences. Ems are relative units; relative units are calculated based on the current font. Other units you can use include points (`pt`), centimeters (`cm`), inches (`in`), and percentages.

To set a margin of 1 em around a specific box, such as an `<h1>`, you'd write a CSS rule like this:

```
h1 { margin: 1em; }
```

Margins are always transparent, meaning that whatever background color is set on the containing box will shine through.

There's one more thing you need to know about margins, and that's *collapsing margins*. The vertical margins—those above and below the element—do something called collapsing, which means that only the largest value of the margins between two elements is used. Margins will collapse only on block elements and only in a vertical direction, not horizontally.

 Think of the collapse of margins as two motor homes parked next to each other. The owner of motor home to the north says, "Don't park within six feet of me." The owner of the southern motor home says, "Don't park within three feet of me." How close to the motor homes would you park? Obviously, you would park six feet away. That's what a `margin` value is like; you take the largest value of the two and use that as the vertical distance between two elements.

The `border` Property

The `border` property is used to draw a border around a box. All boxes have borders, even if the size of the border is 0 pixels or ems, which is the default for HTML elements.

Each border has three qualities associated with it, which can all be set using the `border` property: the size of the border, the style of the border, and the color of the border. A border declaration reads like this:

```
selector { border: size style color; }
```

The *size* of the border is measured the same way as the margin; pixels or ems are the most common units. Border *styles* include `solid`, `dashed`, and `dotted`; you'll use more border styles in Hour 13. The *color* of a border can be any CSS color name or RGB triplet.

So, to set a solid red border that is one-fourth of the current font size around an `<h1>`, you would write a rule like this:

```
h1 { border: 0.25em solid red; }
```

And here's a dashed two-pixel blue border around paragraphs:

```
p { border: 2px dashed #99CCFF; }
```

You can set borders (and margins and padding) around inline elements as well as block elements; this sets a thin black border around `<i>` tags:

```
i { border: 1px solid black; }
```

The `padding` Property

The space surrounding the content is the padding; this could be thought of as whitespace because there's nothing in it (no content or border), but keep in mind that it doesn't have to be white. The padding is always the same background color as the content itself, which means it is the color of the `background-color` set on the box.

Padding is measured in the same way as margins or borders; here's a 3-pixel padding around `<i>` and a 0.5-em padding around `<h1>`:

```
i { padding: 3px; }
h1 { padding: 0.5em; }
```

Want to see the result of all these examples? Figure 6.5 shows what happens if we apply all of the CSS rules listed above to the poem from Listing 6.1. I added a `<style>` section in the `<head>` and added the rules as an embedded style sheet.

6

FIGURE **6.5**
Applying various box styles to the tree poem, as shown in Internet Explorer 5.1 (Mac).

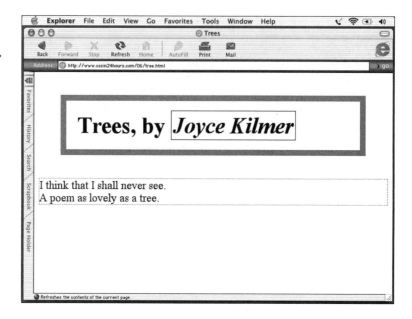

Summary

The visual formatting model of CSS describes how pages should be displayed. An HTML (or XML) element can be block or inline, and the `display` property can change how an element is displayed.

The box model views Web pages as nested boxes based on a tree view of a Web document. Web pages are displayed as CSS properties set on those boxes.

The `margin`, `border`, and `padding` properties define the outer edge of the box. Margins are transparent and surround the box, separating it from other boxes; vertical borders collapse to the largest value. Borders are in specified colors and styles and are within the box's margin. Padding is inside the border and is the same background color as the content.

Browser Support Report Card

CSS Feature	Grade	Notes
`display: block` and `inline`	A-	A few quirks; see Hour 11, "Styling Links"
Basic margins	A	
Basic borders	A	
Basic padding	A	

Everything described in this hour should be reasonably safe to use; specific quirks for `margin`, `border`, and `padding` are described in Hour 13.

Q&A

Q   What kind of element is a table cell? Is that block or inline?

A   It's neither inline nor block. The display value for a table cell (`<td>`) is special; it's `table-cell`. An element that has been set `display: table-cell` is displayed like a table cell. (Of course.) This is a special type of block element, although there are some limitations; a `table-cell` element can't have a `margin`, for example. You'll learn more about tables and CSS in Hour 15, "Styling Tables."

Q   What is an em, anyway? Is it related to the size of a capital M?

A   Not really, although that's where it gets the name from, historically. In CSS, an em is defined as a measure equal to the size of the font; it is a square that is as tall as the font size and as wide as it is tall. It's not related to letter M officially because some fonts—non-English fonts—don't have the letter M, and CSS needs to be able to function with all fonts around the world.

Q   Okay, then what's a pixel? And a point? And how do percentages work?

A   A pixel is basically one dot on a screen; if you've got an 800 x 600 display monitor, it is showing you 800 pixels across and 600 pixels down. A point is 1/72 of an inch in CSS. Percentages are based on the width of the containing block. You'll learn more about CSS's units of measurement in Hour 8, "Fonts and Font Families," and Hour 13.

Workshop

The workshop contains quiz questions and activities to help reinforce what you've learned in this hour. If you get stuck, the answers to the quiz can be found after the questions.

Quiz

1. Is the `<hr>` element block or inline? How can you tell?

2. What is the correct order of the box model, from outside to inside?

    (a.) `border, margin, padding, content`

    (b.) `padding, border, margin, content`

    (c.) `margin, border, padding, content`

    (d.) `margin, padding, border, content`

3. Consider the following style rules:

```
body { background-color: red;
       color: white; }
h1 { color: black;
     padding: 1.5em;
     border: 5px solid green;
     background-color: yellow;
     margin: 0.5em; }
```

What is the color of the margin around an <h1>? What is the color of the padding?

Answers

1. Because horizontal rules are on separate lines and don't occur inline, <hr> must be block. You can check by looking it up in the HTML 4.01 specification. (See Appendix A, "How to Read W3C Recommendations.")

2. (c.) The outermost part of the box is the margin, then the border, and then the padding around the content.

3. The color of the margin would be the background-color of the containing box; assuming the <body> contains the <h1>, the color would be red. The background-color of the <h1> determines the color of the padding, so the padding color is yellow.

HOUR 7

Cascading and Inheritance

The cascade is one of the key concepts of Cascading Style Sheets—so important, in fact, that the language was named after it. The cascade defines how you combine rules, including rules from different sources—some provided by the Web developer, some by the browser, and some from the user. When these are combined, values for properties on individual HTML tags are calculated. Some of these take their values directly from the CSS rules, whereas others are derived from other properties.

In this hour, you'll learn

- What the secret formula behind the cascade really is
- Which CSS rules have the highest weight, and how those relate to HTML attributes
- How you can override the order of the cascade when writing CSS rules
- How the user can supply her own style sheet to express her preferences for display, and how those are balanced with the author's desires

- How to include one style sheet's rules within another style sheet, and which set of rules takes priority
- Which property values are inherited, which are calculated, and what that means for your CSS designs

How the Cascade Works

The cascade is the set of directions that determines what rules apply to a given element on the page. Without a method for determining priority of conflicting rules, it would be impossible to figure out which styles should be used. Take, for example, the style sheet shown in Listing 7.1—different rules with a number of different selectors.

LISTING 7.1 A Colorful Style Sheet

```
/* colors-7.1.css */

body { background-color: white;
       color: black; }

h1 { background-color: blue;
     color: red; }

em { background-color: green;
     color: black; }

#serious { color: purple; }

.yahoo { color: black;
         background-color: yellow; }

#serious { color: maroon; }

h1 em { color: lime; }
```

Now you'll look at a page that uses the style sheet and also has its own embedded CSS rules within a <style> element in the <head>. Such a page is listed in Listing 7.2.

LISTING 7.2 An HTML Page with Tips on Color Use

```
<html>
  <head>
    <title>
      Accessibility of Color
    </title>
```

LISTING 7.2 Continued

```
    <link type="text/css" rel="stylesheet"
          href="colors-7.1.css">
    <style type="text/css">
      .yahoo { background-color: silver;
               color: white; }
      h1 { background-color: yellow; }
    </style>
  </head>
  <body>
    <h2>Accessibility Tip:</h2>
    <h1>Don't
        <em class="yahoo" id="serious"
            style="background-color: white;">Rely</em>
        on Color Alone</h1>
    <p>
      Some Web users may be unable to see color -- they may
      be blind (and use a screenreader program); they may
      be color-blind and unable to easily distinguish colors;
      or they could be using an access device, such as a cell
      phone, which does not display color. For this reason,
      the W3C's Web Accessibility Initiative recommends that
      you not <em>rely</em> upon color as the <em>only</em>
      way of conveying information.
    </p>
    <p>
      This doesn't mean "don't use color" -- on the contrary,
      color is very useful to those who can see it, and will
      help make your page understandable.  What it does mean
      is that color (and other presentational effects) should
      not be the only way you make something special.  For
      example, instead of using a &lt;span&gt; and a color
      style to make something stand out, use the &lt;strong&gt;
      tag (which you can also style) so browsers that
      can't use the visual CSS color rule can at least know
      to emphasize that section -- perhaps by increasing the
      volume when reading the text out loud, for example.
    </p>
  </body>
</html>
```

Now concentrate on the second word in the headline, "Rely." This word is within an
<em> element, which is part of an <h1>. It has a class of yahoo and an id of serious.
What color will the text be, and what color background will it have? You have several
choices from several sources; by using the cascade, you can figure out what a browser
will do with your example.

7

In Table 7.1, I've listed the various sources from which the browser might find the background and foreground colors for the word "Rely."

TABLE 7.1 CSS Rules Applying to the Word "Rely"

Color	Background	Selector	Source
black	white	body	Linked style sheet
red	blue	h1	Linked style sheet
black	green	em	Linked style sheet
purple		#serious	Linked style sheet
black	yellow	.yahoo	Linked style sheet
marooon		#serious	Linked style sheet
lime		h1 em	Linked style sheet
white	silver	.yahoo	Embedded style sheet
	yellow	h1	Embedded style sheet
	white	(implied)	Inline style element

Order of the Cascade

To be able to figure out which properties get applied to the <em> tag in your example, you'll need to think like a Web browser. The first thing you need to do is to realize that many of your rules are combined rules. For example, take this rule:

```
.yahoo { color: black;
    background-color: yellow; }
```

The rule is actually two different rules, which happen to share a common selector, as follows:

```
.yahoo { color: black; }
.yahoo { background-color: yellow; }
```

This is important because each declaration (property name and value) could be overridden separately. A rule that changes the color might not change the background color at all, so the .yahoo background-color rule would continue to stay in effect even if the .yahoo color rule is superceded.

So, you'll need to consider only those rules that are in conflict—in other words, those that designate different values for the same property name, such as those rules that affect the color property.

First, you sort these rules by their *origin*. In the cascade, the origin means one of the following: the author of the page, the user, or the browser. Author rules have priority over user rules, which have priority over the browser's default rules for how to display HTML elements. In this case, all of these rules have the same origin; they come from the author of the page.

Next you order the rules based on the selector and how specific it is. This *specificity* is calculated as follows:

1. An `id` *selector*, or an inline style attribute, is the most specific. If there is more than one `id` in the rule, the rule with the greatest number of `id` selectors wins.

2. If there aren't any `id` selectors, or if there's the same number, count the number of *classes or pseudo-classes* in the rule. The rule with the most classes or pseudo-classes has the higher priority.

3. If there's the same number of classes (or no classes), compare the number of *elements*—the greater the number of elements, the higher the specificity.

4. If the numbers of `id` values, classes, and elements are all the same, whichever was *declared most recently* has the highest priority. If two rules have the same selector and are in disagreement on a specific property, the one listed second is more specific.

Applying these rules to your `<em>` text, you must consider the `color` property separately from the `background-color` property. The most specific rules that set the `color` property are the two rules with an `id` selector—the `#serious` rules. Of these, the second one takes priority, which means the text color will be maroon.

To figure out the `background-color`, you also have to determine the most specific rule. In this case, the most specific rule is the inline style attribute, so the background will be white.

Calculating the colors of the `<h1>` is also a useful illustration; you have two competing `<h1>` selectors, one in the linked style sheet and one in the embedded style sheet. Which one triumphs? The one declared most recently; because your `<style>` comes after your `<link>`, the `background-color` will be yellow. If the order of the `<link>` and `<style>` elements were reversed, the background would be blue.

Cascading and HTML Attributes

In addition to setting `style`, `class`, and `id` attributes, HTML also has presentational attributes that let you affect how the page looks. Examples include `align`, `color`, `face`, `link`, `vlink`, `bgcolor`, and `background`.

When these attributes conflict with a CSS rule, the HTML attribute is considered to be the least specific declaration possible. In other words, the HTML attribute will always be overridden by a CSS rule. However, in many cases you may want to set an

7

HTML presentation attribute in case CSS is disabled or not understood by an older browser. Keep in mind that HTML presentational attributes will be ignored only if there is a corresponding CSS rule; if there's no rule setting the color of an item, for example, the HTML value will be used.

> Remember, you generally can't use HTML presentation attributes with CSS if you are using the Strict variety of HTML. Use HTML 4.01 Transitional (or XHTML 1.0 Transitional) if you need to use HTML attributes along with your CSS styles.

Using !important in Rules

When necessary, an author of a style sheet can designate one rule as explicitly more important than others. To do this, the author adds !important after the specific property name and value declaration, like this:

```
em { color: blue !important; }
```

This overrides the normal order of the cascade by inserting a new requirement: important rules come before rules that have not been designated as important. An !important rule, even one which is not very specific, will always take priority over a non-!important rule even if the latter is extremely specific.

The use of !important also changes one other part of the cascade; !important rules that originate with the user take priority over the author's rules. Normally, the author's rules have higher priority than the user's rules, but this allows users with special needs to define their own style sheets and designate their needs for access as more important than the author's desire for a certain style.

> Those of you who have done programming in a language like C++ or Perl may find this particular part of CSS perplexing. In most programming languages, an exclamation point (!) means "not," so !important looks like it means "not important," which is the exact opposite of the true meaning. Don't be surprised if it takes a while to get used to reading !important as "very important."

User-defined Style Sheets

A *user-defined style sheet* is one created by the user and stored on that person's local computer. The browser automatically loads this file and applies it to Web pages that are viewed.

The purpose of a user-defined style sheet is to let the Web surfer's preferences influence how he views the Web. This is especially useful for certain specific groups of users, including those users with visual disabilities. For example, if you need a high contrast display, your user style sheet could be set with a default black background, white text, and large font sizes.

In theory, user style sheets are quite beneficial; in practice, though, they require each Web user to know how to write CSS in order to see the Web the way she would like to see it! This is a rather high learning curve to simply surf the Web comfortably; you're learning CSS now because you want to design Web sites, not because you simply want to access information. Despite this, user style sheets are incredibly functional for those who know how to use them, or for those who can download and install user style sheets written by others.

A user style sheet can have any kind of CSS rules that could normally be included in a style sheet, and the syntax is exactly the same; it's just another external style sheet, after all. However, there are certain types of rules that make less sense in a user style sheet, and several normal cautions can be relaxed.

In a user style sheet, you won't want to use any selectors that presume specific attribute values will be set, such as `class` or `id`, because you won't know what's in the HTML of each page.

Normally when creating a style sheet, you won't want to use absolute values in your font sizes, such as `9px` or `2cm`, because these don't take the user's preferences into account. A user with poor vision would have problems seeing a 9-pixel font size if you put this on a style sheet for the Web. But because you *know* the exact properties of the final output medium when writing a user-defined style sheet for yourself, it's perfectly fine to use those values in your own user-defined style sheet.

Finally, you will want to declare these as `!important` to give them highest priority because, after all, it doesn't make sense to set your own preferences if the designer's style sheet can just overrule them.

An example of a user-defined style sheet is given in Listing 7.3. This style sheet is designed specifically for a user who needs large print and high contrast (white-on-black).

7

LISTING 7.3 A Sample User-defined Style Sheet

```
/* user-07.3.css */
* { color: white! important;
    background-color: white! important;
    font-family: Verdana, sans-serif !important; }
body { font-size: 24pt !important; }
a:link { color: cyan !important; }
a:visited { color: violet !important; }
```

Once you've created a user-defined style sheet and saved it on your hard drive (some-where you can remember its location), you need to tell your browser to use it. How you do that will depend on which browser you're using. In Internet Explorer for Windows, this is a preference under Accessibility; in Internet Explorer for Macintosh, it's listed under Browser content. If you're using Netscape or Mozilla, you need to add your rules to the user.css file. In Opera, this is a preference under Document that lets you select a user-defined style sheet.

Importing CSS

To make style sheets that are more modular, you may want to *import* another style sheet. Importing, in this context, means that all of the rules in the imported style sheet are included in the style sheet that is doing the importing. In this way, importing is like link-ing an external style sheet.

You can import another style sheet from an embedded style sheet, from a linked style sheet, or from a user style sheet. An imported style sheet can even import additional style sheets.

How do imported style sheets affect the cascade order? You might think that rules are included at the point where the importation is declared, but this actually isn't the case. Any imported style sheets are treated as if their rules had been declared before any of the rules in the importing style sheet.

You can think of the imported style sheet as being more distant, which means it is lower priority if there is a conflict; all other things being equal (same number of id attributes, classes, and elements), the importing style sheet's rules are considered more recently declared, even if the rule happens before the importation.

If you're designing a large Web site and there are some CSS rules that apply to the whole site, whereas the others should be used only with certain sections of the site, you may want to write one site-wide style sheet and then import it into the style sheets you write for each part of the site.

The @import Rule

To import a file, you simply write as a complete rule (with no property declarations or curly braces) an @import statement that looks like this:

```
@import url("filename.css");
```

An alternate way to write the same rule is to leave out the url() function because everything you will @import will be a URL. So you can also write the rule like this:

```
@import "filename.css";
```

You can also give @import an extra parameter, which is a list of media types; like the media attribute on the <link> attribute, the style sheet will load only if the media type is correct for the browser being used. For example:

```
@import "screenorprint.css" screen, print;
@import "allmedia.css" all;
```

Here's an example of @import in action. First, the importing style sheet:

```
h1 { color: red; }
h1, h2, h3, h4, h5, h6
  { font-family: sans-serif; }
@import "sitewide.css";
h2 { color: blue; }
```

And here's the imported style sheet:

```
/* sitewide.css */
h1, h2, h3, h4, h5, h6
  { color: green; }
body { background-color: silver; }
```

What color is an <h1>, <h2>, or <h3> on a page using the importing style sheet? The <h1> would be red and the <h2> would be blue because all of the imported rules are considered to come before the original style sheet's rules. The <h3> would be green because that's the only rule setting its color.

7

Workaround for Netscape 4

Netscape 4 doesn't understand @import; it simply won't import other style sheets. Unfortunately, there's not a good general workaround for this; the solution is to explicitly include all style rules you need in your embedded style sheet or to link to multiple external style sheets.

However, this isn't necessarily all bad; there are certain types of CSS rules that will confuse Netscape 4 and cause it to break horribly—for example, the rules used to position items on the page, which are covered in Hour 16, "Page Layout in CSS." If you ever want to hide something from Netscape 4, but you'd like the other browsers to see it, simply put in an @import rule that imports an "advanced" style sheet. See http://www.hwg.org/styles/ for an example of this in action.

Inheritance

As you've already seen, some property values don't have to be explicitly set on each element if the value is already set on a parent element. For example, if you set a font-family property on the <body>, all other elements on the page will also have the same value unless it's changed by another rule. This is called *inheritance;* the page elements have inherited the property value from their parent element, <body>.

Not all properties will naturally inherit; some simply don't make sense for inheritance. For example, the border, margin, and padding properties from Hour 6, "The CSS Box Model," don't inherit. Otherwise, whenever you'd draw a box, all elements inside it would have the same type of box around them. Each property, when it's defined in the CSS specifications, is designated as either inheriting or not inheriting, by default.

Workaround for Netscape 4

Unfortunately, Netscape 4 has serious problems with inheritance; for example, table cells do not inherit properties set on the <body>. For this reason, to maintain compatibility with Netscape 4, you'll want to write rules like the following:

```
body, th, td { font-family: sans-serif; }
```

Be sure to test all your designs carefully if they rely on inheritance. It may be better to avoid depending on inheritance if you're going to have many users with Netscape 4.

Inherited Values

An *inherited value* is passed along in most cases as if it had been set on the element itself. Thus, if you make an <h1> blue, you're making all its children blue because they'll inherit the color. Other rules—more specific or higher priority—could change this, of course.

Of the properties you've learned so far, font-family and color are inherited. The display, border, margin, and padding properties are not inherited. You might think that background-color is inherited, but actually it's not; the default when background-color is unset is actually the special value transparent, which means the color "underneath" can be seen, so it's not quite the same as inheriting the value.

Calculated Values

The font-size property works a little differently when it comes to inheritance. That's because you don't actually inherit the declaration; you inherit the *calculated value*. Some values are absolute values, such as 12px, but most will be relative values, such as smaller or 3em. When a relative value is inherited, the value is first calculated before being passed on to the child element.

Specifying Inheritance

If you want a property to inherit from its parent, but it doesn't actually do so by default, you can use the special value of inherit in a rule you write. Say that you decide any <div> in the class standout should have a blue border and that any paragraphs inside it should have the same border. You could write these rules:

```
div.standout { border: 1px solid blue; }
div.standout p { border: inherit; }
```

Summary

In this hour, you learned about the cascade, user style sheets, importing style sheets, and inheritance.

The cascade first sorts rules based on source; author style rules take priority over user style rules, which take priority over browser default styles. After that, the more specific a rule, the higher priority it's given. You can add !important to a rule to give it a higher priority.

User style sheets are a crucial part of the cascade that allows the user's preferences to blend with the author's desires. Users with disabilities can often benefit from specific style sheets tailored to their needs.

7

You can include one style sheet's rules in another by using an @import rule. This doesn't work well in Netscape 4, but you may find it a useful way to write style sheets that Netscape 4 won't even try to apply.

Not all values need to be explicitly set; values can be inherited from their parent element. Some properties inherit, and some don't; those that use relative values will pass along the calculated value.

Browser Support Report Card

CSS Feature	Grade	Notes
The cascade	A	
!important	A	
User style sheets	B+	Netscape 4 does not support user CSS
@import	B+	Netscape 4 does not support @import
Inheritance	B+	Netscape 4 has inheritance bugs

Q&A

Q Why is it a big deal that calculated values are inherited, instead of relative values?

A Well, consider this example:

```
...
<div class="footer">
  <p>
    Questions?  Send me email at
    <a href="mailto:kynn@idyllmtn.com">
      kynn@idyllmtn.com
    </a>
  </p>
</div>
...
```

If the font on the page is 20 pixels, and the style rule is div.footer { font-size: smaller; }, anything within the <div> inherits the calculated value 16 pixels, which is 20% smaller than 20 pixels. They do not inherit the relative value smaller.

What if they did inherit the relative value? Well, then the <p> would have to be 20% smaller than the size of the <div> (about 12.8 pixels). The <a> would inherit smaller from its parent and would shrink to 80% of the <p>, so the e-mail address would be 10.24 pixels—incredible shrinking text! This is why calculated values are not inherited.

Q How did the order of the Cascade change between CSS Level 1 and CSS Level 2?

A When CSS Level 1 was published, the author's `!important` styles took precedence over the user's `!important` styles. This was found to be a problem because it meant that users with special needs had no way to insist that the browser meet their needs. In the CSS Level 2 recommendation, this was changed so that the user's `!important` rules beat the author's `!important` rules. Note that this is a special case exception; in most cases, the author's styles will override the user's styles, assuming the user's styles are not flagged as `!important`.

Q Where can I find some examples of user-defined style sheets?

A In my not-so-copious spare time, I have been working on a project called Free User-Defined Style Sheets for You (FUSSY). This is a repository for useful user CSS and includes a generator to create your own user-defined style sheets according to your preferences. You can test it out at `http://fussy.kynn.com/`.

Workshop

The workshop contains quiz questions and activities to help reinforce what you've learned in this hour. If you get stuck, the answers to the quiz can be found after the questions.

Quiz

1. Rank these CSS rules in order from least specific to most specific:

   (a.) `p { font-family: serif; }`

   (b.) `<p style="font-family: fantasy;">`

   (c.) `p#mocha { font-family: monospace; }`

   (d.) `tr td p { font-family: sans-serif; }`

   (e.) `td p.latte { font-family: cursive; }`

2. How would your answer to question 1 change if rule a were rewritten like this?

   (a.) `p { font-family: serif !important ; }`

Answers

1. The least specific is (a.), as it has no `id` selectors, no classes, and only one element. Rule (d.) is more specific because it has three elements instead of one. Rule (e.) is more specific than (d.), even though it has only two elements, because (e.) has one class, and (d.) has none. Rules (b.) and (c.) are equally specific because `id` selectors and inline rules have the same specificity. In practice, (b.) would take precedence over (c.) because the inline rule would occur after a linked or embedded style sheet. Therefore, the paragraph would be in a `fantasy` font.

7

2. With the addition of !important to rule (a.), it becomes more important than the others, and thus the font-family value would be serif. However, the specificity technically did not change; it is still less specific than the others, although it has higher priority. So it's a bit of a trick question; the priority would change, but because question 1 asked you about specificity, not priority, your answer should *not* change.

Activity

One of the best ways to become familiar with the cascade is to set up your own user style sheet. Create your own style sheet, save it on your hard drive, and tell your browser to use it as a user style sheet. You can experiment with !important and other aspects of the cascade by changing your user style sheet.

PART III

Styling with CSS

Hour

Hour **8**

Fonts and Font Families

One of the most effective changes you can make to a Web page using CSS is to simply alter the browser's default font. This can immediately add a more professional look to your Web site, as well as making it easier for users to read and find information.

In this hour, you'll learn

- Which font properties specify bold, italic, stretched, and variant fonts
- How you can set a number of font properties at once using a shorthand property
- What the generic font families are and how to use them
- Which fonts are most commonly installed on various browsers and platforms
- How you can use CSS to tell a browser to download a font from the Web

Specifying Font Properties

In Hour 2, "Getting Started with CSS," you were introduced to two font properties: font-size and font-family. These allow you to specify the size and typeface of the font, respectively. In addition, there are a number of other properties that can be used to further select fonts from within those families. These properties are `font-weight`, `font-variant`, `font-style`, `font-stretch`, and `font-size-adjust`.

To understand how these properties work, it's important to understand how CSS views fonts. A font in CSS is one specific instance of several properties: a specific typeface, size, weight, and other variables. So the font `12pt Arial bold italic` is different from the font `10pt Arial`. They are part of the same font family, of course. It's helpful to remember that when you declare a font family, you're actually selecting a group of fonts to be used. Other properties (or browser defaults) will narrow down the specific font.

Font families generally include a number of variations on the base font, for example, an italic version of the font. In some cases, you will specify a font combination that simply isn't available as a distinct variant. The browser will then have to create a variant on the fly by slanting the text to produce italic effects, for example, or by using the closest available equivalent in the font family.

The effects produced by various font settings are listed in Table 8.1 for reference; this is because it's not always clear which property controls which effect.

TABLE 8.1 Properties Affecting Font Display

Property	Effect
`font-family`	Selects the typeface family
`font-size`	Sets the size of the font
`font-weight`	Makes text bold or lighter
`font-variant`	Creates "small caps" effect
`font-style`	Sets italic font
`font-stretch`	Stretches the font horizontally
`text-decoration` (Hour 9)	Underlines text
`color` (Hour 9)	Changes the color of text
`line-height` (Hour 12)	The height of the line (but not the text height)
`font`	Sets `font-family`, `font-size`, `font-weight`, `font-variant`, `font-style`, and `line-height`

The `font-weight` Property

The `font-weight` property controls how heavy a font appears—in other words, the thickness of the lines used to draw that font, relative to the size of the font. The weight of a font is measured in numbers that range from 100 to 900, in steps of 100. The higher the number, the bolder the font; normal text has a weight of 400 and bold text (as created by the HTML <b> tag) has a weight of 700.

Not all font families have specific fonts at all values; in such a situation, the browser will usually use the closest match. For example, if there's no weight 800 variant for a font, the browser may substitute weight 700.

Many browsers support only two to four font-weight values. Figure 8.1 shows how Opera 6 (Windows) displays each font-weight value of Verdana, whereas Figure 8.2 is from Internet Explorer 5.1 (Macintosh). Notice that they differ on whether weights 500 and 600 should be weighted like 400, 700, or somewhere in between. Keep this in mind; it will be important later on.

FIGURE 8.1

Successive font-weight *values of Verdana font, shown in Opera 6.*

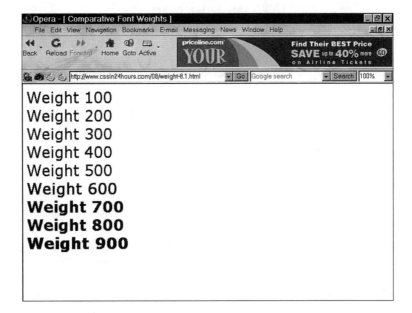

In addition to numeric values, the font-weight property can take named values, as shown on Table 8.2. The font-weight value is inherited from the containing box if any is set. The default value is normal (400) for most HTML tags; some, such as <b>, <strong>, <h1> to <h6>, and <th>, will default to bold (700).

FIGURE 8.2
Successive font-
weight *values of
Verdana font, shown in
Internet Explorer 5.1
(Macintosh).*

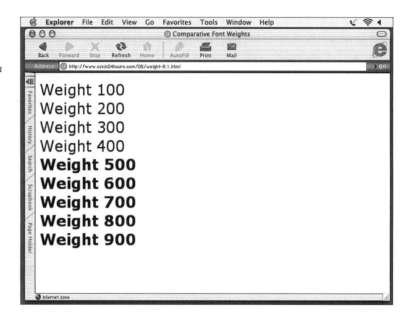

TABLE 8.2 Values for the font-weight Property

Value	Effect
100 to 900	Lightest (100) to heaviest (900) font weight
bold	Same as 700
bolder	One step (+100) heavier than the containing box's font-weight
lighter	One step (-100) lighter than the containing box's font-weight
normal	Same as 400
inherit	Uses the value of the containing box's font-weight property

If a font's weight is already at 900, the value bolder won't make it any heavier; likewise, if the font-weight is 100, lighter has no additional effect.

I noted earlier that browsers aren't consistent about how heavy they make in-between values, such as 500 or 600. Because bolder and lighter move up or down in steps of 100, it's possible that a bolder (or lighter) rule may have no effect. If the default is 400, and the browser does not render 500 as 700 but as 400, an increase of 100 is meaningless. For this reason it's probably better to use explicit numeric values or the keyword bold for cross-browser consistency.

Workaround for Netscape 4

Netscape 4 doesn't understand the font-weight value of lighter. To make fonts lighter in Netscape 4, give explicit numeric values, such as 200.

8

The font-variant Property

Only one type of variant font can be set with the font-variant property, a variant where lowercase letters are represented with smaller versions of capital letters. The three possible values for font-variant are shown in Table 8.3; the default value is normal, and if there is a value set on the containing box, it will be inherited.

TABLE 8.3 Values for the font-variant Property

Value	Effect
normal	Uses normal lowercase letters
small-caps	Uses small capitals instead of lowercase letters
inherit	Uses the value of the containing box's font-variant property

An example of font-variant is shown in Figure 8.3; the rule used is

```
#a { font-family:  Verdana, sans-serif;
     font-variant: small-caps; }
```

FIGURE 8.3

Using font-variant: small-caps *in Opera 6.*

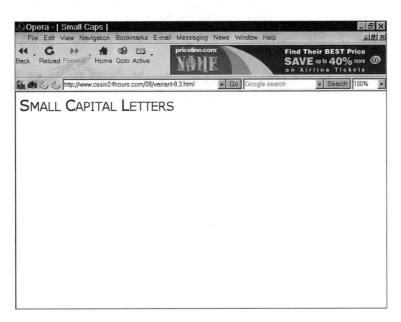

The `font-style` Property

To set something in an italic or oblique font, you can use the `font-style` property; `font-style` is not used for anything else, although the name seems deceptively general. The values for `font-style` are shown in Table 8.4. If there's a `font-style` property set on the containing box, it will be inherited. Otherwise, the default will usually be `normal`, although some HTML properties, such as `<i>`, `<em>`, and `<address>`, are normally italicized by Web browsers.

TABLE 8.4   Values for the `font-style` Property

Value	Effect
italic	Uses an italic font
normal	Uses a non-oblique, non-italic font
oblique	Uses an oblique or slanted font
inherit	Uses the value of the containing box's `font-style` property

What is `oblique`? Although it's a less common term than `italic`, it's a related concept.

Most fonts we see are called *Roman fonts*; these are not slanted, and they correspond to the CSS value of `normal`. An *italic font* is created by making slanted, slightly curly alternate versions of the letters in a Roman font; each letter has been redesigned so that it's essentially a new set of characters within the same font family.

An *oblique font*, on the other hand, is created simply by tilting the Roman font's characters at an angle. This doesn't always require font redesign and can be done automatically by a computer, but often the results are not nearly as nice looking. Many typography books explicitly discourage the use of computer-created obliques.

Browsers will treat `italic` and `oblique` property values the same because they don't really know the difference most of the time. The CSS specification allows for `italic` fonts to be displayed as `oblique` (even oblique fonts generated automatically) if a matching italic font is not available. You'll probably want to simply use `italic`; don't worry about the difference unless you are a professional typographer, in which case you don't need me to explain the difference between oblique and italic.

Figure 8.4 shows the lack of difference between oblique and italic as displayed by current browsers; they're both rendered the same, in slanted text. This is unfortunate for typographers, but for most of us it won't be a major problem. The code used in this screenshot was

```
<div style="font-style: normal;">
  This is Roman text.
</div>
<div style="font-style: italic;">
  This is italic text.
</div>
<div style="font-style: oblique;">
  This is oblique text.
</div>
```

FIGURE 8.4

Oblique versus italic in Netscape 6.

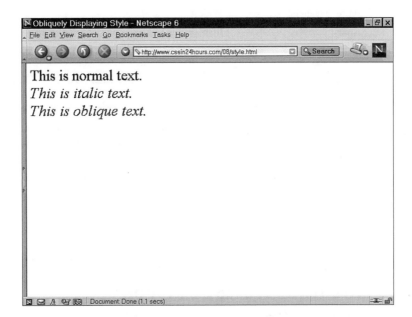

The `font-stretch` Property

You can use the `font-stretch` property to select a thinner or wider font in CSS. Condensed type is narrower and looks as though it's been pressed together from the left and right sides; conversely, expanded type looks as though it's been pulled out and stretched to be wider. Values for `font-stretch` are shown in Table 8.5; the default is `normal`, and this value can be inherited from the containing box.

TABLE 8.5   Values for the `font-stretch` Property

Value	Effect
ultra-condensed	Most narrow
extra-condensed	Very narrow
condensed	Narrow
semi-condensed	Somewhat narrow
normal	Unchanged (default)
semi-expanded	Somewhat wider
expanded	Wide
extra-expanded	Very wide
ultra-expanded	Widest
wider	Increase by one step over inherited value
narrower	Decreases by one step below inherited value
inherit	Uses the `font-stretch` value of the containing box

Unfortunately, no browser currently supports the `font-stretch` property. This is the reason there's no screenshot of these values in action. If you need to use a condensed font, you should name the specific condensed font as one of the fonts in `font-family`, such as

```
h2.compressed {
  font-family: "Arial MT Condensed Light",
               Arial, sans-serif; }
```

See the discussion later this hour on font availability.

The `font-size-adjust` Property

Not all fonts of the same point size look like they're the same size. For example, 12-point Verdana looks much larger than 12-point Times New Roman. Why is that if they're both 12 point?

To understand the reason for that, and to understand how to use `font-size-adjust`, you need to understand how font sizes are measured. A font size is measured from the bottom baseline to the top of the capital letters; this unit is called the em, as we've discussed before and used in our CSS properties for borders, margins, and padding.

Another unit of measure is the *ex*; the ex is the measurement from the bottom baseline up to the top of the lowercase letters (historically, this was measured to the top of a lowercase x).

The ratio of the ex to the em is called the *aspect value* of the font. Fonts with larger aspect values are going to look larger because the uppercase letters will be the same size, but the lowercase letters will be taller and usually wider. This is why 12-point Verdana looks larger than 12-point Times New Roman; Verdana has a larger aspect value. Aspect values of common fonts are given in Table 8.6; these are listed in the CSS Level 2 specification.

TABLE 8.6 Aspect Values for Typical Web Fonts

Font Name	Aspect Value
Verdana	0.58
Comic Sans MS	0.52
Georgia	0.5
Times New Roman	0.46

So for Verdana, 1ex is 0.58em, whereas 1ex in Times New Roman is 0.46em. When you set the font-size property, the ex value is calculated automatically from the em size.

You can use the ex unit in your designs—for example, setting the size of the margin to 3ex—but I advise against it. Because the ex varies considerably depending on the font and isn't easily known in advance (unlike the em, which is based directly on font-size), the ex is a much less reliable measure than the em.

The font-size-adjust property allows you to tweak the size of the ex, changing the aspect ratio to another value. You write a font-size-adjust rule like this:

```
selector { font-size-adjust: aspect-value; }
```

For example, to make your Verdana and Times New Roman fonts look closer to the same size, use this type of CSS rule:

```
body { font-size: 12pt;
       font-family: Verdana, sans-serif;
       font-size-adjust: 0.46; }
```

Like font-stretch, font-size-adjust is not supported by existing browsers. For this level of font control, you'll have to wait for future CSS implementations.

The `font` Shorthand Property

As you've probably noticed this hour, there are quite a few properties that define a font. Rather than typing out each property, the `font` property allows you to set these values at one time.

The `font` property is a *shorthand property* in CSS terminology. A shorthand value has two effects: it sets all affected properties to their default values, and it assigns designated values to the appropriate properties. The `font` property is shorthand for the `font-family`, `font-size`, `font-weight`, `font-variant`, `font-style`, and `line-height` properties. (You'll learn about `line-height` and how to use it with `font` in Hour 12, "Alignment and Spacing.") The `font` property doesn't let you set values for `font-stretch` or `font-size-adjust`; these need to be set in separate rules.

> Don't overlook that first function, resetting to default values! You can easily spend hours trying to debug your style sheet. In addition to anything else a `font` rule does, it also is equivalent to the following declarations:
>
> ```
> font-family: serif; /* or the default browser font */
> font-size: medium;
> font-weight: normal;
> font-variant: normal;
> font-style: normal;
> line-height: 100%;
> ```

A `font` rule looks like this:

```
selector { font: style variant weight size family; }
```

The values for `weight`, `size`, and `family` must be specified in that exact order, but other than that the values can appear in any order. Any values that aren't listed are set to their default values. Here are some examples of `font` shorthand rules:

```
body { font: 12pt normal "Times New Roman"; }
h1 { font: 20pt Arial italic small-caps; }
blockquote { font: bold "Courier New", sans-serif; }
```

When using `font` it's important to keep in mind that the first function of this property is to reset values to their defaults; this means that priority order counts. For example, consider these pairs of rules:

```
#a { font-weight: 700;
     font: large Verdana, sans-serif; }
#b { font: large Verdana, sans-serif;
     font-weight: 700; }
```

In the `#a` rules, the `font-weight` gets set to `700` by the `font-weight` property, but then the `font` property resets it to the default, so the weight is back to `400`. The `#b` rules are in the correct order to make the text bold; first the `font` rule sets everything to default values, and then the specific rule for `font-weight` overrides the default.

> The `font` property can also take values based on the user's operating system fonts; these are discussed in detail in Hour 22, "User Interface and Generated Content."

8

Font Families

As you learned in Hour 2, the `font-family` property is used to select the family of font faces. A `font-family` rule can be written like this:

```
selector { font-family: font1, font2, font3, ...
              generic; }
```

You can give as many alternate fonts as you want; the browser will look through its own list (from the computer's operating system) and locate the closest match. Once it finds one, it will display the text using that font face. For example, consider this rule:

```
h1 { font-family: "MS Sans Serif", Palatino, Helvetica,
     "Bookman Old Style", "Times New Roman", Times,
     Garamond, Chicago, Arial, Geneva, Verdana,
     cursive; }
```

The browser will start looking through the list of fonts, and if it finds a match, it will use that font. So on my Windows computer, it might find `"MS Sans Serif"` and display the `<h1>` in that font; on my Apple iBook, it won't find `"MS Sans Serif"` and will go on to the next one. If the iBook has `Palatino` (which it does), that's the font family that will be used.

> Remember to include quotes around font names that are more than one word!

The Generic Font Families

In the long rule above, I included a generic font family name at the end—`cursive`. In case the browser can't find any of the 11 named fonts, it will use the browser's `cursive` font. The exact value of the `cursive` font will vary a lot from operating system to operating system; also, modern browsers (such as Netscape 6 or Internet Explorer 5.1 for

Macintosh) allow the user to set specific fonts tied to the generic families. So on my Netscape 6, cursive might mean "Apple Chancery", whereas on yours it may be the "Lucida Handwriting" font.

The five generic font families in CSS are serif, sans-serif, cursive, fantasy, and monospace. To show you how different browsers (on two different operating systems) will display the generic font families, I've taken some screen shots. Your browser may display these differently as well; in most browsers you can reconfigure your generic font families depending on which fonts are installed on your system.

In Figure 8.5, you can see the generic font families as shown in Netscape 6, running on my iBook Macintosh laptop.

FIGURE 8.5

Generic font families in Netscape 6 (Macintosh).

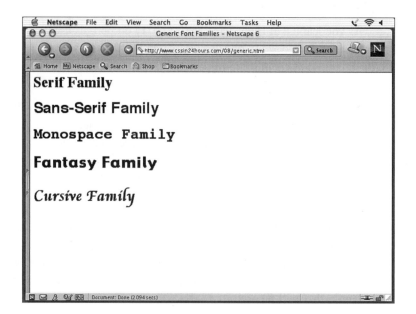

Figure 8.6 shows you what the generic font families look like in Internet Explorer 6, running on my Windows desktop computer. Notice that the serif, sans-serif, and monospace families are consistent with the iBook's families, but the cursive and fantasy families are very different. Some of this is because we're comparing two computers, each on its own operating system.

In Figure 8.7, I've shown the generic font families as displayed by Opera 6 on the same computer I used to create the screenshot in Figure 8.6. Once again, the cursive and fantasy families are the most variable, even on the same computer.

FIGURE 8.6

Generic font families in Internet Explorer 6 (Windows).

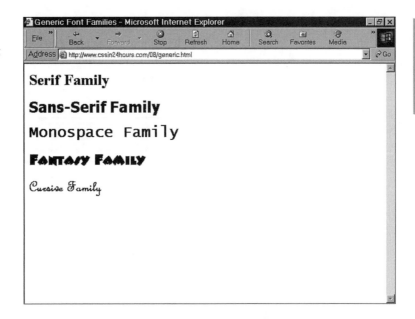

FIGURE 8.7

Generic font families in Opera 6 (Windows).

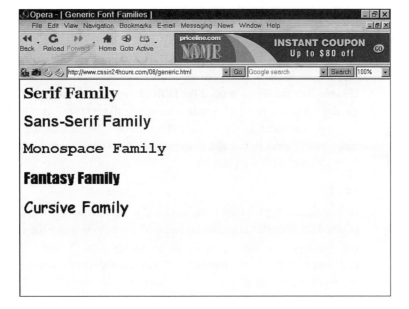

Finally, Figure 8.8 shows how Internet Explorer on the Macintosh interprets the generic
font families. Compare these fonts with those in the previous figures, and you'll find that
there's little regularity across browsers—or even within browsers or operating systems—
when using `fantasy` and `cursive` families.

FIGURE **8.8**

Generic font families in
Internet Explorer 5.1
(Macintosh).

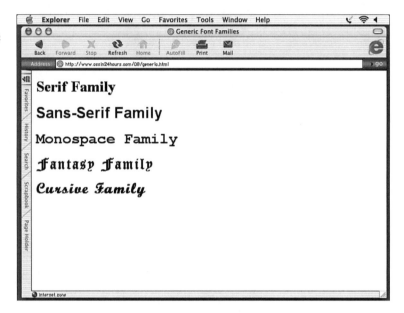

Generic font families are good for fallback; without them, your font face will be the single default of the browser, usually something like `"Times New Roman"`. However, they're
not very consistent, as you can see. They are still better than the basic default, however,
and you will want to include a generic family in each `font-family` property value (or
`font` shorthand property value).

serif

In font terminology a *serif* is defined as the little feet or curved bits added to the end of
the straight lines that constitute a letter. These help to make the characters easier to distinguish when reading, especially when reading print. A serif font makes it much easier
to distinguish among the number 1, the lowercase letter l, and the uppercase letter I, as
shown in Figure 8.9.

FIGURE 8.9

Serif fonts make it easier to distinguish letters.

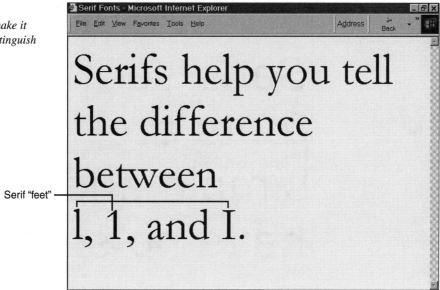

Serif "feet"

Serif fonts are often used for normal body text in Web browsers. The default test font is commonly `"Times New Roman"`, which is usually the generic `serif` family font as well. However, serif fonts tend to display poorly on the screen compared with print, especially at smaller font sizes. Many Web developers will immediately change the font-family to a nonserif font as the first rule of their style sheets.

Other examples of serif fonts include `"Bookman Old Style"`, `"Book Antiqua"`, `"Century Schoolbook"`, Garamond, `"Goudy Old Style"`, Palatino, and Sonoma. The font `Times` is similar to `"Times New Roman"`, and it's often useful to specify both of those fonts together, like this:

```
blockquote { font-family: "Times New Roman",
             Times, serif; }
```

sans-serif

The prefix *sans* means "without," so a sans-serif font is one that does not have serifs. Sans-serif fonts look cleaner and more streamlined than serif fonts, and they often fit better on most Web pages. (Not all Web designs are the same, though, and you can many times find uses of both serif and sans-serif fonts, often within the same style sheet.) A sans-serif font is shown in Figure 8.10.

FIGURE **8.10**

Sans-serif fonts have a more modern look than serif fonts.

The most common sans-serif font is `Arial`; its near relatives are `Helvetica` and `Geneva`. Another important font is `Verdana`, which was specifically developed for on-screen display; it is wider than `Arial` and easier to read, especially at smaller sizes. Other examples of sans-serif fonts are `"Century Gothic"`, `Chicago`, `Futura`, and `Tahoma`.

cursive

The `cursive` generic family is very variable; it refers to any font that was based on the way people handwrite text. There are no real standards on what the default cursive family should be, which is why it is different from computer to computer and even from browser to browser. Examples include `"Script MT Bold"`, `"Apple Chancery"`, `Swing`, and `"Lucida Handwriting"`; in Figure 8.11, you can see one example of a cursive font.

Cursive fonts tend to be very difficult to read onscreen and probably should be avoided unless you have a very specific reason to use one, such as the writer's name after a letter, styled to represent a written signature.

Workaround for Netscape 4

Netscape 4 doesn't recognize the `cursive` font family; therefore, you should specify another generic family, as well, such as `serif`:

```
sig { font-family: "Lucida Handwriting",
      cursive, serif; }
```

FIGURE **8.11**

One browser's cursive font.

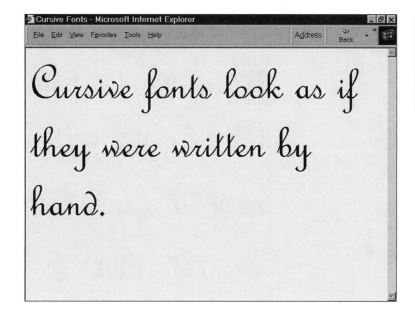

fantasy

The `fantasy` generic family is even more of a grab bag than the `cursive` family; any irregular, somewhat-whimsical font falls into this category. Some are old woodcut-style ornate letters; some are bizarre squiggles; some look like animals; and some look like letters cut from newspapers for a ransom note. Figure 8.12 has an example of a font from the `fantasy` generic family.

Because the `fantasy` generic family is so undefined and because browsers have interpreted this as a catchall for any strange fonts that may come along, a declaration of `fantasy` could produce text that looks like anything. For example, on my browser it may display in a comic book printed font, but on yours it could appear in an old English woodcut font. Because this kind of irregularity makes it hard to design effectively, you'll probably want to avoid using this family.

Workaround for Netscape 4

Because Netscape 4 doesn't understand the `fantasy` generic family, either, use the same workaround you used for `cursive` (adding an additional generic family) if you choose `fantasy`.

FIGURE 8.12

One of many possible fantasy fonts.

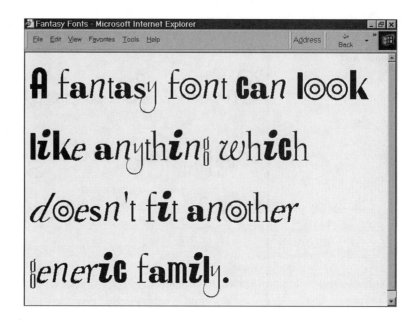

monospace

The term monospace means that each letter is displayed in the same amount of space; columns of text line up, for example, so that the 15th character from the left is always at the same location. This is rather like an old typewriter. (Soon I may be unable to use that analogy!) The code samples in this book are set in a monospace font, as is anything you type, such as property values and the names of properties and selectors. Figure 8.13 is an example of the `monospace` generic family.

The most common monospace font family is `"Courier New"`, and this is the default monospace value on pretty much every browser. `Courier` is an older version of `"Courier New"`; you may want to list both of these to ensure a greater likelihood of a font match.

Other monospace fonts include `"Andale Mono"`, `VT102`, and `Mishiwaka`.

Commonly Installed Fonts

Because there's so much variance among computers, you may not be able to know with certainty whether or not a given font will appear on a user's computer. She might be using Internet Explorer 6 on Windows, but she also could've decided to delete Arial entirely! (Why someone would do this, I'm not quite sure.)

FIGURE 8.13

The letters of monospace fonts line up in columns.

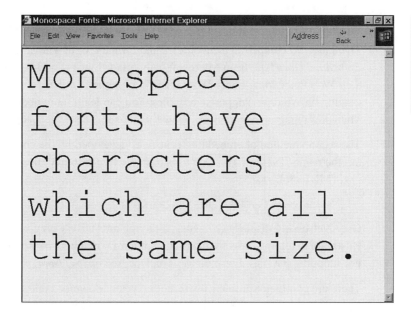

However, it's possible to devise a list of relatively safe fonts—those that are found on most operating systems and browsers. You should continue to use generic families as fallbacks, but these are relatively safe.

The common fonts are "Times New Roman", Times, Arial, Helvetica, Geneva, Verdana, "Courier New", and Courier. Other fonts are less reliable.

Downloadable Fonts and Font Descriptors

To overcome the problem of uninstalled fonts, the Cascading Style Sheets Level 2 specification defines a way to specify *downloadable fonts*. These fonts will be retrieved from the Web automatically and used to display the page.

A downloadable font is declared by a @font-face rule, and various attributes of that font are defined by font descriptors—properties that look like ordinary CSS values but that describe qualities of the font. A @font-face rule looks like this:

```
@font-face { font-family: "name of font";
            src: url("url of font");
            other font descriptors }
```

The list of other font descriptor properties is long and includes all of the font properties from earlier in this hour, as well as other ways to define which characters are covered by the font, exact details of the dimensions, and so on.

Browser Support for Downloadable Fonts

There are two competing technologies and formats for downloading fonts. The first one, *Embedded OpenType* from Microsoft, supports @font-face rules, but you need to use their Web Embedding Fonts Tool (WEFT) to prepare `.eot` files. Only Internet Explorer running on Windows supports `.eot` files. You can learn more about WEFT at the Microsoft typography site, `http://www.microsoft.com/typography`.

The second method of embedding fonts was developed by the company Bitstream and has the name *TrueDoc*. TrueDoc uses portable font resource files (.pfr), which are linked in HTML as follows:

```
<link rel="fontdef" src="url">
```

Only Netscape 4 displays `.pfr` files, although an ActiveX plug-in is available from Bitstream to allow access by Internet Explorer (Windows). Netscape 6 and Mozilla do not support `.pfr` files. For more on TrueDoc, see `http://www.truedoc.com/`.

There are two major problems with both types of downloadable fonts: support and speed. Opera, Netscape 6, and Mozilla do not support downloadable fonts, and neither `.eot` nor `.pfr` are cross-platform compatible; this means there is not a single usable standard that will work on most browsers. As for speed, each additional downloadable font you add increases the download and display time of your Web page, and if it's simply for a presentational effect, including the additional fonts may not be worth it.

Summary

When you specify a font, you're actually selecting a font from a set maintained by the user's browser and operating system. The various font properties, such as `font-weight`, `font-variant`, `font-style`, and `font-size`, narrow down the fonts within a specific `font-family` to find the right one to use. All of these properties can be specified using the `font` shorthand property.

There are five generic font families—`serif`, `sans-serif`, `cursive`, `fantasy`, and `mono-space`—that are used if the user's computer doesn't contain a font you specify. A short list of common fonts is available on all browsers. CSS describes a method for downloading fonts on demand, but unfortunately neither of the two competing methods for downloading fonts is very reliable.

Browser Support Report Card

8

CSS Feature	Grade	Notes
The `font-weight` property	B+	Inconsistencies among browsers
The `font-variant` property	B+	Not supported by Netscape 4
The `font-style` property	A-	`italic` and `oblique` treated the same
The `font-stretch` property	D	Unsupported
The `font-size-adjust` property	D	Unsupported
The `font` shorthand property	B+	See other font properties
The `serif` generic family	A	
The `sans-serif` generic family	A	
The `cursive` generic family	B+	Workaround needed for Netscape 4
The `fantasy` generic family	B+	Workaround needed for Netscape 4
The `monospace` generic family	A	
List of common fonts	A	
Downloadable fonts (`@font-face`)	D+	No standardization or cross-browser support

Q&A

Q I need to have specific fonts on my page, even if the user doesn't have them on his computer. Downloadable fonts don't seem reliable. What can I do?

A In such a case, you may want to create graphics of your text; assume we're talking about headers or navigation buttons. The problem with text-as-graphics is that the images don't scale at all with the user's preferences, which may make it harder for some users with visual disabilities. In any case, you need to remember to set the `alt` attribute on the HTML `<img>` tag to a value equal to the text on the graphic.

Workshop

The workshop contains quiz questions and activities to help reinforce what you've learned in this hour. If you get stuck, the answers to the quiz can be found after the questions.

Quiz

1. Consider the following HTML:

```
<div style="font-weight: bold;">
  That's <span style="font-weight: bolder;">heavy</a>,
  man.
</div>
```

What numeric value (100 to 900) is the equivalent of the font weight on the word heavy?

2. How do you write the following properties using the font shorthand property?

```
.double { font-weight: 700;
          font-family: Verdana, sans-serif;
          font-size: x-large;
          font-size-adjust: 0.55;
          font-style: oblique;
          font-stretch: condensed;
          font-variant: small-caps; }
```

3. What are the generic font families that are closest to each of these fonts?

(a.) Verdana

(b.) Times New Roman

(c.) Lucida Handwriting

(d.) Helvetica

(e.) Courier New

Answers

1. The value bold is inherited from the containing box, and it has a value of 700. The bolder property value increases the inherited value by 100, so the total is 800.

2. Here's one way to write that rule using the font property:

```
.double { font: oblique small-caps 700
                x-large Verdana sans-serif;
          font-size-adjust: 0.55;
          font-stretch: condensed; }
```

Because font-size-adjust and font-stretch aren't included in the font shorthand property, they have to be declared separately. Note that the order of *weight, size,* and *family* is used; hopefully, you remembered that the order does matter for those values.

3. The generic families for each font are:

(a.) sans-serif

(b.) serif

(c.) cursive

(d.) sans-serif

(e.) monospace

Activity

Explore the use of fonts in CSS with these optional projects.

- View the Web page at http://www.cssin24hours.com/10/generic.html with your browser, and see how your browser's generic family fonts compare with those in Figures 8.5 through 8.8. Does your browser have preferences for changing these defaults?

- Create a Web page with a style sheet that uses a number of different fonts for headers, paragraphs, navigation, footers, tables, and anything else. Go overboard with your font choices, and then start decreasing the variety of fonts you use. Discover at what point "a lot" is "too many," and discover how many fonts you really need to make a Web page look right. (My preference? No more than two or three.)

- To use downloadable fonts on your Web page, you'll need to download software to repackage an existing font from your system. Go to http://www.microsoft.com/typography for .eof fonts, or go to http://www.truedoc.com/ for .pfr fonts, and try using these programs to make font files. Are they worth the effort?

HOUR 9

Text Colors and Effects

Use of Cascading Style Sheets can transform a plain, boring page of text into a visual treat, without even using any graphics to do so. The CSS specifications define ways to visually enhance your textual content, from changing the colors to adding drop shadows.

In this hour, you'll learn

- Additional ways to specify the color of text
- How to use color effectively in Web design
- How to add or remove underlines from your text
- How to add lines through or over your text
- Which CSS property allows you to change the case of your letters
- How to do text shadows in CSS, and which browsers support them

Text Colors

Colors are a key part of conveying information in a visual medium. Giving distinct colors to certain types of information on a page can emphasize or de-emphasize the importance; for example, new content can be marked with a bright, vivid color, and outdated content may be presented in a more muted hue.

As you already know, the `color` property is the primary method for setting the foreground color. You can set the background color using the `background-color` property, which we'll look at in detail next hour.

The foreground `color` is also used by other properties as a default color value if none is specified. For example, if a color value is omitted for the `border` property, the foreground `color` will be used.

Specifying Color Values

CSS provides two ways to define a color. The first is to use a color name, such as `green` or `black`; the second is to use a set of three RGB values, corresponding to the amount of red, green, and blue desired. RGB colors were introduced in Hour 2, "Getting Started with CSS," and in this hour we'll tell you other ways to specify a set of RGB values.

Color Names

Back in Hour 2, you learned about the sixteen colors recognized by the CSS specifications. These color names—`aqua`, `black`, `blue`, `fuchsia`, `gray`, `green`, `lime`, `maroon`, `navy`, `olive`, `purple`, `red`, `silver`, `teal`, `white`, and `yellow`—are well-supported by the browsers.

Most browsers will accept other color names as well, such as `pink`, `orange`, `cyan`, and `violet`. However, until a future version of CSS adds those colors to the official specification, it's probably best to avoid using such nonstandard colors. There's no guarantee that a compliant browser will support them, so you're safer with RGB values.

There are some other colors that are accepted by browsers as well; those are based on the user's operating system preferences and are called *system colors*. In Hour 22, "User Interface and Generated Content," you'll learn more about system colors and how to use them in your Web design.

RGB Color Values

To specify a color in RGB notation, you need to know how much red, green, and blue is contained in that color. Web colors are a bit strange at first if you're not used to them; they're not at all like mixing paints as a child. For example, when you're blending paint colors, you mix red and yellow to make orange. When you're making RGB colors, you mix red and green to make yellow! If you did that with paint, you'd get some ugly, muddy gray-brown shade.

This is because paints (and ink, as well as most other physical objects you look at) have color because they selectively reflect light; something that actually emits light, as your monitor does, creates colors by adding together portions of colored light. It's a bit confusing, but you'll get used to it once you've worked with RGB values.

Even more confusing is the way RGB colors are written. All RGB colors are measured based on a scale from 0 to 255. They're usually counted in hexadecimal, which means a base-16 number system where the digits are 0, 1, 2, 3, 4, 5, 6, 7, 8, 9, A, B, C, D, E, and F. The number 32 is written as 20 (two sixteens and zero ones), and the number 111 is 6F (six sixteens and 15 ones).

CSS offers four ways to present RGB values. The first is using straightforward *hexadecimal notation*, as a six-digit number:

```
body { color: #CC66FF; }
```

This means the foreground color should have a red value of CC—204 out of 255, or 80%; 66 green, which is 102 (40%); and FF blue, or 255 (100%). What does this color look like? Kind of a light lavender. The closer you are to white (#FFFFFF) the more pastel the colors, and when you mix large amounts of blue and red, you get a purple effect.

You can also write this in *short hex notation*. This is a three-digit hexadecimal number; to convert a three-digit RGB code to a six-digit one, simply double each letter. So the same rule can be written like this:

```
body { color: #C6F; }
```

The rgb() function provides two more ways to set colors, especially if you don't know hexadecimal numbers well. One of those is to provide a triplet of RGB numbers, rated from 0 to 255, separated by commas. The other is to give percentages. Here's how the lavender rule can be written:

```
body { color: rgb(204, 102, 255); }
body { color: rgb(80%, 40%, 100%); }
```

You can use these color values when setting any color in CSS, not just the color property. For example, you can set a background-color or a border with any of these types of values.

 To design effectively with color, you need a color chart, or else you have to be very willing to experiment with RGB values! I recommend getting a color chart; either a printed one you can keep by your computer or an electronic file you can refer to, or both. A great site for Web color information is Visibone, http://www.visibone.com/, which has a hex color chart arranged by hue.

Using Color Effectively

When you're designing a Web page and adding color by using CSS, it's always helpful to put some thought into the process. The theory and practice of employing color is a topic that could fill an entire book or several books, as not everyone seems to agree! However, here are some pointers which can help you use color more effectively in your designs; most of these are common sense, but it's amazing how many Web designs don't seem to have taken these into account.

- Use colors to visually emphasize important differences among types of content. The presentation of your content should be derived from the meaning of that information. Color your navigation bar differently from your main content. Set sidebars apart visually with background colors that fit well with the rest of the page. Change the color of headings to make them more visible.

- Change colors for a reason, not on a whim. I've seen many Web sites where the developers appear to have discovered color just the day before and change the color for no reason. Be able to justify your color choices.

- Bright colors draw attention; faded colors hide unimportant material. As an example, if some content is more important or changes often, give it a vibrant, bright color, such as yellow or red, to make it stand out.

- Too many colors will make your page seem confusing and unprofessional; a restricted set of hues often works better. If you don't have any experience with graphic design, pick up a good book on color and design, and notice that many great designs have a limited palette.

- You don't have to change the color of everything. Black-on-white is not the enemy. Web users are accustomed to the default colors, and often it's easier to read text if there's high contrast, such as black-on-white (or white-on-black).

- If you're designing for a whole site, use a consistent look across your pages. Consistency helps users recognize that they're still at your site and helps establish a feeling of familiarity. If you change your site too often, regular users may be disoriented.

- If there are identifiable subsites, consider assigning each one a color scheme. Don't create a brand new design for each; it can be disorienting if each section looks like a brand new Web site. Instead, add color that complements the primary site design.

- Make sure your color choices look good together and contrast well. Subtle shades of difference, such as medium blue on dark blue, may not come across well and content could be lost.

- Use colors that complement any images or graphics on your page. You can derive color schemes from your graphical content, or choose graphics that fit your chosen colors. The more coordinated your colors, the better your site will look.

- Test your colors in several browsers and computers; your monitor's settings may be different than someone else's. Try testing with 256 colors instead of thousands, millions, or billions; if you can, try your site in black-and-white.

- Don't employ color as the only way of conveying information; visually impaired users might miss important context. It's fine to use color, but make sure that important distinctions among content are reflected in the markup as well. In Hour 21, "Accessibility and Internationalization," you'll learn more about designing to enable access by people with disabilities.

9

Special Text Effects

In addition to changing the colors of the text, and the font properties from Hour 8, "Fonts and Font Families," Cascading Style Sheets can be used to produce text effects ranging from decorations to drop shadows. These can be used only on CSS elements that actually contain text; on anything else, they have no effect. For example, a `text-shadow` property set on an `<img>` tag won't produce a shadow under the displayed image.

The `text-decoration` Property

CSS uses the term *text decoration* to refer to a specific set of effects that can be applied to text: lines through, under, or around the text, and blinking text. The types of values that can be set for the `text-decoration` property are shown in Table 9.1. The default value for `text-decoration` is usually `none`, although most browsers will automatically use `text-decoration: underline` for hypertext links.

TABLE 9.1   Values for the `text-decoration` Property

Value	Effect
blink	The text blinks off and on
line-through	Draws a line through the middle of the text
overline	Draws a line over the top of the text
underline	Draws a line under the bottom of the text
none	None of the effects listed above
inherit	Uses the value of `text-decoration` on the containing box

The blink property value is not very popular, primarily due to serious abuse of the <blink> tag by designers when it was first introduced by Netscape. The <blink> tag is nonstandard in HTML and highly discouraged. Because of this, text-decoration: blink is specifically stated to be an optional part of the CSS specification; browsers don't have to support it. Netscape 4 and Opera support blink; Netscape 6, Mozilla, and Internet Explorer do not.

The value of text-decoration is technically not inherited, although if it is set on a block element, the decoration should be applied to all text within that block.

The color of the text-decoration—the line through, over, or under the text—is the same as that of the text itself, and so can be set using the color property. The lines drawn are thin, and the exact thickness is up to the browser; you can't change the line thickness with CSS.

Caution for Netscape 4

Netscape 4 doesn't support the overline value for text-decoration. Fortunately, most designers rarely (if ever) have a use for this setting, but if you need it, be advised that it won't work in Netscape 4.

The most common value for text-decoration in style sheets is none; the property is mainly used to turn off underlines rather than add them or any other text decorations. Why is this so? Because you can use text-decoration to turn off the underlines on links by writing a:link and a:visited rules. Many designers find underlined links to be annoyingly ugly and much less elegant than links without underlines.

However, there are some problems with that approach; namely, it makes it harder for the user to know what's a link and what's not. If you're going to remove one of the user's primary cues to find clickable links, you need to make sure that the links are obvious. Color typically isn't enough by itself, even though Web developers like to think it should be.

If you're using inline links—those within paragraphs of text—then you should probably leave the underlines alone. An alternative approach is to set obvious borders or background colors on your inline links.

Navigation bars are a different case; even without underlines, users can tell they're supposed to click on things that look like buttons or a list of options. Removing underlines from navigation bars is acceptable and won't cause problems.

The other side of the link-underlining coin is this: Users think that anything that is underlined is clickable. If you put text-decoration: underline on your <h2> tag, people will try to click it. And they'll get annoyed when it doesn't click. Therefore, you will want to avoid using underlines nearly all the time. If you need to call attention to something, use the <em> or <strong> tags, font effects like font-weight or font-style, or colors.

Listing 9.1 is an HTML file with an embedded style sheet that demonstrates text-decoration in action; you can see the results displayed in Figure 9.1.

9

LISTING 9.1   Text Decorations in an Embedded Style Sheet

```
<!-- decorate-9.1.html -->
<html>
  <head>
    <title>I love to decorate</title>
    <style type="text/css">
      body { font-family: Verdana, sans-serif; }
      h1 em { text-decoration: underline; }
      .navbar { border: 0.3em solid black; }
      .navbar a:link, .navbar a:visited
        { text-decoration: none; }
      .strike { text-decoration: line-through; }
      .eg { border: 1px solid black;
            margin: 2em; padding: 1em; }
      #a { text-decoration: underline; }
      #b { text-decoration: line-through; }
      #c { text-decoration: overline; }
      #d { text-decoration: blink; }
    </style>
  </head>
  <body>
    <table class="navbar" border="0" align="right">
      <tr><th><a href="home.html">Home</a></th></tr>
      <tr><th><a href="info.html">Info</a></th></tr>
      <tr><th><a href="help.html">Help</a></th></tr>
      <tr><th><a href="news.html">News</a></th></tr>
    </table>
    <h1>I <em>love</em> to decorate!</h1>
    <p> I think that decorating
        <span class="strike">cakes</span>HTML is lots
        of fun. Here are some of my favorites: </p>
    <div class="eg">
      <p id="a">
        Underlined text (don't you want to click here?) </p>
      <p id="b">Line-through text</p>
      <p id="c">Overlined text</p>
      <p id="d">
```

continues

LISTING 9.1   Continued

```
              Blinking text (this is hard to show in print!) </p>
        </div>
      </body>
    </html>
```

FIGURE 9.1

*Netscape 6 displays
text decorations.*

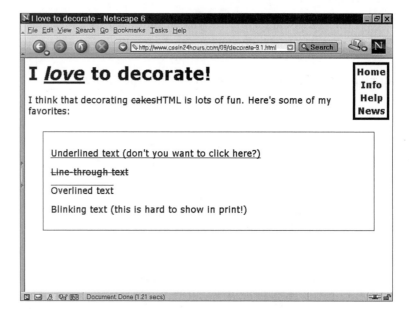

The `text-transform` Property

You can change the case of text from upper to lower case, or vice versa by using the
`text-transform` property. Well, you're actually not changing the text itself, rather how a
CSS-enabled browser displays it. The values you can set for this property are shown in
Table 9.2; the default is none, although if there is `text-transform` property on the containing box, that value will be inherited.

TABLE 9.2   Values for the `text-transform` Property

Value	*Effect*
capitalize	Capitalizes the first letter of each word
lowercase	Changes all uppercase letters to lowercase
uppercase	Changes all lowercase letters to uppercase
none	Doesn't change anything
inherit	Uses the value on the containing box

This property is dependent upon the language and character set being used; if a language doesn't have uppercase or lowercase letters, nothing will be changed.

Here's a short piece of HTML demonstrating text-transform:

```
<div style="text-transform: capitalize;">
  <span style="text-transform: uppercase;">
    hello out there,
  </span>
  can ANYONE
  <span style="text-transform: lowercase;">
    HEAR ME?
  </span>
</div>
```

When a CSS-enabled browser displays this, the case is transformed as shown in Figure 9.2.

FIGURE 9.2

Transformed text is more than meets the eye.

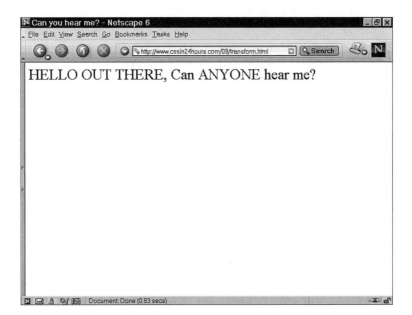

The `text-shadow` Property

To set a shadow effect on your text, you can use the `text-shadow` property—in theory, at least. The `text-shadow` property is written like this:

```
selector {
  text-shadow: color x-displace y-displace diffusion;
}
```

The `color` can be any CSS color. The `x-displace` and `y-displace` values are measurements, usually measured in pixels or ems, which tell the browser how far to offset the shadow from the original text. The `diffusion` affects how blurry the shadow should be; it's also a unit of measurement. If there's no `color` specified, the shadow is the same as the text color, set by the `color` property. If there's no `displacement` or `diffusion` listed, they have values of `0px`. A zero-pixel diffusion means the shadow is as sharp and unblurred as the original.

This seems complex at first, but it's actually pretty easy. Here's an example:

```
h1 { text-shadow: blue 0.1em -0.1em 3px; }
```

This means to create a blue text shadow that is placed 0.1 ems to the right of, and 0.1 ems above, the `<h1>` text. It should blur out up to 3 pixels.

So what's the catch? Well...

> **Caution for Netscape 4, Netscape 6, Internet Explorer (Windows), Internet Explorer (Mac), Mozilla, and Opera**
>
> No browsers support `text-shadow`! So don't bother trying to use it, at least not with Year 2002 browsers. If you use it, it won't hurt anything, but it won't do anything, either. Browser support may exist in the future, but until that happens, there's little point in using `text-shadow`.

Summary

The foreground color of text can be set with the `color` property, as you've seen in previous hours. You can set the color value in several ways, including color names, long or short hexadecimal values, and the `rgb()` function.

Color is a powerful tool for visual communication, but you also need to take care to use it effectively. Consistency and simplicity will help your Web sites convey information better and produce a more professional look.

Other effects you can apply to your text include decorations such as underlines and strikethroughs using the `text-decoration` property; changes of case with `text-transform`; and shadows under the text via `text-shadow` (although there's no browser support for text shadows currently).

Browser Support Report Card

CSS Feature	Grade	Notes
Color names	A	
RGB colors	A	
text-decoration	B+	Limited blink and overline support
text-transform	A	
text-shadow	D	No browser support

9

Q&A

Q I've heard someone mention "browser-safe colors" before. What is that?

A When Web browsers were first created, they couldn't handle the full range of color available. Instead, they displayed only a limited subset of specific colors—216 colors to be precise. Any other colors were displayed poorly, making some backgrounds and images look quite bad. These days, browsers can support a full range of color choices, so the browser-safe color list isn't as important, although you may want to look into it if you are supporting older hardware or software. For more information, see the Visibone site at http://www.visibone.com/.

Q I really want to use text-decoration: blink. Can I?

A No.

Q Are you serious?

A Well, if you *have* to, you can use it. Keep in mind that blinking text is very hard to read and very distracting. Use it only if that's the only way you can get an effect; remember, though, that most browsers don't support it.

Workshop

The workshop contains quiz questions and activities to help reinforce what you've learned in this hour. If you get stuck, the answers to the quiz can be found after the questions.

Quiz

1. Consider the color #FFFF00. How do you write this color in the following ways?

    (a.) Short hexadecimal

    (b.) RGB percentages

    (c.) RGB values

    (d.) Color names

2. You want to transform this text so that the first line is in upper case, the second line is mixed case but with each letter capitalized, and the third is in lower case. What CSS rules do you write?

```
<div id="a">CSS is fun.</div>
<div id="b">I use CSS each day.</div>
<div id="c">Do you like it too?</div>
```

Answers

1. Here are the alternate ways to write #FFFF00:

   (a.) `#FF0`

   (b.) `rgb(100%, 100%, 0%)`

   (c.) `rgb(255, 255, 0)`

   (d.) `yellow`

2. Here's how you transform that text:

```
#a { text-transform: uppercase; }
#b { text-transform: capitalize; }
#c { text-transform: lowercase; }
```

Activity

To get your hands dirty with text colors and formats, try these exercises; you'll know whether you've succeeded because you'll be able to see the desired effect.

1. Make a page with headings that contrast in color with the text. What color combinations work best?

2. See whether you can specify each color in more than one way; first try it with words, and then RGB values. Which approach is easier, and which is more flexible?

3. Turn off underlining of links on a page. Have someone else try it to use it; is it easier or harder to use? Then try overlines.

4. Convert text to uppercase or lowercase, using `text-transform`. Is this more or less useful than just changing the text in the HTML?

Hour 10

Backgrounds and Background Colors

In Hour 2, "Getting Started with CSS," you learned how to use the background-color property to change the appearance of HTML elements. Background colors can be used to good effect in Web design to group related items together or to highlight important parts of the page. In addition to pure colors, you can also use images as backgrounds for the whole page or for any element on the page.

In this hour, you'll learn

- More using about the background-color property
- How to use background and foreground colors together effectively
- How to set a background image and how to control the display of that background
- Which types of images you can use as backgrounds

Setting Background Color

As you've learned already, the background-color property is used to set the background of an HTML element and is written like this:

```
selector { background-color: color; }
```

This property is similar to the bgcolor attribute in HTML. The CSS version of background colors is a lot more useful, if just because it can be applied to anything; the bgcolor attribute can be set only on <body>, <table>, <tr>, <th>, and <td> tags. CSS selectors, such as class selectors, id selectors, and :link and :visited pseudo-class selectors, let you change the background colors for specific parts of the page.

The background-color Property

Like the foreground colors discussed in Hour 9, "Text Colors and Effects," a background-color can be specified in a number of ways: color name, RGB codes, triplets of numbers, or triplets of percentages. Here are some examples of background color declarations:

```
h1 { background-color: white; }
h2 { background-color: #FFFFFF; }
h3 { background-color: #FFF; }
h4 { background-color: rgb(255, 255, 255); }
h5 { background-color: rgb(100%, 100%, 100%); }
```

In addition to color values, there are two other values that background-color can take: transparent and inherit.

The transparent value is actually the default for all elements; transparent means that whatever background already exists will be shown. So if a background-color of blue is set on the <body>, all elements that don't have a background-color setting will be transparent and thus will be blue. This actually isn't the same as inheriting the value because background-color doesn't naturally get inherited from the containing block.

If you really need the background-color property to inherit, you can use the value inherit. In practice, transparent and inherit will almost always have the same effect, although there are a few cases when you'd need to use inherit instead of transparent. Remember that inherit is the same as setting a value equal to that of the containing block's value, whereas transparent just makes the background so that it can be seen through. It is the difference between painting the ceiling blue and installing a window on the roof. If the sky is blue anyway, they'll look about the same.

Backgrounds and Foregrounds

When you're setting background and foreground colors in CSS, it's very important to make sure that your color choices will be usable by your audience. You'll need to worry about both *contrast* and *completeness*.

Lack of contrast between your foreground and background colors can make your page difficult to use by a variety of users. Those who have poor vision will struggle to see the letters, and users of limited or black-and-white displays may be left out as well. Printed pages can also suffer from contrast problems.

When considering contrast, you also have to take the needs of users with color blindness into account; if someone can't distinguish between red and green, they may not be able to make out your green heading on a red background.

> An excellent site for color advice is Bob Stein's VisiBone Web site at
> http://www.visibone.com/. Bob offers color charts as well as suggestions on
> testing your site for use by color-blind users.

10

In addition to contrast, you also have to consider completeness. By this I mean that if you specify a foreground color, you'll also need to specify a background color. Don't assume that all users have the same initial background and foreground colors that you do!

For example, let's say you write the following rule:

```
h1 { color: black;
     font-family: Verdana, sans-serif; }
```

Looks harmless, until you consider that the user's browser settings or style sheet may have set text to be white on a black background. Your <h1> will become invisible black-on-black by this rule!

So if you want it to be visible, you'll have to explicitly set the background color whenever you set the foreground color—something like this:

```
h1 { color: black;
     background-color: white;
     font-family: Verdana, sans-serif; }
```

Using Background Images

In addition to using solid colors as your background, you can also use images. This is similar to the background attribute of HTML; the background attribute can be set only on the <body> tag, but CSS allows you to set a background image on any element.

A background image can be of any type understood by the browser, which means most background images will be GIFs or JPEGs (a few browsers also support PNG background images). Background images are more versatile than a solid color; for example, by using an image with a gradient, you can introduce fades and blends into your backgrounds. Photographic images used as backgrounds can often have a striking effect that can't be achieved with a solid RGB color. However, complex backgrounds also have their price; it is much harder to find text colors that will contrast well with a background image.

The background-image property is used to set a background image on an element. The browser will load the image and then display it behind the foreground content as specified by the CSS properties background-repeat, background-position, and background-attachment. Transparent parts of the background image will show the background color of the element (if any) or the background of the containing element.

In most cases, a background image will *tile,* which means that it repeats both horizontally and vertically across the box containing that element. A background image will fill only the area inside the border (if any), which means the padding and the content itself, as defined by the box model.

> Remember that to set a background image for the entire page, you just need to write a CSS rule for the <body> tag.

A good background image intended to tile both across and down will be created so that it doesn't have visible edges and seems to flow smoothly between one tile and another. If you're going to position text over the graphic, you'll also want to make sure that it's not too busy; you should still be able to read text once that text is placed over the background.

For the examples in this hour, I created a very simple background graphic—a star field. I created a 100 pixel by 100 pixel black square, made a few dots in various colors, and saved it as stars.gif. The background image is shown in Figure 10.1.

FIGURE 10.1

A star-spangled background image.

I also created a simple HTML page with some content, so you can see the effects of using this background image behind text; the page contains the first few lines of the U.S. national anthem, *The Star-Spangled Banner*. Listing 10.1 shows this sample HTML page, which will be used for applying styles learned this chapter.

LISTING 10.1 The Sample HTML Page

```
<!-- anthem-10.1.html -->
<html>
  <head>
    <title>The Star Spangled Banner</title>
  </head>
  <body>
    <h1>The Star Spangled Banner</h1>
    <h2>By Francis Scott Key</h2>
    <h3>HTML markup by <a href="http://kynn.com/">Kynn Bartlett</a></h3>
    <p>
      Oh say, can you see
      <br>
      By the dawn's early light
      <br>
      <!-- rest of the lines omitted here -->
    </p>
  </body>
</html>
```

The `background-image` Property

Values for the background-image property are either an image address URL, none, or inherit. URLs are indicated by the url() function around the address of the image. Quotes around the URL are optional and can be either single or double quotes (but they have to match); the following rules are all identical:

```
selector { background-image: url(image.gif); }
selector { background-image: url('image.gif'); }
selector { background-image: url("image.gif"); }
```

The URL will be calculated relative to wherever the rule appears, not necessarily to the Web page. For example, the page URL might be http://www.CSSin24hours.com/author/index.php, and it links in an external style sheet located at http://www.CSSin24hours.com/styles/site.css. A value in that style sheet, such as url("bg.gif"), refers to something in the /styles/ directory, not the /author/ directory. However, if the same rule were part of an embedded style sheet or an inline style attribute on the index.php page, it would reference something in the /author/ directory because it's all relative to the file that contains the rule.

When you set the background-image, you'll want to set the foreground colors so that they contrast with the background, just like you do when setting the background-color. You should also designate a background-color that is roughly equal to most of the background-image or at least one that contrasts well with the foreground color. If the background-image can't be loaded, the background-color will be displayed instead. If you have a cloudy, sky-blue background-image, set your color property to black (because that contrasts well with the light background) and the background-color to something like #CCCCFF (light blue).

For example, here's a rule to set the stars.gif image as the background-image of the page, along with the appropriate colors:

```
body        { background-image: url("stars.gif");
              background-color: black;
              color:            white; }
a:link      { color:            yellow; }
a:visited   { color:            lime; }
```

You'll notice I set the a:link and a:visited colors as well; otherwise, my links may not be visible against the dark background. You can see these style rules applied to *The Star-Spangled Banner* in Figure 10.2.

FIGURE 10.2

Oh say, can you see the stars.gif *background in Netscape 6?*

As you can see, the image was tiled across and down the page and looks like it fills up the entire page with a star field.

As noted earlier, you can set background images on any element, not just the <body>. This lets you set a background on paragraphs, <div> tags, or any other HTML tags. For example, these rules set the background-image on headline elements:

```
body        { background-color: white;
              color:            black; }
h1, h2, h3 { background-image: url("stars.gif");
              background-color: black;
              padding:          0.5em;
              color:            white; }
```

I've added padding here to make it easier to see the effects of the background behind the text. Apply these rules and you get a different look to the page, as seen in Figure 10.3.

FIGURE 10.3

Background images behind <h1>, <h2>, and <h3>.

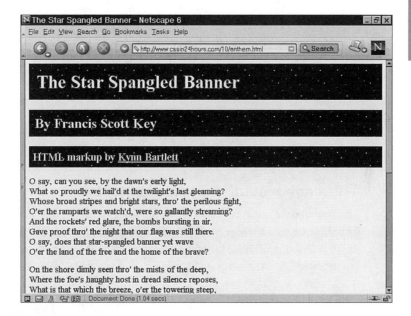

Inline elements as well as block elements can have backgrounds; here's a set of rules that just make the star field appear behind links:

```
body        { background-color: white;
              color:            black; }
a:link      { background-image: url("stars.gif");
              background-color: black;
              padding:          0.5em;
              color:            cyan; }
```

```
a:visited { background-image: url("stars.gif");
            background-color: black;
            padding:          0.5em;
            color:            violet; }
```

You can see these styles at work in Figure 10.4.

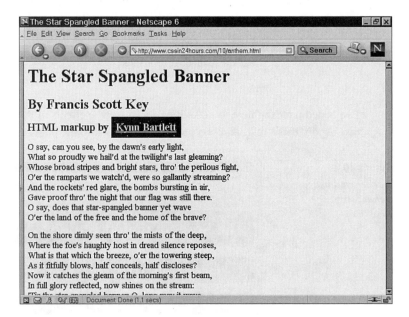

The `background-repeat` Property

The `background-repeat` property allows you to control whether or not the background
image tiles across the screen. Values for `background-repeat` are shown in Table 10.1;
the default value is `repeat`, and `background-repeat` values do not inherit from the containing block.

TABLE 10.1   Values for the `background-repeat` Property

Value	Effect
repeat	Tile horizontally and vertically
repeat-x	Only tile horizontally (along the X-axis)
repeat-y	Only tile vertically (along the Y-axis)
no-repeat	Display the image only once, with no tiling
inherit	Inherit the `background-repeat` value of the containing block

It's easier to demonstrate these in action rather than explain them in text, so let's look at how you use background-repeat. Listing 10.2 is a style sheet that sets a horizontally repeating background on the <body>, which puts a band of stars across the top of the page.

LISTING 10.2 A repeat-x Background Image

```
/* stars-10.2.css */
    body { background-color: gray;
           background-image: url("stars.gif");
           color: white;
           background-repeat: repeat-x;
         }
```

In this example, you'll notice I set the background color to gray; this makes it easier to see where the black image starts and stops. Figure 10.5 shows this style sheet applied to the HTML page in Listing 10.1.

FIGURE 10.5

Horizontal tiling of the background image.

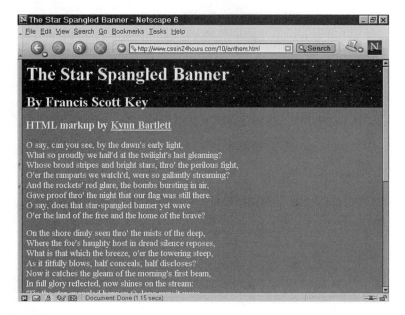

To tile the figure vertically, you use the background-repeat value of repeat-y, as in Listing 10.3.

LISTING 10.3   A repeat-y Background Image

```
/* stars-10.3.css */
    body { background-color: gray;
            background-image: url("stars.gif");
            color: white;
            background-repeat: repeat-y;


        }
```

This will create a stripe down the left side, as shown in Figure 10.6. In the next section of this hour, you'll learn how you can move the stripes created by repeat-x and repeat-y using the background-position property.

FIGURE **10.6**

Vertical tiling of the background image.

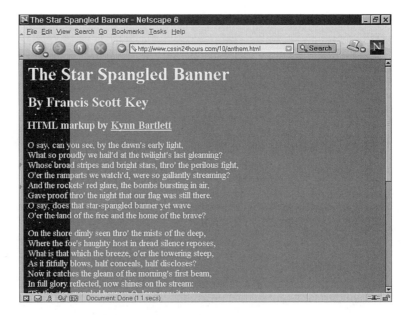

If you don't want the image to repeat at all, use the background-position value of no-repeat, as in Listing 10.4. You'd use this value whenever you want a single placement of an image, such as a watermark or a very large background that shouldn't be repeated.

LISTING 10.4   A Nonrepeating Background Image

```
/* stars-10.4.css */
    body { background-color: gray;
            background-image: url("stars.gif");
```

LISTING 10.4 Continued

```
      color: white;
      background-repeat: repeat-x;
}
```

 When an image doesn't repeat or repeats only in one direction, you have less worries about the sides of the image matching up properly. A no-repeat image won't wrap around, so there's no need to blend the top and bottom, or the left and right, into each other smoothly.

FIGURE 10.7
The background image without tiling.

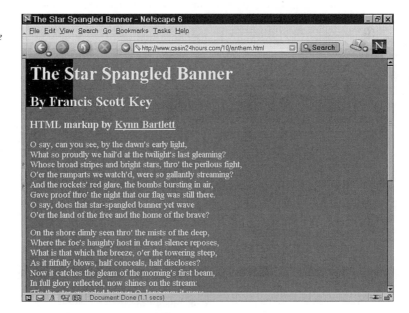

10

The `background-position` Property

As you can see in Figure 10.7, a background image is placed in the upper left corner of the element box it is styling. If tiling occurs, it reproduces itself to the left and right horizontally, or up and down vertically, from that starting position.

You can change the location of the initial image by using the `background-position` property. A `background-position` value consists of two size values or percentages: one indicating the horizontal position and the second indicating the vertical. If only one value is given, it sets the horizontal position.

A size value for background-position is a number and a unit, such as 30px or 4em; this tells where to place the initial image's upper left corner.

A percentage value indicates how far over the image should be aligned; 50% means that the center of the image (horizontally or vertically) aligns with the center of the element being styled. A pair of values, such as 75% 25%, means the spot on the image that's 75% over from the left horizontally and 25% down from the top should be matched with the corresponding location in the element's box.

In addition to sizes and percentages, word values can be used for background-position; these are shown in Table 10.2. Values can be combined together; right center means 100% 50%, for example. However, if only one word value is given, the second value is assumed to be center. Values can be listed in either order, so bottom left is the same as left bottom.

 You can use the background-position property to place repeating stripes across or down your page in conjunction with the background-repeat property. A single faint image can be used as a watermark with the background-repeat value of no-repeat and the background-position of center center.

The default value of this property is top left, which is the same as 0% 0%. Like background-repeat, this property's value is not inherited from the containing block.

TABLE 10.2 Values for the background-position Property

Value	Effect
size size	Place the image at the specified location
percent% percent%	Place the image proportionally
top	Corresponds to 50% 0%
left	Corresponds to 0% 50%
right	Corresponds to 100% 50%
bottom	Corresponds to 50% 100%
center	Corresponds to 50% 50%
top left	Corresponds to 0% 0%
top center	Same as top (50% 0%)
top right	Corresponds to 100% 0%
left center	Same as left (0% 50%)
center center	Same as center (50% 50%)
right center	Same as right (100% 50%)

TABLE 10.2   Continued

Value	Effect
bottom left	Corresponds to 0% 100%
bottom center	Same as bottom (50% 100%)
bottom right	Corresponds to 100% 100%

Listing 10.5 uses the `background-position` property to place an image that is set to tile horizontally.

LISTING 10.5   A Positioned, Repeating Background Image

```
/* stars-10.5.css */
    body { background-color: gray;
           background-image: url("stars.gif");
           color: white;
           background-repeat: repeat-x;
           background-position: 0% 33%; }
```

As seen in Figure 10.8, when this style sheet is applied to Listing 10.1's HTML page, the effect is a stripe across the page.

FIGURE 10.8

Placing an image with `background-position`.

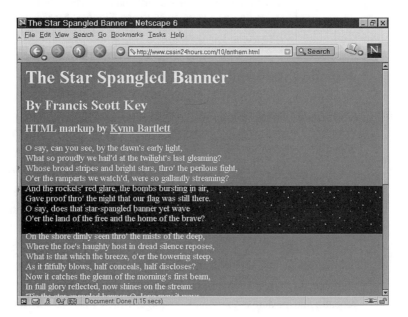

> ### Workaround for Netscape 4
>
> Unfortunately, Netscape 4 doesn't support the background-position property at all. Images can tile only horizontally across the top of the screen or vertically down the left side. An image that is not tiled will be located only in the upper left corner. There's no full workaround for this, but a usable fix is to take advantage of the fact that Netscape 4 doesn't recognize @import directives, as noted in Hour 7, "Cascading and Inheritance."
>
> Create two style sheets: one that works in Netscape 4 but doesn't use a background image (or maybe use a different one—say, a wider one of the type used as a background image) and another one (say, advanced.css) for other browsers with the background-image and background-position you want to use. Use @import to request the second CSS file; Netscape won't load it and will use the first set of values.
>
> One more thing, though: imported styles are considered older than all non-imported styles, so the Netscape-specific style rules take priority over the others. Therefore, you'll want to make the advanced.css rules more specific; set an id attribute on your <body> tag, and in advanced.css, use that id in id selectors, like this:
>
> ```
> body#mybody { background-image: url("stars.gif");
>               background-repeat: repeat-y;
>               background-position: 10% 10%; }
> ```
>
> It's not a pretty workaround! The other choice is to simply make sure your page doesn't fail when Netscape 4 ignores background-position.

The background-attachment Property

Normally, images scroll with the rest of the page; however, you can change that using the background-attachment property. This property can take three values: scroll, fixed, or inherit. The default value is scroll, and the property's value is not inherited from the containing block unless the value is explicitly set to inherit.

A background-attachment value of fixed means that the image doesn't move relative to the original position of the page, even if this means it might not be displayed because the element being styled is not on the screen or is not within the region where the background image could be seen (as determined from the background-repeat and background-attachment properties). If the value of background-attachment is fixed, the location of the image is placed relative to the whole page, not to the element being styled.

An example of using a fixed background image can be seen in Listing 10.6. This is a repeating stripe across the top of the page, which won't move when the page is scrolled.

LISTING 10.6 Style Sheet for a Fixed Background

```
/* stars-10.6.css */
    body { background-color: gray;
           background-image: url("stars.gif");
           color: white;
           background-repeat: repeat-x;
           background-position: top left;
           background-attachment: fixed; }
```

In Figure 10.9, I've scrolled down a little using the scrollbar, but the background image remains at the top of the page where I placed it. You can test this yourself by viewing the page at http://www.cssin24hours.com/10/anthem-10.6.html; you can also download the HTML page, style sheet, and image, for local viewing.

FIGURE 10.9

A fixed background doesn't scroll from its original position even when you scroll the page.

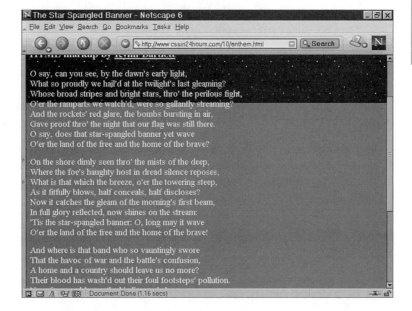

Workaround for Netscape 4

Like background-position, background-attachment is also not recognized by Netscape 4. You can either use a workaround like the one previously described for background-position, or you can choose to simply let the background image scroll with the page in Netscape 4.

Fixed backgrounds are supposed to be placed relative to the page even when set on boxes within the page; however, Internet Explorer positions them relative to the box of the element being styled. This is most clearly illustrated in Eric Meyer's css/edge spiral, which was used as an example in Hour 3, "Browser Support for CSS."

The background Shorthand Property

Like the font property, background is a shorthand property that allows you to set several properties at once. By using background, you can set the background-color, the background-image, the background-repeat, the background-position, and the background-attachment. Simply list the values you want (in any order) as the value for background; any values you don't set will be set to their default values.

The CSS rules used to create Figure 10.9 can be rewritten like this:

```
body { color: white;
       background: url("stars.gif") repeat-x
                   fixed top left gray; }
```

Summary

The background of any element can be set using the background-color and background-image properties. When using backgrounds, make sure there is contrast between the colors you're using (including image colors), and also ensure that you've set the foreground colors as well.

The tiling, position, and scrolling of the background image can be set using the background-repeat, background-position, and background-attachment properties. All of the background properties can be set at once using the background shorthand property.

Browser Support Report Card

CSS Feature	Grade	Notes
background-color	A	
background-image	A	
background-repeat	A	
background-position	B	Workaround needed for Netscape 4
background-attachment	B-	Workaround needed for Netscape 4, plus IE quirks
background	B-	Workaround needed for Netscape 4, plus IE quirks

Note that because the `background` shorthand property sets `background-position` and `background-attachment` properties, it has the same problems as those other properties.

Q&A

Q **What if I want a graphic to tile across the page horizontally and vertically, forming a "T" or "L" shape instead of filling the whole page? Can that be done?**

A No. Well, okay, yes. Here's how you do it: Add a `<div>` tag just inside the `<body>` of your page; have it contain all the content you'd normally put in `<body>` and give it an `id` attribute. Then use the `transparent` value for `background-color`, like this:

```
body { background: gray url("stars.gif") repeat-x;
            padding: 0px;
            margin: 0px; }
    div#mydiv { background: transparent url("stars.gif")
                            center repeat-y;
            color: white;
            padding: 0.5em; }
```

This will make a T-shaped star background. The `padding` and `margin` adjustments are necessary to remove the default padding and margin the browsers put on `<body>` and add it back in for the `<div>`.

Q **Why doesn't the order matter for the `background` shorthand property? That seems confusing. Shouldn't they be in some specific order?**

A Nope; because each of the properties set by the shorthand property have completely different types of values that can be assigned to them, it's pretty easy for a browser to figure out that, for example, the value `green` must go with `background-color` and the value `url("stars.gif")` with `background-image`.

Workshop

The workshop contains quiz questions and activities to help reinforce what you've learned in this hour. If you get stuck, the answers to the quiz can be found after the questions.

Quiz

1. Which of these values for `background-position` places the background image at the middle and bottom of the styled element's display box?

   (a.) `bottom center`

   (b.) `center bottom`

   (c.) `bottom`

   (d.) `50% 100%`

10

2. You have an image named `skyblue.jpg`; it's a graphic that looks like a blue sky with a few wispy clouds. The color is closest to `rgb(75%, 75%, 100%)`. You want it to tile down the right hand side of the page, and the background image shouldn't scroll when the page scrolls. The rest of the page will be white; all of your text will be black or other colors that contrast against the background. What CSS rule would you write, using the `background` shorthand property?

Answers

1. Trick question! They all do; they're all the same value.

2. Because you want the rest of the page to be white, the RGB values of the sky don't matter that much; your black text will contrast nicely with either white or light blue. Therefore, the rule can be written like this:

```
body { background: url("skyblue.jpg") white
                   right top repeat-y fixed; }
```

Activity

The best way to understand background colors and images is to get some hands-on practice. Create yourself a test page, an image or two, and a style sheet. Try the following:

1. Position the graphic in each corner of the page.

2. Tile the graphic along each edge of the page.

3. Create a faded-color watermark in the very middle of the page that doesn't scroll with the page.

4. Set backgrounds on inline and block elements besides just <body>. Make them scroll or tile!

Hour 11

Styling Links

The capability to make hyperlinks is what enables the interconnectedness of the Web; HTML itself is named for the hypertext links. Cascading Style Sheets can be used to style these links beyond the default blue-underlined text. You've already learned how to use :link and :visited pseudo-classes to create CSS rules for link presentation.

In this hour, you'll learn

- What pseudo-selectors let you designate effects for active links, mouseovers, and an element focus
- Which order pseudo-classes follow for link styling and inheritance
- How do to some of the most common link effects, including replacing the attributes on the <body> tag, removing underlines, and creating dynamic mouseovers

CSS for Link Styling

The style rules you write to affect hypertext links are much the same as other CSS rules; you identify the elements to be styled by using a selector, and you write property declarations describing how you want the elements to appear. So why spend a whole hour on links?

One reason is that rules for hypertext links require extensive use of pseudo-selectors, whereas most other rules don't. You can't just use the element name alone and get full functionality; you need to write your rules with a:link and a:visited selectors. In this hour, you'll learn about three more pseudo-classes, as well—:active, :hover, and :focus.

Link styles are very dependent upon the state of the user interface; what the user is doing and has done is at least as important as the content. That's not the case with most styles. You don't have to worry about your paragraph text changing state once the styles have been applied to it. Links require dynamic reapplication of the cascade and inheritance rules as the page is used.

One more reason that links are set off with their own hour is that it's one of the most common questions asked by people learning CSS. Underlines, mouseovers, and special effects on links are some of the coolest simple style effects you can add to a site, along with colors and fonts. Links are active styles, and the pseudo-classes used with them can add unexpected pleasant touches to a page, if done right.

The :link and :visited Pseudo-classes

Although you learned about a:link and a:visited selectors in Hour 5, "Selectors," we'll briefly revisit them here. The :link state and the :visited state are *mutually exclusive,* which means that either one or the other applies, but not both. Neither inherits property values from the other; if you set a style property on a:link, the same property won't be set on a:visited. You'd need to write two rules (or one rule with a combined selector).

A rule based on the <a> tag will be applied to <a> links, visited or unvisited. They'll also be used on anchors set with the <a name="anchor"> syntax. So if you want your links to all have a yellow background, you're better off with a rule based on a:link and a:visited instead of a by itself, or else your anchor points will be yellow, too.

Other styles set on the box holding the <a> tag will be inherited normally if those properties usually inherit. So the font-family and font-size properties, for example, will be inherited from whatever element contains the link tag.

One exception is the default styling on links. Unless explicitly set by a CSS rule to something else, your links will look like whatever the browser thinks they should look like. At least, that's true when it comes to two specific properties: color and text-decoration. The accepted practice is to make unvisited links blue, visited links purple, and both kinds of links underlined. Effectively, browsers have a built-in set of style rules that look like this (although user preferences can change the specifics):

```
a:link              { color: blue; }
a:visited           { color: purple; }
a:link, a:visited   { font-decoration: underline; }
```

To change these default styles, you'll need to explicitly override these style rules with more specific ones of your own. Remember that the cascade counts pseudo-classes as classes, and it gives priority to author styles over browser default styles; that means that your a:link rule will win out.

The :active Pseudo-class

An *active link* is a link that's in the process of being activated by the user in some way. How this activation occurs is dependent on the type of input and output media used. Usually this means that a mouse pointer has clicked on the link, and the page is about to be replaced by a new one reached by following the link. This corresponds to the HTML attribute alink, which can be set on the <body> tag (although alink can change only the color, whereas a CSS rule can do far more). Browsers usually display this as if the following rule were in its default style sheet:

```
a:active { color: red; }
```

The :active state is not mutually exclusive with :link or :visited. In fact, any link that is :active is undoubtedly going to be one or the other: visited or unvisited. Property values set on the :link or :visited state will be inherited by the :active element, as appropriate for each value. For example, if you've already declared that there should be no underlines in your a:link and a:visited rules, you don't need to worry about including it in the a:active rule if you want active links to continue to be underlined.

Cascading is also a consideration. If there's a property value conflict between an a:link and a:active rule, which one wins according to the cascade order? Well, they have the same origin (your style sheet), the same number of id attributes (none, presumably), the same number of classes or pseudo-classes, and the same number of elements, which means it's a tie. Therefore, the winner will be whichever one is declared last, according to the source code. In practice, this means that you'll want to put your a:active rule after your a:link and a:visited links.

You can combine together two or more pseudo-class selectors by simply chaining them together without spaces, like this:

```
a:link              { color: blue;
                      background-color: white; }
a:link:active       { color: white;
                      background-color: blue; }
```

```
a:visited              { color: purple;
                         background-color: white; }
a:visited:active       { color: white;
                         background-color: purple; }
```

These rules display unvisited and visited links in blue or purple as usual, but when the link is clicked, the colors will invert while the page is loading. Combined selectors let us make sure the colors are kept straight. If we didn't write a rule with two pseudo-classes, we'd have to choose either blue or purple as the color we'd use, like this:

```
a:active { color: white; background-color: purple; }
```

Warning for Netscape 4

Netscape 4 doesn't support the :active pseudo-class. Although this is unfortunate, it's probably not that bad, as the cost of failure is pretty small. Netscape 4 will simply turn your text red (or the browser's default active link color) when the link is clicked, but because this is displayed only for a very short time, it's probably not worth worrying about.

The :hover Pseudo-class

Hovering means that the mouse pointer has been positioned over a particular element, but the user has not necessarily clicked a button to activate it. In HTML, this state triggers a mouseover event, which can invoke JavaScript functions set on the onMouseOver attribute; when the mouse is no longer hovering, that's an onMouseOut event.

The CSS approach is to add the state of :hover to any other states currently on the element (such as :link or :visited) and apply an appropriate style. You can change the color, of course, but you can also change the background properties, border, font-family, font-size, or anything else you like. Some of these changes may cause the dimensions of displayed boxes to change, which can be distracting as the page has to redraw itself and shift about as someone moves the mouse, so you probably should avoid major changes such as padding or display.

Warning for Netscape 4

Netscape 4 doesn't support the :hover selector. CSS rules that depend on mouseovers can't count on Netscape 4 to display them. If your audience includes Netscape 4 users, you may want to use :hover effects only for eye-candy and not for essential site tasks. This is probably a good rule of thumb anyway, as some people (such as visually impaired users or Lynx users) may never see your fancy styles. Use CSS to enhance your page, but still allow access to those with older browsers.

Here's an example of the :hover rule in action. I want to make my links change color and background-color when the user moves the mouse. This will point out which link will be followed if the user clicks—a typical mouseover function. Listing 11.1 has an embedded style sheet in the HTML for this example.

LISTING 11.1   A Simple Question That Hovers Ominously

```
<!-- game-11.1.html -->
<html>
  <head>
    <title>Want to play a game?</title>
    <style type="text/css">
      body {
        background-color: black;
        color:           lime;
        font:            xx-large "Boost SSI",
                         monospace; }
      a:link, a:visited {
        color:           lime;
        text-decoration: none; }
      a:hover {
        background-color: white;
        color:            black; }
    </style>
  </head>
  <body>
    <h1>Want to play a game?</h1>
    <h1>
      <a href="yes.html">yes</a> /
      <a href="no.html">no</a>
    </h1>
  </body>
</html>
```

11

Figure 11.1 shows what this looks like in a browser; unlike most of the screenshots in this book, I've included the mouse pointer so you can see where it is. The no option is in black-on-white text when the mouse is over it, and when the mouse is elsewhere, it turns back to lime-on-black.

The CSS specifications are very vague on which HTML tags must be able to take on the :hover state. Can you set a rule with a selector like h1:hover and then change the styling on the <h1> tag whenever the mouse is moved over it? Good question. At the present time, you can't; only items that can be clicked on can enter the :hover state in current browsers.

FIGURE 11.1

How about a nice game of chess? Page shown in Netscape 6.

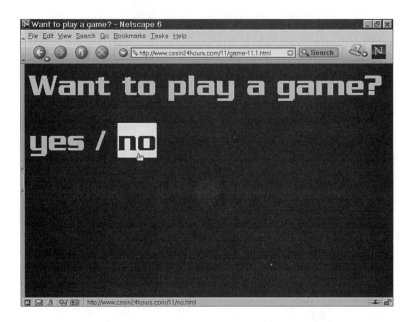

Workaround for Internet Explorer, Opera, Mozilla, Netscape

If you want to add mouseover effects to other items, you can use the HTML event attributes and JavaScript. For example, the following bit of HTML code creates an `<h1>` tag that changes color when the mouse moves over it:

```
<h1 onmouseover="style.color = 'blue';"
onmouseout="style.color = 'red';"
style="color: red; background-color: white;"
>Superman</h1>
```

You'll learn more in Hour 23, "CSS and JavaScript," about using JavaScript with CSS to create dynamic effects.

The :focus Pseudo-class

If you can type something into an HTML element, that element is said to have the *focus*. Focus is an indication of something that's been selected but not necessarily activated. The focus is often indicated by a light dashed line or by a colored glow around part of the page.

Being able to identify the current focus is important for keyboard access to the Web. Web surfers who aren't able to use a mouse will use the tab key to move from link to link or to `<form>` field tags, such as `<input>` and `<textarea>`. The HTML `tabindex` attribute can affect the order of tabbing.

When an element receives the focus, it enters the `:focus` state and applicable styles are applied. In our previous example from Listing 11.1, the background and foreground colors don't change if someone tabs through the links; they change only if the mouse is used. Because we want to provide access to all users—not just those with mice!—we'll add the following rules to our style sheet:

```
a:focus {
   background-color:  white;
   color:            black; }
```

Workaround for Internet Explorer (Windows), Opera

Netscape 6, Mozilla, and Internet Explorer 5 (Macintosh) support the `:focus` pseudo-class, but other browsers don't. You can use the same JavaScript techniques as described for the `:hover` workaround, but you should use the `onFocus` attribute when the element comes into focus and the `onBlur` attribute when it loses focus.

It's possible for an element to be in a state of `:active`, `:hover` and `:focus` all at the same time; none of them are mutually exclusive. An `<a>` link will be either `:link` or `:visited` as well. You should put your `:active`, `:hover`, and `:focus` rules after the `:link` and `:visited` rules because of the order of the cascade and inheritance.

Common Link-styling Techniques

The rest of this hour, I'll show you how to do some of the most common tasks related to styling links. Think of this section as a small cookbook with some key recipes. Armed with these and with your growing knowledge of CSS, you can improvise on your own sites, creating your own style sheet culinary masterpieces.

Replacing HTML `<body>` Attributes

The `<body>` tag in HTML lets you set a number of attributes that affect the appearance of the entire page. Now you can replace those with CSS rules and go further than the capabilities of HTML because you can fine-tune parts of the page separately by using selectors and by having better control over backgrounds and link styles.

Here's a typical <body> tag:

```
<body background="mybg.jpg" bgcolor="#FFFFCC"
      text="#000066" link="red" vlink="#999999"
      alink="#FFCC99">
```

As you can see, this uses presentational HTML attributes—the background, bgcolor, text, link, vlink, and alink attributes—to control the colors and background image on the page. This works in current browsers, but from a CSS point of view, it's a poor idea because the presentation is mixed in with the markup, and that always makes things harder, not easier. For example, if you want to change the appearance of the entire site at once, you'll need to go into every single HTML file and edit the attributes, but if you are using a linked style sheet, it's just a minor tweak to a single style sheet file.

So, how do you write the <body> tag with Cascading Style Sheets rules? Something like this:

```
body { background: #FFFFCC url("mybg.jpg");
       color: #000066; }
a:link { color: red; }
a:visited { color: #999999; }
a:active { color: #FFCC99; }
```

> All browsers, except the very oldest, will understand the CSS rules listed above, but if you need to support those older browsers, you can combine your CSS rules with the HTML attributes. CSS browsers will display the styles from your style sheet, whereas ancient browsers will show the colors as defined in the <body> tag. Netscape 3 is an example of an old browser that won't understand CSS.

Removing Underlines

This seems to be one of the first questions Web developers want to know: How do I turn off the underlines? If you've been reading this book straight through from beginning to end, you learned about the text-decoration property in Hour 9, "Text Colors and Effects." However, you may have just jumped directly to the hours that looked most likely to give you the answers you needed; that's a valid way to use this book, too.

You remove underlines by using the text-decoration property with a value of none. Here's an example:

```
.navbar a:link,
.navbar a:visited
  { text-decoration: none; }
```

Several important cautions were mentioned in Hour 9 about the effects on usability if you remove link underlines; you may want to go back and read that section if it's not fresh in your mind.

Removing underlines from links can be relatively easy. The bigger question is how will you replace them? The reason that links were underlined in the first place was to make them stand out so the Web user doesn't have to randomly guess what can be clicked and what can't. Here are some ideas, which can be used separately or in combination:

- Use very bright colors, set using the `color` property, to make links that much more visible. Links should stand out from the rest of the page and should be easily seen.
- Put borders around the links by using the `border` property so that the links are in boxes. Boxes can draw attention, as color does.
- Employ the `font-weight` property to make your links stand out better. Bold links likewise catch the eye; I have used `font-weight: bold` for unvisited links and `font-weight: normal` for visited links when designing styles for certain sites.
- Make all links italic (or oblique) by using `font-style`, or put them in small caps with `text-transform`. Be careful about readability, though; excessive use of this technique can make your navigation hard to use.
- Add a background color to your links with the `background-color` property. This can often give an effect similar to a highlighter pen; make sure your background stands out against both the visited and unvisited link colors.
- Utilize `class` or `id` selectors to give different styles to different kinds of links; for example, style offsite links differently from local links. Likewise, use different styles for inline links in the body of your text and for navigation links located in a sidebar.

Mouseover Effects

A mouseover effect can be as simple as swapping the colors, as we've seen earlier in this hour, or as subtle as adding back in the underline on a mouseover, as follows:

```
a:link, a:visited { text-decoration: none; }
a:hover { text-decoration: underline; }
```

11

You can also head for the other extreme and get pretty complex. Here's an example of making buttons with CSS and making those buttons change when the mouse rolls over them, all without using JavaScript. Listing 11.2 is the HTML file we'll style, and Listing 11.3 is the style sheet.

LISTING 11.2   An HTML Page with a Navigation Bar

```
<!-- buttons-11.2.html -->
<html>
  <head>
    <title>About the Temecula Writers Group</title>
    <link type="text/css" rel="stylesheet"
          href="buttons-11.3.css">
  </head>
  <body>
    <table width="100%" border="0">
      <tr><td valign="top" align="center" width="150">
          <div class="navbar">
            <a href="/">Home</a>
            <a href="about.html">About Us</a>
            <a href="writers.html">Writers</a>
            <a href="links.html">Links</a>
            <a href="map.html">Map</a>
            <a href="calendar.html">Calendar</a>
            <a href="contact.html">Contact</a>
          </div>
        </td><td valign="top">
          <h1>About Us</h1>
          <p>The Temecula Writers Group is an informal group of
             writers who meet <a href="calendar.html">every other
             Wednesday evening</a> from 7:30 to 9:00, at the
             bookstore in Temecula.</p>
          <p>We don't have rules, dues, officers, or much of anything
             else, except a mutual desire to improve as writers.
             Authors of fiction, nonfiction, travel, technical books,
             poetry, or any other type of writing are welcome! You
             don't have to be a published author to come; many of us
             are amateurs or beginners, and we're very welcoming and
             supportive.</p>
          <p>If you'd like to attend, just stop by for the next
             meeting, or <a href="contact.html">drop a note via
             e-mail</a> to one of our members.</p>
        </td></tr></table>
  </body>
</html>
```

LISTING 11.3   Style Sheet with Mouseover Effects

```
body { font-family: Verdana, sans-serif;
       color: black; background-color: white; }
    h1 { color: navy; }
    .navbar a:link, .navbar a:visited
        { font: bold 12pt Verdana, sans-serif;
          padding: 0.5em; margin: 0.5em;
          display: block; text-decoration: none;
          background: url("button.gif") transparent
                      50% 50% no-repeat; }
    .navbar a:link    { color: yellow; }
    .navbar a:visited { color: lime; }
    .navbar a:hover, .navbar a:focus
        { background-image: url("button_yellow.gif");
          color: black; }
    .navbar a:visited:hover, .navbar a:visited:focus
        { background-image: url("button_green.gif");
          color: black; }
```

The three button images used are shown in Figure 11.2, and the final effect can be seen in Figure 11.3. When the mouse is moved over the navigation bar, the glow graphic is used. You'll notice that I used an a:hover:visited rule, as well, so that visited links glow lime green instead of yellow.

FIGURE 11.2

Background graphics for buttons.

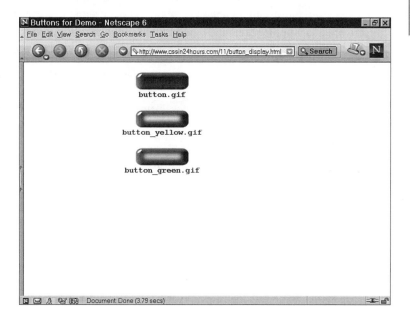

FIGURE 11.3

Mouseovers in action, displayed by Netscape 6.

Summary

CSS rules for styling hypertext links use the same properties as other style rules but extensively utilize pseudo-class selectors. These pseudo-class selectors track the state of various qualities—:link and :visited depend on Web browsing history; :active, :hover, and :focus depend on the user's interaction with the page.

Link styles can be used to replace the <body> attributes in HTML, remove links, and even create complex mouseover effects without requiring JavaScript. Armed with your growing knowledge of CSS, you can now confidently apply styles to your hypertext links.

Browser Support Report Card

CSS Feature	Grade	Notes
The :link and :visited pseudo-classes	A	
The :active pseudo-class	A-	Not supported by Netscape 4
The :hover pseudo-class, on <a>	B+	Not supported by Netscape 4
:hover on other elements	C	Workaround required for most browsers
The :focus pseudo-class	C+	Workaround required for Internet Explorer, Opera

Q&A

Q Now that I know CSS, I can throw away all those `<body>` attributes, such as `vlink` and `bgcolor`, right?

A Well, maybe. If you are using the Strict versions of HTML or XHTML, you'll have to remove them for your markup to be valid. On the other hand, there are a few old browsers still out there that understand only the `<body>` attributes, and it might not hurt to include presentation markup.

Q What about those annoying blue borders around images? How do I get rid of those?

A How about this?

```
a:link img, a:visited img { border: 0px; }
```

Workshop

The workshop contains quiz questions and activities to help reinforce what you've learned in this hour. If you get stuck, the answers to the quiz can be found after the questions.

Quiz

1. Which of these rules makes the text bold when the user tabs to a link using the keyboard?

   (a.) `a:visited { font-weight: 700; }`

   (b.) `a:hover { font-weight: 700; }`

   (c.) `a:active { font-weight: 700; }`

   (d.) `a:focus { font-weight: 700; }`

   (e.) `a:active:hover { font-weight: 700; }`

2. How would you rewrite this `<body>` tag as CSS rules?

   ```
   <body text="white" background="stars.gif"
         bgcolor="black" link="#00FFFF"
         vlink="#FF00FF" alink="#FFFF00">
   ```

Answers

1. (d.) The `a:focus` selector activates whenever a link has the keyboard focus.

2. Here's one way to rewrite the `<body>` attributes in CSS:

   ```
   body { color: white;
          background: url("stars.gif") black; }
   a:link { color: #00FFFF; }
   a:visited { color: #FF00FF; }
   a:active { color: #FFFF00; }
   ```

11

Activity

What makes for good link styles and for bad? Experimenting is the best way to figure out what works for the needs of each Web site. Here are some ideas you can try:

- Eliminate underlines from your inline links, but replace them with another style that makes them stand out. Which works best—background colors, font weight, italics, or something else?

- Build a navigation menu that uses backgrounds, borders, and fonts instead of images. Is it easier to maintain CSS-styled text links than graphical navigation bars?

HOUR 12

Alignment and Spacing

Control over text formatting enables you to replace many HTML tags with CSS rules. Effects that were previously available only as presentational markup attributes are now part of the Cascading Style Sheets specification and can help you separate presentation from content.

In this hour, you'll learn

- How to align, justify, and center content using CSS
- How to indent paragraphs and other HTML elements
- How to make text that rises above or below the rest of the text, such as subscripts or superscripts
- How to control the spaces between letters and words
- How to control line breaks and duplicate the HTML <pre> and <nobr> tags
- How to adjust the spacing between lines

Aligning and Indenting Text

The *alignment* of text defines the way in which the text lines up with the left or right margins. Most things you read (including this book) are left aligned;

left-aligned text is generally easier to read. Centered text is often used on headlines, but it is rarely used on blocks of text because both margins are irregular and jagged; experienced designers usually reserve right-aligned text for special text effects.

An *indent* is the extra space at the start of a line that lets you know you're on a new paragraph. In Web design, new paragraphs are more commonly indicated by extra spacing than by indented text, although you are free to combine both if it suits your needs.

CSS properties allow you to control both the alignment and the indentation, setting them to whatever values you like on HTML block elements.

The `text-align` Property

Alignment of text inside a block property is controlled by the `text-align` property. This property has meaning only on block boxes; the content of inline boxes has no alignment, although the inline boxes themselves will be aligned within the surrounding box. The block box itself is not actually positioned; only the content inside the box is aligned. To position the box, use either the margin properties you'll learn in Hour 13, "Borders and Boxes," or the positioning properties you'll learn in Hour 16, "Page Layout in CSS."

Table 12.1 shows the values that can be given to the `text-align` property; the default value is `left`. The `text-align` property is inherited, so you can use a single `<div>` or even a rule on the `<body>` to center an entire page. There's one exception; for backward-compatibility, browsers usually have a default rule that sets `text-align: left` for `<td>` tags and `text-align: center` for `<th>` tags. Keep this in mind when using tables, especially if you use them for layout.

TABLE 12.1   Values for the `text-align` Property

Value	Effect
center	Centers the content
justify	Justifies text on both sides
left	Aligns content on the left
right	Aligns content on the right
inherit	Uses the value of `text-align` from the containing box

There's an additional kind of value you can use with the `text-align` property, which aligns columns of data in tables. You'll learn more about column alignment values for `text-align` in Hour 15, "Styling Tables."

Text that is *justified* is printed so that both the left and right sides line up; browsers accomplish this by adding extra spaces between words and letters.

A simple style sheet that uses `text-align` is shown in Listing 12.1.

LISTING 12.1   CSS for Alignment

```
/* twain-12.1.css */

body { font-family: Arial, sans-serif;
       font-size: smaller; }
h1 { font-family: Verdana, sans-serif;
     text-align: right; }

#a { text-align: justify; }
#b { text-align: right; }
#c { text-align: center; }
#d { text-align: left; }
```

I've created an HTML file with sample paragraph text in it; you can download it from `http://www.CSSin24hours.com/12/twain.html`. This HTML file is used in this hour's examples; applying the style sheet above results in the effects shown in Figure 12.1.

FIGURE 12.1

Lining up text using CSS.

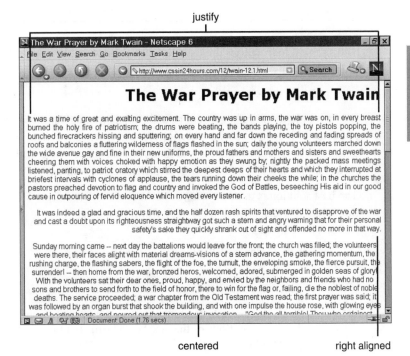

justify

centered

right aligned

12

The `text-indent` Property

Although it's most commonly used on <p> tags, the `text-indent` property can be set on any block element in HTML. (It has no effect if applied to an inline tag.) The effect produced by this property is to indent the first line of the element by adding blank space. This blank space is treated similarly to the `padding` of the displayed box: it is inside the `margin` and `border` of the box, and it is colored with the same `background-color` as the element content.

The values for `text-indent` are shown on Table 12.2; in short, you can give either a measurement value, such as `3em` and `10px`, or a percentage value based on the size of the containing box. The default indentation is `0px`. The value of `text-indent` is inherited by all children elements, but keep in mind that it has no effect on inline elements, only block elements that inherit the value.

TABLE 12.2   Values for the `text-indent` Property

Value	Effect
measurement	Sets an indent
negative measurement	Sets a hanging indent
percentage	Sets an indent based on a fraction of the containing box
inherit	Uses the value of `text-indent` from the containing box

The simplest indentations are the most straightforward; here's a rule to indent all paragraphs by 3 ems:

```
p { text-indent: 3em; }
```

It gets a little trickier if you want to make a hanging indent—one where the first line is not actually indented but the other lines of the text *are* indented. To do this, you can give a negative measurement, but it will then flow off the left side of the element's box, which means it may not be visible or may overwrite other content.

The best solution is to add a `margin` to the box, which indents all of the text except for that initial line that subtracts its value from the `margin`. Here's an example, which creates a `2.8em` hanging indent:

```
p { text-indent: -2.8em;
    margin-left: 3em; }
```

In this example, I used the `margin-left` property, which sets the `margin` just for the left side of the box. You'll learn about this and other properties that affect only one side of the box in Hour 13.

Warning for Opera 5 and 6

For some reason, Opera doesn't display negative indents the same way that other browsers do. To get a proper indent, you need to add on an extra negative length to the `text-indent` that is equal to the `margin-left` value, such as this:

```
p { text-indent: -5.8em;
    margin-left: 3em; }
```

This will create a `2.8em` hanging indent in Opera 5 and 6. Unfortunately, in other browsers it will likely create an unreadable indent that goes off the left edge of the box. Because of these browser irregularities, you may want to avoid using hanging indents.

The style sheet in Listing 12.2 uses several different ways to set indents. Applied to an HTML page (with successive id attributes set on each paragraph), the style sheet produces the effects shown in Figure 12.2.

Listing 12.2 Style Sheet with Several Different `text-indent` Values

```
/* twain-12.2.css */

body { font-family: Arial, sans-serif;
       font-size: smaller; }
h1 { font-family: Verdana, sans-serif; }

#a { text-indent: -3em;
     margin-left: 3em; }
#b { text-indent: 5em; }
#c { text-indent: 15%; }
#d { text-indent: 25px; }
```

12

The `vertical-align` Property

The `vertical-align` property is used to adjust vertical alignment within an inline box. This can be used to make text appear higher or lower compared with the rest of the text on the line; it's most useful for creating superscripts or subscripts. *Superscripts* are bits of text with the baseline above the surrounding text; *subscripts* have baselines lower than the surrounding text.

Except for table cells, only inline elements use the `vertical-align` property. The use of `vertical-align` with table cells is covered in Hour 15.

FIGURE **12.2**

*Internet Explorer 6
(Windows) indents
our page.*

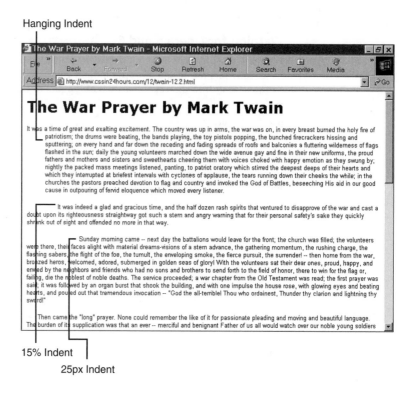

Hanging Indent

15% Indent

25px Indent

The types of values that can be set for the `vertical-align` property are shown in Table 12.3. The default value is `baseline`, and any values set on containing boxes are not inherited.

TABLE 12.3 Values for the `vertical-align` Property

Value	Effect
baseline	Aligns with the surrounding text
bottom	Aligns the bottom with bottom of line
middle	Aligns with the middle of the surrounding text (see comment)
sub	Lowers to subscript level
super	Raises to superscript level
text-top	Aligns with the top of surrounding text
text-bottom	Aligns with the bottom of surrounding text
top	Aligns the top with top of line
measurement	Raises above surrounding text

TABLE 12.3 Continued

Value	Effect
negative measurement	Lowers below surrounding text
percentage	Raises as a percentage of the line-height
negative percentage	Lowers as a percentage of the line-height

Several of these values require further explanation. The middle value aligns the middle of the text with a height that's 0.5ex above the baseline of the surrounding text. An ex is a unit of measure equal to the height of a lowercase letter, usually about half the font-size. Percentages are based on the value of the line-height, which is usually equal to the font-size. The top and bottom values align with the highest and lowest parts of the line, whereas text-top and text-bottom are based only on the containing box's font-size values.

Browser implementation of vertical-align is highly variable and is dependent upon factors such as font-size, ex calculation, and others. The safest values for consistency's sake are sub, super, measurements, and percentages; fortunately, the others are not particularly useful most of the time, anyway.

To create superscripts or subscripts, you use the vertical-align property, probably in combination with font-size; the vertical-align property doesn't affect the size of text, but most subscripts or superscripts are smaller than the surrounding text. Here are some example rules:

```
.atoms { vertical-align: -0.4em;
         font-size: smaller; }
.power { vertical-align: super;
         font-size: smaller; }
```

You'd use these style rules in HTML by setting class attributes, like this:

```
H<span class="atoms">2</span>0
x<span class="power">2</span> - 1 = 63
```

The effects of these styles can be seen in Figure 12.3. You could also use the HTML Transitional elements <sub> and <sup> for the same effects, but CSS affords you more control over the specific presentation details.

12

FIGURE 12.3

*Superscripts and
subscripts in Opera 6.*

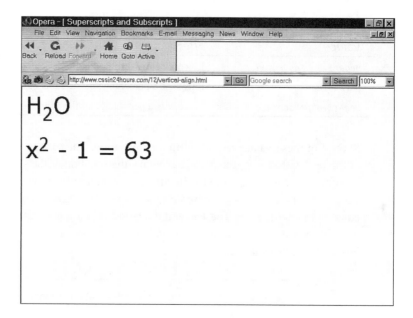

Controlling Text Spacing

The display characteristics of the text can be controlled by a number of properties that
affect the spaces between characters and words. These properties are less useful than
many others, such as the font properties, but if you ever need to fine-tune your text display, these are the properties you will use.

The `letter-spacing` Property

All browsers use default spacing between letters; if there wasn't such a space, the letters
would touch up against each other and would be nearly impossible to read. The `letter-
spacing` property lets you adjust this space by increasing or decreasing the value of the
default spacing. Values for `letter-spacing` are listed in Table 12.4; the default value is
`normal`. If the letter-spacing property is set on the containing box, the value will be
inherited.

In typography, the space between letters is known as the *kerning*. Professionally
typeset text often contains very subtle but important kerning effects. For example, the letters in most logos are not evenly spaced; varying the kerning can
make text look a lot better. Usually this doesn't matter too much on the Web,
but sometimes it is vitally important, especially to professional typesetters.

TABLE 12.4   Values for the `letter-spacing` Property

Value	Effect
normal	Doesn't insert extra spacing between letters
measurement	Inserts extra letter spacing
negative measurement	Reduces spacing between letters
inherit	Uses the value of `letter-spacing` from the containing box

The `text-align` property can also affect the `letter-spacing`; if `text-align` is set to `justify`, the browser will automatically adjust the space between letters so that the text can be justified. If the `letter-spacing` property is set to a measurement, such as `0.1em` or `2px`, the browser isn't allowed to change that space, even if it is justifying text.

The `word-spacing` Property

The `word-spacing` property is similar to the `letter-spacing` property, except, of course, that it controls the space between words. Browsers convert any whitespace (spaces, tabs, line breaks) to a single space and then display that space as a gap between words. The size of the space depends on the browser and the font; the `word-spacing` property adjusts from that initial size.

Values for `word-spacing` are shown in Table 12.5. If there is a value on a containing box, that will be inherited; otherwise, the default value is `normal`. Like `letter-spacing`, if a `word-spacing` value is set, the browser is not allowed to change the spacing even when the `text-align` value is `justify`.

12

TABLE 12.5   Values for the `word-spacing` Property

Value	Effect
normal	Doesn't insert extra spacing between words
measurement	Inserts extra word spacing
negative measurement	Reduces spacing between words
inherit	Uses the value of `word-spacing` from the containing box

Keep in mind that both `letter-spacing` and `word-spacing` add or subtract from the default browser spacing; they don't set it to that value. So if a browser normally has a space of 0.5 em between words, a `word-spacing` value of `0.3em` will make the total gap 0.8 em, not 0.3 em. Examples of letter-spacing and word-spacing rules are shown in Listing 12.3.

LISTING 12.3   Styles Affecting Letter and Word Spacing

```
/* twain-12.3.css */

body { font-family: Arial, sans-serif;
       font-size: smaller; }
h1 { font-family: Verdana, sans-serif;
     letter-spacing: 0.2em;
     word-spacing: 0.5em; }

#a { word-spacing: 1em; }
#b { letter-spacing: 5px; }
#c { letter-spacing: -0.1em; }
#d { word-spacing: -0.5em; }
```

Applying the style sheet in Listing 12.3 to the sample paragraph text gives us the styles shown in Figure 12.4.

FIGURE 12.4

Letter and word spacing in Netscape 6.

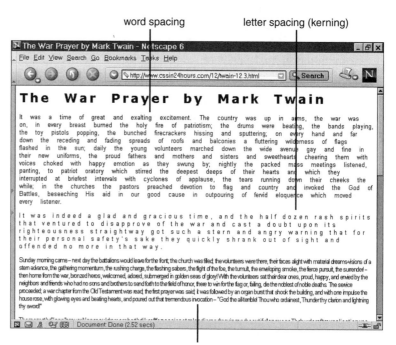

letter spacing (leading)

Warning for Netscape 4

The Netscape 4 browser does not support the letter-spacing or word-spacing properties. Because these properties are used for fine-tuning, the cost of

failure is relatively low, even when Netscape 4 does not display adjusted
letter or word spacing.

The `white-space` Property

As I noted before, Web browsers will condense all whitespace in the source and consider
it as if there's only one space when displaying the page. This is *whitespace condensation*.
If the content exceeds the width of the box allocated to that content, the browser simply
moves down to the next line and continues with the rest of the text. This is called *word
wrapping* because the new lines occur immediately before a new word.

The `white-space` property allows you to control both the condensation of whitespace
and the word wrapping by setting the values shown in Table 12.6. The value of this property is inherited if it is set on a containing box; otherwise the default is `normal`.

TABLE 12.6   Values for the `white-space` Property

Value	Effect
normal	Does normal word wrapping and whitespace condensing
nowrap	Condenses whitespace, but don't wrap lines
pre	Wraps lines as in the source markup
inherit	Uses the value of `white-space` from the containing box

A value of `nowrap` means that any text won't have automatic lines inserted, and that can lead
to horizontal scrolling if you're not careful. The `nowrap` value is similar to the old `<nobr>`
element, which was a nonstandard HTML tag introduced by Netscape to prevent lines from
breaking in the wrong place. The `<nobr>` tag was never adopted as an official part of the
HTML standard; if you need that same effect, use a `white-space: nowrap` rule instead.

Workaround for Netscape 4

Netscape 4 doesn't use the `nowrap` value; if you need to get the same functionality from Netscape 4, you can use the `<nobr>` tag, which will be ignored
by other browsers. However, keep in mind this will disqualify your HTML
from passing validation; you can't use browser-specific tags and still write to
the HTML specifications.

The value `pre` produces an effect quite similar to the `<pre>` tag in HTML, except that
`<pre>` also sets the font to a monospace font. The `white-space: pre` declaration doesn't
change the `font-family` unless you explicitly write a rule to that effect.

12

The HTML file in Listing 12.4 includes an embedded style sheet with `white-space` declarations.

LISTING 12.4   A Poem Dependent upon `white-space` for Proper Display

```
<!-- whitespace-12.4.css -->
<html>
  <head>
    <title>Whitespace Demo</title>
    <style type="text/css">
      body { font-size: large;
             font-family: Arial, sans-serif; }
      .nobr { white-space: nowrap; }
      .poem { white-space: pre; }
    </style>
  </head>
  <body>
    <h1>Trees -- a poem by Joyce Kilmer</h1>

    <p class="nobr">
      Citation:
      <cite>
        Untermeyer, Louis. Modern American Poetry. New York:
        Harcourt, Brace and Howe, 1919; Bartleby.com, 1999.
        www.bartleby.com/104/.
      </cite>
    </p>

    <div class="poem">
I think that I shall never see
A poem lovely as a tree.

A tree whose hungry mouth is prest
Against the sweet earth's flowing breast;

A tree that looks at God all day,
And lifts her leafy arms to pray;

A tree that may in summer wear
A nest of robins in her hair;

Upon whose bosom snow has lain;
Who intimately lives with rain.

Poems are made by fools like me,
But only God can make a tree.
    </div>
  </body>
</html>
```

In Figure 12.5, the browser displays the whitespace example. Notice that the `nowrap` value has caused the citation to scroll off the screen to the right, creating a horizontal scrollbar.

Figure 12.5

The effects of the `white-space` *property.*

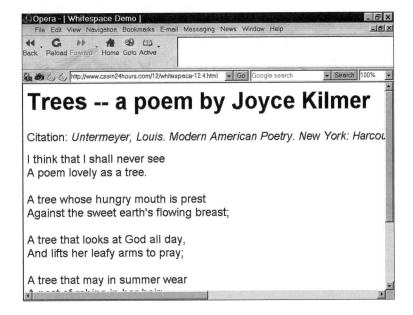

The `line-height` Property

The *line height* of a line of text is initially determined by the `font-size` property's value. A font that is `12pt` tall will have a line height of `12pt` in most cases, although browsers can choose to insert a little extra space to make the text easier to read.

The `line-height` property allows you to adjust the height of the line by using a value listed in Table 12.7. The value `normal` means that the line-height should be calculated using the browser's usual methods for doing so; this is the default value.

TABLE 12.7 Values for the `line-height` Property

Value	Effect
`normal`	Uses the default line height
`measurement`	Sets the line height to a particular value
`multiplier`	Sets the line height based on the `font-size`
`percentage`	Sets the line height based on the `font-size`
`inherit`	Uses the value of `line-height` from the containing box

12

A *multiplier* is a normal number without any units, such as 1.5 or 3, that is multiplied by the font-size value. A multiplier of 1.5 means the same thing as a percentage of 150% and is also the same as 1.5em.

The value of line-height is inherited from a containing box if the property is set; in most cases, the calculated value is inherited. For example, if the font-size is 18pt and the value of line-height is 200%, the calculated value 36pt will be inherited by children boxes. However, if a multiplier value such as 2 is set, that multiplier is passed on directly, and not the calculated value.

A style sheet that changes the line spacing of our sample text is shown in Listing 12.5; in Figure 12.6, this is displayed by a browser. Setting the line-height to a value based on the font-size, such as 2 or 200%, has the effect of equally spacing out the lines, assuming the font-size doesn't change; 200% is double-spacing. To equally space mixed font sizes, use an absolute measurement, such as 32px.

LISTING 12.5 Making Space with line-height

```
/* twain-12.5.css */

body { font-family: Arial, sans-serif;
       font-size: smaller; }
h1 { font-family: Verdana, sans-serif; }

#a { line-height: 80%; }
#b { line-height: 2.5; }
#c { line-height: 2em; }
#d { line-height: 32px; }
```

You can also set the line-height value as part of the font property, which you learned about in Hour 8, "Fonts and Font Families." When setting the font using the font short-hand property, include a slash after the font-size and indicate the desired line-height value. For example, to set a paragraph font that's 12 point Verdana with a line height of 200%, you'd write the following rule:

```
p { font: 12pt/200% Verdana, sans-serif; }
```

FIGURE 12.6

Line spacing in Internet Explorer 6.

80% Line Height

2.5 Line Height

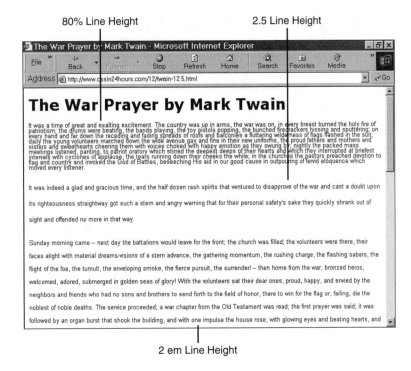

2 em Line Height

Summary

Several CSS properties allow you to adjust the appearance of text when displayed by the browsers, altering the alignment, indentation, and spacing.

The text-align property specifies whether the text should be lined up on the left side, the right side, both sides, or in the center. The text-indent property lets you set a paragraph indent or other indent, although hanging indents are somewhat unreliable across browsers. The vertical-align property lets you specify how text is aligned within an inline box and can create subscripts or superscripts.

Using the letter-spacing and word-spacing properties, you can fine-tune the display of your text, increasing or decreasing the gaps between letters and words. The white-space property controls both the condensation of whitespace and word wrapping. The line-height property can be used to double-space text or otherwise control the distance between each line.

12

Browser Support Report Card

CSS Feature	Grade	Notes
text-align	A	
text-indent, positive values	A	
text-indent, negative values	C+	Unreadable text in Opera
vertical-align, sub and super	A	
vertical-align, other values	B	Inconsistent browser support
letter-spacing	B	Not supported by Netscape 4
word-spacing	B	Not supported by Netscape 4
white-space, pre	A	
white-space, nowrap	B+	Workaround needed for Netscape 4
line-height	A	

Q&A

Q How can I set an exact value for `letter-spacing` or `word-spacing`?

A You can't; you can adjust it only from what the browser uses as a default. Fortunately, most browsers use sensible defaults, but there's no way to set an absolute value for letter or word spacing.

Q The `text-align` property works only on inline content. So how do I align a block element?

A You can align a block element in two ways: with margin properties and `float`. To place a block element on the left side of its containing block, use the `margin-right` property with a value of `auto`, and to align it on the right, use a `margin-left` value of `auto`. To center it, set both `margin-left` and `margin-right` to `auto`. You'll learn more about the right and left margins in the next hour.

Alternatively, set the `float` property to either `left` or `right`; subsequent content will flow around the floating block. Hour 16 covers the use of `float`.

Workshop

The workshop contains quiz questions and activities to help reinforce what you've learned in this hour. If you get stuck, the answers to the quiz can be found after the questions.

Quiz

1. Which of these rules sets a paragraph indent equal to 300% of the `font-size`?

    (a.) `p { text-indent: 300%; }`

    (b.) `p { text-indent: 30px; }`

    (c.) `p { text-indent: 3em; }`

2. The default word spacing in a hypothetical browser is 0.5 ems, and you'd like to put a full em between each word. Which of these declarations accomplishes that?

    (a.) `word-spacing: 0.5em;`

    (b.) `word-spacing: 1em;`

    (c.) `word-spacing: 200%;`

3. You want to evenly space out each line of <p> text so they are double-spaced, 16-point Arial font. How do you write this using a `line-height` rule, and how do you write it without using `line-height`?

Answers

1. Rule (c.) is the correct answer. `1em` equals the `font-size` measurement; if the `font-size` is `12pt`, `3em` will be 36 points. Percentages in `text-indent`, such as rule (a.), are based on the containing block's size; so `text-indent: 300%` means to have a first line indent that is 3 times larger than the box holding the paragraph! A more reasonable value would be between `0%` and `50%`.

2. Declaration (a.) will produce a total word spacing of 1 em if the browser's default is 0.5 em, but remember that you can't set the exact value. If the browser's default is 0.75 em, a will result in a gap of 1.25 em, and (b.) will produce a 1.75 em gap. Percentages, such as (c.), aren't valid values for `word-spacing`.

3. Here's one way to write the `line-height` rule:

        p { line-height: 200%; }

    You could also write the same rule with a `line-height` value of 2, 2em, or even `32pt`. Without using `line-height`, you'd use the `font` property:

        p { font: 16pt/32pt Arial, sans-serif; }

12

Activity

Your own experiments with the properties in this hour will help you master how to use them to style your text. Try the following to expand your understanding:

- Align some paragraph text to the right, justify it, and center it. Which is easiest to read? Now try it with headlines; is there a difference between paragraph text and headlines?

- Use a variety of indents, and decide which one you like better. Does 5em look good? 10%? 40px?

- Using vertical-align: super, create some links that are anchors to footnotes at the bottom of the page. What makes a good-looking footnote reference? Experiment with smaller font size and adding or removing underlines.

- Try adjusting the kerning between letters in your headlines. Create <span> tags that enclose only adjacent letters, and try moving them closer or farther from each other.

Hour 13

Borders and Boxes

Within the CSS visual formatting model, all HTML elements are displayed as either inline boxes or block boxes. Property values in CSS rules affect the way these boxes are displayed by applying the styles to the content of each box.

You learned about the box model in Hour 6, "The CSS Box Model," and how you can use the margin, padding, and border properties to affect how a box is displayed. Those core properties allow you to manipulate the edges of the box itself, from the space around the content, to the border around the box, and finally to the space surrounding the content of the box.

In this hour, you'll expand on that knowledge and learn

- What the four sides of each box are called, and how to refer to them in CSS rules
- How to use the margin shorthand property to specify margins for specific sides of a box
- Which margin values to set to center boxes horizontally
- How to set the padding on each side of a box
- Which width, color, and line styles can be used on box borders

- How to set borders for specific sides of the box
- Which properties and values allow you to hide the display of a box and its contents
- How to add a message that can be seen only by non-CSS browsers

Adjusting Boxes

As you've seen before, CSS browsers view all Web pages as a series of nested boxes. Block boxes contain inline boxes or other block boxes; inline boxes contain content, usually text. Styles are applied on a box-by-box basis, using selectors that identify boxes or groups of boxes.

Each of these boxes consists of the inside of the box, which is where you can find the content or any child boxes and the edge—the margin, border, and padding. As you learned in Hour 6, these can be adjusted by using properties known as the *edge properties*. You use the margin property to set the blank space just within the limits of the box; the border property to set a line surrounding the content, within the margin; and the padding property to add spacing between the content and the other edge properties.

Changing these properties lets you affect the appearance and placement of a display box so that you can better control how your content is shown to the Web user.

In Hour 6 when I introduced the margin, padding, and border properties, I didn't mention that they are actually shorthand properties, as are the font and background properties. A shorthand property is one that sets several properties at once, first resetting them to their default values (as defined by the W3C specification) and then setting individual values as given in the declaration. Each of the edge shorthand properties sets the edge characteristics of all four sides of the box.

A box in CSS has four sides: top, bottom, left, and right. The edge properties for each side are displayed in Figure 13.1.

FIGURE 13.1

The edge properties surrounding the content in the box model on four sides.

Edge properties for each side allow you either to set the margin, padding, and border separately for every side or to set several at once with a shorthand property. When using a shorthand property, you can specify between one and four values; the results of these values are shown on Table 13.1.

TABLE 13.1 Shorthand Values for Edge Properties

Shorthand Values	Effect
value	Sets all four properties to the same value
value1 value2	Sets the top and bottom properties to *value1* and the right and left properties to *value2*
value1 value2 value3	Sets the top property to *value1*, the right and left properties to *value2*, and the bottom property to *value3*
value1 value2 value3 value4	Sets properties in clockwise order: top, right, bottom, left

Values can also be set with individual properties, such as `margin-left` or `padding-bottom`. A shorthand value will always set all appropriate values; no sides are left unset, even if fewer than four values are specified.

Setting the Margins

Take a look at setting the margins first. You can set all the margins to a single value with the `margin` property, like this:

```
#content p { margin: 3em; }
```

This would put a margin space of 3 ems around any paragraphs identified by this selector. Remember that vertical margins collapse, so the nearest vertical content will be 3 ems away, unless the other content has a greater margin.

When collapsing margins, you compare the bottom margin of the first box to the top margin of the second. If both are positive, the distance is the greater of the two; if one is negative, the distance is the difference between them. If both vertical margins are negative, the distance between the boxes is the largest negative value. Negative distances mean overlapping display boxes, which is allowable in CSS, albeit often confusing.

Imagine that you just want to set the horizontal margins. Here are four ways to do that:

```
#content p { margin-left: 3em;
             margin-right: 3em; }
#content p { margin: 0em 3em; }
#content p { margin: 0em 3em 0em; }
#content p { margin: 0em 3em 0em 3em; }
```

All of these rules are identical in effect; they set the right and left margins to 3 ems.

13

Nearly any displayed element box has margins that can be adjusted; the exceptions are table cells. Table cells, represented by <td> or <th> in HTML, don't have margins. See the discussion of table styling in Hour 15, "Styling Tables," for more about this.

Margin values are not inherited; unless otherwise set, a box's margin will be zero. The types of values you can set for margins are shown in Table 13.2.

TABLE 13.2   Values for the `margin` Properties

Value	Effect
measurement	Sets the margin(s) to a specified size
negative measurement	Reduces the margin(s) of touching boxes by a specified size
percentage	Sets the margin(s) to a percentage of the containing box's width
auto	Automatically calculates the margin(s)
inherit	Uses the margin value(s) of the containing box

Note that percentages are always based on the width of the containing block, even vertical margins. You'd expect them to be determined relative to the height of the containing box, but this just isn't the case in CSS.

The `auto` value bears some explanation. If it is set on an inline element's margins, the value is calculated to 0. If set on a box element's left or right margin, the margin is set to be all remaining space within the containing box; this will move the box with the margin to one side or another. If both the left and right margins are set to `auto`, the box will be centered within its containing box. A value of `auto` for a top or bottom margin has no effect.

Actually, a value of `auto` for any margin can mean more than what I've described here, but only when you're using CSS to position content on the screen. We'll revisit `auto` margins in Hour 17, "Advanced CSS Layout," in the discussion on CSS positioning.

Setting the Padding

Setting values for padding in CSS is simpler than setting margin values because there are no auto values and no negative measurements. The only values for padding are measurements and percentages.

Percentage values for padding, such as margin percentages, are based on the containing box's width, even for the top and bottom padding properties.

Here are four different ways to set the top padding to 4 pixels, the left and right padding to 0 pixels, and the bottom padding to 8 pixels:

```
#content p { padding-top: 4px;
             padding-bottom: 8px; }
#content p { padding: 4px 0px 8px; }
#content p { padding: 4px 0px 8px 0px; }
#content p { padding: 4px 0px;
             padding-bottom: 8px; }
```

Note that in the last rule, the padding-bottom was set twice, once as part of the padding shorthand rule, to 4px, and later separately to 8px. Because the second rule comes later (and all other priority factors are the same), the bottom padding will be 8 pixels.

Setting the Border

Borders in CSS have three distinct values associated with them: the width, or thickness of the border; the color of the border; and the style, or type of line drawn. With four sides, that means that there are actually 12 properties associated with the borders: the width, color, and style for top, bottom, left, and right. Each is written as border-*side-property*, such as border-left-style or border-bottom-color.

The border shorthand property sets all 12 of these properties at once. Using the border property, you'd write a rule like this:

```
#nav div { border: solid purple 3px; }
```

This defines the border as a solid purple line that is 3 pixels wide. This is the same as the following rule:

```
#nav div { border-top-style: solid;
           border-top-color: purple;
           border-top-width: 3px;
           border-right-style: solid;
           border-right-color: purple;
           border-right-width: 3px;
           border-bottom-style: solid;
           border-bottom-color: purple;
           border-bottom-width: 3px;
```

13

```
border-left-style: solid;
border-left-color: purple;
border-left-width: 3px; }
```

Unlike `margin` and `width`, you can't set one to four different values for each side's border using the `border` shorthand property; instead, you can use one shorthand property per side, as in the following:

```
#nav div { border-left: 1em solid green;
           border-right: 2em dashed blue;
           border-top: 1.5em dotted red;
           border-bottom: 0.5em solid purple; }
```

Alternately, you can use other shorthand properties to set all the `border-width`, `border-color`, and `border-style` values at once. You also can set the 12 border-style properties individually or combine these approaches using normal CSS cascading rules to resolve priorities.

Warning for Netscape 4

Netscape 4 doesn't recognize the `border-left`, `border-right`, `border-top`, and `border-bottom` shorthand properties. (It does understand `border`, however.) For compatibility with Netscape 4, you will need to spell out all your rules explicitly, such as `border-left-style`, `border-left-width`, and so on. Also, Netscape 4 doesn't allow you to set different border colors for various sides of the same box; see the warning under `border-color` later in this hour.

Border Width

The thickness of the border is set by a `border-width` value; possible values are shown in Table 13.3. If no `border-width` value is specified in a shorthand property, the default is `medium`. For a border to be displayed at all, the `border-width` value for each side must be set to something, even if it's simply set to the default with a shorthand property.

TABLE 13.3   Values for the `border-width` Properties

Value	Effect
medium	Sets a medium thickness border
thick	Sets a thick border
thin	Sets a thin border
measurement	Sets a border as wide as the specified measurement
inherit	Uses the inherited `border-width` value of the containing box

The values thin, medium, and thick are relative values whose exact measurements are left up to the browser. The browser can determine the precise thickness however it likes, though within certain constraints; thin can't be thicker than medium, thick can't be thinner than medium, and when displaying a page, all borders of a given thickness must be the same width. One browser's interpretation of these values is shown in Figure 13.2.

FIGURE 13.2

Each border-width *value displayed in Netscape 6.*

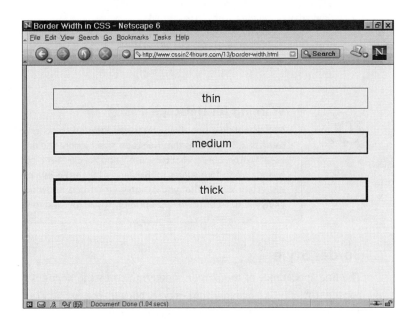

The thickness of each side's border doesn't have to be the same; each can be set to a different value if you like. To set different thicknesses, you can either use multiple values with the border-width shorthand property, or you can use the border-width property for each side. Here are some examples:

```
#nav div { border-width: 3px 2px 3px 4px; }
#nav div { border-top-width: 3px;
           border-right-width: 2px;
           border-bottom-width: 3px;
           border-left-width: 4px; }
#nav div { border-width: 3px 4px;
           border-right: 2px; }
```

These all set the same effect; a top border of 3 pixels, a right border of 2 pixels, a bottom border of 3 pixels, and a left border of 4 pixels.

Border Color

The color of all borders can be set at once with the border-color shorthand property or set individually with the border-top-color, border-right-color, border-bottom-color,

13

and `border-left-color` properties. If no color is specified, the default color value will be the foreground text color set by the `color` attribute.

You can specify the border color as you would any other colors in CSS: by RGB hex values, numeric values, or percentages, or by color name. Examples of setting border color are

```
#nav div { border-color: red white blue; }
#nav div { border-top-color: red;
           border-right-color: white;
           border-bottom-color: blue;
           border-left-color: white; }
```

> **Warning for Netscape 4**
> Netscape 4 does not allow you to set different colors on different sides of the same box. This means that Netscape 4 will ignore the `border-top-color`, `border-right-color`, `border-bottom-color`, and `border-left-color` properties. Also, giving two to four values for `border-color` results in a rule ignored by Netscape. It's recommended that you design your borders knowing that Netscape 4 will likely fail to color them appropriately if you mix and match colors on the sides.

Border Style

The line appearance of the border is determined by the `border-style` properties: `border-top-style`, `border-right-style`, `border-bottom-style`, and `border-left-style`. These can be set with the `border` shorthand property or with the `border-style` shorthand property that sets the style for all four of the borders.

Valid border types are shown in Table 13.4. Hour 6 introduced the `solid`, `dashed`, and `dotted` values. This hour adds the three-dimensional border values `groove`, `ridge`, `inset`, and `outset`, as well as the `hidden` and `double` values.

TABLE 13.4   Values for the `border-style` Properties

Value	Effect
dashed	A dashed border.
dotted	A dotted border.
double	A solid double line border.
groove	The border appears to be carved into the page.
hidden	No border displayed; borders collapsed in tables.
inset	The entire box appears to be carved into the page.
none	No border displayed.
outset	The entire box appears to rise up from the page.

TABLE 13.4 Continued

Value	Effect
ridge	The border appears to rise up from the page.
solid	A solid single line border.
inherit	Use the value of the border-style from the containing box.

The none and hidden values are identical—no border is displayed—except in table styles. In Hour 15, we'll cover the use of hidden with table cells.

The exact rendition of each border style is left up to the browser, though within the definitions of each style; obviously, a dashed border should be made up of dashed lines. Examples of each type of border are shown in Figure 13.3.

FIGURE 13.3

Each border-style value displayed in Netscape 6.

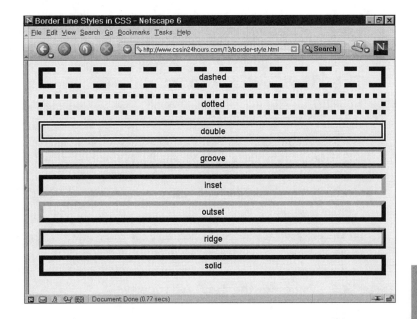

Not all browsers support all border styles; in fact, the CSS specifications explicitly support this. Browsers that don't display all border styles can instead choose to show them as solid.

Warning for Netscape 4

Netscape 4 does not recognize the dashed or dotted values for border styles and instead displays them as solid. This is allowed by the specification but is rather annoying, so it pays to know about this.

Displaying Boxes

In addition to changing the properties of the box edge, you can also set certain boxes to not be displayed at all or to display differently. The properties controlling this are the `display` and `visibility` properties.

Why wouldn't you want a box to display? Well, in most cases you'll want them to show up; this is why they're in the page content, after all. However, you may want to hide a display box if that content is inappropriate for the type of output medium being used. For example, a navigation bar may not make sense on the printed page because you obviously can't click on paper. The `display` and `visibility` properties are also useful with JavaScript to produce Dynamic HTML effects.

 You'll learn more about style sheets for printers in Hour 20, "CSS for Printing," and in Hour 23, "CSS and JavaScript," you can read about Dynamic HTML.

The `display` Property

As you've seen before, you can use the `display` property to change a box from a block element to an inline element or vice versa; you can also use it to make something display as a list item. In general, you'll want to avoid overriding the default display rules for HTML in browsers; there are too many things that can get confused if you do this, such as the default margins on certain elements. However, setting the `display` property is very useful when you're dealing with XML, as we'll discuss in Hour 24, "CSS and XML."

There are going to be some times when you're going to want to use the `display` property with HTML, especially if you need to hide some content. The values you can assign to `display` are shown in Table 13.5, and the one we're primarily concerned with is the value `none`.

TABLE 13.5 Values for the `display` Property

Value	Effect
block	Displays as a block box
compact	Displays as a compact box
inline	Displays as an inline box
list-item	Displays as a list item, with marker box
marker	Defines a marker box; see Hour 22, "User Interface and Generated Content"
none	Doesn't display the box or its children boxes
run-in	Displays as a run-in box
inherit	Uses the display value of the containing box

In addition to the values listed above, there are several values for display that apply only to tables, such as `inline-table` or `table-row-group`; these are covered in Hour 15.

The value none means that any selected elements won't be displayed; their boxes (and the boxes of their children) won't even appear. This value technically isn't inherited, but if you set one box to `display: none` and then try to set one of its children to `display: block` (or `display: inline`), the inner box still won't appear.

The `display` property is a handy way to include messages for users with browsers that don't support CSS, such as Lynx. (This won't work with browsers that have buggy CSS support but support `display` anyway, such as Netscape 4.) For example, if you're using a specific color to mark new entries, you can add some text explanations with `display: none`. Here is an example:

```
New courses are marked in red<span class="hidden">
or with the word New</span>:
<ul>
   <li><span class="hidden">New:</span>
       <span class="new">Accessible Web Design</span>
   </li>
</ul>
```

You'd then write CSS rules to support those classes, like this:

```
.hidden { display: none; }
.new { color: red; }
```

Theoretically you could use this trick to tell someone to get a better browser, but honestly, that's just plain rude.

The values compact and run-in are displayed as either block or inline depending on context. A compact box will try to fit itself into the left margin of a following block element. If it can do this, it displays as an inline element; otherwise it will display as a block element. A run-in box will display as a block element unless there's another block element (which isn't positioned using CSS positioning) after it, in which case it will become the first inline block of that subsequent block element.

13

Warning for Netscape 4, Netscape 6, Mozilla, Internet Explorer

Both compact and run-in are poorly supported by these browsers and generally should be avoided. Only Opera supports both of these; Internet Explorer supports run-in. If you need to do effects like these, consider instead using `display: inline` or CSS positioning techniques.

The `visibility` Property

Both the `visibility` and `display` properties affect whether or not the element's display box is shown. The difference between the two is that `visibility` sets aside a place on the page for an undisplayed box, whereas `display` does not. The place where the box (and its contents) would normally be displayed is instead shown as a transparent box of the same size. The values for `visibility` are shown on Table 13.6.

TABLE 13.6   Values for the `visibility` Property

Value	Effect
collapse	Collapses only table cells; see Hour 15
hidden	Doesn't display the box, but reserve the space in the layout
visible	Displays the box normally
inherit	Uses the visibility value of the containing box

The `visibility` property is most useful in Dynamic HTML and JavaScript, where you can interactively change the `visibility` of a box in response to user actions. For more on this, see Hour 23.

Warning for Netscape 4

Netscape 4 doesn't understand the `visibility` property, so this can't be used to make boxes invisible in Netscape 4. If you want to use this to put a message suggesting an upgrade to a better browser, I won't condemn you for it.

Summary

Each side of a display box is named; top, right, bottom, and left. You can set the margins and padding space for each using shorthand properties or individual properties. If you use shorthand properties and specify one value, it applies to all sides; two values assign the top/bottom and left/right; three designate top, left/right, and bottom; and four values set the properties in clockwise order.

There are also 12 properties that control the borders, and a number of shorthand properties exist to set all of those in various combinations. The width, color, and line style of the borders can be set all at once, or they can be set individually for each side.

You can also control whether or not a box is displayed at all. To hide a box entirely, use the `display: none` value. If you want to reserve space for the box, but not actually show it or its content, use the `visibility` property with a value of `hidden`.

Browser Support Report Card

CSS Feature	Grade	Notes
`margin` shorthand (1 to 4 values)	A	
`margin-side`	A	
`border-side`	B+	Not understood by Netscape 4; use individual properties
`border-width` shorthand	A	
`border-width-side`	A	
`border-color` shorthand (1 value)	A	
`border-color` (2 to 4 values)	B	Not understood by Netscape 4
`border-color-side`	B	Not understood by Netscape 4
`border-style: dashed` or `dotted`	B	Not understood by Netscape 4
`border-style:` other values	A	
`border-style-side`	B	See `dashed` or `dotted`
`display: none`	A	
`display: compact` or `run-in`	D+	Not recognized by most browsers; avoid
`visibility`	B	Not recognized by Netscape 4

Q&A

Q How can I align a box using `margin` properties?

A Here's how it works. First, don't use `text-align` unless you want the content of the box to be aligned. Instead, use `margin-left` and `margin-right` properties as shown here:

```
.left   { margin-right: auto; }    /* align left */
.right  { margin-left:  auto; }    /* align right */
.center { margin-right: auto;
          margin-left:  auto; }    /* center */
```

Q I tried setting a black border that should be `inset`, `groove`, `outset`, or `ridge`, and it showed up as `solid`! What gives?

A When you set a border with those three-dimensional border types, the third dimension is added by adjusting the base color. The edges "facing the light" are colored lighter, and the edges "in shadow" are darker. The CSS specification doesn't say how to derive those colors, so browsers are free to use their own methods. If a browser decides that the light color is 20% brighter and the dark color is 20% darker, that works unless your color is zero to begin with, like black (`#000000`). If

13

you want to be certain that your border colors appear properly three-dimensional, you should set the border style to `solid` and manually choose your own lighter and darker side colors, setting them individually on each side border.

Workshop

The workshop contains quiz questions and activities to help reinforce what you've learned in this hour. If you get stuck, the answers to the quiz can be found after the questions.

Quiz

1. These two shorthand properties set the margin and padding. What are equivalent declarations that don't use shorthand properties and instead use properties such as `margin-left`?

   ```
   #demo { margin: 0em 1em 1.5em;
           padding: 5px 7px; }
   ```

2. Likewise, these border shorthand properties can be written as 12 separate property value declarations. What are they?

   ```
   #demo2 {
           border: 3px groove black;
           border-style: dashed dotted double solid;
           border-left: medium inset green;
           }
   ```

3. A box that looks like it's depressed into the page has been styled with which border line style?

   (a.) `border-style: emboss;`

   (b.) `border-style: groove;`

   (c.) `border-style: inset;`

   (d.) `border-style: sunken;`

4. What's the difference between these two rules?

   ```
   .hide1 { visibility: hidden; }
   .hide2 { display: none; }
   ```

Answers

1. The equivalent declarations are

   ```
   #demo { margin-top: 0em;
           margin-right: 1em;
           margin-bottom: 1.5em;
           margin-left: 1em;
           padding-top: 5px;
   ```

```
                     padding-right: 7px;
                     padding-bottom: 5px;
                     padding-left: 7px; }
```

2. Here's how to write those rules as separate properties:

```
#demo2 { border-top-width: 3px;
         border-top-color: black;
         border-top-style: dashed
         border-right-width: 3px;
         border-right-color: black;
         border-right-style: dotted;
         border-bottom-width: 3px;
         border-bottom-color: black;
         border-bottom-style: double;
         border-left-width: medium;
         border-left-color: green;
         border-left-style: inset; }
```

3. The correct answer is c, inset. The groove value makes the line appear carved but not the box itself, and there are no such values as emboss or sunken for border styles.

4. With the first rule, empty (transparent) space will be reserved for the box, but with the second, there will be no space reserved, as the box won't be displayed at all.

Activity

The border properties can be used in conjunction with color, background-color, and font properties to create "buttons" that look like graphics but are really HTML tags with styles applied. Here are some ideas you could try for practice:

1. Create a menu bar using a simple table HTML. (The margin property doesn't work with table cells, so use the HTML cellspacing attribute on <table> to spread your table cells out.)

2. Set the font characteristics and size, the foreground and background colors, and the text-decoration on any links present.

3. Draw a border around each table cell using an inset or outset border-style.

4. Finally, change the border style to solid and try setting your own colors on each border to give a different three-dimensional effect. If you set the colors explicitly, you have more control over the resulting button's appearance. To make a button stand out from the page, use a light color on the top and left and a darker color on the right and bottom.

13

HOUR **14**

Lists

Not all information is organized into paragraphs of text. Many types of Web content are actually lists of information, including navigation menus, product feature lists, glossaries, and step-by-step instructions. Because of the way information is read on the Web, the use of lists can be one of the most effective and direct methods of conveying information to an audience. Styling lists well can also enhance their usefulness.

In this hour, you'll learn

- How lists are formatted in CSS
- What the different types of lists are, and how they're coded in HTML
- How other elements can be displayed as lists
- Which CSS properties change the shape and appearance of bullets
- How to set the counting methods of numbered lists

List Formatting

Before I discuss how CSS browsers display lists, I'll define some terms that will be important this hour.

A *list* is just a set of information that has been organized into discrete pieces called *list items*. A list can be *ordered,* which means that the order in which the items are presented is important, or it can be *unordered,* indicating that there isn't any specific order to the items or that order isn't important. A third type of list is the *definition list* (also called a *dictionary list*); these consist of pairs of shorter words and longer explanations.

Types of HTML Lists

Lists in HTML are usually indicated by appropriate list markup, which means a list tag such as `<ol>`, `<ul>`, or `<dl>` and then list items marked up with `<li>`, or `<dt>` and `<dd>` for definition lists. It's also possible to create a list using non–list tags, such as `<div>` or `<a>`, and convert them into lists using CSS.

Within a CSS context, an element is a list item if it has the `display` property value `list-item`. When that value is set, the element is treated as an `<li>` tag by the browser, no matter what the tag really is. The `list-item` value designates the element as a block element, except that it also allows for a *list marker*. A list marker is a symbol before each list item that indicates it's a list.

In Listing 14.1, you can see each of the three types of HTML lists, along with a fourth "list" done without using HTML list markup.

LISTING 14.1   Four Lists in HTML

```
<!-- lists-14.1.html -->
<html>
  <head><title>List-O-Rama</title></head>
  <body>
    <table border="0" width="100%">
      <tr><td valign="top" width="50%">
          <h2>Ordered List: Tallest Mountains</h2>
          <ol><li>Everest</li>          <li>K2</li>
              <li>Kangchenjunga</li>  <li>Lhotse</li>
              <li>Makalu</li>          <li>Cho Oyu</li>
              <li>Dhaulagiri</li>
          </ol></td>
          <td valign="top" width="50%">
            <h2>Unordered List: Flavors of Soda</h2>
            <ul><li>Peach</li>
                <li>Berry:
                  <ul><li>Raspberry</li>
                      <li>Blackberry</li>
                      <li>Boysenberry</li>
                  </ul></li>
                <li>Orange</li> <li>Kiwi</li>
            </ul></td>
```

LISTING 14.1 Continued

```
        </tr>
        <tr><td valign="top" width="50%">
            <h2>Definition List: Common Abbreviations</h2>
            <dl> <!-- definition list -->
              <dt>CSS</dt>  <dd>Cascading Style Sheets</dd>
              <dt>HTML</dt> <dd>Hypertext Markup Language</dd>
              <dt>W3C</dt>  <dd>World Wide Web Consortium</dd>
            </dl></td>
          <td valign="top" width="50%">
            <h2>Non-List: Links</h2>
            <div id="nav"> <!-- not done with list markup -->
              <a href="/">Home</a>
              <a href="info/">Info</a>
              <a href="shop/">Shop</a>
              <a href="map/">Map</a>
              <a href="contact/">Contact</a>
            </div></td>
        </tr>
  </table></body></html>
```

The four lists are shown in a browser in Figure 14.1; this HTML file will be used in the examples later this hour to illustrate how CSS can be used to style lists.

FIGURE 14.1

Four different lists displayed by Netscape 6.

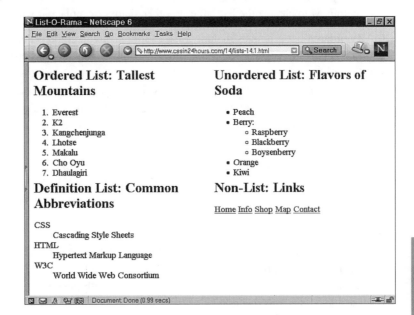

14

Ordered (Numbered) Lists

Ordered lists are displayed by putting a *number marker* of some kind before the list items. Usually number markers are ordinary numbers, such as 1, 2, 3, and so on, but later in this hour you'll learn to change those to other counting methods.

Examples of ordered lists include the top ten best-seller list at a bookstore or a set of instructions for making a cake. In both cases, the specific order of the list items is significant.

Ordered lists in HTML are created by the <ol> element, which contains <li> tags for each list item.

 Users with visual disabilities often find ordered lists easier to navigate than unordered lists because they have a better sense of context; the numbers can be used to keep track of location in a list. Using ordered lists on your page is very helpful to these users.

Unordered (Bulleted) Lists

An unordered list is commonly displayed with a *bullet marker*. This is a symbol placed before each item of the list; it commonly looks like a solid circle. During this hour you'll learn how to change the list bullet to other shapes or replace it with an image.

Unordered list examples include a list of toppings you could order on a pizza or a roster of students in a class. Even though the class roster may have an order—usually alphabetical by last name—the order probably isn't significant; it's arbitrary. For example, the list isn't ordered by the tallest or the shortest in the class. In most cases, the significance of a list's order depends on how the list is meant to be used. A list's order may not matter in one case but might in another.

To create an unordered list in HTML, you use the <ul> element, and each bullet point gets an <li> tag. There are two other HTML tags that create bulleted lists, <dir> and <menu>, but these are deprecated in HTML 4, which means that you should use the <ul> tag instead, as newer browsers may not support the deprecated tags.

Definition Lists

Definition lists consist of pairs of content—a shorter *term* and a longer *definition*. The term is displayed first, and then the definition is displayed on a new line with an indented left margin. A definition list in HTML is created with the <dl> element, with several <dt> and <dd> tags inside it.

A definition list doesn't have to be a glossary; although that's a common use, it could be anything from a listing of features in a car to a menu of desserts that describes each treat. A definition list can be used whenever you have pairs of shorter text and longer explanations or descriptions of that text.

Unlike the <li> tags in the <ol> or <ul> elements, the <dt> and <dd> tags do not have the property display set to list-item. Instead, they have the display value of block, although the <dd> tag usually has an extra margin-left value of 1.33em.

> Sometimes Web developers use the <ol>, <ul>, or <dl> tags to create indented texts or margins. Using structural tags, such as the list elements, for presentational effects like margins reduces the separation of content from presentation. To create margin effects, use the CSS properties in Hour 13, "Borders and Boxes," not list markup.

Changing List Type with `display`

Using the CSS display property, you can override the default presentation of a tag and create a list from non–list elements or change a list into a nonlist.

If you change the value of the display property, it changes only how it's presented—block or inline—and in the case of the list-item value, it sets aside space for a marker. Changing the display property doesn't affect any other values, such as the inherent margin-left on <ol> or <dd>.

Examples of setting display properties can be seen in Listing 14.2, a style sheet to change the appearance of your HTML lists. Notice that I set margin-left values to remove the left margins when changing the display value to block, and I add margin-left when setting display: list-item.

LISTING 14.2   Several Lists with Type Changed

```
/* lists-14.2.css */
ul li { display: inline; }

ol { margin-left: 0px; }
ol li { display: block; }

dd { display: list-item;
     margin-left: 0px; }

div#nav a { text-decoration: none;
            margin-left: 2em;
            display: list-item; }
```

14

The effects of this style sheet can be seen in Figure 14.2, which applies the style sheet to the HTML lists from Listing 14.1. Because the type of list marker is not set, the exact marker used will vary from browser to browser, depending on what the browser chooses to use for a default; your browser may show some of the lists differently than in Figure 14.2. To ensure consistency across browsers, you'll want to set the list item properties described later this hour whenever you change the `display` of an element to `list-item`.

FIGURE **14.2**

Displaying alternate list formatting in Netscape 6.

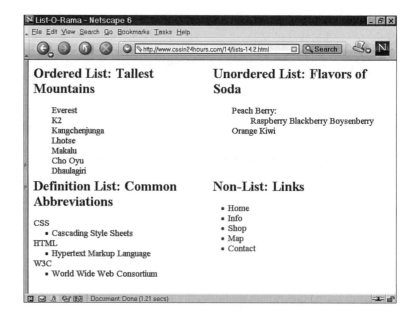

The `list-style-type` Property

The type of list marker can be changed by using the `list-style-type` property. This property is used only on elements that have the `display` value of `list-item`, but it can be set on any tag, and the value will be inherited by children that are list items. Most commonly, it's set on the `<ol>` or `<ul>` tags that enclose the `<li>` list items; this way you can set different styles for each list.

The most common values for `list-style-type` are shown in Table 14.1; additional values allow for internationalization of list markers and are discussed in Hour 20, "CSS for Printing." The default value for `<ol>` is `decimal`, and for `<ul>` and lists created using `display: list-item`, the default is `disc`.

TABLE 14.1   Values for the `list-style-type` Property

Value	Effect
`circle`	A hollow circle bullet
`decimal`	Decimal number markers (1, 2, 3, . . .)
`decimal-leading-zero`	Decimal number markers with leading zeros (01, 02, 03, . . .)
`disc`	A solid circle bullet
`lower-alpha`	Lowercase alphanumeric markers (a, b, c, . . .)
`lower-roman`	Lowercase roman numeral markers (i, ii, iii, . . .)
`none`	Don't display any marker before the list
`square`	A square bullet
`upper-alpha`	Uppercase alphanumeric markers (A, B, C, . . .)
`upper-roman`	Uppercase roman numeral markers (I, II, III, . . .)
`inherit`	Use the value of `list-style-type` from the containing box

There are two types of values: those that set bullet markers, and those that set number markers. It is possible to set a bullet `list-style-type` for ordered lists or to set a number marker on unordered lists, but generally speaking, this should be avoided. As a rule of thumb, you should use number markers only with ordered lists and bullet markers only with unordered lists.

One list contained within another list is called a *nested list*. Most browsers will display nested, unordered lists by changing the bullet type from `disc` to `circle` and then to `square`. Using `list-style-type` you can control the marker with appropriate descendant rules. Topical outlines created using <ol> tags can be styled as well, like the following:

```
ol { list-style-type: upper-roman; }
ol ol { list-style-type: upper-alpha; }
ol ol ol { list-style-type: decimal; }
ol ol ol ol { list-style-type: lower-alpha; }
ol ol ol ol ol { list-style-type: lower-roman; }
```

A style sheet that changes list markers is shown in Listing 14.3.

LISTING 14.3   Setting the `list-style-type` in CSS

```
/* lists-14.3.css */

ol { list-style-type: upper-roman; }

ul { list-style-type: square; }
ul ul { list-style-type: circle; }
```

14

continues

LISTING 14.3   Continued

```
#nav a { display: list-item;
         margin-left: 2em;
         list-style-type: square; }
```

The results of applying this style sheet to your sample lists can be seen in Figure 14.3.

FIGURE 14.3

Lists displayed in Netscape 6.

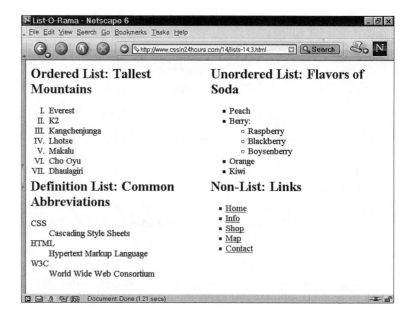

Markers (bullet or number) are displayed with the same font characteristic as the list item. If you want to change a property—for example, the color—set the property on the list item, and then use a <span> or other inline element to change the text, like the following:

```
<ol>
 <li><span>Noam Chomsky</span></li>
</ol>
```

To change the color of the list marker but not the list text, write rules like these, which put the number in red:

```
ol { color: black; }
ol li { color: red; }
ol li span { color: black; }
```

The `list-style-image` Property

You aren't restricted to bullets that are circles or squares; you can actually use any image you like by using the `list-style-image` property. Naturally, you'll want to use only small images, which can function as bullets, for this purpose; images that are too large will overwhelm the text. As an approximate rule, you should use bullets that are between 12 and 20 pixels in size.

I created a simple one-bullet image in a graphics program by first creating a 16-pixel by 16-pixel blank image, then drawing a black circle, and then adding a green plus sign in the middle of it; this is shown in Figure 14.4.

FIGURE 14.4

Creating a simple list bullet image.

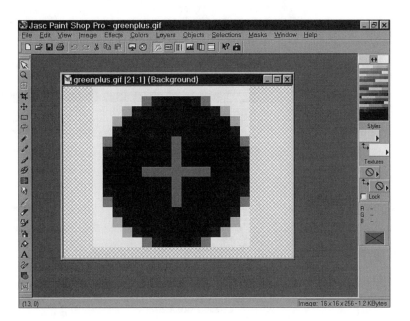

To use this image as a bullet, I simply need to set the `list-style-image` property in a rule, as in the following:

```
selector { list-style-image: url("graphic");
```

An example of a style sheet that uses bullet images is shown in Listing 14.4. Notice that I also set the `list-style-type` property to `circle`; if the image can't be loaded for any reason, the `circle` will be displayed instead.

14

LISTING 14.4   Setting a `list-style-image`

```
/* lists-14.4.css */

ol { list-style-type: upper-roman; }

ul { list-style-type: square;
     list-style-image: url("greenplus.gif"); }
ul ul { list-style-type: circle; }
        /* This will inherit the list-style-image above */

#nav a { display: list-item;
         margin-left: 2em;
         list-style-type: square;
         list-style-image: url("greenplus.gif"); }
```

Applying this style sheet to the sample lists gives the results in Figure 14.5.

FIGURE 14.5

Bullet lists displayed in Netscape 6.

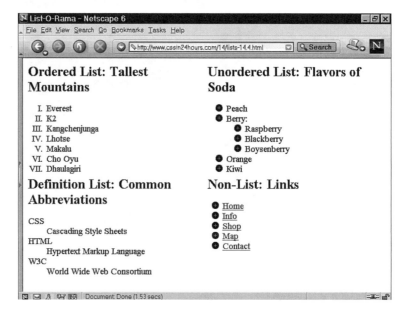

Workaround for Netscape 4

Netscape 4 doesn't use the `list-style-image` property, which makes it harder to use images as bullets. You can get a similar effect using `<img>` and an imported style sheet; Netscape 4 doesn't understand `@import` either.

Here's how you do it:

1. Make your list bullets the same color as the background color, using a `<span>` within your `<li>`, and using appropriate `color` rules.

2. Add an `<img>` tag before each `<span>` that loads your bullet image; give each tag a `class` of `bullet`.

3. Create a style sheet named `advanced.css` (or anything else you like) and add rules with `list-style-image` for non-Netscape 4 browsers, plus the following: `.bullet { display: none; }`.

4. Put a line at the start of your style sheet to import the advanced style sheet: `@import url("advanced.css")`.

For an example of this workaround in action, see `http://www.cssin24hours.com/14/workaround-14.1.html` on the Web. It's not a perfect match for `list-style-image`, but it gets the point across.

The `list-style-position` Property

When a bullet or number marker is placed, it's normally located outside the main content to the left of the list element's box. A *virtual marker box* is created; the box inherits the text properties of the list item, although the background is always transparent.

The browser determines the placement of this virtual marker box; as a Web developer, you can't affect the exact placement of the marker. You can control one thing, though; you can move the marker box inside the list element's box, so it functions as an inline box instead. This is done by setting the `list-style-position` property.

Three values are possible for `list-style-position`: `outside` (the default), `inside`, and `inherit`. Any value set on a containing box will be inherited, so you can set it on `<ol>` or `<ul>` selectors, and it will apply to list items within them.

The effects of `list-style-position` are clarified in Listing 14.5 by adding `border` properties to make the list item display boxes clear.

LISTING 14.5   Setting the Position of the List Bullet or Number

```
/* lists-14.5.css */

ol { list-style-type: upper-roman;
     list-style-position: inside; }

li { border: 1px solid black; margin: 2px; }
ul { list-style-type: square;
     list-style-image: url("greenplus.gif");
     list-style-position: outside; }
```

14

continues

LISTING 14.5 Continued

```
ul ul { list-style-type: circle;
        list-style-position: inside; }

#nav a { display: list-item;
         list-style-position: inside;
         list-style-type: square;
         list-style-image: url("greenplus.gif");
         border: 1px solid black; margin: 2px; }
```

The repositioned markers are shown in Figure 14.6.

FIGURE 14.6

List positioning in Netscape 6.

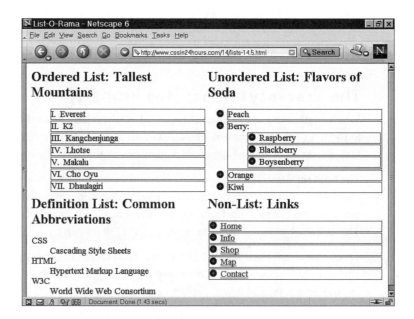

The `list-style` Shorthand Property

Like other shorthand properties, the list-style property lets you set multiple CSS properties at once. A list-style rule is written like the following:

```
selector { list-style: type position image; }
```

The values for *type*, *position*, and *image* can appear in any order; any values that aren't specified are set to their default values. For example, to set the image to greenplus.gif, the bullet type to square, and the position to inside, you can use the following rule:

```
ul li {
  list-style: url("greenplus.gif") square inside;
}
```

Summary

HTML defines three types of lists: ordered lists, unordered lists, and definition lists. Ordered and unordered lists contain `list-item` elements, which are a special type of `block` content.

Any HTML element with the CSS property display set to `list-item`—including `<li>` tags, thanks to browsers' default style sheets—will generate a virtual marker box. This marker box contains a marker of some kind; ordered lists have number markers, and unordered lists have bullets.

The type of marker can be set using the `list-style-type` property; a variety of number schemes and bullet types are available. Bullet images can also be used with the `list-style-image` property. The location of the marker box is set with the `list-style-location` property. All of these properties can be set at once using the `list-style` shorthand property.

Browser Support Report Card

CSS Feature	Grade	Notes
Changing list type with `display`	A	
`list-style-type`	A	
`list-style-image`	B+	Workaround required for Netscape 4
`list-style-position`	B	Not supported by Netscape 4
`list-style`	B	

Q&A

Q How do I set styles on definition lists? You've mostly talked about `<ol>` and `<ul>`, not `<dl>`.

A That's because from the CSS perspective, definition lists aren't lists at all! They're simply `block` content, not `list-item` elements. That means that you can just create style rules for `<dl>`, `<dt>`, and `<dd>` normally, as you would for any block elements. I personally like to do the following:

```
dt { font-weight: bold; }
```

Q How do I set the starting values for ordered lists using CSS?

A Unfortunately, you can't set those with CSS. In order to set specific number values for ordered lists, you'll need to use the HTML `start` attribute on the `<ol>` element or the `value` attribute on `<li>`. Both of these values are deprecated in HTML 4.01, which means you can't use them in Strict HTML documents.

14

Workshop

The workshop contains quiz questions and activities to help reinforce what you've learned in this hour. If you get stuck, the answers to the quiz can be found after the questions.

Quiz

1. Which of these rules will make an ordered list count in lowercase letters?

   (a.) `ol { list-style-type: alphabet; }`

   (b.) `ol { list-style-type: lower-case; }`

   (c.) `ol { list-style-type: lower-letters; }`

   (d.) `ol { list-style-type: lower-alpha; }`

2. Assuming the following style rules, what color will the numbers before a list item be?
   ```
   ol { color: green; }
   ol li { color: blue; }
   li { color: black; }
   ol li span { color: red; }
   ```

3. You want your bullet list items to be marked by a graphic, `bullet01.jpg`, which looks like a small box. You also want the graphic to be placed inside the list item's display box. How do you write this using the `list-style` shorthand property?

Answers

1. The correct answer is (d.); the `lower-alpha` value starts counts list items with (a.), (b.), (c.), and so on.

2. The numbers will be the same color as the `<li>`; in this case, that color is `blue`. (If you think it's `black`, you're forgetting that the second rule is more specific than the first in cascade order.)

3. Here's one way to write such a rule:
   ```
   ul { list-style: square inside url("bullet01.jpg"); }
   ```

Activity

Some projects you can undertake to investigate list styles on your own include the following:

- Build an outline using `<ol>` and `list-style-type` properties. Adjust the margins and padding to suit taste.

- Design several list bullet graphics for your Web pages, and add these using the `list-style-image` property. Which kinds of bullets are best at capturing the user's attention?

- Create a navigation bar in a layout table that consists of `<a>` links changed to list items using display. Add two list bullets—one for unvisited links, one for visited links.

HOUR 15

Styling Tables

Tables in HTML are a staple of Web development and are used for everything from schedules and calendars to page layout. Although CSS offers the ability to replace tables for visual design of the page, it's a more common scenario to find tables and CSS styles used together for best effect.

In this hour, you will learn

- What the HTML table model is, and how it is used with CSS
- How tables are laid out on the screen
- What the layers of a table are, and how CSS rules can be used to affect cells in those layers
- How the borders, padding, and spacing of table cells can be affected by CSS
- How to use other CSS properties with table layout

Table Formatting

Tables are ubiquitous on the Web and constitute the primary way of visually formatting output; they were intended originally for pure data but have evolved to serve as a rudimentary page-layout sublanguage within HTML.

In Hours 16, "Page Layout in CSS," and 17, "Advanced CSS Layout," I'll tell you how you can eliminate tables entirely from your Web designs and use pure CSS for the positioning of page elements. In this hour, I'm going to assume that you are using tables either for data or layout; the properties here can be used for either. The examples given are for data tables but apply equally well to layout tables.

> **Warning for Netscape 4**
>
> Netscape 4 recognizes none of the CSS properties related to table markup that are described in this hour.

HTML Table Model

The way HTML browsers display tables should be familiar to anyone who has done Web development work. Tables are employed not only for displaying columns of tabular data, but also for graphically laying out entire pages on the screen.

To do any serious Web development, you'll need to know how tables are used in HTML. This same knowledge will serve you well in CSS because the CSS table model is based on the HTML table model. Hopefully, you've worked with tables before, and this explanation will be a review for you.

An HTML table is defined by the <table> element. Within the opening and closing tags of the <table> can be found a number of table rows, designated by the <tr> tag. Each row is composed of one or more table cells. A table cell can either be table data, <td>, or a table header, <th>. Table headers are generally assumed to convey some sort of information about the corresponding table data cells; at least, if the markup is used properly, this will be true.

More complex tables can be built by grouping table rows into groups, using the <thead>, <tbody>, and <tfoot> elements. Each of these tags defines a container that holds one or more table rows and identifies them as a group. The <thead> tag is used to designate table header rows; if a printed table spans more than one sheet of paper, the <thead> should be repeated on the top of each page. The <tfoot> is the complement of the table header rows; it is a group of rows that serves as a footer and should also be repeated if the table spans multiple pages. Table body sections, marked with <tbody> tags, group together related rows; a table can have one or more <tbody> sections.

An example of a data table built using table row groups can be seen in Listing 15.1; this is an HTML file that contains a weekly listing of scheduled events. In fact, it's my current schedule, as I'm writing this book; you can assume that all other time is taken up with either writing or sleeping, and often with very little of the latter!

LISTING 15.1 A Simple HTML Table

```
<!-- schedule-15.1.html -->
<html>
  <head>
    <title>Weekly Schedule</title>
  </head>
  <body>
    <table>
      <caption>My Schedule</caption>
      <thead>
        <tr>
          <th></th>
          <th>Mon</th>
          <th>Tue</th>
          <th>Wed</th>
          <th>Thu</th>
          <th>Fri</th>
        </tr>
      </thead>
      <tbody>
        <tr>
          <th>Morning</th>
          <td>Class</td>
          <td></td>
          <td>Class</td>
          <td></td>
          <td></td>
        </tr>
        <tr>
          <th>Afternoon</th>
          <td></td>
          <td></td>
          <td>Gym</td>
          <td></td>
          <td>Gym</td>
        </tr>
        <tr>
          <th>Evening</th>
          <td>Online Gaming</td>
          <td></td>
          <td>Writers Group</td>
          <td>Class</td>
          <td></td>
        </tr>
      </tbody>
    </table>
  </body>
</html>
```

15

This sample table also contains a `<caption>` tag; the caption is used to provide a label for the table. You could have specified table columns, as well, by using the `<colgroup>` and `<col>` tags, but for now, this table will serve as an effective example for your table-related style properties. Later in this hour, I'll cover columns and column groups.

Because an HTML browser understands the table markup, it can display it with default styling. Borders typically aren't drawn between cells or around the table; table data cells are left-justified in normal text; table header cells are center-justified and set in bold font; and captions are centered over the table. This can be seen in Figure 15.1, which shows the default styles Netscape 6 uses to display a table.

FIGURE 15.1

Schedule table with default HTML styling in Netscape 6.

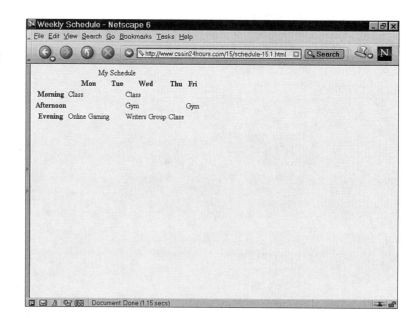

CSS Table Layout

The Cascading Style Sheets model for tables is based on the HTML model; CSS was specifically built to be compatible with HTML as used on the Web. Style sheets can be used in conjunction with HTML markup to style and present columns and rows of information or to lay out the whole page on the screen.

Just because you can do something, that doesn't mean you always should. HTML tables were not originally designed for page layout; in Hours 16 and 17 you'll learn how you can use CSS positioning properties to create powerful and flexible layouts without using <table> tags. You may still want to use layout tables for backwards-compatibility with older browsers, but you should also be aware that tables, as a visual way of conveying information, may sometimes leave behind people who have vision-related disabilities. For more on users with disabilities, see Hour 21, "Accessibility and Internationalization."

The link between the HTML and CSS table models is the display property in CSS. Each table tag corresponds to a value for display; the default style sheet within a CSS-based browser specifies how each item should be shown to the user. The list of additional display values is shown in Table 15.1.

TABLE 15.1 Table-related Values for the display Property

Value	Effect
inline-table	As <table>; displayed as an inline box
table	As <table>; displayed as a block box
table-caption	As <caption>; displayed before, after, or beside the table
table-cell	As <td> or <th>; an individual table cell
table-column	As <col>; not displayed but can be used for formatting
table-column-group	As <colgroup>; not displayed but can be used for formatting
table-footer-group	As <tfoot>; designates a group of footer rows
table-header-group	As <thead>; designates a group of header rows
table-row	As <tr>; a row of table cells
table-row-group	As <tbody>; designates a group of rows

Because these values are built into the browser, you won't ever actually need to change the display property to work with tables, but it is useful to know how CSS considers each. For example, CSS classifies <td> and <th> as the same type of display property.

Table cells in CSS are treated as block boxes; they can contain inline or block content and are contained by table-row block boxes. Table rows and groups of table rows are used primarily for grouping. Usually, styles can't be applied to them directly, although properties that are inherited can be set on rows or groups of rows and will apply to cells (<td> or <th>) within those rows.

In general, applying styles to table cells is straightforward and follows all of the normal rules of the cascade and inheritance; nearly any CSS properties can be set on table cells. There are a few exceptions, however, and so before you go on, I'll spend some time looking at how CSS styles interact with HTML tables.

Layers and Inheritance

One key way in which tables differ from other block boxes is the introduction of table layers into the inheritance method. Each cell is considered to be a descendant of several other layers of markup, as shown on Table 15.2.

TABLE 15.2   Table Layers, in Order from Most Specific to Most General

Layer	Equivalent HTML
cells	`<td>`, `<th>`
rows	`<tr>`
row groups	`<thead>`, `<tbody>`, `<tfoot>`
columns	`<col>`
column groups	`<colgroup>`
table	`<table>`

The most surprising thing about table layers is that they exist even if the actual tags do not! For example, all cells are part of a row group, even if there are no `<thead>`, `<tbody>`, or `<tfoot>` tags in the document. It is assumed that there is an unstated, invisible `<tbody>` surrounding all table rows that aren't already within a row group. Likewise, all cells are part of columns and column groups.

When considering the appearance of a table cell, you need to take into account the effects of these table layers. For example, the `background-color` property is normally transparent unless otherwise specified. This means that the background of the containing box of the `<table>` will be visible. If `background-color` is set on a `<tbody>`, that will be the cell's background color, unless the property is set on a `<tr>` or a table cell, which are more specific, according to the table layers model.

Automatic and Fixed Layouts

The browser usually automatically determines the dimensions of the table's box and of the box sizes of each cell within it. Browsers generally follow the same method of calculating the size, but this is not a requirement, and in fact the CSS Level 2 specification allows

15

browsers to use whatever method they like to size a table and its cells. This is called an *automatic layout.*

However, in many cases you will want more control over the dimensions of the table. At those times, you'll want to use a *fixed layout,* one where the width and cells of the table are specified in the CSS rules. To tell the browser you're working with a fixed layout, use the `table-layout` property. Values for `table-layout` are shown in Table 15.3; the default is `auto`. This property can be set only on table elements.

TABLE 15.3   Values for the `table-layout` Property

Value	Effect
auto	Lets the browser determine the dimensions of the table and table cells
fixed	Explicitly designates the width of each table cell
inherit	Uses the value of `table-layout` set on the containing block

Once you have informed the browser that you're using a fixed layout, you then need to define the widths of each column. You do this by setting the `width` property on the table and on each table cell. The value of the `width` property can be either a measurement, such as `300px` or `6em`, or a percentage value.

> The `width` property can be used with other block elements, as well; you'll learn more about this useful property in Hour 17.

The style sheet in Listing 15.2 sets the `table-layout` property to `fixed` and provides width values for the table and for each table cell. A border is drawn around each cell to make the widths more apparent.

LISTING 15.2   Style Sheet with Fixed Layout

```
/* schedule-15.2.css */

table { table-layout: fixed;
        width: 90%; }
td, th { width: 15%;
         border: 2px solid silver; }
```

Applying this style sheet to your schedule table from Listing 15.1 gives us the effects shown in Figure 15.2. The primary advantage of a fixed layout is that it displays faster because the browser doesn't have to calculate the column widths.

FIGURE 15.2

Netscape 6 displays a schedule with a fixed layout.

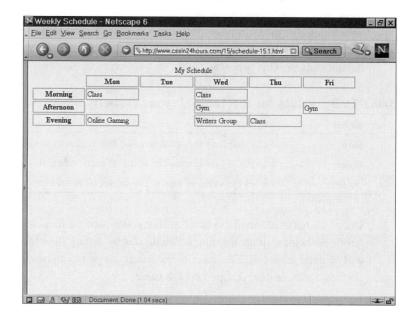

Table Borders, Padding, and Spacing

Like other block display boxes in CSS, table cells can be surrounded by borders and can have internal padding. Unlike other block boxes, though, a table cell never has a margin on any side.

The appearance of a table cell's borders is affected by several properties that determine which cells display borders and how adjacent borders interact with each other.

Displaying or Hiding Empty Cells

If you looked carefully at Figure 15.2, you might have noticed something unusual: Only cells that contained content had borders drawn around them. This can be an effective way of presenting information in some circumstances, but in others you are going to want a border drawn around all table cells, even those that are empty. You can control the display of borders around table cells by using the empty-cells property.

The `empty-cells` property can be set only on table elements, and the valid values for this property are shown in Table 15.4. The default is `hide`, which means borders aren't shown for empty cells.

TABLE 15.4   Values for the `empty-cells` Property

Value	Effect
hide	Doesn't display borders for empty cells
show	Displays appropriate borders for empty cells
inherit	Uses the value of `empty-cells` set on the containing box

By setting `empty-cells` to `show`, you are telling the browser that if a cell is empty, it can go ahead and apply whatever `border` style would be used if the cell contained content. If there is no applicable border to use, the cell won't be displayed. Setting only the `empty-cells` property without the appropriate border properties (or the border `shorthand` property) is ineffective.

Listing 15.3 contains rules for several styles of borders, along with an `empty-cells: show` declaration on the table.

LISTING 15.3   Turning on Borders around Empty Cells via the `empty-cells` Property

```
/* schedule-15.3.css */

table { table-layout: auto; width: 90%;
        font-size: large;
        empty-cells: show; }
td, th { width: 15%; }
thead th { border: 0.20em dashed gray; }
tbody th { border: 0.25em solid black; }
td { border: 0.10em solid gray; }
```

In Figure 15.3, you can see the results of applying this style sheet to Listing 15.1; a border surrounds all table cells, in contrast to Figure 15.2.

FIGURE 15.3

Empty cells become visible, as shown by Netscape 6.

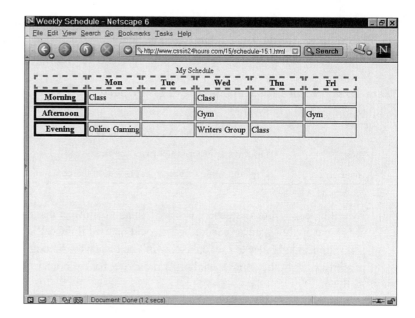

Collapsing Borders

Within CSS you can have two options for how you want table cell borders to be handled: They can either collapse or remain separate. You can choose which of these two display models to use by setting a value for border-collapse on your <table> element; appropriate values are shown in Table 15.5.

TABLE 15.5   Values for the border-collapse Property

Value	Effect
collapse	Collapses adjacent borders together
separate	Keeps adjacent borders separated
inherit	Uses the value of border-collapse set on the containing box

In the *collapsed border model,* two cells that are adjacent, horizontally or vertically, share a single, common border line between them. There is no space between the cells; one ends where the other begins. You'd use this to produce a clean, simple table presentation where the cells aren't separated within distinct boxes. This is a style choice you'd make based on how you envision the final look of the table.

If two adjacent cells have different border properties set on them, the border will be based on the most visible border of the two. A wider border takes precedence over a narrow border. If two borders are the same width, the border-style determines which one is chosen; in order from most important to least important, a border-style value of double takes precedence over solid, dashed, dotted, ridge, outset, groove, and inset. If two border declarations have the same width and style and differ only in color, a rule set on a more specific layer takes precedence; a style on a table cell will beat a row, row group, column, column group, or table rule. Otherwise, normal CSS cascading order is followed.

Warning for Netscape 6, Internet Explorer (Mac)

Neither Netscape 6 nor Internet Explorer on Macintosh supports the margin-collapse property.

An example of collapsed borders is shown in Listing 15.4. This table has different border values for <td> and <th> elements in the table heading and body.

LISTING 15.4 Style Sheet to Collapse Borders between Cells

```
/* schedule-15.4.css */

table { table-layout: auto; width: 90%;
        border-collapse: collapse;
        font-size: large; empty-cells: show; }
td, th { width: 15%; }
thead th { border: 0.20em dashed gray; }
tbody th { border: 0.25em solid black; }
td { border: 0.10em solid gray; }
```

The effect of collapsing these borders can be seen in Figure 15.4.

FIGURE 15.4

*Collapsed cell borders
displayed by Opera 6.*

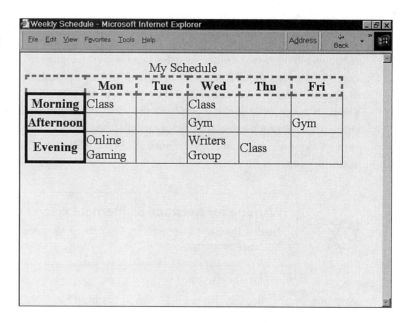

Separated Borders

Table cells can also be displayed with space between them. This is known as the *separated borders model* and is selected by a rule on the `<table>` cell setting the `border-collapse` property to `separate`. You'd choose this stylistic approach if you want cells presented as a distinct box, with a background surrounding each one. For example, a table meant to look like a telephone keypad would use separated borders.

In HTML, the spacing between cells is set by the `cellspacing` attribute; in CSS the same effect is accomplished by the `border-spacing` property. The `border-spacing` property sets the distance between the outer edge of adjacent cells—in other words, the spacing between each border. Table 15.6 indicates the possible values for `border-spacing`; if one value is given, that sets both the horizontal and vertical border-spacing; if two are supplied, the first is the horizontal spacing and the second is the vertical. The space between cells displays the background of the table.

TABLE 15.6   Values for the `border-spacing` Property

Value	Effect
`measurement`	Sets the horizontal and vertical cell-spacing to the same value
`measurement measurement`	Sets the horizontal and vertical cell-spacing, respectively
`inherit`	Uses the value(s) for `border-spacing` set on the containing box

Warning for Internet Explorer

Current versions of Internet Explorer for Macintosh and Windows do not support the `border-spacing` property.

15

Listing 15.5 is a style sheet that you can apply to your schedule from Listing 15.1; it displays the cells with a horizontal spacing of `0.45em` and a vertical spacing of `1em`.

LISTING 15.5 Increasing the Spacing between Cells Using the `border-spacing` Property

```
/* schedule-15.5.css */

table { table-layout: auto; width: 90%;
        border-collapse: separate;
        font-size: large; empty-cells: show;
        border-spacing: 0.45em 1em; }
td, th { width: 15%; }
thead th { border: 0.20em dashed gray; }
tbody th { border: 0.25em solid black; }
td { border: 0.10em solid gray; }
```

As you can see from Figure 15.5, the applied style sheet spaces out the cells appropriately in your schedule.

FIGURE 15.5

Netscape 6 displays spacing between cells.

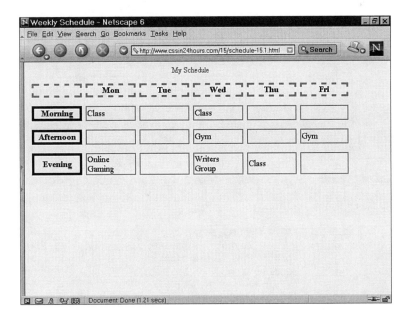

Table Captions

The HTML <caption> tag gives the *caption*, which is a label for a table. This appears within the <table> element as the first child, and it is usually presented before the table. The display box containing the <caption> is as wide as the table itself.

The location of the caption isn't fixed; the CSS caption-side property can be used to place the caption on a different side of the table box. The values for caption-side are shown in Table 15.7. This property can be set only on <caption> elements, and the default value is top.

TABLE 15.7 Values for the caption-side Property

Value	Effect
bottom	Caption appears after the table.
left	Caption appears to the left of the table.
right	Caption appears to the right of the table.
top	Caption appears before the table.
inherit	Uses the value of caption-side set on the containing box.

Warning for Internet Explorer (Windows), All Browsers

Internet Explorer for Windows does not support the caption-side property. All other browsers (except Netscape 4) support caption-side: bottom and caption-side: top. Only Opera supports caption-side: left or caption-side: right. Unfortunately, using left or right values in Opera often results in unreadable text, so caption-side values other than top or bottom should be avoided in all browsers.

The style sheet in Listing 15.6 moves the caption from the top to the bottom and sets specific font and box properties on the caption, as well. The default styling for <caption> in most browsers is default text, centered above the table.

LISTING 15.6 Style Sheet to Move the Caption to the Bottom of the Table

```
/* schedule-15.6.css */

table    { table-layout: auto;        width: 90%;
           border-collapse: separate; font-size: large;
           border: 6px double black;
           padding: 1em;
           margin-bottom: 0.5em; }
```

LISTING 15.6   Continued

```
td, th   { width: 15%; }
thead th { border: 0.10em solid black; }
tbody th { border: 0.10em solid black; }
      td { border: 0.10em solid gray; }

caption  { caption-side: bottom;
           font-size: x-large;        font-style: italic;
           border: 6px double black;
           padding: 0.5em 0em;
           margin-top: 0.5em; }
```

The results of applying this style sheet to the schedule from Listing 15.1 can be seen in Figure 15.6; notice that the widths of the table and the caption are the same.

FIGURE 15.6

The caption displayed after the table in Netscape 6.

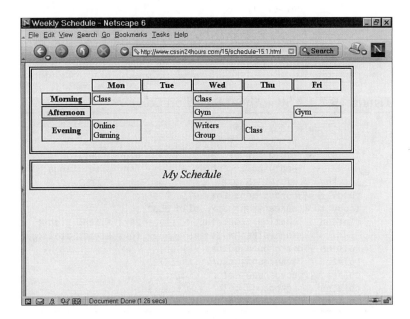

Styling Columns

As noted before, each cell in a table is part of a column in addition to being in a row. Cascading Style Sheets can be used to affect the presentation of columns, but only within certain parameters. If you need to apply a set of style rules to a specific column, such as making the third column of cells have a black background, there are two approaches. The first way to do this is to set the third cell of every row to the same `class` and then to write a `class` selector. The second is to write selectors based on columns.

To designate a column or a group of columns, you use the <col> and <colgroup> tags. These can be given class or id attributes to be used in selectors, or they can have style attributes for inline styles.

You'll extend your schedule markup by adding the <colgroup> and <col> tags in your example. Add the following lines to the HTML file from Listing 15.1 immediately after the <caption> tag in order to define the columns:

```
<colgroup>
  <col id="time">
</colgroup>
<colgroup id="days">
  <col id="mon">
  <col id="tue">
  <col id="wed">
  <col id="thu">
  <col id="fri">
</colgroup>
```

These tags define specific identifiers for columns, which you can use in your CSS rules with id selectors. Listing 15.7 contains several examples of these types of selectors.

LISTING 15.7   A Style Sheet Based on Columns

```
/* schedule-15.7.css */

table    { table-layout: auto;        width: 90%;
           empty-cells: show;         font-size: large; }
td, th   { width: 15%; }
tbody th { border-top: 2px solid black; }
tbody td { border-top: 2px solid black; }
caption  { caption-side: top;         text-align: right;
           font-size: x-large;        font-style: italic; }
col#mon { background-color: silver; }
col#tue { background-color: lime; }
col#wed { background-color: violet; }
col#thu { background-color: yellow; }
col#fri { background-color: #CCF; }
```

Only certain types of properties are allowed in column or column group rules; other properties are ignored. The appropriate properties are background and related properties; width; visibility; and the border properties. The visibility property can take the value of collapse to hide an entire column; the border properties are respected only if the collapsing border model has been chosen with the border-collapse property.

Warning for Netscape 6, Opera box

Warning for Netscape 6, Opera

Only Internet Explorer (on both Macintosh and Windows platforms) supports the use of columns and column groups as selectors.

15

The effects of applying the style sheet from Listing 15.7 to the modified HTML page, with added column markup, can be seen in Figure 15.7.

FIGURE 15.7

The effects of applying the columnar style sheet as shown in Internet Explorer.

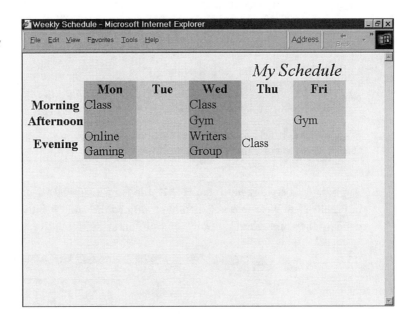

Applying Other Styles to Tables

Nearly any other styles that can be applied to block elements can be applied to tables or table cells; the primary exception is that table cells never have margin properties. To set the spaces between table cells, you would instead use a separated-borders model, as described earlier, and set the border-spacing property on the table. The effect is the same as setting the margin between the cells.

Horizontal Alignment

As with other block boxes, the alignment of inline elements inside a table cell can be set with the text-align property. Use of text-align can easily make tables more readable, lining up columns to the left, right, or center as appropriate. Because <th> cells are center-aligned and <td> cells are left-aligned, columns can look a bit disorganized;

`text-align` rules can correct this. For example, if you have a table listing movie show dates, you'd want to align the columns to the right, so that the times line up.

A sample style sheet using `text-align` is shown in Listing 15.8.

LISTING 15.8   Setting the Horizontal Alignment of Table Cells

```
/* schedule-15.8.css */

table     { table-layout: auto;       width: 90%;
            border-collapse: separate; border-spacing: 0.25em;
            empty-cells: hide;         font-size: large;
            margin-left: auto;         margin-right: auto; }
td, th    { width: 15%; }
th        { border: 2px solid black; }
td        { border: 2px solid gray; }
caption   { caption-side: top;         text-align: right;
            font-size: x-large;        font-style: italic; }

tbody th { text-align: right; }
tbody td { text-align: center; }
```

Applying this style sheet to the HTML file from Listing 15.1 gives the effects shown in Figure 15.8. Note that you also have aligned the table itself in the center, using the `margin-left` and `margin-right` values of auto.

FIGURE 15.8

Aligning cells horizontally in Opera 6.

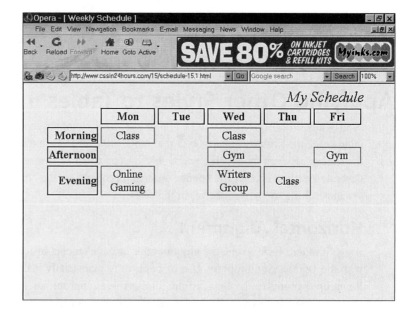

In addition to the normal left, right, center, and justify values for text-align, another alignment system can be used with tables. By supplying a text string as a value, you instruct the cells to be horizontally aligned so that the specific string lines up in a column. This is especially useful for monetary figures and other values with decimal points. This is easiest to illustrate with an example; Listing 15.9 is an HTML file with styles to center the prices on the decimal point.

LISTING 15.9 Alignment Based on a Text String

```
<!-- prices-15.9.html -->
<html>
  <head>
    <title>Menu</title>
    <style type="text/css">
      .price { text-align: "."; }
    </style>
  </head>
  <body>
    <table>
      <tr><th style="text-align: left;">Item</th>
          <th>Price</th>
      </tr>
      <tr><td>Hamburger</td>
          <td class="price">$2.99</td></tr>
      <tr><td>~~ Add Cheese</td>
          <td class="price">.25</td></tr>
      <tr><td>Lobster Dinner</td>
          <td class="price">$25.</td></tr>
      <tr><td>Soft Drinks</td>
          <td class="price">$1</td></tr>
    </table>
  </body>
</html>
```

Unfortunately, no major browsers currently support aligning with a text string, so you will probably not find this feature very useful.

Vertical Alignment

The vertical-align property in CSS is the equivalent of the HTML valign property; browsers often will align table cells to the vertical middle, and this can make cell contents look clumsy if the text wraps. Most of the time you are going to want to vertically align data cells so that the first line of each row is lined up on the top. Column header cells may look better aligned along the bottom. You can use the vertical-align property to affect these styles.

15

Listing 15.10 is a style sheet that lines up the baselines of each cell, so that the first line of each row is aligned with each other line in that row.

LISTING 15.10 Setting the Vertical Alignment of Table Cells

```
/* schedule-15.10.css */

table    { table-layout: auto;         width: 90%;
           border-collapse: separate; border-spacing: 0.25em;
           empty-cells: hide;          font-size: large;
           margin-left: auto;          margin-right: auto; }
td, th   { width: 15%; }
th       { border: 2px solid black; }
td       { border: 2px solid gray; }
tbody th { text-align: right; }
tbody td { text-align: center; }
caption  { caption-side: top;          text-align: right;
           font-size: x-large;         font-style: italic; }

td, th    { vertical-align: baseline; }
thead th  { vertical-align: bottom; }
```

The results of this style sheet, when applied to the HTML file from Listing 15.1, are shown in Figure 15.9.

FIGURE 15.9

Aligning cells vertically in Opera 6.

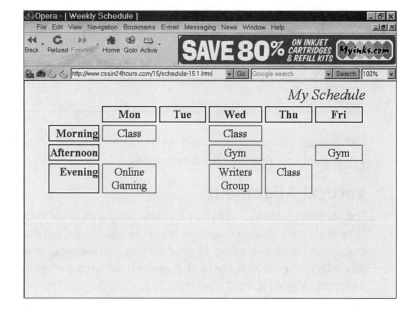

Summary

CSS rules can be used in conjunction with HTML tables to create a pleasing presentation of columnar data or layout tables. CSS browsers conceptualize tables as a series of layers; in order from most specific to least, those are the table cells, the table rows, the groups of table rows, the table columns, the groups of table columns, and the table itself. Inheritance follows these layers, as can be seen in background property effects.

Nearly any CSS property can be applied to table elements, although table cells don't have margins. Borders are of special importance when dealing with tables, and CSS offers two models for displaying tables: collapsed and separated. Both are set via the border-collapse property.

Table cells in the collapsed border model share a common border, whereas in the separated border model, a distance defined by the border-spacing property separates all cells from each other. In both models, the empty-cells property defines whether or not borders around empty table cells are displayed or not.

The caption, a label for the content of the table, can be located on any side of the table and styled separately. Rules can also be set by column rather than by row or cell by using the <col> and <colgroup> tags, although the types of properties available for column styling are limited. The appearance and usability of a table can be improved by adjusting the text-align and vertical-align properties of the cells.

Browser Support Report Card

CSS Feature	Grade	Notes
Fixed layout model	B+	
Display of empty cells	B+	
Collapsed borders	C	Not understood by Internet Explorer (Mac), Netscape 6
Border spacing	B-	
Captions on the bottom	B	Not understood by Internet Explorer (Windows)
Captions on the left or right	D-	Understood only by Opera; often illegible
Styles on table columns	C-	Understood only by Internet Explorer (Mac, Windows)
Horizontal cell alignment	A-	
Aligning cells to a string	D	Not supported by major browsers
Vertical cell alignment	A-	

In addition, note that none of these styles works with Netscape 4.

Q&A

Q When would I ever want to change the `display` property value of a tag to a different type of table element?

A When using HTML, you pretty much don't ever want to do that. The browsers all understand what the default display values for each table element are supposed to be, and they will ignore attempts to change those values. The table-related `display` values are intended for use with XML, which doesn't have specific tags that are shown as tables. Using the `display` property, you can make XML elements show up as tables with rows, columns, and cells. For more information on using XML with CSS, see Hour 24, "CSS and XML."

Workshop

The workshop contains quiz questions and activities to help reinforce what you've learned in this hour. If you get stuck, the answers to the quiz can be found after the questions.

Quiz

1. All of the following rules apply to a certain cell in a table. What color will the background of that cell be?

```
tbody { background-color: green; }
table { background-color: blue; }
tr    { background-color: transparent; }
col   { background-color: yellow; }
```

2. You want to set the spacing between table cells to 10 pixels in both the horizontal and vertical directions. Which one of the following CSS rules accomplishes that?

   (a.) `table { cell-spacing: 10px; table-layout: separate; }`

   (b.) `table { cell-spacing: 10px; border-collapse: collapse; }`

   (c.) `table { border-spacing: 10px; border-collapse: separate; }`

   (d.) `table { cell-spacing: 10px; border-collapse: separate; }`

3. How would you write a rule to make the caption appear after the table in a smaller, italic font with a thin black border around it?

Answers

1. The background color will be green. In order from most specific to least specific, the selectors are `<tr>`, `<tbody>`, `<col>`, and `<table>`. Because the background color of the table row is `transparent`, the next selector's `background-color` shows through, and that is the `green` of the `<tbody>`.

2. The correct answer is (c.). There is no `cell-spacing` property; the correct name is `border-spacing`.

3. Here is one such rule:

```
caption { caption-side: bottom;
          font-size: smaller;
          font-style: italic;
          border: thin solid black; }
```

Activities

To get your hands dirty with table styles, why not make your own weekly schedule?

1. Create an HTML table containing your weekly schedule. You can break it down into the hours of each day, and then group morning, afternoon, and evening using `<tbody>` elements.

2. Set specific styles for the `<th>` and `<thead>` elements that are the headers for your columns and rows.

3. Select border styles that fit your personal preferences. Try both the separated and collapsed border models, and see which one you like best. Do you want to display borders around empty cells?

4. Add `<colgroup>` and `<col>` elements, and apply styles based on columns as well as on horizontal rows.

5. Adjust the colors, fonts, and alignment to suit your taste, and now you've got your own calendar!

Hour 16

Page Layout in CSS

Proper use of layout to position content on the visible page is essential to creating effective Web designs. Through the proper use of layout, Web pages can be broken down into visually distinct sections, columns, and boxes. Cascading Style Sheets offer an alternative to traditional `<table>`-based HTML design, in the form of properties that can create page layouts.

In this hour, you'll learn

- Which types of properties allow you to change the layout of the page
- How to design around a common browser that poorly supports layout properties
- The types of positioning schemes available for placing a display box on the screen
- How to place an HTML element in relation to its containing box
- How to move an HTML element relative to its original position
- How to fix an HTML element on the screen, even if the page scrolls
- How to float content of any type on the right or left of its containing box so that text wraps around the side of it

Visual Formatting in CSS

In previous hours of this book, you have learned how to use Cascading Style Sheets to produce minor stylistic effects, such as font types, letter spacing, and paragraph indenting. More extensive effects can be created by setting foreground and background colors or by manipulating box model properties, such as `margin` or `border`. These are all examples of visual formatting—styles used to create or enhance the visible presentation of a page's content.

The most significant visual formatting effects are those that change the *layout* of the page. The layout is the two-dimensional representation of the content placed on the screen or printed page. Placing boxes of information physically close together emphasizes relationships within that content, and setting something off to the side, as in a sidebar, draws attention to content while stressing its secondary importance.

Many Web page developers have used HTML `<table>` elements to create layout effects. Because HTML lacks tags that are explicitly meant to be used for page layout, tables, which were originally meant only for columns and rows of data, have been employed to give a measure of control over the page's layout.

Cascading Style Sheets can be used to affect the layout of the page and produce significant changes in appearance. Display boxes can be shifted from their original positions or placed anywhere on the page. The flow of text can be wrapped around other elements, or a display box can be fixed so that it doesn't move when the rest of the page scrolls. And perhaps most usefully, CSS properties can be used to replace `<table>` tags in defining a page's layout.

 Why would you want to lay out your page using CSS and not `<table>` tags? The primary reason is that by doing so, you're explicitly separating the content of the HTML page from the presentation styles. This is a good thing for a number of reasons, not least of which is the accessibility benefit to people with visual disabilities. (You'll learn more about designing for users with disabilities in Hour 21, "Accessibility and Internationalization.") Also, CSS-based layout is more flexible than `<table>`-based layout, allowing for more creative and usable formatting designs.

There are two methods of visual formatting used in CSS to affect the layout. The *positioning properties* are used to specify the exact placement of a display box, in relation to a specific context within the layout. The *float properties* move display boxes to the left or right side, and subsequent content is adjusted to flow around those boxes. You'll learn both of these methods in this hour.

Listing 16.1 is a Web page for a fictional bookstore, which I'll use to demonstrate the concepts of CSS-based layout. As you can see from the HTML listing, this page doesn't even attempt to use presentational or layout CSS; instead, the design of the page will be created using positioning styles and floating boxes.

LISTING 16.1 An HTML File without Layout Formatting

```
<!-- bookstore-16.1.html -->
<html>
  <head>
    <title>Kynn's Bookstore</title>
  </head>
  <body>
    <div id="structure">
      <div id="headline">
        <h1><span class="name">Kynn's</span>
          <span class="store">Bookstore</span></h1>
      </div>
      <div id="main">
        <div id="founder">
          <img src="kynn-face.jpg" alt="Kynn">
          <br>"our founder"
        </div>
        <p>Welcome to Kynn's Bookstore! This
          online bookstore is here to assist
          you with all your book-shopping
          needs.  </p>
        <div class="pullquote">
          "I found everything
          <br>I wanted at Kynn's
          <br>bookstore!" --Kynn </div>
        <p>We feature a wide variety of books
          on topics as diverse as graphic novels
          and accessibility; cascading style
          sheets and current politics. Why
          don't you browse through our offerings
          and see for yourself? </p>
        <h2>Some Featured Books:</h2>
        <p>All of our featured books come with Kynn's
          highest recommendations. Take one home
          with you today!</p>
        <ul> <li><a href="yablt/">You Are Being
              Lied To</a></li>
          <li><a href="ng/">Northern Gothic</a></li>
          <li><a href="/">SAMS Teach Yourself Cascading
              Style Sheets in 24 Hours</a></li>
          <li><a href="chomsky/">The Essential
              Chomsky</a></li>
          <li><a href="uc/">Understanding Comics</a></li>
```

16

continues

LISTING 16.1 Continued

```
        <li><a href="whiteout/">Whiteout</a></li>
      </ul>
      <div id="mainmenu">
        <a href="books/">Featured Books</a> |
        <a href="reviews/">Reviews</a> |
        <a href="news/">News</a> |
        <a href="mailto:kynn@kynn.com">Email Me</a>
      </div>
    </div>
    <div id="sitemenu">
      <img src="k.gif" alt="[K]"> <br>
      <a href="http://kynn.com/">kynn.com</a> <br>
      <a href="http://kynn.com/nav/people.html">People</a> <br>
      <a href="http://kynn.com/nav/causes.html">Causes</a> <br>
      <a href="http://kynn.com/nav/work.html">Work</a> <br>
      <a href="http://kynn.com/nav/fun.html">Fun</a> <br>
      <a href="http://kynn.com/nav/books.html">Books</a>
    </div>
  </div>
 </body>
</html>
```

You can see this rather ordinary-looking page displayed in Figure 16.1. Not very impressive, but at least all of the page information is conveyed in a direct, if pedestrian, manner.

FIGURE 16.1

A lack of layout styles makes this page boring, as shown by Netscape 6.

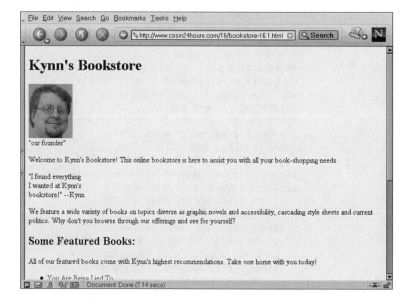

What can CSS styles do to spice up the appearance of the page? Well, take a look at Figure 16.2 for an example. This screenshot shows the HTML from Listing 16.1 redisplayed with layout styles in effect. In addition, color and font rules have been used to make the page nicer to look at.

FIGURE 16.2

CSS rules for layout, plus a few more styles, transform the HTML page, seen here in Netscape 6.

Some things you should notice about this new layout:

- The dual-color headline "Kynn's Bookstore" overlaps itself.
- The navigation bar with featured books, reviews, news, and a contact link is now located at the beginning of the page, not near the end as it appears in the source code.
- Text flows around the mug shot picture and the pull quote, like a stream of water around boulders.
- The site menu granting access to the rest of the kynn.com Web site is located on the left side, over the colored margin, rather than at the bottom of the page. Even more unexpected is that the site menu remains fixed in place when the page is scrolled.

All of these effects were created using CSS rules. The HTML source wasn't altered, and neither tables nor presentational attributes created these effects. This layout example illustrates the types of effects that can be created with visual formatting CSS.

Where's the style sheet for this? Have no fear, you'll see it in due time, but first I will introduce the separate concepts and properties used in this style sheet. By the time you reach the end of the hour, you'll have learned the properties to create this layout. If you absolutely can't wait, you can find it on the Web at http://www.cssin24hours.com/16/bookstore-16.12.css, or at the end of this hour.

Browser Support for Visual Formatting

As with most other CSS properties, those that affect the visual layout of the page are subject to the vagaries of browser support. All of the newest browsers—Opera 5 and 6, Netscape 6, Mozilla, and Internet Explorer and 5 (Mac)—support the styles used to create the example shown in Figure 16.2. Netscape 4, as you may guess, has problems interpreting some of the layout code. Figure 16.3 shows the same example as that in Figure 16.2, but displays it in Netscape 4.

FIGURE 16.3

Layout is a lot less reliable in Netscape 4.

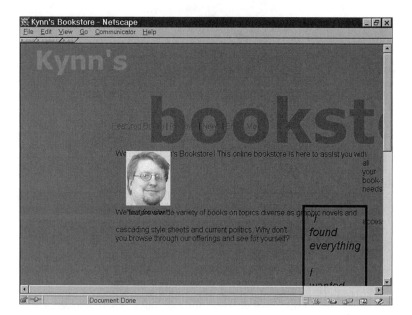

A Workaround for Netscape 4

As you can see in Figure 16.3, that layout is less than useful, and in fact makes it actively difficult to use the content of the Web page. In Netscape 4, you're better off trying to use the default styling shown in Figure 16.1 than the version with the layout styles.

In fact, that's one of the best strategies for dealing with Netscape 4's problems with layout styles—simply don't let Netscape 4 even attempt to display layout rules. Trying to code your CSS-based layouts to function in Netscape 4 is honestly more trouble than it's worth, and it will limit your ability to use valid and effective CSS with other browsers. Instead, you can use an @import rule to hide layout styles from Netscape 4.

As noted in Hour 6, "The CSS Box Model," Netscape 4 doesn't understand @import rules and thus will ignore them completely. You can create one style sheet that contains only safe (or harmless) styles that are understood by Netscape 4 as well as by newer browsers and, at the beginning of that style sheet, @import another style sheet that contains the positioning style rules.

16

This works only if your HTML is carefully designed so that the content is still accessible and understandable even without the style sheets to provide layout, as with the example in Listing 16.1. Users of newer browsers will receive the well laid out version, and those with Netscape 4 will still be able to use the page's content.

Positioning Content

Whenever you include an HTML element on a page, it generates a display box, as you learned in Hour 6. Normally, these boxes are simply placed one after another, or within another, based on the structure of the document and whether the box is an inline or block box. This is known as *normal flow* in the CSS specifications. Whenever you move an element's display box to a new location, you are disrupting the normal flow to create a new layout.

The first way to lay out the page with CSS is to use styles that position an element relative to a specific context on the page. The position property is used to choose that context. Positioned content is offset from the context by a specific amount that you can set using the top, right, bottom, or left properties.

As a historical footnote, the positioning properties in CSS were originally introduced in a draft produced between the CSS Level 1 and CSS Level 2 recommendations and were called CSS-P, for CSS Positioning. CSS-P properties were partially implemented by the browsers and were formally added to the CSS language when CSS Level 2 was released.

The position Property

To properly place a display box using positioned content, you must establish the context of that position. This is accomplished by using the position property, which defines how a box should be positioned. The default value is static, which means that the box is placed according to the normal flow of the document. Other properties for position are shown in Table 16.1. Unless inherit is specified, this property's value is not usually passed along to child boxes, although those children will be displayed within their containing box if that containing box is repositioned.

TABLE 16.1 Values for the position Property

Value	Effect
absolute	Position the box relative to the context box.
fixed	Position the box relative to the entire page, and don't move it even if the page scrolls.
relative	Position the box relative to its normal position.
static	Position the box where it should normally be placed.
inherit	Use the position value of the containing box.

To explain the differences among the different position values, I've created a simple HTML page that I'll use to illustrate each type of positioning. Listing 16.2 contains two nested <div> elements, along with some embedded styles to make their display boxes visible.

LISTING 16.2 Simple HTML to Demonstrate the Types of Formatting Available

```
<!-- demo-16.2.html -->
<html>
  <head>
    <title>Demonstration of layout formatting</title>
    <style type="text/css">
      body   { font-size: 20pt;            font-weight: bold;
               font-family: Verdana, sans-serif; }
      #outer { border: 3px solid black;   padding: 1em;
               background-color: silver;  margin: 1em; }
      #inner { border: 5px dashed black;  padding: 1em;
               background-color: white;   margin: 1em; }
    </style>
  </head>
  <body>
    <div id="outer">
      <p>This is the outer box.</p>
      <div id="inner">
        <p>Inside, you can find the inner box.</p>
      </div>
      <p>And this is more content within the outer box.</p>
    </div>
  </body>
</html>
```

Without positioning rules, these <div> boxes follow normal flow, as shown in Figure 16.4. This is the same as the static value for position.

FIGURE 16.4

Box demo without any positioning applied.

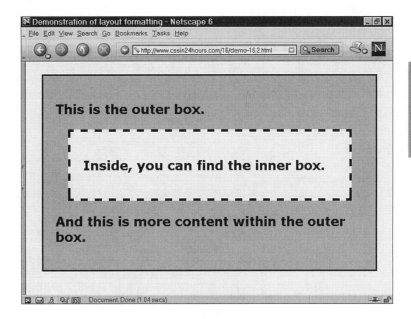

The Context Box

When you set the position property to a value besides static, you are taking the element out of the normal flow of text and locating it relative to another box called the *context box*. The positioned element is placed relative to this context box based on the offset properties top, right, bottom, and left.

The context box is determined by the value of the position property. If the value of position is relative, the context box is the original position of the element. If the position value is absolute, the context box is the display box of the <body> tag. For a value of fixed, the context box is the display window.

Relative Positioning

A box that has been placed according to *relative positioning* has been located according to the position in which that box would normally appear. Unlike absolutely positioned boxes, the space for a relatively positioned box is still allocated, and then the box is moved in relation to that context box.

Listing 16.3 is a style sheet to relatively position the inner box. A complete explanation of the left and top properties (as well as right and bottom) is given later this hour; in short, they define the offset from the upper left corner of the context box.

LISTING 16.3   Relative Positioning Shown via a Style Sheet

```
/* demo-16.4.css */
#inner { position: relative;
         left: 4em;
         top: 4em; }
```

As seen in Figure 16.5, the space that would be taken up in normal flow has still been set aside for the box, although it is now located 4 ems to the right and 4 ems down from where it would normally be.

FIGURE 16.5

Relative positioning is based on the static location of the element.

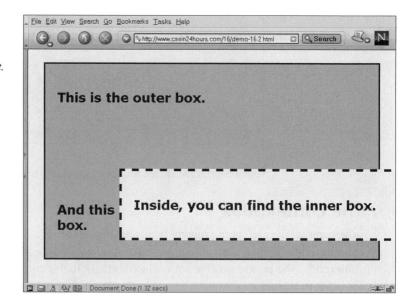

Absolute Positioning

In *absolute positioning,* the display box is placed in relation to the context box, offset by a certain amount. The box is removed from the normal flow, and in fact the space normally taken up by the absolutely positioned box isn't even allocated for it. Instead, it appears somewhere else, possibly even overlaying existing content.

The context box in absolute positioning is initially set to be the box of the <body> tag, and absolutely positioned elements will be placed relative to the rest of the page. However, if an ancestor box of an element is positioned (with absolute, relative, or fixed positioning), that positioned box becomes the new context box for absolute positioning.

To reset the context box easily, just use a relatively positioned box with no specified offset. For example:

```
div#outer { position: relative; }
```

All children of the `<div id="outer">` element will use the box of that `<div>` as their context box for absolute positioning.

Listing 16.4 is a CSS style sheet that sets the inner `<div>` to use absolute positioning and specifies an offset of 4em on the left and top from the outer box, which has been set to `position: relative` to make it the new context box for its children.

LISTING 16.4   A Style Sheet That Demonstrates Absolute Positioning

```
/* demo-16.3.css */
#inner { position: absolute;
         left: 4em;
         top: 4em; }
#outer { position: relative; }
```

So what effect does this style sheet have? Take a look at Figure 16.6, which is the result of applying the style sheet in Listing 16.3 to the HTML file in Listing 16.2. The inner box has been placed so that its upper left corner is 4 ems down and to the right of the upper left corner of the context box.

FIGURE 16.6

Absolute positioning is based on the context box.

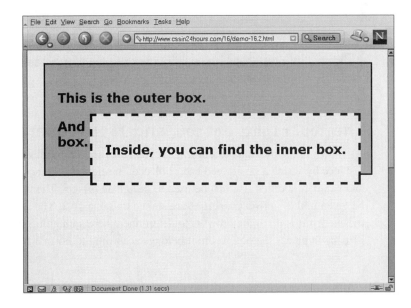

16

Fixed Positioning

In *fixed positioning,* a box placed on the screen doesn't move even if the rest of the page moves; it seems to float on top of the page in a fixed location. This is useful if you want to create a menu bar or graphic that never leaves the page. A box placed according to fixed positioning is located in relation to the whole page, not to its containing block or its original position. Like absolute positioning (and unlike relative positioning), no space is set aside for the box in its normal flow location.

The style sheet in Listing 16.5 uses fixed positioning and also adds a very large bottom margin to the outer box. This is so that the effects of the fixed positioning can be seen by using the scrollbars to move the page.

LISTING 16.5   Style Sheet Using Fixed Positioning to Prevent an Element from Scrolling

```
/* demo-16.5.css */
#inner { position: fixed;
         top: 4em;
         left: 4em; }
#outer { margin-bottom: 25em; }
```

The effects of fixed positioning are shown in Figure 16.7. I recommend testing this yourself at http://www.cssin24hours.com/16/demo-16.5.html to see how it works, using one of the newer browsers that support CSS positioning.

Warning for Netscape 4 and Internet Explorer 4 and 5

Older versions of Netscape and Internet Explorer don't support fixed positioning.

The top, right, bottom, and left Properties

As shown in the previous examples, the top and left properties can be used to set the distance by which a positioned box is placed, in relation to the context box. The bottom and right properties also can be used to designate offsets. The types of values that can be given to these offset properties are shown in Table 16.2. The default is auto, which means that it is up to the browser to determine where something should be placed, which is to say it places the box where it belongs according to normal flow.

FIGURE 16.7

Objects fixed in position don't move when the rest of the page scrolls.

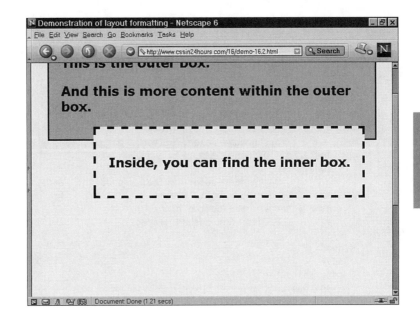

16

TABLE 16.2 Values for the Offset Properties

Value	Effect
measurement	Offset the box by some amount, toward the "inside."
negative-measurement	Offset the box by some amount, toward the "outside."
percentage	Offset the box by a percentage, toward the "inside."
negative-percentage	Offset the box by a percentage, toward the "outside."
auto	Calculate the offset automatically.
inherit	Use the value of the offset property from the containing box.

Because positive values are toward the center point of the context box, some of these off-sets can seem backward in effect from what you'd expect. For example, setting a left value of 4em actually moves the box to the right, a right value of 4em moves the box to the left, and a top value of -4em moves the box up, not down. You will need to remember this when placing boxes.

More examples are helpful to illustrate this in action, so the HTML page in Listing 16.6 contains three boxes that can be positioned on the page with different offset values.

LISTING 16.6   Three Boxes for Positioning

```
<!-- offsets-16.6.html -->
<html>
  <head>
    <title>Offset Values in Positioning</title>
    <style type="text/css">
      body   { font: 20pt bold Verdana, sans-serif; }
      #outer { border: 3px solid black;
               background-color: silver;  margin: 1em; }
      #outer p { padding: 1em; }
      #one, #two, #three
             { background-color: white;   padding: 1em; }
      #one { border: 5px solid black; }
      #two { border: 5px dotted black; }
      #three { border: 5px dashed black; }
    </style>
  </head>
  <body>
    <div id="outer">
      <p>This is the outer box.</p>
      <div id="one">One</div>
      <div id="two">Two</div>
      <div id="three">Three</div>
      <p>And this is more content within the outer box.</p>
    </div>
  </body>
</html>
```

Listing 16.7 is a style sheet that uses relative positioning to move the boxes a specified number of ems from their original positions.

LISTING 16.7   Relative Offsets Set via em Lengths

```
/* offsets-16.7.css */
#one   { position: relative; top: 0px; right: 0px; }
#two   { position: relative; top: 2em; left: 4em; }
#three { position: relative; bottom: 5em; right: 4em; }
```

The effects of applying Listing 16.7 to the HTML page of Listing 16.6 are shown in Figure 16.8. The first box hasn't been moved from where it should be; the second box has been moved down and to the right; and the third box has been moved up and to the left, creating some overlap. Notice that the word "Three" is cut off, as it has been moved off the left side of the screen.

FIGURE 16.8

Boxes placed using relative offsets, shown in Netscape 6.

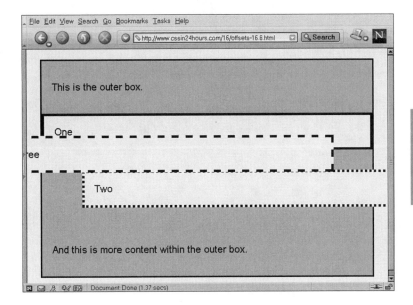

The style sheet in Listing 16.8 differs from that in Listing 16.7 only in using absolute instead of relative positioning. Therefore, the numbered boxes will be placed in relation to the gray outer box that contains them all, and not relative to their original positions in normal flow.

LISTING 16.8   Absolute Offsets Measured in em Lengths

```
/* offsets-16.8.css */
#one    { position: absolute; top: 0px; right: 0px; }
#two    { position: absolute; top: 2em; left: 4em; }
#three { position: absolute; bottom: 0em; right: 4em; }
#outer { position: relative; }
```

The effects of absolute positioning can be seen in Figure 16.9. One thing you will notice here is that the boxes are not as wide as in Figure 16.8. A block box is normally as wide as its containing box, but when that box is removed from the normal flow, it will become as wide (or as narrow) as its content.

Figure **16.9**

*Absolutely positioned
boxes, à la Netscape 6.*

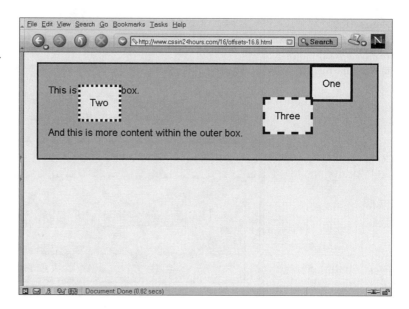

 In Hour 17, "Advanced CSS Layout," you'll learn how to explicitly set the size of display boxes by using the width property.

The examples so far have used ems as units. Percentages can also be used to specify the offset, as in Listing 16.9. These boxes will be absolutely positioned as a fraction of their containing box.

LISTING 16.9   Absolute Offsets as Percentages

```
/* offsets-16.9.css */
#one    { position: absolute; top: 0%; right: 0%; }
#two    { position: absolute; top: 20%; left: 20%; }
#three  { position: absolute; bottom: -10%; right: 30%; }
#outer  { position: relative; }
```

The positioned boxes are shown in Figure 16.10.

FIGURE **16.10**

Percentages used to absolutely place boxes, displayed in Netscape 6.

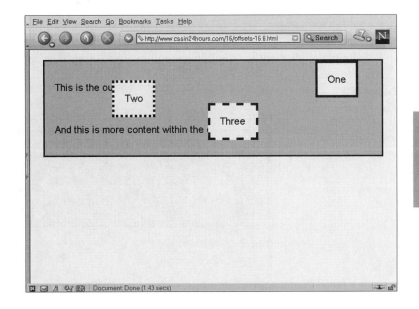

 It's entirely possible to position a box off the visible part of the page. For example, if you use a value of `-1000px` for `left` and `-800px` for `top`, the box will probably be displaced completely off the page. Such a box still "exists" but just won't be seen. This problem is especially likely when using `fixed` positioning and values for `right` or `bottom`, based on how browsers interpret `right` and `bottom` offsets, as described next.

A fixed box doesn't scroll, and is fixed with respect to the whole display. Unfortunately, browsers don't agree on what this means in terms of offset values for `right` and `bottom` properties. Listing 16.10 is an example of those values in a style sheet.

LISTING 16.10   Fixed Positioning and Vertical Offsets

```
/* offsets-16.10.css */
#one   { position: fixed; top: 0%; right: 0%; }
#two   { position: fixed; top: 20%; left: 20%; }
#three { position: fixed; bottom: 2em; right: 2em; }
#outer { margin-bottom: 30em; }
```

Now take a look at Figure 16.11, which applies those styles to the HTML file from Listing 16.6. Where did boxes one and three go? Well, they're offset from the right or bottom somewhere. But because a Web page could (theoretically) scroll infinitely in either direction, they're offset to 0% of infinity, or 2em from the corner of infinity and infinity. In other words, they're fixed out someplace they'll never be seen.

FIGURE **16.11**

Fixed positioning is often fraught with trouble, as in Netscape 6.

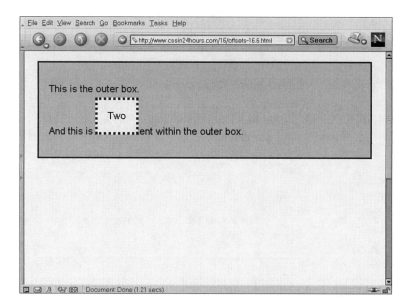

Not all browsers will do it this way; Internet Explorer will position them according to the current width of the viewing window. But because of these irregularities, I recommend using fixed positioning only when setting the top and left properties.

Floating Content

Another way to place content within the page layout is to float it. Floating boxes move to one side or another according to the value of the `float` property, and other content flows around them in a liquid fashion. The `clear` property can be used to indicate when the rest of the content should stop flowing around the floating box.

An example of floating content can be seen in Figure 16.12; the picture is positioned on the left, and the subsequent text content wraps around it on the right side and then flows back out to the full width when the picture ends. (I'll present the HTML and style sheet for this page shortly.)

FIGURE 16.12

Floating content to the left.

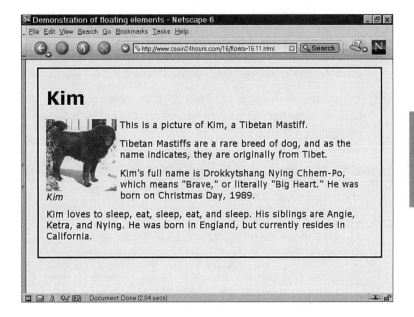

This effect should be familiar to experienced HTML developers who have used the align attribute on <img> or <table> tags to position floating content on either side of the page layout. The clear attribute on the <br> tag has been used to control when the floating should end. The CSS properties float and clear can be used on any HTML elements and therefore greatly extend the types of content that can be set to float or to stop flowing.

Floating content is especially useful for pictures (with or without captions), pull quotes, and sidebar text.

The float Property

The values for the float property are shown in Table 16.3; the default value is none, meaning that the box and subsequent content are laid out according to the normal flow.

TABLE 16.3 Values for the float Property

Value	Effect
left	The box moves to the left, and text flows around the right side.
none	The box doesn't move, and text is not flowed around it.
right	The box moves to the right, and text flows around the left side.
inherit	Use the float value of the containing box.

When a box is floated, it is positioned within its containing box's content section. Unlike absolute positioning, the floating box remains within the margin, border, and padding of the containing box; it simply moves to the right or left side as appropriate. Any subsequent content is placed alongside the floating box for the length of that box.

The source for the page in Figure 16.12 is shown in Listing 16.11. The paragraphs have `id` attributes so that you can refer to them later when setting rules using the `clear` property.

LISTING 16.11   An HTML File with a Picture That Will Be Floated

```html
<!-- floats-16.11.html -->
<html>
  <head>
    <title>Demonstration of floating elements</title>
    <style type="text/css">
      body  { font-family: Verdana, sans-serif; }
      #outer { border: 3px solid black;   padding: 1em;
              background-color: white;   margin: 1em; }
      #inner { font-style: italic; }
    </style>
    <link type="text/css" rel="stylesheet"
          href="floats-16.11.css">
  </head>
  <body>
    <div id="outer">
      <h1>Kim</h1>
      <div id="inner">
        <img src="kim.jpg" alt="[Kim]">
        <br> Kim</div>
      <p id="a">This is a picture of Kim, a Tibetan Mastiff.</p>
      <p id="b">Tibetan Mastiffs are a rare breed of dog, and as
              the name indicates, they are originally from
              Tibet.</p>
      <p id="c">Kim's full name is Drokkytshang Nying Chhem-Po,
              which means "Brave," or literally "Big Heart."
              He was born on Christmas Day, 1989.</p>
      <p id="d">Kim loves to sleep, eat, sleep, eat, and sleep.
              His siblings are Angie, Ketra, and Nying. He
              was born in England, but currently resides in
              California.</p>
    </div>
  </body>
</html>
```

The screenshot in Figure 16.3 was created by adding the following line to the embedded style sheet:

```css
#inner { float: left; }
```

To place the dog's picture on the right side of the text, you can simply change that rule to read float: right instead. This is shown in Figure 16.13.

FIGURE 16.13

Floating the content to the right.

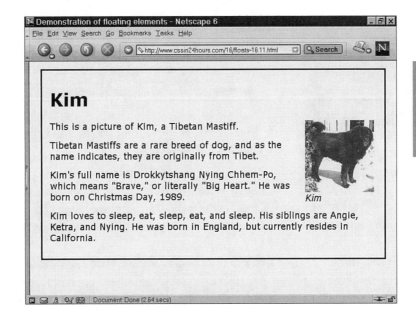

16

>
>
> Other properties can be set on floated elements, of course, and some of the most useful are the margin properties, which can be used to affect how close subsequent content will flow. For example, margin-left on a right-floating element will keep the flowing text at a respectable distance.

The clear Property

To stop subsequent text from flowing around a floating box, you can set the clear property on the first element you don't want to flow. This will move that element down far enough so that it won't be wrapped around the floating box. This effectively increases the top margin of the element with the clear property on it by an amount calculated by the browser to provide enough space to make it past the floating box.

The values for clear are shown in Table 16.4; naturally, the default value is none. Other values specify whether the content should stop the flow around all floating boxes or only boxes on either the left or right side.

TABLE 16.4   Values for the clear Property

Value	Effect
both	Move this box down enough so it doesn't flow around floating boxes.
left	Move this box down enough so it doesn't flow around left-floating boxes.
none	Don't move this box; allow it to flow normally.
right	Move this box down enough so it doesn't flow around right-floating boxes.
inherit	Use the clear value of the containing box.

To use this property with the dog example from Listing 16.11 requires only adding rules such as these to the embedded style sheet:

```
#inner { float: right; }
#b { clear: right; }
```

This floats the dog's head to the right, but causes the second paragraph to start once it has cleared all floating content on the right side as shown in Figure 16.14.

FIGURE 16.14

Clearing the floats at the second paragraph.

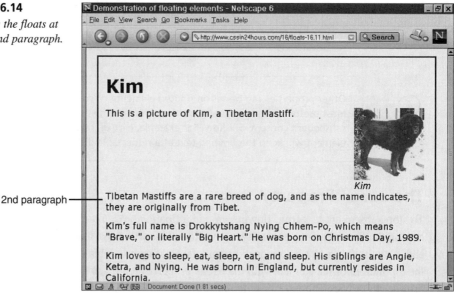

Sometimes, if you float multiple boxes of content, you'll get a staggered effect down the page, where one box is positioned against the lower right corner of another. This is because floated content tries to locate itself as high as possible in addition to moving to the left or right. To avoid this problem, set a `clear` property on your floating content, like this:

```
div#sidebar { float: right; clear: right; }
```

Laying Out the Page

To bring this hour to a close, you'll look at how you created the layout from the start of this hour, as shown in Figure 16.2. The specific layout effects you will use are the following:

- Combine absolute and relative positioning to make an overlapping headline.
- Move the navigation bar from the bottom of the page to the top using absolute positioning.
- Float the founder's picture on the left and `pullquote` on the right, using the `float` property. So that `pullquote` doesn't scrunch up your `<h2>`, you'll insert a `clear` on headlines.
- Place the site menu on the rest of the `kynn.com` site by using fixed positioning, so that it is always on screen even if the page scrolls.

Why did I put the navigation bar at the end of the page, anyway? You'd think it would make more sense to place it at the beginning of the HTML, rather than using CSS to move it. Well, if you put it at the start, sight-impaired readers with screenreaders will have to sit through the navigation menu before hitting the content of the site because it comes first in the source code. That's not so bad, until you consider that on the average Web site, a screenreader user needs to listen through the navigation bars multiple times for each new link she follows to a new page. That can be a real chore, and so if possible, it's best to put the navigation menu last on the page, rather than first. Using positioning CSS you can do both—put it last in order in the source but up front for visual users. This is a simple example of how CSS can be used to meet the requirements of users with special needs while still preserving the graphic design for users with more typical needs.

You should know how to create all of the effects necessary from what you learned this hour. If you want to test yourself, skip this next listing and come back to it in the activity. The style sheet I used to create the layout in Figure 16.2 is shown in Listing 16.12.

LISTING 16.12   The Style Sheet for the Layout Shown in Figure 16.2

```
/* bookstore-16.12.css */

body
   { font-family: Arial, sans-serif;
     margin: 0px;                    padding: 0px;
     background-color: green; }
h1, h2, h3
   { clear: both;
     font-family: Verdana, sans-serif; }
#structure
   { margin-left: 10em;
     background-color: white;        color: black; }

#headline /* These create the overlapping headline effect */
   { padding: 1em;                   margin-bottom: 1em; }
#headline .name
   { position: absolute;             left: 1.75em; top: 0em;
     font-size: 3em;                 color: red; }
#headline .store
   { position: relative;             left: 1em; top: 0.5em;
     text-transform: lowercase;      font-size: 2em;
     color: blue; }

#main { padding: 3em 1em 1em 1em; }

#founder /* A floating image and caption */
   { margin: 0em 1em;                float: left;
     font-style: italic; }

.pullquote /* A floating pullquote on the right */
   { float: right;
     margin: 0.25em;                 padding: 0.25em;
     font-size: large;               font-style: italic;
     border: 5px solid black; }

#mainmenu /* Moves the main menu up near the top */
   { position: absolute;             top: 9em; left: 11em; }

/* These styles are based on the (current) kynn.com style
   sheet at http://kynn.com/styles/k.css */
#sitemenu
   { position: fixed;                left: 1.5em; top: 1.5em;
     background-color: #CCA580;       border: 2px solid white;
     font-family: Garamond, Georgia, serif;
     margin: 0.5em;                  padding: 0.25em; }
#sitemenu a:link
   { color: #000066;                 text-decoration: none;
     font-weight: bold; }
```

LISTING 16.12   Continued

```
#sitemenu a:visited
   { color: #006600;                    text-decoration: none;
     font-weight: bold; }
#sitemenu a:hover { color: white; }
```

16

Summary

Layout is essential for the creation of any effective Web design. CSS layout properties can replace misused HTML <table> tags, allowing for better separation of presentation from content while preserving visually attractive designs.

Display boxes can be moved from their original positions in the normal flow of layout by using the position property. The position property selects among four different types of positioning schemes. Static positioning is the normal way in which HTML elements are placed. Relative positioning shifts a display box relative to its normal position by a given amount. Absolute positioning places the HTML element in a new location within or relative to its containing box. Fixed positioning locates the display box on a set position on the screen, even if the page scrolls.

Placement of boxes in the context of their positioning schemes is determined by the values of the offset properties: left, right, top, and bottom. These can be measurements or percentages, with a positive value moving in the direction of the center of the context box, and a negative value moving away from it. Care needs to be taken when placing boxes so that content isn't obscured or moved off the visible part of the page entirely.

The normal flow of layout also can be affected by the float property, which positions a display box on either the right or left side of its containing box's content area. Subsequent text then flows around the floating box, wrapping around the outer margin. The clear property can be used to move content down the page until it is no longer flowing.

Browser Support Report Card

CSS Feature	Grade	Notes
Relative positioning	B+	Unreliable in Netscape 4
Absolute positioning	B+	Unreliable in Netscape 4
Fixed positioning	B-	Unreliable in Netscape 4, unsupported in Internet Explorer (Windows)
Offsets based on bottom or right	F	Can result in lost content in some browsers
Floating content	B+	Unreliable in Netscape 4
The clear property	B+	Unreliable in Netscape 4

Because of poor Netscape 4 support for layout properties, a workaround is suggested, as noted earlier in this hour. This workaround uses @import to exempt Netscape 4 from displaying CSS layouts; without the use of such a workaround, CSS layout properties would rate a D at most, due to poor Netscape 4 support.

Q&A

Q **How can I get better control over the height and width of my display boxes, like I can with HTML tables?**

Q **I also use frames for page layout. Can CSS replicate the functionality of HTML frames?**

Q **In your example, one part of the "Kynn's Bookstore" headline overlays another. Are there any properties to layer one tag over another?**

A Hour 17 covers a number of additional properties that can be used to get even more control over the layout and appearance of a page.

Workshop

The workshop contains quiz questions and activities to help reinforce what you've learned in this hour. If you get stuck, the answers to the quiz can be found after the questions.

Quiz

1. Which of the following best describes relative positioning?

    (a.) Subsequent text is flowed around the positioned box, relative to the box's new left or right location.

    (b.) The box is held in location relative to where it is located, even if the page is scrolled.

    (c.) Relative to the box's original location, the box is offset by a certain distance.

    (d.) The box is placed relative to its containing box.

2. Which of these offset declarations will move a display box 20 pixels to the right?

    (a.) `right: 20px;`

    (b.) `left: 20px;`

    (c.) `left: -20px;`

    (d.) `right: -20px;`

3. Part of your Web page consists of an image followed by text; the next section begins with an <h3> tag. You want the image to be located on the left and the text to flow around it, but you don't want the next section's header to be placed next to the image. What CSS rules would you write to do this?

Answers

1. Choice (c.) is a description of relative positioning, (a.) describes floating content, (b.) describes fixed positioning, and (d.) defines absolute placement.

2. Both (b.) and (d.) shift a box to the right. Remember that positive offsets are toward the middle of the box, and negative offsets are away from it.

3. Here's an example of the type of rules you would write; in practice you'd probably use class or id selectors to make these more specific:

```
img { float: left; }
h3 { clear: left; }
```

Activities

As with other CSS properties and concepts, hands-on experience is invaluable for working out the nuances of CSS-based layout. Especially remember to test in various browsers to see how they choose to interpret the CSS specifications. Here are some ideas for projects:

- If you haven't looked at Listing 16.12 yet, try to construct your own version of a style sheet that will transform Listing 16.1 into the layout shown in Figure 16.2. You can check your work by looking at my style sheet in Listing 16.12; you may even be able to improve on what I've done!

- Create your own style sheet for the bookstore (and change the founder's name to your own if you wish!). Can you make a completely different layout using the same HTML source code?

- Take a page you've worked on before that uses <table> to lay out the page, and try to recreate it using <div> and CSS. You will probably run into problems because the properties in this hour aren't enough to fully encompass the functionality of layout tables. Keep track of what difficulties you encounter and then go on to Hour 17 to learn how to gain even more control over the appearance of your page.

HOUR 17

Advanced CSS Layout

Last hour, you learned about basic layout using CSS properties to position content on the page. The position property, the offset properties, the float property, and the clear property can all produce effective layouts, but they don't come close to matching the layout capabilities that Web developers expect.

In this hour, you'll learn

- How browsers calculate the width and height dimensions of a display box
- Which properties can control the dimensions of a box
- What browsers will do if a box's content exceeds the dimensions of the box
- How to layer content upon other content and control the stacked order
- How to replace an HTML layout <table> with CSS rules

Sizing Content

When laying out a page, it's not always enough to specify only where content should be placed, as you can do with the position property and the offset properties. To create effective layouts, you need the capability of setting the size of display boxes. In HTML, this is done with the height and width attributes; unsurprisingly, those are the names of the CSS properties that control a content box's dimensions.

To illustrate the necessity of the width and height attributes, I've created a sample HTML page that we'll use for most of this hour. You can see this in Listing 17.1, or you can download it from http://www.cssin24hours.com/17/sizes-17.1.html.

LISTING 17.1   This HTML Page Has Unsized Boxes

```
<!-- sizes-17.1.html -->
<html>
  <head>
    <title>Size Matters</title>
    <style type="text/css">
      body { font-family: Verdana, sans-serif; }
      #banner { position: relative; }
      #menu { position: absolute; left: 0px; top: 0px;
              border: 1px dotted black; }
      #menu a.toc { display: block; text-align: center; }
      #headline { border: 2px dashed black;
                  position: absolute; right: 0px; top: 0px; }
      #maincontent { position: relative; }
      #text1, #text2 { border: 2px dotted gray; }
      #text1 { position: absolute; top: 0px; left: 10%; }
      #text2 { position: absolute; top: 0px; left: 55%; }
    </style>
  </head>
  <body>
    <div id="banner">
      <div id="menu">
        <a class="toc" href="int.html">International News</a>
        <a class="toc" href="nat.html">National News</a>
        <a class="toc" href="loc.html">Local News</a>
        <a class="toc" href="wea.html">Weather</a>
      </div>
      <h1 id="headline">Idyll Mountain News</h1>
    </div>
    <div id="maincontent">
      <div id="text1">
        <h2>Welcome Laura Bishop</h2>
        <p>
          Idyll Mountain Internet is pleased to introduce
          our newest employee, Laura Bishop, who is actually
          not new to IMI at all! Laura worked part-time for
          Idyll Mountain in 1996. She rejoined us in April
          2002 as a Site Maintenance Specialist,
          supporting our Web clients.
        </p>
      </div>
      <div id="text2">
        <h2>Kynn's Book Now Available!</h2>
        <p>
```

LISTING 17.1   Continued

```
    <cite>SAMS Teach Yourself Cascading Style Sheets
    in 24 Hours</cite>, written by IMI's co-founder and
    Chief Technologist, Kynn Bartlett, was published
    recently and is available at finer bookstores
    everywhere. Add CSS skills to your repertoire;
    pick up a copy today!
  </p>
  </div>
  </div>
 </body>
</html>
```

The intent of the embedded style sheet within Listing 17.1 is to create a very simple "newspaper" layout, with a list of links in the upper left corner, a headline in the upper right, and two columns of textual information. To help you keep track of the display boxes involved, I've added some borders.

When a browser displays this page, it determines the layout based on the space available. Because the two context boxes, id="banner" and id="maincontent", are set with position: relative, their descendants will be located in relation to those context boxes. Unfortunately, once you remove the absolutely positioned descendants, each of these boxes has no height, which means that they will overlap horribly. You can see this in Figure 17.1—an obvious failure to create an effective layout.

FIGURE 17.1

The browser tries to determine the size and placement of each box and doesn't do very well.

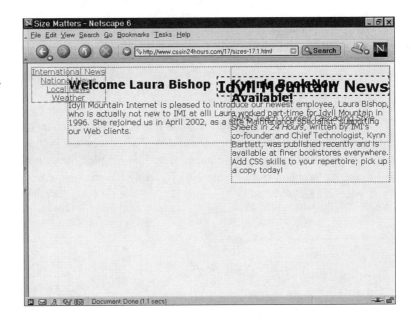

The `width` and `height` Properties

To correct the problem displayed so clearly in Figure 17.1, we'll need to use the `width` and `height` properties. Hour 15, "Styling Tables," briefly introduced `width`, and in this hour you'll learn to use it with all block content, as well as with its fraternal twin, `height`.

A CSS display box actually has two widths, the content width and the box width. The *content width* is, as you might imagine, the width of the box's content area; it is the area where the box's content exists, within the padding, the border, and the margin. The *box width* is the width of the entire box, including the left and right padding, the left and right border, and the left and right margin, as well as the content width. You can see this visually displayed in Figure 17.2.

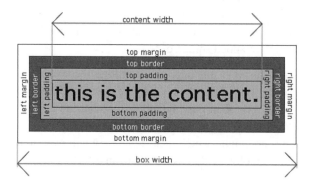

The content height and box height are likewise determined in this manner. The CSS properties `width` and `height` are used to control the size of the content width. The box width and box height can't be directly set; instead, you can control the box width and height by setting appropriate padding, border, and margin values that add to the content width and height.

Values for `width` and `height` can be measurements, such as `3em` or `5px`. They can also be percentage values, such as `20%`. The percentage is based on the height or width of the parent box's content area. Listing 17.2 shows a style sheet that fixes the overlap problem from Figure 17.1 by using `height` and `width` properties to help lay out the page.

LISTING 17.2 Setting `height` and `width` Values via CSS

```
/* sizes-17.2.css */
#banner { height: 5.5em; }
#menu { width: 40%; }
#headline { width: 55%;
            margin-left: 45%; margin-top: 0px; }
#text1, #text2 {width: 30%; padding: 5%;}
```

This sets a height on the #banner box, which means that it won't overlap with the columns of text. The #maincontent box has no height set, but that's okay because it's the last thing on the page. If we had another element, such as a copyright notice, following the #maincontent box, we'd want also to set a height for #maincontent.

In Figure 17.3, you can see the result of applying this style sheet to the HTML page of Listing 17.1.

FIGURE 17.3

Boxes set to specific heights and widths, as shown by Netscape 6.

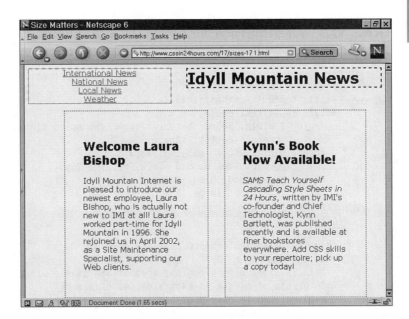

The Internet Explorer `width` Bug

Unfortunately, previous versions of Internet Explorer for both Windows and Macintosh have a bug that miscalculates content width. Internet Explorer doesn't consider the content width to be just the width of the content area of a box; instead, it includes the padding and the border width, as well. This is shown in Figure 17.4.

FIGURE **17.4**

*How Internet Explorer
calculates widths.*

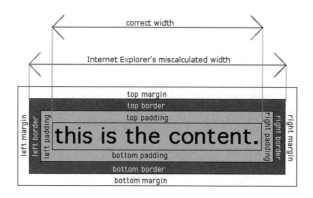

Internet Explorer's nonstandard interpretation of the width tag can produce problems in your layout. An example of this is given in Listing 17.3; this is a simple HTML page that displays a box according to the embedded style sheet.

LISTING 17.3   An HTML Page Illustrating the IE Width Bug

```
<!-- bug-17.3.html -->
<html>
  <head>
    <title>Content Widths</title>
    <style type="text/css">
      #ruler { width: 500px; border-bottom: 2px solid black;
               margin-bottom: 10px; }
      #one { width: 350px; padding: 40px;
             border: 10px dashed black; margin: 25px;
             background-color: silver;
             font-size: large; }
    </style>
  </head>
  <body>
    <div id="ruler">Ruler (500 pixels wide)</div>
    <div id="one">
      This is a box with a content area of 350 pixels wide, with
      25 pixels of margin on each side, 40 pixels of
      padding, and 10 pixels of border. The box width
      of this element is 500 pixels.
    </div>
  </body>
</html>
```

To calculate the size of the box width, you simply add the content width (350) to the margins (25 twice), borders (10 twice), and padding (40 twice). 350 + 25 + 25 + 10 + 10 + 40 + 40 = 500 pixels. Netscape 6 displays this correctly in Figure 17.5.

FIGURE **17.5**

Netscape 6 shows this box according to the specification.

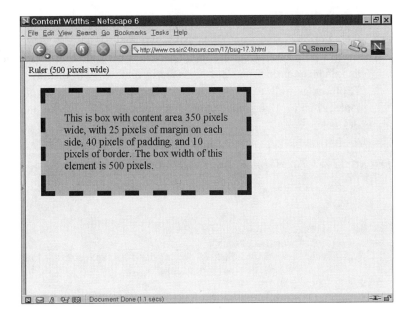

Internet Explorer incorrectly displays this box because it assumes the 350-pixel figure for width consists of the content width, padding, and borders. So the actual width of the content, as shown by Internet Explorer, is 350 minus the borders (10 twice) and padding (40 twice), or 250 pixels. The box width is 350 pixels plus the margins (25 twice), or 400 pixels. You can see this miscalculation illustrated in Figure 17.6; the box is much narrower than that shown in Figure 17.5, as the 500-pixel ruler shows.

FIGURE **17.6**

Internet Explorer displays this box at the wrong width.

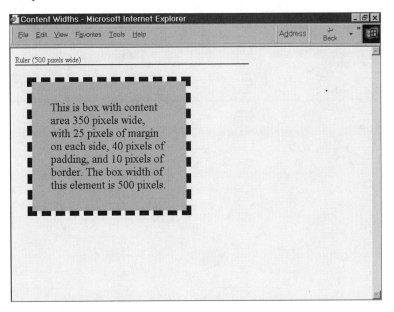

17

Fortunately, there is a workaround for this bug. The trick is to create two `<div>` elements instead of just one, thus using two boxes. The first `<div>` box has `width` and `margin` properties set on it. The second box is located inside the first and has `border` and `padding` properties. Boxes nested in this way will display properly in Internet Explorer, as well as in properly compliant browsers, such as Netscape 6, Mozilla, and Opera. Listing 17.4 is an example of how to use this workaround to fix our previous example.

LISTING 17.4 An HTML Page Illustrating How to Work Around the IE Bug

```
<!-- bug-17.4.html -->
<html>
  <head>
    <title>Content Widths</title>
    <style type="text/css">
      #ruler { width: 500px; border-bottom: 2px solid black;
               margin-bottom: 10px; }
      #one { width: 450px; margin: 25px;
             background-color: silver;
             font-size: large; }
      #two { padding: 40px; border: 10px dashed black; }
    </style>
  </head>
  <body>
    <div id="ruler">Ruler (500 pixels wide)</div>
    <div id="one">
      <div id="two">
        This is box a with a content area 350 pixels wide, with
        25 pixels of margin on each side, 40 pixels of
        padding, and 10 pixels of border. The box width
        of this element is 500 pixels.
      </div>
    </div>
  </body>
</html>
```

The boxes are displayed properly when viewed by Internet Explorer, as seen in Figure 17.7.

FIGURE 17.7

The workaround has solved the problem in Internet Explorer.

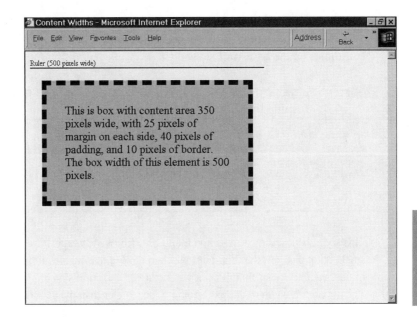

17

 This bug was fixed in Internet Explorer 6 for Windows; however, to get correct `width` calculations, you need to use a correct `DOCTYPE` statement at the beginning of your document. If you don't use a `DOCTYPE` statement, IE 6 will display the page using a backward-compatible method identical to IE 5, which means the buggy version. For more on `DOCTYPE` switching, see `http://msdn.microsoft.com/library/default.asp?url=/library/en-us/dnie60/html/cssenhancements.asp`. Keep in mind that many Internet Explorer users are not using IE 6, so the type of workaround described in this hour may still be necessary on your site, even if you use the correct `DOCTYPE`.

Minimum and Maximum Dimensions

Sometimes you might not want to set specific sizes for dimensions; instead, you might want more flexible designs that allow something to range in size between two values. For example, you might want a navigation bar to be as wide as 20% of the screen most of the time, but if the browser's window is only 500 pixels across, this may be too small to display your navigation links. A minimum size of 10em would therefore be a constraint placed on the width.

A *constraint* is a value beyond which a box isn't allowed to grow or shrink; if the size is smaller than the minimum constraint, the size will be that minimum, and if it's larger than the maximum constraint, the size will be that maximum value.

The constraints for width are set using the min-width and max-width properties; for height, the values are min-height and max-height. Listing 17.5 is a style sheet that sets constraints on the boxes in Listing 17.1.

LISTING 17.5 A Style Sheet to Constrain the Maximum and Minimum Sizes of Display Boxes

```
/* sizes-17.5.css */
#banner { height: 5.5em; }
#menu { min-width: 200px; width: 5%; }
#headline { width: 55%; min-height: 60px;
            margin-left: 45%; margin-top: 0px; }
#text1, #text2 {width: 30%; max-width: 125px; }
```

This style sheet sets the navigation menu a width of 5%, which would normally be much too small, but it also sets the minimum width to a more reasonable number. The minimum height of the headline means that the box will be larger, but there's no extra text to fill up the space. The maximum width of 125px is going to be smaller than the 30% width in nearly every case, so the text columns will look narrow. You can see all of these styles in action in Figure 17.8.

FIGURE 17.8

Minimum and maximum dimensions are shown in Netscape 6.

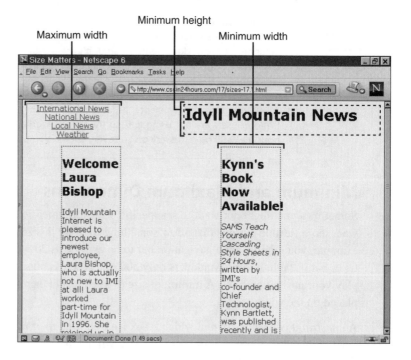

Content Overflow

If a display box's height hasn't been set by using the `height` property, the height will automatically be calculated to take up enough room for all the content. But what happens if a `height` property has been set that doesn't allow enough space for all the content? This creates a situation called *overflow*. Listing 17.6 is a style sheet specifically designed to create overflow.

LISTING 17.6   A Style Sheet Where the Size of the Content Exceeds the Height

```
/* sizes-17.6.css */
#banner { height: 5.5em; }
#menu { min-width: 15em; width: 10%; }
#headline { width: auto;
            margin-left: auto; margin-top: 0px; }
#text1, #text2 {width: 35%; height: 12em; }
```

As seen in Figure 17.9, the content of the columns simply spills out the bottom of the box because there's not enough room. This is the default behavior for overflow, but you can change it by using the `overflow` property.

FIGURE 17.9

Sometimes content just won't fit inside a box, and it overflows.

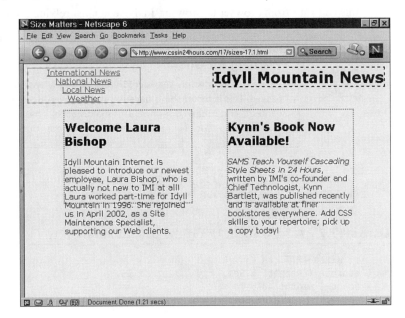

17

The `overflow` Property

To change what happens when a box's content overflows, you can set the `overflow` property to one of the values shown in Table 17.1. The default value is `visible`, which has the effect shown in Figure 17.9.

TABLE 17.1   Values for the `overflow` Property

Value	Effect
auto	The browser determines what to do with overflowing content, choosing either `scroll` or `visible`.
hidden	Overflowing content is clipped and not displayed.
scroll	A scrollable box is used to provide access to all content.
visible	The overflowing content spills out of the box.
inherit	Use the value of `overflow` set on the containing box.

The `scroll` value provides scrollbars at the edges of the display box that let the user access all the content. The `hidden` value prevents that content from being displayed, so it should be used with care. A value of `auto` leaves the decision up to the browser; because this can vary from browser to browser, I advise against relying on it.

Warning for Opera

Opera doesn't display the `scroll` value correctly; instead it shows it as `hidden`. This is a bad thing because `scroll` gives access to overflowing content, and `hidden` does not. This makes `scroll` much less reliable; if you use that value for `overflow`, Opera users will miss out on information.

Two examples of the `overflow` property are shown in Listing 17.7, a style sheet that sets one column to `scroll`, and the other to `hidden`.

LISTING 17.7   A Style Sheet Using the `overflow` Property

```
/* sizes-17.7.css */
#banner { height: 5.5em; }
#menu { width: 40%; }
#headline { width: 55%;
            margin-left: 45%; margin-top: 0px; }
#text1, #text2 { width: 35%; height: 12em; }
#text1 { overflow: scroll; }
#text2 { overflow: hidden; }
```

As you can see in Figure 17.10, scrollbars allow access to the content in the left column. Only the content that fits in the box is shown in the right column. This is known as *clipping*, a term that refers to cutting away all the extra content that won't fit.

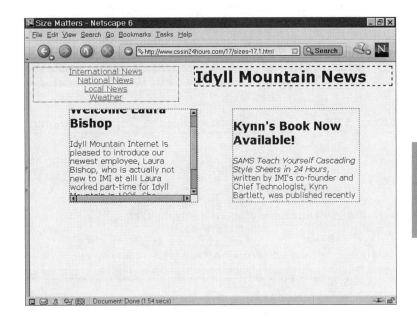

The clip Property

Normally, only content that extends outside the display box is clipped. However, the clip property allows you to define a *clipping area*, outside of which the content will be clipped. The types of values that can be set for the clip property are shown in Table 17.2. The clip property is used only if the box's overflow value is not visible.

TABLE 17.2 Values for the clip Property

Value	Effect
auto	The clipping area is defined by the box's edges.
rect(top, right, bottom, left)	The clipping area is a rectangle defined by four measurements.
inherit	Use the value of clip set on the containing box.

When using the rect() function to define a clipping area, you're defining a sub-box relative to the display box. The values *top*, *right*, *bottom*, and *left* are measurements that define where each edge begins, relative to the upper left corner of the box.

The easiest way to think of these values is to consider them a pair of points, the first in the upper right corner and the second in the lower left, which define the clipping area.

For example, if you have a 300px by 300px box, and you want a clipping area that is 100px tall and 100px wide in the upper middle of the box, you'd set the upper right corner at 0px, 200px and the lower left corner at 100px, 100px. Therefore, you'd write the rect() function as those two coordinates, as follows:

```
#box { overflow: hidden;
        clip: rect(0px, 200px, 100px, 100px);
```

In Listing 17.8, I added a background color to the clipped areas because the clipping effect will cut out the borders; the background color lets you see where the clipped content ends.

LISTING 17.8   A Style Sheet That Clips the Displayed Columns

```
/* sizes-17.8.css */
#banner { height: 5.5em; }
#menu { width: 40%; }
#headline { width: 55%;
            margin-left: 45%; margin-top: 0px; }
#text1, #text2 { width: 35%; height: 12em;
                  overflow: hidden;
                  background-color: silver; }
#text1 { clip: rect(0px, 200px, 150px, 15px); }
#text2 { clip: rect(35px, 150px, 175px, 30px); }
```

As you can see in Figure 17.11, the display box itself doesn't move, but only the content within the clipping area is displayed.

FIGURE 17.11

Clipped content, displayed in Netscape 6.

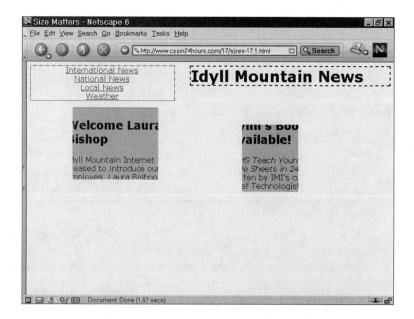

Warning for Opera

Neither the Windows nor the Macintosh version of Opera supports the `clip` property. In most cases this won't cause information to be lost, due to the way `clip` works to hide content. If `clip` fails, the information will still be accessible.

Layered Content

As you saw in the bookstore example from Hour 16, "Page Layout in CSS," positioned elements can be placed on top of each other. Transparent areas of each element—such as the background, unless it's been set to a color or an image—let the "lower" image show through.

Each of the overlapping display boxes can be thought of as existing in a third dimension, as if it were printed on a piece of clear plastic. This is commonly referred to as a *layer*.

Netscape 4 also uses the term *layer* to refer to the nonstandard `<layer>` tag. The `<layer>` tag should be avoided because it is not part of the HTML specification and is not widely supported by browsers. In this book, *layer* refers to creating distinct, overlapping boxes using CSS and does not refer to the `<layer>` tag.

In Listing 17.9, you can see an example of overlapping layers that create a splash page about a dog. The intent is to have the name appear behind the picture and to have a small caption appear over it.

LISTING 17.9 Content to Be Displayed in Overlapping Layers

```
<!-- layers-17.9.html -->
<html>
  <head>
    <title>Layers in CSS</title>
    <style type="text/css">
      #name { position: absolute; top: 0px; left: 75px;
              font-size: 300px; font-family: Verdana, sans-serif;
              color: black; }
```

continues

LISTING 17.9   Continued

```
        #name2 { position: absolute; top: 15px; left: 85px;
                 font-size: 300px; font-family: Verdana, sans-serif;
                 color: gray; }
        #kimpic { position: absolute; top: 145px; left: 250px;
                  border: 5px outset black; }
        #text1 { position: absolute; top: 240px; left: 200px;
                 font-family: Verdana, sans-serif; font-size: large;
                 background-color: white; border: 3px solid black;
                 text-align: center; width: 250px; }
    </style>
  <link type="text/css" rel="stylesheet"
        href="layers-17.10.css">
  </head>
  <body>
    <div id="name">Kim</div>
    <div id="name2">Kim</div>
    <div id="text1">This is my dog Kim. He is a Tibetan Mastiff.</div>
    <img src="kim.jpg" alt="Kim" id="kimpic">
  </body>
</html>
```

In this listing, the dog's name appears twice, in the #name and #name2 elements. Why? Because the positioning CSS locates the second name offset from the first by a small amount, producing a drop-shadow effect. As you may remember from Hour 9, "Text Colors and Effects," current browsers do not support the text-shadow property. The drawback of the approach in Listing 17.9 is that the shadowed text appears twice in the markup, which means it will be displayed twice by browsers that don't support CSS.

In Figure 17.12, you can see the layered effect, as each display box is placed over another. However, there's a problem! The boxes are not in a sensible order. The dog's picture blocks the caption, and the shadow effect is backward.

FIGURE 17.12

*One box is laid over
another, as seen in
Netscape 6.*

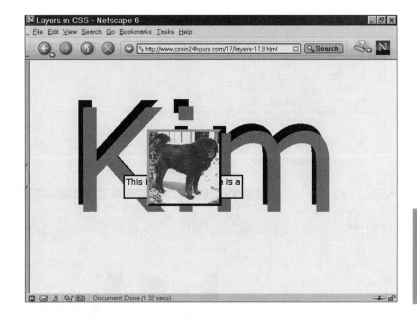

The z-index Property

Each layer is placed in the order it appears in the HTML source code, with subsequent
layers placed on top of earlier ones. This order can be changed using the z-index property. Values for z-index are numbers that indicate the layering order. A lower number
goes on the bottom, and a higher number goes on the top.

> The property name z-index comes from basic geometry. Horizontal
> placement is said to be along the x-axis, vertical along the y-axis, and
> third-dimensional placement—out of the page or the screen—is along
> the z-axis.

The style sheet in Listing 17.10 reassigns the layering order by using the z-index property.
As you can see, you can skip numbers, so you don't have to assign them sequentially; all
of the layers will be considered and then sorted so the highest are on top, even if there are
gaps in the sequence.

LISTING 17.10　Style Sheet to Change the Order of Layering

```
/* layers-17.10.css */
#name   { z-index: 2; }
#name2  { z-index: 1; }
#kimpic { z-index: 10; }
#text1  { z-index: 15; }
```

Applying this style sheet to the HTML page in Listing 17.9 results in the layering order shown in Figure 17.13.

FIGURE 17.13

The layers are now in the desired order.

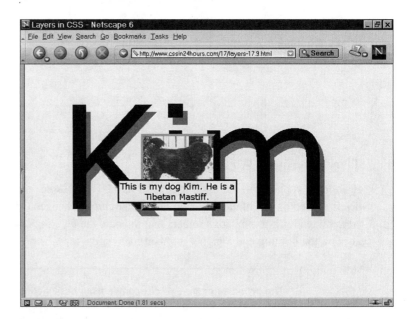

Replacing HTML Layout Tables with CSS Rules

One of the ultimate goals many people have in learning CSS is to fully separate content from presentation, and that includes the layout presentation. Positioning CSS, floating and flowing content, layers, and content sizing can all be used in combination to remove <table> markup from your HTML pages.

Why replace your tables with CSS? That's a good question and one that warrants a serious answer. Tables for layout were originally a hack themselves, a workaround for the fact that HTML provided no actual page-layout capabilities. Graphical layout is a good thing, you see, because a well-done design can aid usability and comprehension. It's a failing of early HTML that this capability wasn't included in the language, and thus it's unfair to blame Web developers for finding a clever way of getting that capability by abusing <table> tags in ways they weren't meant to be used.

From a dogmatic standpoint, CSS layout is pure. From a practical point of view, CSS layout accomplishes separation of presentation from content, a goal that enhances accessibility, but it also can be irregularly supported by browsers, especially Netscape 4.

In the near future, CSS properties will likely be used exclusively for layout, and tables will be used exclusively for columns of data. Right now it's not as cut-and-dried; there's "the correct way," and then there's "the way that works." I recommend using CSS for layout, but only cautiously and only after lots of testing. My own personal site doesn't use CSS layout, although this book's site does, at http://CSSin24hours.com/. My personal site is in good company, though; the W3C's homepage (http://w3.org/) also uses tables for layout!

17

To update an existing page from tables to CSS, you'll first need to do some thinking and planning. What I've provided here is a short list to help you through the process of converting from table layout to CSS. This is a valuable exercise, and I highly recommend you give it a try.

1. First, you'll need to remove your entire table markup from your HTML page and replace each table cell with <div> elements.

2. Don't assume, however, that all <tr> tags will equate to a <div> element, as well. Positioning CSS allows you to place your content wherever you like.

3. Before you start positioning your content, take a look at the order of the information in the source code. The source code order is the same order in which the content will be presented to a screenreader used by a blind user. In Hour 16, I placed the navigation bars at the end of my source code and used CSS to move them to the top of the layout.

4. Draw a grid on paper, and start placing your content where you want it to be. Columns won't automatically be built for you; you will need to give each one a width and a position using absolute positioning. You will probably want to create a <div> for each of your columns.

5. Be consistent about what you are using for measurements. I recommend using percentages or ems, but you may be able to use pixels in some designs, especially if you use those values on maximum and minimum constraints.

6. To create the equivalent of table `rowspan` or `colspan` cells, you simply need to change the `height` or `width` properties appropriately. There is no concept of spanning in CSS layout, just of position and size.

7. To convert the `align` and `valign` table attributes, just use the `text-align` and `vertical-align` properties covered in earlier hours of this book.

8. You might find yourself deviating from your table layout when converting it to CSS. That's fine, and in fact it's perfectly natural; there are many capabilities available only in CSS, such as trimming or scrolling boxes, that you can't do with HTML no matter how hard you try. Feel free to take advantage of these new CSS abilities; it's your Web site, after all!

9. Test, test, and test again. You can never test too much when designing in CSS, and when doing layout, it's even more important. What's more, get some friends to help test, too. The more eyeballs the better, especially if they have diversity in their operating systems and browsers.

 If you'd like to read a good case study of converting to a CSS layout, including how to overcome a number of CSS bugs, check out the account of duplicating the Web Reference layout in CSS at `http://www.webreference.com/authoring/style/sheets/layout/advanced/`.

Summary

The CSS language provides a number of properties for fine-tuning your layout, giving functionality that actually exceeds that of HTML layout tables, such as scrollable display boxes.

These properties include the `width` and `height` properties for setting a box's dimensions, as well as the `min-width`, `min-height`, `max-width`, and `max-height` properties that constrain a box's dimensions.

Content that naturally exceeds the dimensions of its display box is said to have overflowed. The `overflow` and `clip` properties can be used to determine whether the excess content is shown, clipped, or shown with a scrollbar.

In addition to existing in two dimensions, CSS boxes occupy a third dimension, as well, that determines which boxes are layered on top of other boxes if the content overlaps. The order of layering can be set with the `z-index` property.

Browser Support Report Card

CSS Feature	Grade	Notes
The `width` property	B	Workaround required for Internet Explorer
The `height` property	B	Workaround required for Internet Explorer
Minimum and maximum box dimensions	C	Not supported by Internet Explorer or Netscape 4
`overflow: scroll`	D	Not supported by Opera
`overflow: hidden`	A	
`overflow: auto`	C	Variable results in different browsers
The `clip` property	C	Not supported by Opera
The `z-index` property	A	

17

Q&A

Q I like the idea of text in columns, as shown in the newspaper-style layout. But how do I know when a column ends and thus when to start a new `<div>`? I'd rather have CSS automatically create columns. Is that possible?

A Unfortunately it's not possible in the Level 2 version of CSS, as supported by current browsers. Future CSS specifications will probably include this ability, but for now you have to decide on column breaks by hand. In other words, you just choose where you think the text should end. For more on column layout in CSS, see Eric Costello's excellent Web site at `http://www.glish.com/css/`.

Q My `clip` rule isn't working right, and I am following the CSS spec exactly! The clipped element doesn't appear at all. What's wrong?

A The problem here is an unclear specification. You might assume that the dimensions for `rect()` are like those of `relative` offsets—that each one specifies how to adjust the sides, with positive changes being toward the middle of the box. This is a natural assumption when you're working with positioning CSS, but it's not the case at all. Instead, a `rect()` defines a rectangle within the content box. As explained in this hour, it's easiest to think of the `rect()` values as a pair of coordinates for the upper right and lower left corners.

Q **You told me how to replace `<table>` markup with CSS. What about frames? Can those be replaced by CSS, too?**

A Yes and no. Some aspects of frames can be duplicated by using `position: fixed` display boxes or `overflow: scroll` display boxes. Respectively, these provide scrollbars and allow content to remain on the screen. However, neither allows content to be reloaded only in a single window; if you follow a link, you need to reload a new HTML page containing the fixed and scrollable content. Using frames, you could load just the changed information. So CSS can't be used to exactly duplicate frames, although it provides some of the functionality.

Workshop

The workshop contains quiz questions and activities to help reinforce what you've learned in this hour. If you get stuck, the answers to the quiz can be found after the questions.

Quiz

1. The browser's display window is 500 pixels wide. How wide will an `<h1>` be, assuming it's the first element of the `<body>` and applying the following CSS rule?

   ```
   h1 { width: 20%; min-width: 125px;
   max-width: 200px; }
   ```

2. The three `<div>` elements in the following snippet of HTML are placed with absolute positioning. What letter will be seen and why?

   ```
   <div style="position: absolute; top: 0px; left: 0px;
      background-color: white; width: 2em; z-index: 10;">K</div>
   <div style="position: absolute; top: 0px; left: 0px;
      background-color: white; width: 2em; z-index: 1;">L</div>
   <div style="position: absolute; top: 0px; left: 0px;
      background-color: white; width: 2em; z-index: 6;">B</div>
   ```

3. You have an `<img>` tag that is 450 pixels wide and 300 pixels tall. The graphic is composed of nine images of television actors in a three by three grid, each cell 150 pixels wide by 100 pixels tall. You want to show only the face of the youngest one, in curls, in the lower left cell. How do you use `clip` to show only that portion of the image?

4. Which of these rules will make scrollbars on a `blockquote`?

   (a.) `blockquote { height: 175px; scroll: auto; }`

   (b.) `blockquote { overflow: scroll; }`

   (c.) `blockquote { scroll: overflow; }`

   (d.) `blockquote { height: 175px; overflow: scroll; }`

Answers

1. The `<h1>` tag will be 125 pixels wide, the minimum width. The calculated width, 100 pixels (20% of 500), is smaller than the `min-width` value, so it is increased to the value of `min-width`. Because it is not larger than the `max-width` value of `200px`, the final size is 125 pixels.

2. The letter *K*. Since they are all placed in the same location, the one that is displayed will be the `<div>` on the top of the stacking order. The highest `z-index` value is `10`, and so the letter *K* will be visible. (Technically, the other letters are visible, too; we just can't see them.)

3. Here is the type rule you would write:

```
img#bunch {
    overflow: hidden;
    clip: rect(150, 200, 0, 300); }
```

Did you remember that you needed to change the `overflow` value from the default of `visible` to be able to use `clip`? The values for `rect()` were calculated by figuring out the coordinates for the upper left corner and the lower right corner of the portion that should be displayed—the points (150,200) and (0,300), respectively.

4. The correct answer is (d.) There is no CSS property named `scroll`, and the `height` property is necessary or else the content won't overflow.

Activity

To complete your education in CSS layout, you'll obviously need to do some hands-on layout work.

- If you worked on a page layout last hour, update that with the new knowledge you've gained this hour, and solve some of the problems you encountered.

- Take one of your existing sites and try to redesign it with CSS, as they did with the Web Reference site.

- Design a new layout from scratch, and use positioning, floats, layered content, overflows, and more. Experiment with design effects, and see what you can create.

- Create a CSS logo, using CSS and no images. Combine colors, fonts, text effects, `z-index`, block sizes and positioning to make a "button" you can place on your page that indicates you designed it using Cascading Style Sheets. How creative can you get?

17

HOUR 18

Web Design with CSS

The Web developer's role is more than just that of a programmer or code-author. In addition to understanding properties, values, selectors, and the cascade order, a CSS developer needs to be conversant in the art of design and the craft of usability.

In this hour, you'll learn

- Why it's important to design for your audience and to test carefully
- How to incorporate style sheets into your Web design practices
- Which questions you need to ask yourself before starting on a style sheet
- How to organize your style sheets to make them easier to use and edit
- What the benefits of validating your style sheet are

Basic Principles of Web Design

In previous hours, you've learned the "what" of using Cascading Style Sheets. You can write your own rules, set your own fonts, choose your colors, and lay out a page.

In this hour, you'll look at the question of "when," which is what design is all about. It's not enough to know the method of doing something; you also need to know the right times to do it and when it's best to not do it.

Web development is a complex field, even if some of the component parts seem simple at first. Designing a Web site is all about balance; it's a complicated balancing act between the desires of the site operator and the needs of the audience. Even basic issues, such as how much content to place on each page, require finding the right balance between too much and too little. Web developers spend a lot of time making compromises, often choosing an alternative that isn't necessarily the absolute best but which works for the greatest amount of people.

Designs that reflect an understanding of the audience and put their needs first are referred to as *user-centric* designs. Some site designs are *designer-centric,* meaning that the Web developer's need for artistic expression comes first; for some sites, such as a personal Web site, this may make sense. More common are *content-centric* designs, which are focused on the site information and functionality. Content-centric sites are usually more effective than designer-centric sites, but their designs sometimes fail to fully understand how their content is used in practice. An effective designer will utilize all of these techniques to create Web designs.

Color, Fonts, and Layout

Presentation isn't everything, but it's a whole lot of something. In an information-intensive medium like the Web—accessed visually by most users—it's important to have an effective presentation that supports the purpose of the site. Rather than being mere window dressing, style sheets can be an integral part of a Web site, crucial to understanding and using the site.

Some people think that because the Web is a completely new medium, the old rules of offline design don't apply. Although the Web does introduce new challenges due to the nature of the medium, it's not so revolutionary that everything can be discarded. The disciplines of graphic design and user-interface design have a lot to teach, which few Web developers learn. For example, graphic design can tell you much about the effective use of color and whitespace, and user-interface design informs you how computer users make choices.

On the other hand, some designers make the opposite mistake of assuming they can just put the same design on the Web as on paper, and this often leads to disastrous results. "Brochure" Web sites gained a bad reputation early, and in most cases it was deserved, based on sites that were barely more than a scanned pamphlet posted on the Internet. The flexible nature of Web design, where the user's choices can influence the final presentation as much as the author's, can prove frustrating and incomprehensible to graphic artists who are used to working in a fixed, printed medium.

As noted in previous hours, font and color rules should be used sparingly; don't go nuts simply because you can. A restrained presentation usually looks better than an overly complex one that is awash in every hue under the sun and set with dozens of fonts.

CSS rules can be used for a number of effects in combination, including simulating buttons and logos with styles. This is generally a good idea, although in some cases you'll be unable to get the exact effect you want. For example, if you need a rare font with a drop shadow, you're in trouble because downloadable fonts are still unreliable, and the text-shadow property is unsupported by the major browsers. In those cases, you'll want to use a GIF or JPEG with text to gain the desired effects.

> Navigation menus created with CSS instead of graphics are much easier to maintain and load faster than images. If you need to add a new link, just add the HTML—no need to open a graphics program.

Usability

Not all attractive Web pages are created equal. Some great-looking sites are hard to use, whereas others are elegantly straightforward and a joy to use. The difference isn't found in the appearance alone—although the visible look can affect ease of use—but in a somewhat nebulous quality called *usability*. The usability of a Web site is a measure of how easy it is for people to use that site. Usability is also the name of a field of study concerned with understanding and improving how people use computers, Web sites, and other technologies.

18

> Jakob Nielsen's Web site at http://www.useit.com/ has good information on usability. You may also notice that his site is very plain. This is more a reflection of Jakob's personal aesthetic than of a strict usability principle. A Web site can (and should) employ good visual design in addition to adherence to usability; there's not a conflict between the two, and a great visual design is actually a boon to usability.

Cascading Style Sheets can be used to enhance usability by producing Web presentations that are simple and distinct. Your styles should reflect how the information is used, highlighting information that is most essential to the site's purpose and the user's needs while still allowing access to all the content.

For example, you can make your site's navigation system stand out by giving a distinct appearance to that part of the page—visible enough that it can be found, but not intrusive enough that the design overwhelms the rest of the content.

Many popular conventions you find on the Web are so widespread that they are second nature to use, making your site easier for visitors. As an example, placing a row of links with distinct styles on the left or top of your page will let users instantly recognize those as navigation links. Don't be afraid to reuse existing Web design elements in this manner; often a site that is too creative can inadvertently become amazingly difficult to use.

Knowing Your Audience

To create user-centric designs, you need to be aware of who your audience is. In some cases, you may be in luck, because you may know everything there is to know about your users. For example, if you are working on an intranet site for your employer, and the company has standardized on Internet Explorer 6, your task suddenly becomes a lot easier. You can use advanced features found only in Internet Explorer 6 and you don't have to worry about workarounds for Netscape or Opera.

However, there's a danger in taking intranet "freedom" too far. You may have to recode your entire site if there's a policy change mandating a new browser or a new version of the same browser. Some users may prefer to use familiar software, such as the Netscape browser they used at their last job. Employees with disabilities might employ special assistive technologies to access the intranet. It will usually save you time and effort in the long run if you design your site to be generally accessible by everyone and not dependent upon a single browser.

If you don't know exactly who your audience is, you can still make some educated guesses. Web servers dutifully record all accesses, and the information they save includes the browser type (name, version, and platform) of each person who downloads a file. These are stored in a Web server log, a long listing of all connections to the server; you can then run a log analysis program, such as Analog (http://www.analog.cx/), to collate and summarize this information. If your ISP or Web host doesn't provide you with this information, ask for it; it's important data for anyone running a Web site.

The information you're looking for is not only the type of browser, but also which pages are being used. By looking at site usage patterns you can discern which pages are most popular and also measure the effectiveness of your navigation systems.

Another useful tactic for getting information on your users is to simply ask for it. Put up a survey on your site to gather responses from your current users so you can serve their needs better. In addition to technical browser information, other demographics can also affect the way you design the site. For example, generational differences among audiences can influence whether you build your site for younger or older users. Users with disabilities or users from foreign countries may have specific needs; in Hour 21, "Accessibility and Internationalization," you'll find out more about how to satisfy those needs.

Organization and Planning

Before you write one line of HTML or CSS code, you need to spend some time planning out your site and organizing the information contained on it. A carefully planned site is much easier to maintain and update than one that grows organically, out of control. Web sites have a natural tendency to evolve, and this is a good thing, but planned growth is always better than accidental growth.

You may want to draw your site out on paper; you might want to create a diagram using software that creates flow charts. The exact way in which you plan your site will depend on your own preferences. Building a chart of your Web content and the links between pages will help you visualize the information and group it into natural sections. The better you organize the page, the easier it will be for users to find your content.

Testing Your Web Site

Once you've got the site up and running, it's time for testing. The first testing will be your own browser tests using your suite of browsers. In Hour 3, "Browser Support for CSS," I recommended building up a standard set of browsers, ideally on different platforms if you can manage it, which represent a broad spectrum of Web users. After you start using a browser with decent CSS support, like Opera, Netscape 6, or Internet Explorer, you may not want to use older or broken browsers regularly. However, it's still important to test on those because, for whatever reason, people are still out there using them!

After you've given your pages a once-over, you're not really done. For the same reason that writers can't edit their own work, you can't be the only one to test your Web pages. A writer will often miss mistakes she's generated, because she knows how something's supposed to be written, and her mind fills in the correct version instead of what's really on the page. For the same reason, you'll want to have others test your site.

One thing you can do is to ask some fellow Web developers for a critique. Because they understand the code behind the designs, they can often point out not only mistakes, but also how to fix them. If you don't know any other Web developers, consider joining a local group or a mailing list; it's no fun being the Lone Ranger of HTML, and even the Lone Ranger had Tonto.

18

The HTML Writers Guild runs a number of mailing lists, including two that are especially useful for testing: HWG-Critique and HWG-Test. You can join these lists and request an evaluation of your site from fellow developers; HWG-Critique is for general design and HWG-Test is for applications. You can also contribute your own opinions on sites. For more information see `http://www.hwg.org/lists/`.

Another way to test your site is by doing user testing, one of the core techniques employed by usability experts. In a formal usability test, you get a number of people and have them attempt to use specific site features, filming them and taking notes from behind a one-way mirror. As explained by Jakob Nielsen, a formal usability test may be overkill; a small sample of around five representative users should be enough, and you can get by without the camera and the mirror.

Here's how you do it:

1. Look over your site and choose several primary functions that users would want to accomplish. Write up several of them (five is a good number again) as tasks or questions; select a variety of functions ranging from easy to difficult. For example, to do such a test on `http://www.cssin24hours.com/`, I might choose "who is the technical editor of this book?" and "order this book from Amazon.com" as two of the questions. (On the latter task, I wouldn't require the transaction actually be completed.)

2. Find your test subjects. Ask them politely, and if possible, offer them compensation or a latte. As much as possible, choose representative users, but don't get obsessed about making sure they're "really" representative. For example, I wouldn't choose my mom for a test of this book's site because she's not a Web developer and won't be using CSS, but I might ask my dad, the Webmaster for the Model A Ford Club of America (`http://www.mafca.com`). If you work for a large company, find some users outside your workgroup who can spare a few minutes.

3. Invite each user to access the Web site and have them attempt the list of tasks you've created. Stress to your users that you're testing the site, not them; if they get something wrong, that's great because it points out a weakness in your design. Watch the users and take notes as they move around your site. No matter how strong the temptation, don't jump in and help them; if they can't figure something out, write that down.

4. When the test is over, thank your test subject, and buy that latte. Then sit down with the results and make sure your ego is safely locked away; every site can be made better. Look at all of the comments and notes you made, and look for patterns across your users. If a certain function is hidden or confusing for several of them, it's likely a good candidate for redesign.

As you can see, this kind of easy user testing isn't a formal science, but it can still produce very useful results. It's certainly better than doing no user testing at all, which is sadly the case for many Web sites.

The Role of CSS in Web Design

As a Web developer, skilled in HTML, Cascading Style Sheets, and possibly other Web languages and technologies, you have a Web development process. Even if you haven't planned it out formally, you've got a method that works for you, whether it's as simple as sitting down and designing whatever strikes your fancy or as complex as a multi-developer corporate development system for a large employer.

Adding CSS to your repertoire has made you an even better Web developer than before; your skill set has expanded and the types of designs you can create are nearly limitless. The next step is to integrate your CSS skills into your Web development process. I'm not going to tell you exactly how you'll do that, as everyone has their own methods, but I'll help you think about how you can go about using CSS in your Web designs.

In a few cases, you may be able to develop your style sheets completely separately from your HTML pages. More commonly, you'll employ an iterative process, where you make changes to the style sheet, then changes to the HTML page, and then go back to the style sheet for a few more tweaks until you're satisfied with the results. The adaptive nature of style sheets makes it easy to create these kinds of changes, and you may find yourself continuing to perfect your styles even after you post your content on the Web.

You may not be starting with a blank slate and an uncreated Web site when you begin using CSS. Redesigns are very common in Web development, and you may want to take advantage of a new site design to convert to a CSS-based presentation. It's harder, but certainly possible, to keep the same look and feel of your site but convert it to use CSS. If you're using a content management system (CMS) that automatically generates your Web site from a database, converting to style sheets may be a snap. On a conceptual level, CSS is pretty compatible with the idea of templates as used by content management systems.

Decisions, Decisions

As mentioned at the start of this hour, CSS design involves balancing a number of factors to arrive at the best compromise for your site and its users. Questions will arise as you work on any site using CSS, and you'll need to answer them before you go on. I've listed several of these key questions here, to help you plan your site:

- Will you use Cascading Style Sheets, and if so, to what effect? You certainly aren't required to use CSS, even after reading this entire book. You can create Web sites that are usable, accessible, attractive, and effective without a single CSS property anywhere in evidence. However, using CSS will make your site more flexible and easier to maintain and will give you access to presentation effects you couldn't get through HTML alone.

- What "flavor" of HTML will you use? As you may recall from Hour 4, "Using CSS with HTML," there are three varieties of HTML: Strict, Transitional, and Frameset. The Strict variety relies upon CSS for all styling effects, whereas Transitional (and Frameset) HTML can mix CSS rules with presentational markup. If you're concerned about older browsers that don't understand CSS, you may want to choose Transitional.

- Which browsers will you support? By "support," I mean investing the effort to work around the quirks of certain browsers. (By "certain browsers," I mostly mean Netscape 4.) This book has a number of workarounds, plus ways to exclude certain browsers from viewing styles. If you are designing just for CSS-enabled browsers, such as recent Netscape, Internet Explorer, or Opera versions, those workarounds become less important.

- Are you using positioning CSS for layout? It's relatively easy to use CSS for formatting text, controlling fonts, and setting colors. Using it for layout is trickier, especially with inconsistent browser support among some of the older versions. Don't assume that you must use positioning CSS; as of early 2002, many sites, including the W3C, were using tables extensively for page layout, even though they recommend CSS for that purpose. Positioning CSS is still less reliable than the <table> tag.

- Will you use embedded or linked style sheets? Here, I'll give you advice: Use linked style sheets whenever you can. Some of my examples in this book use embedded style sheets, but that's mainly because it's easier to give you one listing than two.

The preceding list isn't exhaustive; you'll encounter more choices to make when designing using CSS, but hopefully you've learned enough by now to answer them. In section 4 of this book, you'll learn some advanced techniques that may make it easier to meet all of your goals for your site using CSS.

Style Sheet Organization

The way you organize your style sheet can affect how easy it is for you to use and maintain your CSS, even if the effects are not evident in the presentation. This becomes even more critical if you're in a situation where someone else may have to use your styles in the future. You may work with an organization where multiple people will be working on the same site, or perhaps when you've moved on to another job your successor will inherit your style sheets.

To make a great style sheet, be organized and clear in what you're doing, and above all, use comments. Web developers often overlook comments in CSS, but if you have to come back later and try to figure out why you did something, they're invaluable. Comments can also be used to group related styles together into sections.

Reasonable names for class and id attributes can make your style sheet easier to read; choose names for these important selectors that reflect the function of the elements. If you can, avoid selectors based solely on appearance characteristics, such as the boldtext or redbox classes; instead try something descriptive of why you've chosen those styles, such as worddef or sidebar. That way, if you change your page styles later, you won't have to rewrite your HTML; there are few things as confusing as a rule like the following:

```
.redbox { color: blue; background-color: white; }
```

In what way is that box red? Well, it probably was red in some prior incarnation, but not now.

When you list your rules in your style sheet, do them in a sensible order. Generally speaking, it's best to start with the body rules first and then proceed down from there, but because the cascade order matters only in case of conflict, it's not strictly necessary to mirror the page hierarchy. What's more important is that you are able to locate the rules that apply to a given selector and to discern which styles should be applied.

An example of bad style sheet organization is shown in Listing 18.1. This is part of the style sheet I use on my personal Web site, http://kynn.com/, but with the rules in a scrambled order. How hard is it for you to figure out what is going on here?

LISTING 18.1   A Randomly Organized Style Sheet

```
/* k-messy-18.1.css */

.ulhc  { color: black; vertical-align: top; }
.menubar { border: 2px solid white; }
.rhs   { color: black; }
.content { position: relative; border: 2px solid white;
           padding: 1em 5% 1em; }
.horiz { }
```

continues

LISTING 18.1 Continued

```
.urhc  { color: black; vertical-align: top; }
A:active { color: black; font-weight: bold; }
.menubar a:hover { color: white; }
body { font-family: Garamond, Georgia, Times,
                 "Times New Roman", serif; }
.inter { }
.lhs   { color: black; }
h1, h2, h3, h4. h5, h6, dt, .heading
  { color: black; font-variant: small-caps; }
.lhrc a:link, .lrhc a:visited {
        text-decoration: none; font-weight: bolder;
        color: black; }
.urhc H1 { color: white; text-align: center;
        border: none; padding: 0% 5%;
        margin: 0px; line-height: 75px; }
A:link { font-weight: bold; color: #000066;
        text-decoration: none; }
.lrhc  { color: black; }
.ulhc img { border: 2px solid white; padding-left: 15px;
        padding-right: 15px; }
.llhc  { color: black; }
h1, h2, h3, h4, h5, h6, .heading
  { border-bottom: 1px solid white; }
body {   background-color: #cca580;
        background-image:
        url("/photos/feb2002/arizona/painted-desert_sm.jpg");
        background-position: top right;
        background-repeat: no-repeat; }
.vert  { }
A:visited { font-weight: bold; color: #006600;
        text-decoration: none; }
```

If that was a bit hard to follow, don't feel bad; that was intentional. On the Kynn.com site, I use tables to divide the page into six content cells that can each be styled independently. Vertical and horizontal bars separate these cells, and the bars, as well as their intersections, can also have styles applied to them.

The layout is shown in Figure 18.1, which indicates the class attribute for each cell. The classes have names like urhc for "upper right hand corner" and lhs for "left hand side."

FIGURE 18.1

The layout of cssin24hours.com, done with tables.

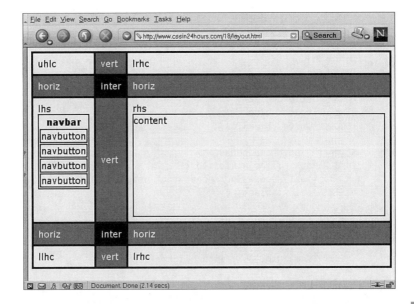

The current style sheet, as given in Listing 18.1, actually eliminates the bars between the content cells by not giving them a distinct background color, but you can't tell that by skimming the style sheet.

The style sheet in Listing 18.2 is really the same as before; both produce the same results when applied to the Web page, but the second one is easier to understand. Comments make clearer what each section of the style sheet does, and the order is much easier to understand.

LISTING 18.2 A Better-organized Style Sheet

```
/* k-orderly-18.2.css */
/* For kynn.com */
/* By Kynn, 6-22-1999 */
/* Last tweaked 02-20-2002 */

/* Default styles */
body { background-color: #cca580;
      background-image:
        url("/photos/feb2002/arizona/painted-desert_sm.jpg");
      background-position: top right;
      background-repeat: no-repeat; }

/* Styled cells */
.ulhc  { color: black; vertical-align: top; }
.urhc  { color: black; vertical-align: top; }
```

continues

LISTING 18.2 Continued

```
.vert  { }
.horiz { }
.inter { }
.lhs   { color: black; }
.rhs   { color: black; }
.llhc  { color: black; }
.lrhc  { color: black; }

/* lower right hand corner */
.lhrc a:link, .lrhc a:visited {
        text-decoration: none; font-weight: bolder;
        color: black; }

/* upper right hand corner */
.urhc h1 { color: white; text-align: center;
           border: none; padding: 0% 5%;
           margin: 0px; line-height: 75px; }

/* upper left hand corner */
.ulhc img { border: 2px solid white; padding-left: 15px;
            padding-right: 15px; }

/* fonts */
body { font-family: Garamond, Georgia, Times,
                    "Times New Roman", serif; }

/* Distinct headings */
h1, h2, h3, h4. h5, h6, dt, .heading
  { color: black; font-variant: small-caps; }
h1, h2, h3, h4, h5, h6, .heading
  { border-bottom: 1px solid white; }

/* Link styles */
a:link    { font-weight: bold; color: #000066;
            text-decoration: none; }
a:visited { font-weight: bold; color: #006600;
            text-decoration: none; }
a:active { color: black; font-weight: bold; }

/* Menu bar */
.menubar { border: 2px solid white; }
.menubar a:hover { color: white; }

/* Primary content */
.content { position: relative; border: 2px solid white;
           padding: 1em 5% 1em; }
```

Site-wide Style Sheets

The style sheet given in Listing 18.2 was created to be used on the entire site, not just on one page. The ability to link in an external style sheet makes this an easy choice to apply styles over your entire site by setting each page to use the style sheet with the `<link>` tag. An example of a Web page on the Kynn.com site, which uses this style sheet, is shown in Figure 18.2; the original page is at `http://kynn.com/nav/causes.html`.

FIGURE 18.2

The Kynn.com style sheet applied to a Web page.

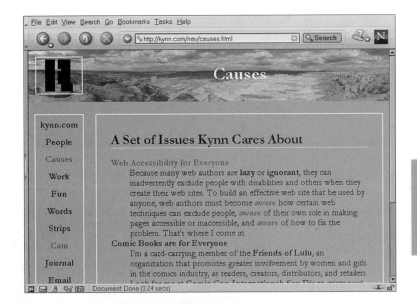

A style sheet that is referenced from all pages on a site makes it a very simple task to change the appearance of the entire Web site. For example, Figure 18.3 shows the same page as in Figure 18.2, but with a different style sheet. Changing the single external file altered the look of the whole Web site instantly. If you're curious, you can view this other style sheet at `http://www.cssin24hours.com/18/k-alt.css`.

A site-wide style sheet can be used to enforce a consistent appearance on the Web site, even if you have multiple Web developers working on the same site. Additional styles can be added in embedded style sheets or in additional linked CSS files that are created for each department or business unit. For example, the City of Fullerton's Web site (`http://www.ci.fullerton.ca.us/`) uses style sheets to give a consistent appearance to the whole site but different colors to each city department's subsite, as shown in Figure 18.4.

FIGURE **18.3**

A different style sheet applied to the Kynn.com site.

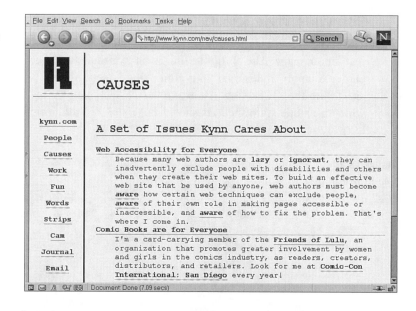

FIGURE **18.4**

Style sheets set the appearance of the city Web site in Fullerton, California.

Validating Your CSS

Everyone makes mistakes, even you and me. Mistakes in writing CSS can be benign, producing a minor effect such as putting a block of text in the wrong font, or they can be much more serious and prevent people from using your page at all.

As you learned in Hour 4, you can validate your HTML using the World Wide Web Consortium's HTML validator at `http://validator.w3.org`. The W3C provides a free CSS validation service, as well, for checking your CSS syntax. This is located at `http://jigsaw.w3.org/css-validator/`.

> Another CSS validator from the Web Design Group can be found at `http://www.htmlhelp.com/tools/csscheck/`.

To use the W3C CSS validator, you can specify a Web page that contains CSS code, give the direct URL of a style sheet, or paste your style rules directly into a text box. The validator will analyze your CSS rules and notify you of errors. It will also give useful warnings.

An example of CSS validation is shown in Figure 18.5, which shows the results of validating the style sheet in Listing 18.2. As you can see, it caught an error and gave a warning about some possible errors.

18

FIGURE 18.5

The results of validating Listing 18.2.

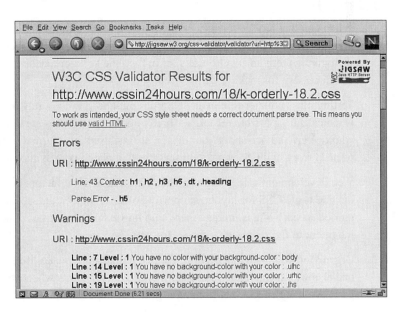

Why Validate?

Validation is a useful strategy for a number of reasons. The biggest benefit is that it allows you to spot errors in your style sheet syntax. For example, in Figure 18.5, the CSS validator noticed a problem with the style sheet. The following line can be found in both Listing 18.1 and Listing 18.2:

```
h1, h2, h3, h4. h5, h6, dt, .heading
```

The error is the punctuation after the h4; it should be a comma, but here I've put a period. That kind of error is hard to spot when you're just skimming the page. In fact, it was there for months before I noticed it! Did you spot it earlier?

The warnings issued by the CSS validator are quite useful for spotting accidental omissions, such as setting a foreground color without a contrasting background color. However, you have to interpret those results carefully. The CSS validator can't fully account for inheritance and transparency in your Web page, and so you'll need to determine for yourself if a warning is an actual problem.

A validator is like a spell-checker or grammar-checker in a word processor. They can spot potential problems and you wouldn't think of submitting a document without checking it first, but blind reliance on an automated checker without using human judgment is just as bad.

Summary

When creating any Web pages, whether using CSS or not, it's important to keep the needs of your users in mind. Providing them with an attractive Web site is not in conflict with giving them an easy-to-use site. In fact, the two approaches are both complementary and necessary for making a truly great site.

Testing plays a major role in any CSS design, and you can't rely on your own judgment when catching possible mistakes. Three important resources are other Web developers who can give advice about your design efforts, users in informal tests who point out unexpected errors, and CSS validation services that check your syntax and warn of omissions.

Web development using CSS is a balancing act, and the factors you'll have to weigh include using CSS for layout, supporting older browsers, and accounting for browser quirks. As each site is unique, there's no universal answer; you'll need to use your own judgment to figure out what works for you.

Organizing your style sheets in a sensible manner will make life easier for you and anyone else who has to read your style sheet. Use comments whenever you think of it, and group your styles together in natural groupings. You'll thank yourself later; believe me.

Browser Support Report Card

There's no report card in this hour because no new CSS features were introduced. The strategies for Web development you learned in this hour can be applied to all style sheets.

Q&A

Q Your personal Web site doesn't use CSS for layout. What gives?

A It's a pretty old design, and when I created it, there were even fewer browsers that understood positioning CSS. If I were doing it from scratch today, Kynn.com would be done using CSS for layout, using the @import trick described in Hours 16, "Page Layout in CSS," and 17, "Advanced CSS Layout," to avoid Netscape 4 problems. This is much easier to do on a new site than on an existing one, especially if you're spending your time writing a book! The CSSin24hours.com site does use CSS for layout because that's a new site.

Workshop

18

The workshop contains quiz questions and activities to help reinforce what you've learned in this hour. If you get stuck, the answers to the quiz can be found after the questions.

Quiz

1. Colors and fonts should be used to

    (a.) Make the page harder to read, so people spend more time on your site.

    (b.) Hide content from the real users while tricking search engine spiders.

    (c.) Present the content in an attractive, usable manner.

    (d.) Make you seem really cool to all your friends.

2. What do you need for effective user testing?

    (a.) Nothing. Just follow your own instincts because you are a user too.

    (b.) Five people, five tasks, and five lattes.

    (c.) A usability lab with one-way mirrors, video cameras, and a million-dollar budget.

3. If you submit the following style sheet to the W3C's CSS validator, which errors or warnings will it give?

```
p, td. th, li { color: black;
bakground-color: white; }
```

Answers

1. The correct answer, of course, is (c.), unless you're making a site to show your friends how cool you are.

2. The answer is (b.), but the lattes are optional. I prefer a nice cold cherry cola, myself.

3. The validator will point out two errors: the period instead of the comma after the `td` and the unknown property name `bakground-color`. Also, because there is no `background-color` value given to contrast with the `color` value, a warning will be generated.

Activity

Here's a list of projects you can undertake to reinforce what you've learned this hour:

- Write up five tasks that could be accomplished by a user of a specific Web site. Make sure you have a few you think are easy and a few you think are hard; you might find yourself surprised in an actual test.

- In fact, if you've got the time and the inclination, do an informal user test as described earlier this hour. The results are always educational, even if they just tell you that you're on the right track.

- Subscribe to the HWG-Critique mailing list at the HTML Writers Guild, and post a site for review. Then, give your own critique in response to someone else's request. Remember to be both polite and constructive, of course!

- Look at some of the style sheets you've worked on, and see if you can reorganize them to be easier to understand. Comments, comments, comments!

- Validate your style sheets, and if they don't pass, fix them until they do. Consider each warning; is it a valid potential problem, or can you safely ignore it?

PART IV

Advanced Cascading Style Sheets

Hour

Hour **19**

Advanced Selectors

The CSS Level 2 specification introduced a number of additional selectors that are not yet fully supported by all browsers. These advanced selectors greatly increase the functionality and power of CSS, allowing rules based on complex relationships to be written. Full support of these new selectors, when available, will greatly extend the utility and power of CSS.

In this hour, you'll learn

- How to create CSS rules that select only those tags that have a specific attribute
- How to create rules based on the values of those attributes
- How to create rules that select direct children of another element and why you'd want to do that
- How to select an element that directly follows another element
- Which browsers support these advanced selectors

Attribute Selectors

An *attribute selector* tests for the existence, and possibly the values, of any specific attributes set on an element. You'd use an attribute selector if you wanted all elements with a certain attribute to be styled a certain way. For example, noshade is an HTML attribute for the <hr> tag; it means that there shouldn't be any shading effects applied to the tag. If you wanted all of those <hr> tags to be colored silver, you'd use an attribute selector based on the noshade attribute. The simplest form of attribute selector is simply the attribute within square brackets, as follows:

```
element[attribute] { declaration; }
```

For example:

```
hr[noshade] { color: silver; }
```

This rule would declare that all <hr> elements with the noshade attribute should be colored silver.

You can write an attribute selector rule so that it selects all elements with the chosen attribute by using the universal selector (*). For example, you could set a specific rule for all tags that have a title attribute to indicate which parts of the page will pop up a tooltip when you move the mouse over them, as in the following:

```
*[title] { background-color: yellow; }
```

This will mark with a yellow background all tags with title attributes. Because the universal selector is optional, you can also write the rule like this:

```
[title] { background-color: yellow; }
```

Workaround for Netscape 4, Internet Explorer 4/5/5.5 (Windows), Internet Explorer 4/5/5.1 (Macintosh)

Only Opera, Netscape 6, and Mozilla support attribute selectors. For compatibility with other browsers, you should use an explicit class attribute and class selector rule. (If you're using more than one class at once, you may need to add additional <div> or <span> tags for compatibility with Netscape 4.) For example, to make the two attribute selector examples work in Netscape 4, you'll need to write your HTML like this:

```
<hr class="unshaded" noshade>
<a href="summer2001.html" class="hastooltip"
   title="What I Did for Summer Vacation">Summer 2001</a>
```

Your CSS rules would then look like this:

```
hr[noshade], hr.unshaded { color: silver; }
*[title], .hastooltip { background-color: yellow; }
```

Selecting by Attribute Value

In addition to checking for the existence of the attribute, you can also select by attribute value. There are three ways to do this:

```
element[attribute="value"]  { declaration; }
element[attribute~="value"] { declaration; }
element[attribute|="value"] { declaration; }
```

The first version designates an exact match; it selects only those elements for which the attribute has the given value. The second registers a match if the value in the rule is one of several values given in the HTML, separated by spaces. The third matches the rule's value against the HTML's value and compares the characters before hyphens. (This is to allow matching of language groups, which are written as en-us, en-uk, en-au, and so on.) Table 19.1 shows several types of selectors and attribute values and indicates whether or not each selector would match the HTML.

TABLE 19.1 Testing Attribute Values

CSS Selector	HTML Snippet	Match?
table[summary="layout"]	`<table summary="layout">`	Yes
table[summary~="layout"]	`<table summary="layout">`	Yes
table[summary|="layout"]	`<table summary="layout">`	Yes
div[class="bar"]	`<div class="foo bar baz">`	No
div[class~="bar"]	`<div class="foo bar baz">`	Yes
div[class|="bar"]	`<div class="foo bar baz">`	No
*[lang="en"]	`<span lang="en">`	Yes
*[lang~="en"]	`<span lang="en">`	Yes
*[lang|="en"]	`<span lang="en">`	Yes
*[lang="en"]	`<span lang="en-us">`	No
*[lang~="en"]	`<span lang="en-us">`	No
*[lang|="en"]	`<span lang="en-us">`	Yes
*[lang="en"]	`<span lang="english">`	No
*[lang~="en"]	`<span lang="english">`	No
*[lang|="en"]	`<span lang="english">`	No

19

Workaround for Netscape 4, Internet Explorer 4/5/5.5 (Windows)

As many browsers don't support attribute value selectors, you will have to use the same tricks with `class` listed in the previous workaround—creating class selector rules that explicitly identify tags that have the values you need to style.

Let's look at an example of attribute selectors in action. Listing 19.1 is an HTML page consisting of a table of departure times for airline flights. I've chosen to use the `axis` attribute on table cells to group similar types of flights. Those flights that fly through Saint Louis have been assigned an `axis` value of `stlouis`, whereas those going through Chicago are labeled with an `axis` value of `ord`.

LISTING 19.1   HTML Table Marked Up with the `axis` Attribute

```
<!-- flights-19.1.html -->
<html>
  <head>
    <title>Flights from Los Angeles to New York</title>
    <link type="text/css" rel="stylesheet"
          href="flights-19.2.css">
  </head>
  <body>
    <h1>Schedule of Flights</h1>
    <h2>Los Angeles to New York</h2>
    <table border="1">
      <tr>
        <th>Monday</th>
        <th>Tuesday</th>
        <th>Wednesday</th>
        <th>Thursday</th>
        <th>Friday</th>
      </tr>
      <tr>
        <td axis="ord">09:13</td>
        <td axis="ord">09:13</td>
        <td>10:17</td>
        <td axis="ord">09:13</td>
        <td>10:17</td>
      </tr>
      <tr>
        <td axis="stlouis">12:05</td>
        <td axis="stlouis">12:05</td>
        <td axis="stlouis">12:05</td>
        <td axis="stlouis">12:05</td>
        <td axis="stlouis">12:05</td>
      </tr>
```

LISTING **19.1**   Continued

```
        <tr>
          <td axis="ord">17:15</td>
          <td axis="stlouis">13:44</td>
          <td axis="ord">17:15</td>
          <td axis="stlouis">13:44</td>
          <td>14:30</td>
        </tr>
        <tr>
          <td></td>
          <td axis="ord">17:15</td>
          <td>19:20</td>
          <td axis="ord">17:15</td>
          <td axis="ord">17:15</td>
        </tr>
      </table>
    </body>
</html>
```

The cascading style sheet for this example is shown in Listing 19.2; you'll use attribute selectors to set up rules on each flight type to show them with different background colors. This effect is shown in Figure 19.1.

LISTING **19.2**   This Style Sheet Uses Rules Based on the axis Attribute Selector

```
/* flights-19.2.css */

td {
    color: black;
    background-color: white;
  }
td[axis="stlouis"]
  {
    background-color: yellow;
    color: navy;
  }
td[axis="ord"]
  {
    background-color: black;
    color: lime;
  }
```

19

FIGURE **19.1**

Using attribute selectors in Netscape 6 to make axis *values visual.*

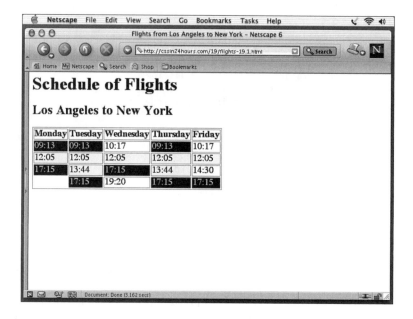

You've actually been using shorthand versions of some attribute selectors for some time now; the class and id selectors are actually just special cases of an attribute value selector. The following pairs of rules are equivalent:

```
.apple                  { color: green; }
*[class~="apple"]       { color: green; }
#banana                 { color: yellow; }
*[id="banana"]          { color: yellow; }
```

Multiple attribute values can be combined together by simply adding on another attribute test. Here's an example of a rule that selects all table cells that are right aligned and vertically aligned to the bottom:

```
td[align="right"][valign="bottom"]
  { font-size: small; }
```

You can use attribute selector rules with a user style sheet to create some very simple but powerful testing tools for Web development. For example, to make anchors visible, create a style sheet, set it as your user style sheet in your browser, and add the following rule:

```
a[name], [id]     { border: 1px dotted red; }
```

This will put a dotted line around your anchors and anything else with the `id` attribute set. You can use this same trick to make table borders, form boundaries, field `<label>`s, and other block elements visible because they're outlined with a `border`. Here's a pair of rules to make it very clear which of your images don't have `alt` attributes on them:

```
img { border: 5px solid lime; }
img[alt] { border: none; }
```

For more of these useful user CSS recipes, see an article by Eric Meyer at `http://www.oreillynet.com/pub/a/network/2000/07/21/magazine/css_tool.html`.

Family Relationships

Family-based selectors in CSS choose elements based on the relationships between the HTML tags; these relationships are named after family relationships. You've already used one of the family relationship selectors: the descendant selector, which selects elements descended from another tag. Other relationship selectors include child and adjacent sibling selectors.

Child Selectors

A *child selector* is a special case of descendant selectors, which were covered in Hour 5, "Selectors." A child selector identifies only those elements that are immediate children of another element, not any "grandchildren" or other descendants. A child selector is indicated by a greater-than symbol (>) between the parent element and the child:

```
parent > child { declaration; }
```

For example, consider the following snippet of HTML:

```
<blockquote>
  <div class="opinion">
    <p>I'm voting Green next year.</p>
    <p>I'm wearing green, too!</p>
  </div>
</blockquote>
```

Here are some style rules, but only a few of these will be applied to the code sample:

```
blockquote p   { font-size:   large;              }
blockquote > p { font-family: Arial, sans-serif; }
.opinion > p   { font-color:  green;              }
```

The first rule will be used on the quote; it's a normal descendant selector, and both of the paragraphs are within a `<blockquote>`. The second rule will not be applied; there are no `<p>` tags that are direct children of a `<blockquote>` tag; both of them are direct children of the `<div>`. (They're *descendants* of the `<blockquote>`, of course, but only direct children,

19

not grandchildren, count for child selectors.) The third rule will be applied to the <p> text because both paragraphs are direct children of a tag with class="opinion". So the total effect will be two green paragraphs, both in the default font face.

> **Workaround for Netscape 4, Internet Explorer 4/5/5.5 (Windows), Internet Explorer 4/5/5.1 (Mac)**
>
> Many browsers won't recognize child selectors. For compatibility with these older browsers, use descendant selectors; if you're unable to get the effects you want with just descendants, use class selectors too. Here's how you would rewrite your green quote style sheet rules:
>
> ```
> blockquote p    { font-size:   large; /* same */  }
> blockquote p.childofblockquote
>                 { font-family: Arial, sans-serif; }
> .opinion p      { font-color:  green;             }
> ```
>
> You'll notice I added a class called childofblockquote; I'll have to add that to every <p> that is a direct child of a <blockquote>. I won't add it to the <p> inside the <div> tag because they shouldn't be in Arial, according to the original style sheet.

Adjacent Sibling Selectors

Two HTML tags are siblings if they have the same parent; they are adjacent siblings if the second occurs directly after the first in the source code. Here's some HTML to illustrate a sibling relationship:

```
<h1>Our Dogs</h1>
<ul>
  <li id="ang">Angie</li>
  <li id="kim">Kim</li>
  <li id="nyi">Nying</li>
  <!-- id attributes are included for reference -->
</ul>
```

The <li> elements containing Angie, Kim, and Nying are all siblings of each other. The id="ang" and id="kim" <li> tags are adjacent siblings, and the id="kim" and id="nyi" <li> tags are adjacent as well. The id="ang" and li="nyi" tags are not adjacent.

An *adjacent sibling selector* makes a selection based on two adjacent siblings, but it applies the declared style only to the second of the two. This is very important to remember; you are not selecting the pair, you are selecting only the final one in the list.

You write an adjacent sibling rule by listing the first sibling, a plus sign (+), and then the second sibling. A rule such as the following will turn only the Kim and Nying names blue:

```
li + li { color: blue; }
```

Workaround for Netscape 4, Internet Explorer 4/5/5.5 (Windows), Internet Explorer 4 (Macintosh)

Like many other advanced selectors in CSS, the usefulness of adjacent sibling selectors has been crippled by a lack of browser support. Using the same techniques described previously in this hour, you can add a number of class attributes and selectors and approximate the behavior for those older browsers that don't support CSS Level 2 selectors. This isn't the best solution, but it's the only one that you currently have.

Adjacent sibling selectors are useful for removing margins, padding, and borders when siblings are meant to flow together visually. An example of this is shown in Listing 19.3.

LISTING 19.3   A Definition List with Adjacent <dt> and <dd> Elements

```
<!-- acronyms-19.3.html -->
<html>
  <head>
    <title>
      Common Acronyms
    </title>
    <style type="text/css">
* { font-family: Arial, sans-serif; }

dt { margin-top: 1em;
    font-weight: bold;
    font-variant: small-caps;
    padding-top: 1em;
    border-top: 1px solid black; }

dt:first-child { border-top: none;
                 padding-top: none;  }

dt + dd { margin-top: 0.5em; }

dd + dd { font-style: italic;
          border: 1px dashed black;
          padding: 0.1em;
          display: inline; }
</style>

  </head>
  <body>
    <h1>Common Acronyms</h1>
```

19

continues

LISTING 19.3 Continued

```
  <dl>
    <dt>AWARE</dt>
    <dd>Accessible Web Authoring Resources and Education Center</dd>
    <dd>See also: HWG</dd>
    <dt>HWG</dt>
    <dd>HTML Writers Guild</dd>
    <dt>WAI</dt>
    <dd>Web Accessibility Initiative</dd>
    <dd>See also: W3C</dd>
    <dt>WCAG</dt>
    <dd>Web Content Accessibility Guidelines</dd>
    <dt>WebAIM</dt>
    <dd>Web Accessibility In Mind</dd>
    <dt>WWW</dt>
    <dd>World Wide Web</dd>
    <dt>WWWC -- <cite>see W3C</cite></dt>
    <dt>W3C</dt>
    <dd>World Wide Wide Consortium</dd>
    <dd>See also: WAI</dd>
  </dl>
  </body>
</html>
```

The embedded style sheet in Listing 19.3 uses styles based on adjacent-sibling rules; the effects of these style rules can be seen in Figure 19.2.

FIGURE 19.2

Adjacent siblings displayed in Internet Explorer 5.1 (Macintosh).

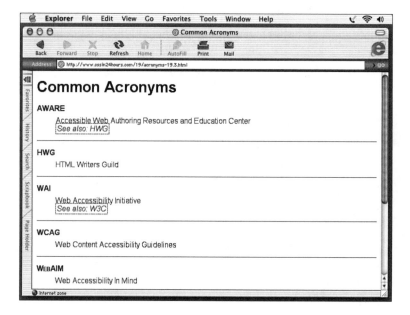

Summary

Although unsupported by all but the newest browsers, advanced selectors add considerably to the CSS developer's toolbox. Attribute selectors allow styles to be set based on specific attribute values or even the existence of an attribute on the tag. Relationships between elements can be expressed in CSS by the child selector, which applies to direct children of a specific element, and by the adjacent sibling selector, which chooses the second of a pair of specified tags.

Browser Support Report Card

CSS Feature	Grade	Notes
Attribute selectors	C–	See text
Child selectors	C–	See text
Adjacent sibling selectors	C–	See text

Unfortunately, there is little browser support for any advanced selectors except from the newest browser versions. For this reason, it is suggested that you should avoid using them unless you know your audience is using a newer browser. Workarounds exist in the form of class attributes, but this is not an elegant solution.

Q&A

Q Can I do pattern matching in attribute values? Suppose I want to select all `<a>` tags that are `mailto` links. Can I use `a[href="mailto:*"]` as my selector?

A Nope. The CSS specifications don't define a way to do this type of pattern matching. Future versions of CSS based on XPath and XPointer might allow this, but for now there is no way to use pattern matching in CSS. To make your `mailto` links stand out, set a `class` attribute on them, and use a `class` selector.

Q If I could use either a child selector or a descendant selector, which should I use? Which should I use if, for example, I want to select all `<img>` tags within `<a>` links?

A In theory, it's better to use a child selector if you know you're dealing with a direct child because it's quicker for the browser to calculate child selectors. It doesn't have to look over the full tree of the HTML document, just up one level. In practice, though, you are better off sticking with the descendant selector due to poor browser support; don't rely on a child selector alone. You can use both, if you like.

19

Q Can I combine advanced selectors with simple selectors or other advanced selectors?

A Certainly! This is a valid CSS rule:

```
.chap > th + td img[alt] { border: 2px solid green; }
```

What would match this? Basically, anything that meets the following criteria:

- An image element
- With an `alt` attribute set (to any value)
- Where that image is a descendant of a table cell
- Assuming that table cell has a table header cell as a sibling
- Which is a direct child of an element in the `chap` class

Workshop

The workshop contains quiz questions and activities to help reinforce what you've learned in this hour. If you get stuck, the answers to the quiz can be found after the questions.

Quiz

1. What does the + symbol indicate, in a selector?

2. Which selector will select the HTML element `<h1 align="right">Welcome</h1>`, and why?

    (a.) `h1[align~="right"]`

    (b.) `*[align="right"]`

    (c.) `[align|="right"]`

    (d.) `h1[align]`

3. You're using Netscape 6 and you want to write a rule in your user style sheet to hide banners that are 468 pixels across and 60 pixels high. How do you write that rule?

Answers

1. The + symbol designates a direct sibling selector.

2. It's kind of a trick question. All of them will select the `<h1>`. The first will select it because `right` is one of the values listed in the attribute. (It's the only value, too.) The second will select it because it's exactly the value (and the selector's type is universal). The third is also a universal selector, and it will compare values before a dash; because there is no dash, it will just compare `right` with `right`. The last matches with any value because the `<h1>` tag has an `align` attribute.

3. Here's one way to zap away those annoying banners:

```
img[height="60"][width="468"] { display: none; }
```

Activity

To understand more about advanced selectors, look at some of the style sheets you have already created, and see if they could be improved by replacing class or descendant selectors with adjacent sibling, direct child, or attribute selectors. Remember that these will work only in recent browsers, so you'll want to test with one of those.

19

Hour **20**

CSS for Printing

Most style sheets are written for onscreen display in a Web browser. However, CSS isn't restricted only to screen display; style sheets can be applied to printed versions of a page as well as to other media types.

In this hour, you'll learn

- How to specify rules for specific media types
- Which media types are supported by CSS and when they are used
- How to set the dimensions and orientation of the printed page
- How to set page breaks
- Which print properties 2002's browsers support
- What kinds of things to consider when making a print style sheet

Media-specific Style Sheets

Using CSS, you can create style sheets that are media specific, meaning that they should be applied only to one particular type of output device. An *output device* is any physical hardware device that can present Web content—visually or otherwise—as well as the software necessary to allow for that presentation, such as a printer driver or a screenreader.

In Hour 4, "Using CSS with HTML," you learned the basics of the `<link>` element and its attribute `media`, which allows you to tie style sheets to categories of output media. In this hour, you'll expand your knowledge of media types and learn how to write rules within one style sheet that apply to different media.

Categories of Media Types

The full list of media types defined in CSS is listed on Table 20.1. A given browser is required to support only those media types appropriate for that browser. For example, a set-top box doesn't need to support screen, aural, or print media types. The typical visual browser uses two media types: `screen` and `print`. Opera also supports the `projection` media type in full-screen kiosk mode.

TABLE 20.1 Media Types in CSS

Media Type	Description
aural	Pages read out loud by synthesized voice; for example, screenreaders for the blind
braille	Content represented by raised dot characters on Braille terminals for blind users
emboss	Pages printed out as raised dots in Braille, on thick paper
handheld	Content displayed on a limited-size handheld screen
print	Pages printed out on paper
projection	Content displayed as slides or transparencies projected on a large screen
screen	Pages displayed on a color monitor
tty	Content printed on teletype devices or other media with limited display capabilities, which print only characters of a fixed size and type
tv	Pages displayed on a television screen, possibly taking advantage of sound capabilities but with limited interaction

Media type values are used in `<link>` tags and `@import` rules for the purpose of specifying which style sheets to use, and they will also be used to classify certain rules within a style sheet as applicable.

The media types described here are obviously not enough to fully capture the diversity of access methods available to Web users of the 21st Century. For example, the `handheld` media type assumes that a handheld device will be monochrome, but we've already seen a number of color handheld devices available. Also, there is a large difference between a PDA, a pocket computer, and a cell phone, although these are all grouped under the term "handheld."

The W3C realizes these deficiencies and is developing a better classification system for the CSS Level 3 recommendation; you can read the current drafts at `http://www.w3.org/Style/CSS/current-work`. Also, the W3C's Composite Capabilities/Preferences Profile (CC/PP) work is moving toward a standardized way of describing end user device characteristics; see `http://www.w3.org/Mobile/CCPP/` for more.

Linking and Importing Media-specific Style Sheets

You've already seen, in a previous hour, how to use a media type with the `<link>` tag in HTML:

```
<link type="text/css" rel="stylesheet"
      media="print, emboss" href="paged-output.css">
```

Such a link would load only the style sheet if the browser were currently printing to a standard or Braille printer.

Warning for Netscape 4

The Netscape 4 browser simply does not support media types beyond `screen`, and it supports `screen` only for `<link>`. In fact, it mistakenly applies a linked `screen` style sheet to printed materials. In short, it's impossible to make a specific style sheet for other media types, such as `print`, that will be recognized by the Netscape 4 browser. If you need to do this in Netscape 4, create an alternate version of the page that differs from the original only in the style sheet file used with `<link>`.

20

An `@import` rule at the beginning of a style sheet can also be set to specify style sheets applicable to certain media types:

```
@import url("site.css");
@import url("screen.css") screen, tv;
@import url("dots.css") braille;
```

These rules always load the `site.css` file and will load `screen.css` for display on a computer or television screen and `dots.css` for a Braille display terminal.

> **Workaround for Internet Explorer (Windows)**
>
> Internet Explorer on Windows does not support `@import` rules with media types. For compatibility with Internet Explorer, you should use some other method of linking media-specific style sheets, such as the `<link>` tag or the `@media` rule described next.

Using the `@media` Rule

Within the same style sheet, you can mix rules for different media types by using a `@media` rule. This is a special type of rule that surrounds your other CSS rules and applies them only to certain media types. The basic form of this rule is

```
@media media-type {
    selector { declaration; }
    selector { declaration; }
    ...
}
```

That last curly brace is important because it marks the end of the `@media` rule. Any rules within the `@media` rule's braces are applied only to the media type listed. Listing 20.1 has several examples of the `@media` rule limiting certain rules only to certain types of output devices.

LISTING 20.1   A Style Sheet with `@media` Rules

```
/* media-rules-20.1.css */                      '

@media print {
  body    { font: 10pt "Times New Roman", serif;
            color: black; background-color: white; }
  .footer { border-top: 1px solid black;
            font-size: 8pt; }
  }

@media screen {
  body    { font-family: Verdana, sans-serif;
            color: white; background-color: #330000; }
  .footer { padding: 2em; font-size: smaller;
            border: 1em solid green; color: #330000;
            background-color: white; }
  }
```

> **Warning for Internet Explorer (Mac)**
> Internet Explorer on the Macintosh platform does not support @media rules.
> To use media-specific style sheet rules with IE for Mac, put those rules in a
> separate file and apply them with <link> or @import.

CSS Properties for the `print` Medium

By far the most common medium you'll be concerned with—besides screen—is print.
Nearly all computers have printers attached, and it's common for users to print a page as
a way of making a permanent copy of the content.

CSS rules can be used to format the appearance of the printed page. You can control the
layout, fonts, line-spacing, display characteristics, and more, separately from the way a
page is displayed on the screen. A specific style sheet for printing is a nice addition to
any CSS-based Web site.

Browsers and Printing

Printing a Web page is often a risky proposition. The combination of text, tables, style
rules, frames, and low-resolution GIF images often results in a poor-looking printed document. Most of the time, browsers don't print nearly as well as they display onscreen.
You can overcome some of these problems with a print style sheet.

To link in a style sheet for printing, simply use the HTML <link> tag as described previously. You can also use an @import rule or a @media rule in the main style sheet with the
appropriate media type. Multiple <link> tags let you provide one style sheet for rules common to all media types—one for screen display and one for printing, like the following:

```
<link type="text/css" rel="stylesheet"
    media="all" href="all.css">
<link type="text/css" rel="stylesheet"
    href="screen.css">
<!-- default value for media attribute is screen -->
<link type="text/css" rel="stylesheet"
    media="print" href="print.css">
```

20

Measurements for Printing

When you're creating a style sheet for printing, you can use additional units of measurement that would be inappropriate or meaningless on a computer monitor. These
units correspond to real-world units of measurement used in printing and are listed
in Table 20.2.

TABLE 20.2   Units of Measurement Appropriate for Printing

Unit	Measurement
cm	Centimeters
in	Inches (`1in = 2.54cm`)
mm	Millimeters (`1mm = 0.1cm`)
pc	Picas (`1pc = 12pt`)
pt	Points (`72pt = 1in`)

These units can be used with any CSS property that requires a measurement value. For example, the following rule sets a padding value in centimeters:

```
@media print { h1 { padding: 1cm 2cm 1cm 1cm; } }
```

Defining the Page with `@page`

The size of a printed page can be set with a `@page` rule. Such a rule creates a page box, which then can have various styles applied. A page box is similar to other CSS boxes, except that although it does have an adjustable `margin`, it does not have a `border` or `padding`.

A `@page` rule looks like the following:

```
@page { declarations; }
```

The `size` property can be used to set the dimensions of the page box. The default value is `auto`, which means to set the value equal to the dimensions of the paper type, as understood by the browser or by the operating system's printer driver. Other values are shown on Table 20.3.

TABLE 20.3   Values for the `size` Property

Value	Effect
measurement	Square page box of the specified size
measurement measurement	Rectangular page box
auto	Use whatever page dimensions already exist (in the browser or printer settings)
landscape	Use a landscape (wide and short) orientation
portrait	Use a portrait (tall and long) orientation

For example, the following defines a page that is 8.5 by 11 inches:

```
@page { size: 8.5in 11; }
```

If the page box is smaller than the size of the sheet of paper, the CSS specification says the browser can place it wherever it likes on the sheet—for example, in the upper left corner—but recommends centering the page box on the sheet. If the dimensions of the page box exceed those of the sheet of paper, the browser can ask the user for a preference to rescale the page box to fit the sheet or switch from portrait to landscape (or vice versa) if that solves the problem.

Another property that can be set is marks; this creates printer marks outside the printable area of the page. These can be used to crop or align the pages. Values for marks are shown on Table 20.4.

TABLE 20.4   Values for the marks Property

Value	Effect
crop	Crop marks around the page edge
cross	Cross marks at the page edge
crop cross	Both crop and cross marks
none	Neither crop nor cross marks

Here is an example of the marks property, which sets crop and cross marks around a square box:

```
@page { size: 5in; marks: crop cross; }
```

If the value auto, landscape, or portrait has been set for size, the page box fills the entire piece of paper, which means there is no room for printing marks. Thus, marks appear only when measurements have been given for the page box.

Three special pseudo-classes can be used to define page box characteristics that apply only to certain pages. These are :first, :left, and :right. These pseudo-classes are used after the @page keyword and are separated from it by a space.

According to the way Cascading Style Sheets understand printed pages, each page alternates between being a left page and a right page. Depending on the writing direction, the first page will be left or right. In English, the first page is a right page, the second a left, and so on. The :right and :left pseudo-classes let you define styles for those types of pages.

Here are some examples of rules set using these pseudo-classes:

```
@page :first { margin: 4in 2in 4in 3in; }
@page :right { margin: 0.5in 1in 0.5in 2in; }
@page :left  { margin: 0.5in 2in 0.5in 1in; }
```

20

The margins are set up this way so that if the page is printed on a double-sided printer—or printed on a single-sided printer and photocopied onto alternate sides of sheets of paper—there will be an extra inch on the "inside" margin to punch holes.

> **Warning for All Browsers**
>
> As of this writing, no current browsers support the @page rule and size property correctly. Opera 6 comes close (although not close enough), but the rest ignore it. Opera 6 can correctly understand landscape or portrait, but it does less well on exact dimensions. The bottom line is that @page is generally not reliable.
>
> If you choose to use the marks property, you are basically preparing for the future, as no existing browsers (as of early 2002) support this. No browsers support the :first, :right, or :left pseudo-classes correctly.

Page box formats can also be given a *page name*. A page name is a single word, used in a fashion similar to an element, after the keyword @page in a @page rule. For example, here are two page box formats, which are named square and rectangle:

```
@page square { size: 8.5in; }
@page rectangle { size: landscape; }
```

You use these page names when setting page breaks, as I'll explain shortly.

Setting Page Breaks

A page break is the point at which the browser decides it has placed enough on a given page and goes on to the next sheet of paper (and a new page box). Usually this is calculated automatically, although CSS rules let you control exactly when this happens. The rules that do this are page-break-after, page-break-before, and page-break-inside.

The page-break-after property means that a page break should (or shouldn't) occur after a given element, whereas page-break-before naturally deals with breaks before an element. The page-break-inside property can be used to prevent page breaks within an element. Values for these properties are shown on Table 20.5; the default values are auto.

TABLE 20.5   Values for Page-break Properties

Value	Effect
always	Always page break here (only page-break-after and page-break-before).
avoid	If at all possible, don't page break here.
auto	Determine page breaks automatically, as normal.

TABLE 20.5 Continued

Value	Effect
left	Break to produce a left page (only page-break-after and page-break-before).
right	Break to produce a right page (only page-break-after and page-break-before).

The values right or left will, if necessary, insert one or two blank sheets of paper to produce the given type of page.

Listing 20.2 has a style sheet that avoids page breaks within tables, forces <h1> tags to start a new right page (as chapter headings are formatted), and prevents page breaks after any headings.

LISTING 20.2 Controlling Page Breaks with CSS

```
/* page-breaks-20.2.css */
@page { size: auto; }
table            { page-break-inside: avoid; }
h1               { page-break-before: right; }
h2               { page-break-before: always; }
h3, h4, h5, h6 { page-break-before: avoid; }
hr               { page-break-before: avoid; }
```

Another way to force a page break is to use a page name with the page property. If a block box contains inline elements and the previous block box has a different value for page, the second box will begin on a new page. The properties of the page box will be those defined by the page name. Here are example rules illustrating this:

```
@page square { size: auto; }
@page square { size: 8.5in; }
@page rectangle { size: landscape; }
.box { page: square; border: 1px solid black; }
.wide { page: rectangle; }
```

Any block elements with class="box" will be printed in an 8.5in square page box; any block elements with class="wide" will be on a landscape page box.

Sometimes when printing a page with paragraph-style text, a single line will appear by itself, either at the bottom of one page or at the top of another. These are called orphans and widows, respectively. Printed pages look better if orphans and widows are avoided; the solution is to move the paragraph or part of it to the next page.

20

In CSS, orphans and widows can be avoided by the use of the `orphans` and `widows` properties. Each of these properties takes a numeric value, which is the minimum number of lines of the paragraph that must be left at the top or bottom of the page. The default value is 2.

Warning for All Browsers

Nearly all browsers ignore these properties. Internet Explorer recognizes the `page-break-before` and `page-break-after` properties with the `always` value, and Opera respects all three page-break properties.

Designing CSS for Print

When creating style rules or style sheets for the print medium, it's important to remember how the medium differs from the computer screen. The point of using a different style sheet for print is to make the resulting hardcopy easier to read and use.

Many printers out there will be black-and-white, although color printers are often used. However, many users will avoid printing in full color simply to save ink. Therefore, you want to make sure you're not relying on color entirely.

A printed page is clearly not interactive. When someone is printing a page, they're usually doing it for the content. Therefore, things like navigation bars and hypertext links are pretty useless. You can't click on a piece of paper.

The `display`, `visibility`, and `text-decoration` properties can help with this. You may want to enclose your navigation bar in a `<div class="nav">` and set rules like the following:

```
.nav { display: none; }
a:link, a:visited { text-decoration: none; }
```

Areas with dark backgrounds and light colors will consume a lot of black ink. Changing these to black ink on white paper, possibly with a border, is a friendly thing to do.

As described earlier in the hour, you can use exact units such as centimeters or inches when printing, as well as points for font sizes. Be careful not to assume that your users' paper will be the same size as yours, though.

The lack of browser support for most of the page-size and page-break properties is obviously a big problem when it comes to detailed control. You can set these properties if you like, and a few browsers will use some of them, but really it will matter only when browsers catch up to the CSS specification. Fortunately, none of these is harmful, so you can use them without fear of something unexpectedly breaking.

Summary

Alternate style sheets for different access devices are classified by the media types they apply to. You can set the media type of a CSS rule in several ways: by linking to a style sheet containing the rule with the `<link>` element in HTML; by importing a style sheet with that rule using `@import`; or by wrapping the CSS rule in a `@media` rule.

Visual browsers support the `screen` media type, and nearly all of them also support the `print` media type. The print medium uses page boxes, which are defined by `@page` rules. The size, margins, and other properties can be set on pages. Page breaks can also be set using CSS rules.

Designing for the print medium requires a different approach than screen designs. Scrolling, links, interactivity, and paging are all changed, so you'll need to think carefully about how to devise your print styles.

Browser Support Report Card

CSS Feature	Grade	Notes
`<link media="screen">`	A	
`<link media="anything else">`	B	Not supported by Netscape 4
`@import` with media type	B-	Not supported by Netscape 4; workaround required for IE (Windows)
`@media` rules	B-	Not supported by Netscape 4; workaround required for IE (Mac)
Units of measurement	A	
`@page`	D	Barely supported by Opera
`size`	D	Barely supported by Opera
`marks`	D-	Not supported
`:first`, `:left`, and `:right`	D-	Not supported
Page break properties	D+	Partially supported by Opera, Internet Explorer (Mac)
`orphans`, `widows`	D	Not supported

20

Q&A

Q Hold on a sec. I can't use `@import` with a media type for Windows Internet Explorer, and I can't use `@media` with Mac Internet Explorer. What can I do?

A Well, the easiest solution is to use `<link>` with a media type, which is supported by both. Another idea is the following:

```
@import url("print.css") print;
@media print { @import url("print.css"); }
```

This is a bit redundant, but it guarantees your `print.css` style sheet will be loaded in all browsers.

Q I need more control over the print layout than what CSS gives me (and the browsers don't support). What other options are there?

A As an alternative to CSS's print-related properties, you may want to investigate Extensible Stylesheet Language Formatting Objects (XSL-FO). Formatting objects use XML elements with attribute values related to CSS and are usually created by applying an Extensible Stylesheet Language Transformations (XSLT) sheet. Obviously, this is advanced stuff, but if you need advanced layout capabilities for print, this may be what you are looking for. See the W3C's XSL page at `http://www.w3.org/Style/XSL/` for more.

Workshop

The workshop contains quiz questions and activities to help reinforce what you've learned in this hour. If you get stuck, the answers to the quiz can be found after the questions.

Quiz

1. Your navigation bar has a `class` of `navbar`, and you've decided you don't want it to appear when the page is printed. How do you write such a rule using `@media`?

2. Which of the following is NOT a unit of measurement in CSS?

    (a.) `in`

    (b.) `mm`

    (c.) `ft`

    (d.) `pc`

3. The ISO metric paper size A4 is often used outside the United States and measures 210 by 297 millimeters. Assuming you're designing for a browser that supports the `@page` rule and the `size` property, how would you define the page box size for A4 paper?

Answers

1. Here is one way to write a rule to hide the `navbar` class:

   ```
   @media { .navbar { display: none; } }
   ```

2. (c.) Feet are not a valid unit of measurement in CSS; inches, millimeters, and picas are.

3. Well, assuming you're printing on A4 paper, you should be able to simply do the following:

   ```
   @page { size: auto; }
   ```

   This would automatically set the page box to be determined by your printer software. However, let's assume you want to explicitly set absolute values for the size of A4 paper; you would write

   ```
   @page { size: 210mm 297mm; }
   ```

Activity

As most browsers don't have good support for printing CSS styles, it can be rather hit-and-miss designing a print style sheet. However, this is still probably one of the best exercises, as it forces you to think through some of the assumptions you make when designing a page. For example, you've probably laid out your page in percentages or pixels, for online display. Do those measurements work well in print, or would it be better to use centimeters or inches? What do you want to do about links on the page? Present them as underlined text, even though they can't be clicked on? Remove the underlines? Or remove the navigation bar entirely? Choose a style sheet you've worked on in the past, and redesign it for printed output.

20

Hour **21**

Accessibility and Internationalization

The promise inherent in the name "World Wide Web" is an information network that can be used by everyone across the entire world. To a large degree this promise has been fulfilled, although there are still many groups of users whose needs aren't adequately met. To address these needs, the Cascading Style Sheets recommendations include specific support for accessibility by people with disabilities and for internationalization and non-English languages.

In this hour, you'll learn

- What hurdles people with disabilities face and how your use of CSS design can increase their accessibility to the Web
- Which standards relating to accessibility the W3C and the U.S. government have published
- How Aural Cascading Style Sheets are used, and which browsers for visually impaired users support them
- Which CSS features support internationalization and non-English languages
- How to write rules or style sheets that apply only to specific languages in your HTML

What Is Accessibility?

When we talk about Web accessibility, we're talking about the interaction between content and presentation and about ensuring that people who may have disabilities can use the result of that interaction. The content is the information we want to convey to our audience; it's not even necessarily the HTML code, but rather the information embodied by the HTML code—or by a Flash animation, GIF image, or multimedia movie. The presentation is the specific way we've chosen to express that information to our audience.

A basic principle of accessibility is that these two types of information, the content and the presentation, should be separated from each other. This allows for alternate versions of the presentation to be constructed that convey the information in a way that the user can perceive it. If the content cannot be easily extracted from the presentation, an alternate version can be provided.

The classic example of this is the `alt` attribute on the HTML `<img>` tag (and the `<area>` tag as well). The content of a visual image is obviously going to be inaccessible to a user who is blind; she simply can't see it. However, if a text equivalent of the image is supplied, using the `alt` attribute, her computer has information about what the image means, and it can provide that to the user—for example, by reading it out loud to her.

Users with disabilities will often use assistive technology (AT) to enable access. Assistive technology is a broad category that not only includes Braille terminals and screenreaders for blind users, but also includes magnification devices, voice recognition software, specialized input devices for those who can't type or use a mouse, and other hardware and software solutions.

Although assistive technology can solve many problems for users with special needs, it can't solve all of them because it can work only with the information that is available. For example, if there is no `alt` attribute for an image, the assistive technology has no clue what to tell the user about the image's function and purpose. AT alone can't enable access; it requires cooperation from the Web developer as well.

How People with Disabilities Use the Web

Most of the time when you hear about Web accessibility, the focus is on blind and visually impaired users. The Web is commonly thought of as a visual medium; however, it's more accurate to say that it's an information medium, and the visual representation of information is simply the most common way the majority of people use the Web. A mistaken insistence that the Web is meant to be only visual can lead many Web developers to inadvertently create Web sites that are inaccessible to users who can't see well.

A user who is blind will commonly use a screenreader, a software program that uses a synthetic voice to read the output of other programs. Examples of common screenreaders include JAWS for Windows (`http://www.freedomscientific.com/`) and WindowsEyes (`http://www.gwmicro.com/`). Screenreaders depend on a Web browser to retrieve and process Web pages; for example, JAWS is integrated with Internet Explorer for Web display.

Another option is a speaking Web browser, which is essentially a browser with a specialized screenreader built into it; examples are IBM's Home Page Reader (`http://www.ibm.com/able/`) and EmacSpeak for Linux/Unix (`http://emacspeak.sourceforge.net/`). Also in use are Braille terminals, which display around 40 characters at a time using raised dots in a row.

All of these access solutions for blind users dramatically change the experience of using the typical Web site. Instead of experiencing the content as a two-dimensional visual display, a user hears (or feels) the content in a sequential, linear order. On most page designs this means having to wade through the navigation options and banner ads before finally reaching the main content of the page.

Users who have the ability to see, but not necessarily see well, often employ other solutions to access Web content. For some, screen magnification software, which allows sections of the screen to be increased to many times their original size, may be necessary for ease of reading. A user with less severe requirements may simply increase his default font size to allow for comfortable reading.

Color blindness may cause someone to be unable to distinguish content within color graphics or to have difficulty discerning text against the background colors. The use of color as the only means of conveying information can restrict access by users who are color-blind or who can't see at all.

Compared with users with visual disabilities, deaf or hearing-impaired users are relatively fortunate when using the Web because most sites don't make heavy use of sound. However, those users can miss sound cues, audio files, and the sound tracks of multimedia presentations.

Users who are unable to use a keyboard or a mouse will often employ creative means to provide equivalent input to their computers. For example, a quadriplegic user who is unable to use his arms or hands may move the mouse pointer by moving a pointer wand worn on his head.

One of the broadest groups of users with disabilities is also the least understood when it comes to Web accessibility—users with cognitive disabilities. This wide category includes everything from relatively simple dyslexia to extreme mental retardation. Many individuals with varying cognitive impairments regularly use the Web as a primary information source, and they should not be discounted as a potential audience for your site simply because of their disabilities.

21

CSS Enables Access

Because the W3C created the CSS specifications with the needs of disabled users in mind, Cascading Style Sheets, if applied correctly, have great potential to meet the needs of those users. The primary benefit of using CSS is the separation of presentation from content; using CSS with HTML (especially Strict HTML) makes it clear which code is meant for presentational effects and which is the structured information of the page.

The CSS language has many features specifically intended to benefit users with visual disabilities, mainly because style sheet properties primarily define visual appearance. Media-specific alternate style sheets and rules can be created for screenreaders, Braille terminals, and Braille printers. Aural CSS properties, described later in this hour, give control over the pitch, frequency, and even apparent location of synthesized speech.

The use of relative measurements, such as em instead of absolute font sizes, allows your style sheets to adapt to user preferences, either in browser settings or in a user style sheet. This lets users with special needs for font or color choices continue to access your site even if the author's CSS isn't sufficient for their needs.

Style sheets do little to benefit deaf, hard of hearing, physically restricted, or cognitively impaired users, although a CSS-styled Web site based on sound usability and design principles will provide benefits for users both with and without these disabilities. Many cognitively disabled users specifically benefit from nontextual information cues, such as color, layout, and graphics.

Accessibility Standards and CSS

To fully test your CSS designs on all possible Web browsers and AT devices, you'd have to spend a fortune; you already know how hard it can be to fully test a CSS design on mainstream browsers, and adding assistive technology software and hardware to the mix makes the task nearly impossible. So what is a Web developer to do?

The answer has been for those with expertise in assistive technologies to gather information on accessibility and create a set of recommendations for Web developers to follow. By learning these standards, a Web developer won't have to spend time researching every possible access method but can instead be reasonably sure that a page created according to those principles will be accessible to a broad audience of users.

W3C's Web Content Accessibility Guidelines

The World Wide Web Consortium, in addition to publishing CSS, HTML, XHTML, XML, and other language specifications, also established the Web Accessibility Initiative (WAI). The purpose of the WAI is to create and distribute information on making the

Web more accessible to people with disabilities. The WAI has issued guidelines for browser programmers, Web editing tool programmers, and Web developers that suggest how to improve Web accessibility.

Most of us aren't programming browsers or authoring environments, so the WAI recommendation we're concerned with is the Web Content Accessibility Guidelines (WCAG), a list of checkpoints that can be used to measure the accessibility of your Web site.

Each WCAG checkpoint has a priority rating of one, two, or three, where priority one checkpoints are the most important and priority three the least. The WCAG checkpoints most applicable to CSS design are shown in Table 21.1.

TABLE 21.1   WCAG Checkpoints

Checkpoint	Priority	Explanation
Provide text alternatives for nontext elements.	one	Most CSS images, such as backgrounds or list bullets, are purely decorative, though, so they don't require additional alternatives.
Don't use color as the only way to convey information.	one	Make sure that the content can be understood if CSS colors aren't displayed.
Design pages that function even if style sheets are turned off.	one	Test your page in Lynx or with styles turned off to ensure functionality is maintained.
Use CSS to style text instead of creating text images.	two	If you can make an effect with CSS rules, you should do that instead of using a graphic.
Style sheets should be used instead of presentational markup.	two	After reading this book, this should be an easy one to meet!
Use relative values for styles instead of absolute values.	two	For example, use `x-large`, `smaller`, or `3em` instead of pixels or points.
Use foreground and background colors that contrast well with each other.	three	Colors that don't stand out from each other cause problems for users with poor vision or color blindness.

21

Table 21.1 is far from complete, but these are the checkpoints that are most relevant for CSS developers. If a Web page or site conforms to all of the priority one checkpoints (not just those listed here), it is said to be Single-A accessible. Meeting the priority one and two checkpoints equates to Double-A accessibility, and Triple-A accessibility means that all checkpoints of any priority level are met.

Many governments, schools, and other public institutions around the world have adopted Double-A accessibility as a standard for their sites; Single-A accessibility is considered the minimum for a public Web site.

> You can measure the accessibility of your Web site by going to the Center for Applied Special Technology site and using their Bobby program at `http://www.cast.org/bobby/`. Bobby is an automatic checker that can catch many of the most common accessibility mistakes, and also helps you manually check those problems that can't automatically be detected.

U.S. Government's Section 508

As part of employment and civil rights regulations, the U.S. government requires all agencies to make their public and internal sites accessible to people with disabilities. Known as Section 508 (from the applicable section of the Rehabilitation Act), these regulations affect how agencies can purchase and use information technology—accessibility is a requirement for hardware, software, and Web sites employed by the government.

> If you're not a U.S. citizen or don't work for the U.S. government, you might think these rules don't apply to you—and you're right. Section 508 is not an attempt to regulate the private sector, just federal agencies. However, because the U.S. government is the largest employer of information technology in the world, these rules have far-reaching influence and may be considered as a model for future accessibility standards. Therefore, it's important to be familiar with these requirements and how they apply to Web development using CSS.

The requirements for Web page accessibility are based on the W3C's Web Content Accessibility Guidelines; specifically, most of the priority one checkpoints with a few additions. These include the following:

- Make online forms compatible with assistive technology.
- Inform users whether a timed response is required, and if so, allow for extra time to be requested.

- Allow users to skip over lists of repetitive links, such as a navigation bar. A common way to do this is to create a link that jumps ahead in the page to the main content.

Many of these requirements—and the WCAG checkpoints—don't deal directly with Cascading Style Sheets and should be handled by the way you create your HTML (and are thus beyond the scope of this book). However, even in those cases, CSS can still be used to enhance the style and accessibility of your page.

CSS can be especially useful for hiding the "skip navigation" link required by Section 508. First create the link like the following:

```
<a href="#content" id="skip">Skip navigation</a>
```

Create an anchor point at the start of the content:

```
<a name="content"></a>
```

Then write a style rule like

```
#skip { display: none; }
@media aural, braille {
        #skip { display: inline; }
}
```

These CSS rules mean that the "skip navigation" link will be hidden on most browsers but will still be displayed by screenreaders, Braille terminals, and browsers that don't support CSS at all.

Aural Casacading Style Sheets

Aural properties for Cascading Style Sheets were first proposed as an extension to CSS Level 1 and were incorporated into the CSS Level 2 specification. These properties allow you to control the sound properties of spoken text, just as the visual properties control the visual properties of text and other elements.

Browsers That Understand Aural CSS

Unfortunately, this list is quite short. There are no mainstream browsers that support aural CSS properties. The EmacSpeak browser, developed for Linux and Unix by one of the primary authors of the aural properties of the CSS Level 2 specification, is the only browser that supports aural CSS.

21

If you're running a Unix-based system, you can download EmacSpeak from T.V. Raman's Web site at http://emacspeak.sourceforge.net/.

Currently, screenreaders and speaking browsers, such as JAWS for Windows and Home Page Reader, do not support aural CSS either; they use their own rules, which are not CSS based, to determine how to speak each page. Future versions may support aural CSS, though.

Because of this lack of support, there's little reason today to spend much time with aural style sheets; this is unfortunate because many of the properties are quite useful both for disability access and potentially for general use. Because these properties don't cause any problems in existing browsers—they're all completely ignored—it doesn't hurt anything to include them; there is a very low cost of failure when an aural CSS property is not supported.

Future versions of browsers, sreenreaders, and other access methods may support aural CSS; one particularly interesting proposal is for multi-modal access methods that would provide both visual and aural renditions simultaneously.

Aural CSS Properties

Rules using aural CSS properties are written just like rules for any other property, with a selector and a declaration of property names and values. You can use the @media selector from Hour 20, "CSS for Printing," to limit these rules only to media type aural, although by their very nature these properties will apply only to text that is spoken by the computer.

Because aural CSS is so poorly supported, I won't give an extensive tutorial on each property; if you want specifics, you can consult the aural properties section of the CSS specification. In this hour I'll just tell you enough to know the general capabilities of aural CSS.

Volume and Voices

The characteristics of the voice speaking the content of the page are determined by several properties relating to volume, pitch, and other qualities. These properties are listed in Table 21.2 along with the range of values allowed.

TABLE 21.2 Volume and Voice Aural Properties

Property Name	Values
pitch	*frequency*, x-low, low, medium, high, x-high, inherit
pitch-range	*variation-number*, inherit
richness	*richness-number*, inherit
speech-rate	*words-per-minute*, x-slow, slow, medium, fast, x-fast, faster, slow, inherit
stress	*stress-number*, inherit
voice-family	*specific-family*, *generic-family*, inherit
volume	*volume-number*, *percentage*, silent, x-soft, soft, medium, loud, x-loud, inherit

The voice-family property is similar to font-family; you can define a specific voice, which may or may not be supported by the aural CSS browser, or you can use one of three generic voice families: male, female, or child. There's no standard list of voice types beyond this, and so the use of specific voices (such as robot, Spock, or "Britney Spears") depends on the browser.

Pausing and Cues

Aural CSS properties allow you either to insert pauses to break up the aural reading, either before or after an element, or to insert specific sound files, called audio cues. These properties are shown on Table 21.3.

TABLE 21.3 Pausing and Cues Aural Properties

Property Name	Values
cue	Shorthand property, setting cue-after and cue-before
cue-after	*sound-url*, none, inherit
cue-before	*sound-url*, none, inherit
pause	Shorthand property, setting pause-after and pause-before
pause-after	*time-measurement*, percentage, inherit
pause-before	*time-measurement*, percentage, inherit

Cues are normal sound files, usually .wav or .au files, and are indicated by url() notation. Pauses are measured in seconds (s) or milliseconds (ms), such as 2s or 30ms.

21

Three-dimensional Sounds

Most humans hear in three dimensions if we have the use of both ears. Aural Cascading Style Sheets allow you to designate a specific location, within three dimensions, from which a sound could originate. Consider a transcript of an interview, marked up with voice properties similar to those of the appropriate speakers, where the interviewer's voice is heard on the left side, and the subject of the interview is heard on the right. A question from the audience could come from behind and below while an overhead announcement originates from directly above the listener.

The properties that place each sound in a specific location are shown on Table 21.4.

TABLE 21.4   Three-dimensional Sound Aural Properties

Property Name	Values
azimuth	*angle*, left-side, far-left, left, center-left, center, center-right, right, far-right, right-side, behind, leftwards, rightwards, inherit
elevation	*angle*, below, level, above, higher, lower, inherit

Angles are measured in degrees (deg), grads (grad), or radians (rad), such as 90deg, 100grad, or 1.571rad, which are all (approximately) a right angle. A 0deg azimuth is directly in front of the listener, and 0deg elevation is level with the listener.

Choosing What to Speak

Just as the display and visibility properties let you hide what is shown visually, aural CSS also lets you control what is vocalized and how that's done. You can even add the equivalent of a background image by specifying a background sound to be played while an element is spoken. These properties are shown in Table 21.5.

TABLE 21.5   Speaking Method Aural Properties

Property Name	Value
play-during	*background-sound*, mix, repeat, auto, none, inherit
speak	normal, none, spell-out, inherit
speak-header	always, once, inherit (table cells only)
speak-numeral	continuous, digits, inherit
speak-punctuation	code, none, inherit

The play-during property allows you to specify whether a background file is mixed in with any other background sounds already playing (from a containing element) or whether it replaces the other sound.

A Sample Aural Style Sheet

Listing 21.1 is an example aural style sheet. Lack of support for aural properties makes this a less-than-practical example, but this should give you an idea of how you can use aural CSS properties in action. Because these styles are purely aural, there's no printed screenshot for this example.

LISTING 21.1   An Aural Style Sheet

```
/* aural-21.1.css */
/* An aural style sheet for a public debate transcript */

#nav { speak: none; }    /* don't speak the navbar */

.intro { volume: loud;
         voice-family: neutral, male;
         azimuth: center;
         elevation: above;
         play-during: url("theme.wav") mix;
         pause-after: 3s; }

/* Two candidates and a moderator */
.mod { voice-family: Fred, male;
       azimuth: center;
       elevation: 15deg;
       pause-before: 1s; }
.rep { voice-family: Bruce, male;
       azimuth: right;
       elevation: 15deg; }
.dem { voice-family: Victoria, female;
       azimuth: left;
       elevation: 15deg;

/* audience questions */
.aud1 { voice-family: Agnes, female;
        azimuth: behind center-right;
        elevation: below; }
.aud2 { voice-family: Ralph, male;
        azimuth: behind center-left;
        elevation: below; }

/* events, moods, numbers, and letters */
.outoftime   { cue-after: url("bong.wav"); }
.angry       { pitch: high; volume: loud; stress: 75; }
.embarrassed { volume: soft; speech-rate: slower; }
abbr         { speak: spell-out; }
span.phone   { speak-numeral: digits; }
span.dollars { speak-numeral: continuous; }
```

21

Internationalization

Internationalization—sometimes abbreviated as i18n—"the letter i, 18 other letters, and the letter n" —is the practice of making content available in a variety of languages, not simply one. With a truly worldwide World Wide Web, the standards that are used on the Web simply can't support only the English language. The Cascading Style Sheets language has been partially internationalized, which means it can be used, with varying degrees of success, with many languages and local variants.

On the Web, languages are indicated by a two-letter code, sometimes followed by a dash and an additional country code for regional versions of a language. Some of these languages are shown in Table 21.6; for a complete list, see `http://www.cssin24hours.com/21/lang.html`.

TABLE 21.6 Several Language Codes

Code	Language
de	German
en	English
en-ca	Canadian English
en-uk	British English
en-us	American English
fr	French
jp	Japanese
ru	Russian

The choice of language can dictate a number of factors, including the direction of the text, the fonts used, or even the dictionary for pronunciation used by a screenreader. The CSS language doesn't allow you to set the language, which must be done in the HTML or in an HTTP header, but it does let you create rules or style sheets that apply only to certain languages.

To set the language within an HTML document, you simply have to use the `lang` attribute on the `<html>` tag. Sections of a second language embedded within the document can be indicated with the `lang` attribute on a `<span>` or any other appropriate HTML element, such as `<blockquote>` or `<div>`.

The :lang() Pseudo-class

The CSS Level 2 specification defines a special pseudoclass, :lang(), for indicating rules that should be applied only to elements that match a certain language. Such a rule is written like the following:

```
:lang(en-uk) { background-color: #CCCCFF; }
```

This would display anything written in British English with a light blue background color. How does the browser know which parts of the text are written in British English? It needs to be set in the HTML, like the following:

```
<p>He cried out in a bad Monty Python imitation,
  <span lang="en-uk">He's pinin' for the fjords!</span>
</p>
```

By itself, :lang() is not particularly useful, but when combined with other CSS rules and properties, it can be quite powerful. Some of those that involve generated content will be discussed in the next hour.

List Markers

One way in which :lang() rules can be used is to set an appropriate marker for ordered lists. You'll recall that you can set the list marker to count using Roman numerals, numbers, or letters, but what about languages that don't use the same alphabet? A list of additional values for the list-style-type property is shown in Table 21.7.

TABLE 21.7 International Values for the list-style-type Property

Value	Effect
armenian	Traditional Armenian numbers
cjk-ideographic	Ideographic numbers (Asian languages)
georgian	Traditional Georgian numbers
hebrew	Traditional Hebrew numbers
hiragana	Japanese hiragana numbers
hiragana-iroha	Japanese hiragana-iroha numbers
katakana	Japanese katakana numbers
katakana-iroha	Japanese katakana-iroha numbers
lower-greek	Lowercase Greek letters

21

You don't have to use a :lang() selector to utilize these values; you could use a normal element selector, a class or id selector, or anything else that fits your markup. Here are two examples:

```
li:lang(jp) { list-style-type: hiragana; }
ul.alphabeta { list-style-type: lower-greek; }
```

> These are supported only for those browsers and operating systems that support these character sets and appropriate fonts. This is highly dependent upon the specific version and language support on each computer. Although you should feel free to use these with content in the appropriate language, you should also expect that browsers without support for such a given language will display these as list-style-type: decimal.

Bidirectional Text

Most languages are read in one direction—left to right, as in English, or right to left. Some languages, such as Arabic or Hebrew, sometimes mix text direction within the same document; this is called bidirectional text (bidi for short). In most cases, the browser will have enough information to determine the direction based on the characters used and the language settings.

Two CSS properties, direction and unicode-bidi, are used to affect the calculation of the correct direction. In most cases, you won't need to use these properties, but if you find yourself needing to change the direction of text, you first use the unicode-bidi property to create an additional level of embedding or to set up an override. Then the value of direction can be set to either ltr (left-to-right) or rtl (right-to-left). For more details, see the CSS Level 2 specification. Browsers are not required to support changing direction of HTML text using these properties.

Summary

Users with disabilities are as entitled to use the Web as anyone else, but often they are unable to access sites due to careless Web design. Using Cascading Style Sheets is an excellent first step toward developing a site that can be used by everyone, as style sheets separate presentation from content.

Assistive technology devices and software can often enable access by disabled users, but only if sites are designed in accordance with Web accessibility standards. The W3C has produced Web Content Accessibility Guidelines that are an invaluable resource for Web developers and that form the basis of the U.S. government's Section 508 regulations for federal agency sites.

Aural CSS properties let you determine qualities of the voice used to read content out loud, such as the pitch, speed, and "family" of the voice. Unfortunately, almost no browsers support aural CSS currently, thus limiting its usefulness.

In addition to users with disabilities, users in non-English-speaking countries also use the Web. CSS is designed with internationalization in mind; for example, rules can be made for specific languages with the `:lang()` pseudo-element, and the `list-style-type` property can produce a number of non-English number markers.

Browser Support Report Card

CSS Feature	Grade	Notes
All Aural CSS properties	C-	No mainstream browser support
`:lang()` pseudo-class selectors	C	Variable support
International list markers	C	Variable support
Bidirectional text	n/a	Avoid changing text direction

Q&A

Q Is Section 508 the same as the Americans with Disabilities Act (ADA)? What are the ADA requirements for Web accessibility?

A Section 508 and the ADA are different sets of regulations. Section 508 applies only to federal agencies, whereas the ADA is applicable to a number of private and public sector entities. Unlike Section 508, the ADA contains no formal regulations for Web accessibility; however, the ADA requires organizations to avoid discrimination on the basis of disability when providing services. For detailed commentary on legal requirements for accessibility, see Cynthia Waddell's essays on the Web site of the International Center for Disability Resources on the Internet (http://www.icdri.org/).

Q Can tables be made accessible? Frames? JavaScript? Java? Flash? PDF?

A Yes. Tables and frames can be made accessible by using HTML markup carefully and by providing additional attributes or elements, such as `<noframes>`. If a certain technology or file format can't be directly made accessible, the content within it can be presented in an alternate, accessible format, such as a transcript or HTML version.

21

Workshop

The workshop contains quiz questions and activities to help reinforce what you've learned in this hour. If you get stuck, the answers to the quiz can be found after the questions.

Quiz

1. Do the Web Content Accessibility Guidelines suggest that color should be avoided in Web design?

2. Which of the following is NOT an aural CSS property?

    (a.) `voice-family`

    (b.) `stress`

    (c.) `accent`

    (d.) `speak-numeral`

3. How would you write a CSS rule to make all ordered lists written in French display a numeric marker that counts in Greek letters?

Answers

1. No. This is a common misunderstanding; the restriction is on using color as the only way to convey information. If you also provide that information in the HTML tags or the text content, your colors are not a problem at all.

2. (c.) There is no `accent` property in CSS.

3. Here is one way to write such a rule:

    ```
    ol:lang(fr) { list-style-item: lower-greek; }
    ```

Activity

Expand your skills with Web development by learning more about Web accessibility. Here are some sites you can visit to get started:

- Test your site's accessibility at the Center for Applied Special Technology using Bobby (`http://www.cast.org/bobby/`).

- Web Accessibility in Mind (`http://www.webaim.org/`) has tutorials and mailing lists for understanding Web accessibility issues.

- Download the free A-Prompt program for Windows computers from the University of Toronto (`http://aprompt.snow.utoronto.ca/`). A-Prompt interactively locates Web accessibility errors and corrects them for you.

- The HTML Writers Guild's AWARE Center (`http://www.awarecenter.org/`) features essays and online courses in Web accessibility.

HOUR 22

User Interface and Generated Content

The CSS properties defined in the Cascading Style Sheets Level 2 specification allow you to do more than simply place and present content. Specific properties also allow you to directly shape the user's experience through interaction with the operating system and browser; other properties let you add to the content of the page to build an appropriate presentation for the user.

In this hour, you'll learn

- How you can change the appearance of the mouse pointer
- Which properties allow you to create outlines, and how an outline is different from a border
- How to use the system colors and fonts in your design, and why you'd want to in the first place
- How you can add additional content to a page, before or after specific elements
- Which properties let you control the appearance of quotation marks
- How counters and markers can be used to automatically number lists and other elements

User Interface Properties

The *user interface* (UI) of a computer program is the part that interacts with the person using the program. This interaction includes not only the visual output, but also the method of providing information to the program via mouse, keyboard, or other input device.

When talking about Web content, there are several layers of user interface we're dealing with. The operating system—be it various versions of Windows, Mac OS, Linux running XWindows, and so on—provides a basic graphical user interface (GUI) layer, which creates the windows, menus, and boxes onscreen. The browser's user interface is built upon the operating system's UI and generally is designed to mesh with the operating system while adding appropriate controls for Web surfing. A third layer of user interface is created by the content itself; a Web page can be thought of as a UI for the information contained in the markup.

CSS Level 2 has several user interface properties that we'll examine in this part of the hour. These are not enough to fully control all interactions with the user, but they do allow you to alter some UI components and use information provided by the operating system to style the page.

Changing the Cursor Appearance

A key part of the Web-user experience is showing what part of the GUI is currently being pointed to by a pointing device, such as a mouse. The mouse cursor could be controlled by a mouse or by another method, such as a track-ball, a joystick, or a virtual mouse via the keyboard, for people who can't operate a normal mouse. For users with extreme disabilities, mouse control can be approximated by pointer wands attached to the head, or even by eye-tracking sensors.

A mouse cursor is applicable only in certain contexts; in print or Braille, for example, there is no mouse cursor. The mouse cursor is disabled or ignored by screenreaders for blind users, and it's also inapplicable for kiosk systems with touch panels or for small devices with touch screens, such as Palm or Pocket PC organizers.

It's important to keep in mind that a mouse cursor is just an indicator of potential action and not necessarily a choice that's been acted on; the cursor's location corresponds to the :hover pseudo-class in CSS, not to the :active or :focus pseudo-classes.

The CSS property cursor can be used to change the appearance of the mouse cursor; this change occurs whenever the mouse cursor is over the part of the page display corresponding to the display rule's selector. Because :hover is implied, it's not necessary to use that pseudo-class with the selector.

A cursor rule is written like this:

```
selector { cursor: cursor-type; }
```

The values that can be assigned to the cursor property are shown in Table 22.1. The default value is auto, and if this value is set on a containing box, it will be inherited by that box's children elements.

TABLE 22.1 Values for the cursor Property

Value	Effect
auto	Lets the browser decide the shape of the cursor
crosshair	Displays a crosshair cursor
default	Displays the default cursor (usually an arrow)
e-resize	Indicates that the object can be resized "eastward"
help	Displays a help-available cursor (usually a question mark)
move	Indicates a movable object's cursor (usually crossed arrows)
n-resize	Indicates that the object can be resized "northward"
ne-resize	Indicates that the object can be diagonally resized to the northeast
nw-resize	Indicates that the object can be diagonally resized to the northwest
pointer	Displays a link pointer cursor (usually a pointing hand)
s-resize	Indicates that the object can be resized "southward"
se-resize	Indicates that the object can be diagonally resized to the southeast
sw-resize	Indicates that the object can be diagonally resized to the southwest
text	Displays a text editing cursor (usually an I-shaped bar)
wait	Displays a waiting cursor (usually an hourglass)
w-resize	Indicates the object can be resized "westward"
url(address)	Displays a cursor image from a given URL
inherit	Uses the cursor value for the containing box

The url() value is written in a special format; you can write as many url() values as you like, and the browser will display the first one it is able to load and understand. After the last url() value, you should provide a "generic" cursor value from the list in Table 22.1, in case the url() cursors can't be displayed; for example, if the file format isn't understood by the browser. The concept of a generic default is similar to that of the font-family property and so should be familiar to you.

As there is not a universal format for cursor files, you should provide cursor images in several file formats using multiple url() values. For example, give a version of the cursor in .tiff, .cur, and .gif formats, in addition to supplying a generic value. Cursor images should usually be small—no more than around 40 by 40 pixels, and usually around 16 by 16.

> **Warnings for Opera, Internet Explorer 5, Internet Explorer (Mac), Netscape 4, and Netscape 6**
>
> Only Internet Explorer 6 for Windows supports the url() method for specifying a cursor image, so be sure to provide a backup cursor type as you would for fonts. Current versions of Opera don't allow you to change the cursor appearance using CSS, nor does Netscape 4.

Listing 22.1 is an HTML file that demonstrates the various cursors available in CSS. You can test these out yourself at http://www.CSSin24hours.com/22/cursors-22.1.html and see how your operating system and browser display each cursor type.

LISTING 22.1   The Different Styles of Cursors

```
<!-- cursors-22.1.html -->
<html>
  <head>
    <title>Changing Cursors</title>
    <style type="text/css">
      h3 { margin: 0.5em; padding: 0.25em;
           text-align: center;
           background-color: silver; color: black; }
    </style>
  </head>
  <body>
  <table width="100%"><tr><td valign="top">
    <h3 style="cursor: crosshair;">Crosshair</h3>
    <h3 style="cursor: default;">Default</h3>
    <h3 style="cursor: help;">Help</h3>
    <h3 style="cursor: move;">Move</h3>
    <h3 style="cursor: pointer;">Pointer</h3>
    <h3 style="cursor: text;">Text</h3>
    <h3 style="cursor: wait;">Wait</h3>
    <h3 style="cursor: url('maus.cur'),
                       url('maus.tiff'),
                       url('maus.gif'), auto;">URL</a>
    </td><td valign="top">
    <h3 style="cursor: n-resize;">North</h3>
    <h3 style="cursor: s-resize;">South</h3>
    <h3 style="cursor: e-resize;">East</h3>
```

22

LISTING 22.1 Continued

```
        <h3 style="cursor: w-resize;">West</h3>
        <h3 style="cursor: nw-resize;">Northwest</h3>
        <h3 style="cursor: ne-resize;">Northeast</h3>
        <h3 style="cursor: sw-resize;">Southwest</h3>
        <h3 style="cursor: se-resize;">Southeast</h3>
    </td></tr></table>
    </body>
</html>
```

The screenshot in Figure 22.1 is actually a composite of several screenshots; obviously, only one cursor can usually be displayed at a time, so I've combined images together to show you how one browser displays these cursors.

FIGURE 22.1
Internet Explorer 6 on Windows displays various cursors.

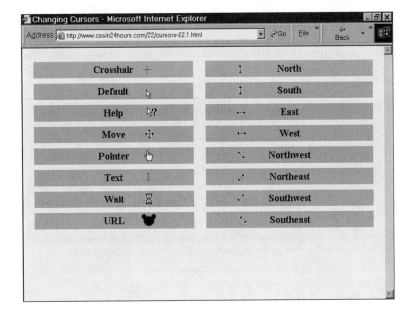

Now you know how to change the cursor, but why would you want to? In most cases, the style of the cursor is automatically set to something sensible by the Web browser, and it actually serves as a useful cue to the user. A pointer finger cursor, for example, lets the user know that they are over a link. In general, you should change the cursor appearance only if you've got a very good reason. For example, if you've used JavaScript to create a Dynamic HTML effect that lets you move something onscreen, you could change the cursor to indicate this. If you're using graphics for cursors, don't just set one for the whole page; create different graphics for links and input fields, and write appropriate rules to call them.

Creating Outlines

An outline is a visual line surrounding an element. This sounds similar to a border, doesn't it? Unlike a border, an outline doesn't actually take up any space in the box model. Instead, it's laid over other elements. The outline is placed just outside of the border, and thus it will be displayed over the margin or even over other content if the margin is small and the outline is wide.

The appearance of the outline is set with the `outline-width`, `outline-style`, and `outline-color` properties, or an `outline` shorthand property that sets all of them at once. The `outline-width` property can take the same types of values as the `border-width` property; the `outline-style` can accept `border-style` properties. The `outline-color` value can be any normal color value, or `invert`, which means the outline is displayed in the opposite colors of the margins (or other content) it lays over. Unlike borders, there is only one outline; you can't set separate outlines for different sides of the outlined element.

An outline is most useful for indicating focus or hover, although you can use it without the `:focus` or `:hover` pseudo-classes to simply draw an outline around anything. For example:

```
:focus, :hover { outline-width: medium;
                 outline-style: dotted;
                 outline-color: invert; }
h2 { outline: green 1px solid; }
```

Warning for All Browsers Except Internet Explorer (Mac)

Current browsers don't seem to support the `outline` properties, with the exception of Internet Explorer 5 for Macintosh. Although the `outline` properties are not harmful to use, they're not very useful at this time, either.

Using the System Colors and Fonts

The CSS language allows you to access certain qualities of the system or browser user interface and use these for color or font values. This is done by using special keywords that correspond to the current system settings.

The system color keywords can be used with any CSS property that can be set to a specific color value—`color`, `background-color`, `border-color`, and so on. These are listed in Table 22.2. These keywords are traditionally written in mixed case, with capital letters at the beginning of words for greater legibility. However, CSS is not case sensitive for color values, so if you write `activeborder` or `ACTIVEBORDER`, it means the same thing as `ActiveBorder`.

TABLE 22.2   System Color Keywords

Value	Effect
ActiveBorder	The border color around the active window
ActiveCaption	The background color of the caption on the active window
AppWorkspace	The background color within the application's main window
Background	The background color of the desktop
ButtonFace	The background color of a three-dimensional button
ButtonHighlight	The border color for the dark edge of a three-dimensional button
ButtonShadow	The shadow color of a three-dimensional button
ButtonText	The text color for a three-dimensional button
CaptionText	The text color in a caption
GrayText	The text color for disabled options (grayed out)
Highlight	The background color for selected items
HighlightText	The text color for selected items
InactiveBorder	The border color around an inactive window
InactiveCaption	The background color of the caption on an inactive window
InactiveCaptionText	The text color of the caption on an inactive window
InfoBackground	The background color for tooltips
InfoText	The text color for tooltips
Menu	The background color for menu items
MenuText	The text color for menu items
Scrollbar	The color of the scrollbar
ThreeDDarkShadow	The dark shadow for a three-dimensional element
ThreeDFace	The background color for a three-dimensional element
ThreeDHighlight	The highlight color for a three-dimensional element
ThreeDLightShadow	The border color for the light edge of a three-dimensional element
ThreeDShadow	The shadow color for a three-dimensional element
Window	The background color of a window
WindowFrame	The border color of the frame around a window
WindowText	The text color within a window

For each of the values in Table 22.2, a descriptive adjective such as highlight, border, background, or text is given before the word *color*. These describe how the colors are used within the system user interface, but you don't have to use them for only those purposes in your style sheet. For example, you could set the text color to Window, and the `background-color` to `WindowText`; the `AppWorkspace` value could be used to set a box's border. Here are examples of how to use these values:

```
.showthis { color: window;
            background-color: windowText;
            border: 2px solid AppWorkspace; }
```

Warning for Netscape 4

Netscape 4 doesn't understand these values and will try to interpret them as malformed hex values, leading to very strange results. Therefore, you can't use these with Netscape. If you want to use system colors, write your rules so that Netscape 4 won't process them; for example, by including them with an @import rule.

You can also use the system font settings for various types of text within your style sheet. These are accomplished by setting the font shorthand property to one of the system values shown in Table 22.3. For example, to make a `<div>` use the font qualities for a system message box, use the following:

```
div { font: message-box; }
```

TABLE 22.3 System Values for the `font` Property

Value	Effect
caption	Uses the same font values as system captions
icon	Uses the same font values as system icons
menu	Uses the same font values as system menus
message-box	Uses the same font values as system message boxes
small-caption	Uses the same font values as small system captions
status-bar	Uses the same font values as the status bar

Each use of font in this manner sets the `font-size`, `font-style`, `font-weight`, `font-variant`, and `font-family` to the same values as the specified kind of system text. Subsequent rules can change those values, as shown here:

```
div { font: message-box;
      font-weight: bold;
      font-size: larger; }
```

Why would you want to use system colors and fonts? Usually you wouldn't. Web sites have good reason to express their own individuality and style, and utilizing the user's system appearance doesn't mesh well with that. However, there are some cases, such as alert boxes, where you may very well want to mimic the effects of an operating system prompt.

There are accessibility considerations as well; in general, you can be sure that system colors will be usable by anyone with visual impairments because otherwise they couldn't operate their computer at all. However, the benefits of system styles are small compared with the negative effects of "sameness" and bland design. User style sheets or alternate style sheets provide better accessibility options for all users in the long run.

Creating Content

In CSS terminology, *generated content* consists of text or images that aren't present in the HTML markup but are added through CSS rules. The ability to generate content allows for even more flexibility in designing style sheets and alternate style sheets that effectively convey the information of the page to the user.

In overview, generating content depends on using the `:before` and `:after` pseudo-classes as selectors for rules with `content` property declarations. Text, attribute values, images, quotation marks, and numbered counters can all be added to HTML using CSS content generation.

Because generated content is not always going to be available due to browser deficiencies, users who have turned off style sheets, or devices that can't display CSS, you shouldn't rely on generated content unless you know the browser on the other end can display it. In other cases, you can use generated content to enhance the presentation without being dependent upon it to convey information.

The `:before` and `:after` Pseudo-classes

To generate content, you must use the `:before` and `:after` pseudo-classes. These pseudo-classes define the point at which you will add additional material. Content can be added at the beginning or the end of an element.

To add content at the beginning of an element, you would write a rule like this:

```
element:before { declarations; }
```

To insert the content after the element, the rule looks like this:

```
element:after { declarations; }
```

You can combine this with any other CSS selectors, such as `class`, `id`, attribute, relationship, or pseudo-class selectors. You can't write a single rule that has both `:before` and `:after` selectors, but you can write one rule putting content before the element and another adding content after it.

The content Property

The material generated at the insertion point (either before or after the selector) is defined by the `content` property. This CSS property can be used only within a rule with a `:before` or `:after` pseudo-class selector. The values for content are shown in Table 22.4.

TABLE 22.4 Values for the content Property

Value	Effect
`"quoted-text"`	Inserts the specified text
`attr(attribute)`	Inserts the value of the specified attribute
`close-quote`	Inserts an appropriate closing quote mark
`counter(name)`	Inserts a counter's value
`counter(name, marker-style)`	Inserts a counter's value
`counters(name, string)`	Inserts a counter's value and a string
`counters(name, string, marker-style)`	Inserts a counter's value and a string
`no-close-quote`	Suppresses the printing of a closing quote mark
`no-open-quote`	Suppresses the printing of an opening quote mark
`open-quote`	Inserts an appropriate opening quote mark
`url(address)`	Inserts the contents of the specified URL

The `content` property allows for multiple values, separated by spaces; for example, the following is allowed:

```
.note:before { content: url('note.gif') "Note "
              counter(notes) ": (" attr(title) ")"; }
```

The content inserted consists of an image, quoted text, a counter reference, another bit of quoted text, an attribute value, and a final snippet of quoted text.

The specified content is added at the designated insertion point and becomes a virtual child element. Although the generated content inherits all appropriate properties from the element it was inserted into, it can also be styled separately, as well.

Warnings for Netscape 4, Internet Explorer

Netscape 4 and Internet Explorer don't display generated content. As suggested before, you should use generated content only if you can be certain which browser will be used or if you are using the generated content only to enhance, rather than to provide the full presentation.

The remainder of this hour will examine how the values in Table 22.4 create content, so I've created a simple HTML file to which we'll add styles. This is shown in Listing 22.2 and is a brief (and incomplete) list of books by J.R.R. Tolkien.

LISTING 22.2 A Simple HTML File Listing Some Works of Tolkien

```
<!-- generated-22.2.html -->
<html>
  <head>
    <title>Generating content</title>
  </head>
  <body>
    <h1>J.R.R. Tolkien</h1>
    <div class="book">The Hobbit</div>
    <div title="Lord of the Rings">
      <div class="book">The Fellowship of the Ring</div>
      <div class="book">The Two Towers</div>
      <div class="book">Return of the King</div>
    </div>
    <div class="book">The Silmarillion</div>
  </body>
</html>
```

The HTML file in Listing 22.2 defines a simple structure wherein book titles are identified by the book class, and related books are grouped within titled <div> tags. There is no styling information provided, so the list appears plain and straightforward, as shown in Figure 22.2. Note that the division title "Lord of the Rings" isn't shown because it is an attribute value and not text content.

FIGURE 22.2

*No styles applied to
the Tolkien book list.*

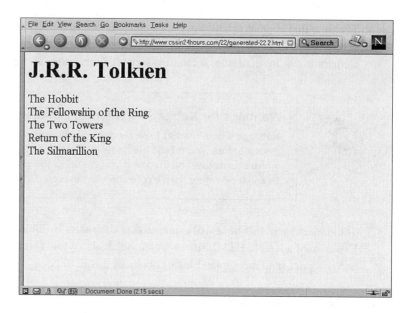

Adding Text and Images

Text can be inserted into a page by giving a quoted text value to the content property.
Quotes can be either double quotes (") or single quotes ('); they have to match, though.
You can use double quotes to surround single quotes, or single quotes to surround double
quotes. For example:

```
h1:before { content: "Kynn's Headline: "; }
h2:before, h2:after { content: '"'; }
```

Text can also be inserted by using an attribute's value via the attr() function. Here is
an example combining quoted text with an attribute value to make the alternative text
of an image visible:

```
img:after { content: " [ALT: " attr(alt) "]"; }
```

To insert an image before or after an element, you give a url() value. This is similar to
providing a bullet image with the list-style-image property, although it can be done
with any element.

Warning for Opera

Opera doesn't display images inserted with the url() function, although it
displays text and attribute values just fine.

Listing 22.3 adds explanatory text, as well as a small graphic, to our HTML file's presentation. The `div[title]` selector is an attribute selector, as covered in Hour 19, "Advanced Selectors."

LISTING 22.3   Style Sheet Generating Text for Book List

```
/* generated-22.3.css */

h1:after { content: ": author index"; }
div[title]:before { content: "Series: " attr(title);
                    font-weight: bold; }
div[title] { margin-top: 0.5em; margin-bottom: 0.5em; }
div[title] div { margin-left: 2em; }
div.book:before { content: url('option.gif'); }
```

Not all browsers support generated content, but Netscape 6, Opera 5 (Mac), and Opera 6 (Windows) do. The results of applying our style sheet to the Tolkien listing are shown in Figure 22.3.

FIGURE 22.3

Netscape 6 generating content for Tolkien list.

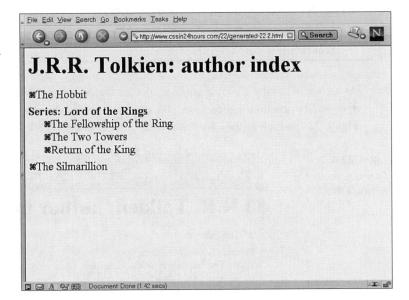

Generating Quotation Marks

You can use CSS to add quotation marks to your Web page. This is most useful when you're dealing with multiple languages on the same site, where different languages have different quotation symbols. It's also applicable if you use the HTML element <q> to mark up your quotations.

To add quotations, first you must define which quotation marks should be used by using the quotes property. The values for quotes are pairs of symbols enclosed in double-quotes themselves (or single-quotes if they contain double-quote characters). The first pair is considered the outer pair of quotation symbols; inner quotes use the next pair in, and so on. Listing 22.4 gives an example, using doubled left-ticks and right-ticks for some quotes and square brackets for others. Your values for quotes don't have to be actual quotation marks; you can use any symbols or text.

LISTING 22.4   Style Sheet That Adds Quotes to the Book List

```
/* generated-22.4.css */

h1:after { content: ": author index"; }
div { quotes: "``" "''"; }
div[title] { quotes: "[" "]"; }
div[title]:before { content: "Series: " open-quote
                    attr(title) close-quote;
                    font-weight: bold; }
div[title] { margin-top: 0.5em; margin-bottom: 0.5em; }
div[title] div { margin-left: 2em; }
div.book:before { content: url('option.gif') open-quote; }
div.book:after { content: close-quote; }
```

As shown in Listing 22.4, the quote marks are included in generated content by the open-quote or close-quote values for content. You can see the effect of these rules in Figure 22.4, which applies the updated style sheet to the HTML file from Listing 22.2.

FIGURE 22.4

Quotes generated by Netscape 6.

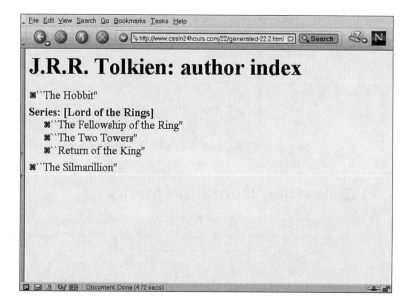

Counters, Numbering, and Markers

22

Generated content can also consist of counter values. A CSS counter is like a very simple variable from a programming language. Each counter is identified by a name and holds a numeric integer value, such as 1, 2, 335, or –5. The counter can be set to a specific value, increased or decreased by a certain amount or displayed as part of a `content` rule.

A counter is set to a specific value by using the `counter-reset` property; whenever a CSS rule containing `counter-reset` is applied to a selector, the counter is reset to the specified value, or to zero if no value is given. The name of the counter must be specified in the `counter-reset` declaration. The counter increases whenever a `counter-increment` property is applied that designates a counter of the same name. The general syntax for `counter-reset` and `counter-increment` looks like this:

```
selector { counter-reset: name amount name amount ... ; }
selector { counter-increment: name amount name amount ...; }
```

The *amount* can be omitted; for `counter-reset` this resets the counter to zero, and for `counter-increment` this increases the counter by one. You can reset or increment multiple counters by giving *name-amount* pairs (or just multiple counter names if you want to use the default *amount* values).

To display the counter value, use the function `counter()` or `counters()` within a content declaration. Each counter has a scope over which the counter applies, which consists of the element in which it was declared and its children; you can have multiple counters with the same name. The value of the current counter with a given *name* is specified by `counter(name)`; the values of all counters with that *name* within the scope are given by `counters(name, delimiter)`. The *delimiter* option specifies a string to be displayed between values. This lets you create nested lists with proper numbering.

An additional option can be supplied to the `counter()` and `counters()` functions, which select a list style to be applied to the display of the counter. This can be any `list-style-type` value as covered in Hour 11, "Styling Links."

An example of counters in a style sheet can be seen in Listing 22.5. This example counts books within a series and the total numbers of books from our HTML Tolkien book list.

LISTING 22.5　Style Sheet for Adding Counters to the Book List

```
margin-top: 1em;
/* generated-22.5.css */

h1:after { content: ": author index"; }
div { quotes: "``" "''"; }
```

continues

LISTING 22.5 Continued

```
div[title] { quotes: "[" "]"; }
div[title]:before { content: "Series: " open-quote
                    attr(title) close-quote;
                    font-weight: bold;
                    counter-reset: BooksInSeries; }
div[title] { margin-top: 0.5em; margin-bottom: 0.5em; }
div[title] div { margin-left: 2em; }
div[title]:after { content: "Books in Series: "
                   counter(BooksInSeries, decimal);
                   margin-left: 2em; font-weight: bold; }
div.book:before { content: url('option.gif') open-quote; }
div.book:after { content: close-quote;
                 counter-increment: BooksInSeries Total; }
body:after { content: "Total books in index: " counter(Total);
             margin-top: 1em; display: block; font-weight: bold; }
```

Most browsers do not support counters; only Opera 5 (Mac) and Opera 6 (Windows) support it reliably. Figure 22.5 shows how Opera displays our HTML file from Listing 22.2 with the style sheet applied.

FIGURE 22.5

Opera 6 displays counts for Tolkien's books.

Summary

Cascading Style Sheets allow your Web designs to incorporate elements of the user interface into the presentation. Through CSS, you can change the cursor using the cursor property or draw highlights around certain items with the outline properties.

Colors and fonts can be tuned to fit the operating system or browser preferences of the user by employing special keywords for the color, background-color, border, and font properties.

Additional information can be added to the HTML by style sheets using content generation. Quoted text, attribute values, images, quotation marks, and counters can be included via the content property. The quotes property specifies the styles of quotes to be used, and the counter-reset and counter-increment properties manage the values of the counters.

As with all advanced CSS features, content generation is not widely supported by the browsers. If the primary content of the site is supported or explained only by generated content, users without access to the style sheet will be left out, so care should be taken whenever using these techniques.

Browser Support Report Card

CSS Feature	Grade	Notes
The cursor property	B+	Not recognized by Opera 5 (Mac), Netscape 4
cursor: url()	C-	Not understood by any browser
The outline properties	C-	Not understood by any browser
System colors and fonts	B+	Workaround required for Netscape 4
Generated content	D	Unreliable
Generated quotation marks	D	Unreliable
Counters	D-	Unreliable

Although generated content is quite useful in theory, in practice it is not currently reliable enough that you can count on it. Depending on content generation to convey key site content is quite dangerous and should always be avoided.

Q&A

Q Form fields are a type of user interface component, right? How can I apply styles to those?

A HTML <form> fields and buttons are called *replaced content* in the CSS specification. This means that the box model doesn't strictly apply to them; the browser can decide how they should appear. Most browsers allow CSS properties to be applied to the textual portions of replaced content; for example, the following style sheet will work in many browsers:

```
textarea { color: white; background-color: black;
           font-family: Courier New, Courier, monospace; }
input    { font-family: Verdana, sans-serif; }
```

However, it's not guaranteed that this will work, because the CSS specification doesn't address the styling of replaced content. You should feel free to use styles on form fields, but be sure to check carefully, and don't rely on those styles appearing as you desire.

Q Can I use content generation to insert HTML tags before and after an element? That would be really cool.

A It would indeed be cool, but the answer is no, you can't. Quoted text is inserted directly as text, not as markup, which means that if you wrap HTML tags around something, they won't be interpreted by the browser. Instead you'll just see those tags, in angle brackets, when viewing the page.

Q Generating content doesn't sound reliable. It would be easier to just add the content to the HTML, and that works in Netscape 4 and every other browser! Why would I ever use generated content?

A Content generation is useful and powerful, but as you say, it can be unreliable. In general, you're right; if you need to include some text in your output, you should put it in the HTML. There are a few cases where generated content is particularly useful, though, including sites where you may not have access to the content but can style it; alternate style sheets for specific presentations, such as a screenreader style sheet for visually impaired users; and XML files that don't inherently contain explanatory text. For more on XML and generated markup, see Hour 24, "CSS and XML."

Workshop

The workshop contains quiz questions and activities to help reinforce what you've learned in this hour. If you get stuck, the answers to the quiz can be found after the questions.

Quiz

1. Which of these options is not a valid declaration for the `cursor` property?

   (a.) `cursor: hourglass;`

   (b.) `cursor: ne-resize;`

   (c.) `cursor: url('target.cur'), crosshair;`

   (d.) `cursor: text;`

2. Your HTML contains `<a>` links of the class `button3d` that you want to style to look like three-dimensional buttons. How do you make members of this class appear as such using the system color and `font` properties?

3. What does each of the following content rules accomplish?

    (a.) `a[href]:after { content: "[LINK: " attr(href) "]"; }`

    (b.) `h1:before { "#" counter(item); counter-increment: item; }`

    (c.) `blockquote p:before { content: open-quote; }`

Answers

1. (a.) `hourglass` is not a proper value for `cursor`; to display an hourglass or timer cursor, use the value `wait`.

2. Here is one way to write the appropriate style rules:

```
a.button3d:link {
display: block;
font: menu;              color: ButtonText;
background-color: ButtonFace;
border-width: medium;    border-type: outset;
border-color: ButtonHighlight; }
```

3. The rules generate the following types of content:

    (a.) All links are followed by an indication of their link target. This is a very handy rule if you are printing out documents.

    (b.) This numbers all `<h1>` elements.

    (c.) This starts all paragraphs within a `<blockquote>` with the opening quote character.

Activities

Here are some projects that will help you get practice using the properties from this hour:

1. Experiment with changing the cursors on your Web site. Does it make it easier to use or harder to use if the cursors aren't set by the browser?

2. Using the `:active` pseudo-class, extend the style rules from Quiz question 2 to create three-dimensional buttons that visually appear to depress when clicked.

3. Use content generation to add additional notes to a Web page explaining the function of each element. Style these notes in a different color or with a border around them.

HOUR 23

CSS and JavaScript

In addition to HTML and Cascading Style Sheets, JavaScript is one of the primary languages spoken by Web browsers. The HTML code provides the structure of the content, the style sheet provides the presentation, and the JavaScript provides the interactivity and actions. JavaScript and CSS go hand-in-hand in building the user's experience with the Web site. A full tutorial on JavaScript goes beyond the scope of this book, but nevertheless, in this hour you will learn

- The basic concepts of JavaScript
- How to trigger JavaScripts in Web pages using HTML events
- How CSS can be used with JavaScript to produce Dynamic HTML
- How to move content around the screen using JavaScript and positioning CSS
- How to detect specific browsers using JavaScript and provide an alternate style sheet for each

What Is JavaScript?

JavaScript is a programming language originally created by Netscape but now used by nearly all Web browsers, including Netscape, Mozilla, Opera, and Internet Explorer.

> JavaScript actually goes by several names. The original name was LiveScript, but they changed it to JavaScript because Java was a hot buzzword at the time. (The less cynical reason is that the syntax of JavaScript is very loosely based on the Java programming language.) The standardized version of JavaScript is called ECMAScript and is published by ECMA, the European Association for Standardizing Information and Communication Systems (http://www.ecma.ch/). Microsoft uses the term JScript to refer to the specific type of JavaScript supported by Internet Explorer.

JavaScript has something in common with Cascading Style Sheets; each browser has quirks in how it understands JavaScript. Just as a CSS designer has to be aware of browser support issues, so does a JavaScript programmer need to take special care to account for browser limitations.

In this hour, there's not enough time to cover everything you need to know about JavaScript; that could take a whole book itself. Instead, I'll tell you about what JavaScript can do and hopefully whet your appetite for learning more if you haven't worked with it before. If you already know JavaScript, this hour will show you how to use it with CSS styles. Some example scripts in this hour will show you specific cases of JavaScript and style sheets working together to produce the end result.

> In fact, there are several good books about JavaScript. If you like the *Sams Teach Yourself* approach to learning, you'll want to pick up *Sams Teach Yourself JavaScript in 24 Hours*, written by Michael G. Moncur (ISBN 0672320258).

JavaScript runs on the browser-side, which means that it doesn't run on a Web server but within a Web browser. Scripts can be written that produce a wide variety of effects, from validating form input to creating animation. The ones we are most concerned with in this hour are those that interact with CSS—setting styles, hiding or displaying content, or positioning elements on the screen.

As a programming language, JavaScript has a different feel than either CSS or HTML. A script is a set of instructions that are executed by the browser in a specific order, rather than a set of style rules or marked-up content. Execution means that the browser follows the instruction, and then the browser goes on to the next instruction in the script. In general, a script starts running when the browser encounters it on the page. Similar to CSS, JavaScript instructions are separated by semi-colons, and distinct sections are contained in matching curly braces.

> What about other scripting languages? Why would you want to use JavaScript instead of another language? In short, JavaScript is the only browser-side language that's well supported by all major browsers. Many other Web programming languages, such as Perl, ASP, PHP, or Cold Fusion, run on the Web server instead of on the browser, and they may require your Web host to install specific software on the server. Server-side programming languages can be used with CSS because they produce normal HTML files, no matter how that code is generated by server code.
>
> Scripts that execute within the browser are written in client-side languages, such as JavaScript, and don't require anything special on the back end. Other examples of languages that execute on the client-side include VBScript and Java. VBScript functions only on Internet Explorer, whereas Java is many times more complex than JavaScript. For these reasons, JavaScript is the language of choice for client-side programming on the Web.

A script contains constructs found in programming languages, such as functions, variables, and conditional statements. If you haven't programmed before, these might not be familiar concepts. A *function* is a part of the script that doesn't immediately execute when the browser encounters it but instead defines a section of code that can be executed upon request elsewhere in the script. A *variable* is a named "storage bin" that holds a value that may be accessed within the script. A *conditional statement* creates a branch in the execution order; if a given condition exists, one set of instructions is executed, and if not, either nothing is executed or another set of instructions is executed.

To use JavaScript with HTML, you use the <script> tag. The <script> tag can be placed in either the <head> section or the <body> section of the Web page. An example of JavaScript in HTML is shown in Listing 23.1, which is a very simple number quiz.

LISTING 23.1   A Simple Interactive Page Created with JavaScript

```
<!-- demo-23.1.html -->
<html>
  <head>
    <title>JavaScript Demo</title>
    <script type="text/javascript" language="JavaScript">
      var magicNumber = Math.floor(Math.random()*100+0.5);
      var isOdd = magicNumber % 2;
      function pressOdd() {
        if (isOdd) { window.alert("Correct!\n\n" +
                      magicNumber + " is odd."); }
          else    { window.alert("Try again!"); } }
      function pressEven() {
        if (isOdd) { window.alert("Try again!"); }
          else    { window.alert("Correct!\n\n" +
                      magicNumber + " is even."); } }
    </script>
  </head>
  <body>
    <script type="text/javascript" language="JavaScript">
      document.write("<h1>The magic number is..." +
                      magicNumber + "</h1>");
    </script>
    <p>Do you think that number is odd or even?</p>
    <form> <button onclick="pressOdd()">Odd</button>
           <button onclick="pressEven()">Even</button>
           <button onclick="document.location.reload()"
                  >Choose Another</button></form>
  </body>
</html>
```

There are two scripts in Listing 23.1. The first is within the <head> element of the page, and when the page loads, that script randomly picks a number, assigns it to the magicNumber variable, determines whether it is odd or even and assigns the result of that determination to the isOdd variable, and finally sets up two functions, pressOdd() and pressEven(). Those functions don't do anything until they are triggered elsewhere in the page.

The second script, in the <body> of the page, creates HTML using the built-in document.write() function to add an <h1> tag and show the value of the magicNumber variable.

The <button> elements are used to create form buttons that display "odd," "even," or "choose another." The onclick attribute on the first <button> triggers the pressOdd() function; the onclick attribute on the second <button> triggers the pressEven() function. The third button has an onclick attribute that reloads the current location. These onclick attributes are HTML intrinsic events, and you'll learn more about them later this hour.

When the pressOdd() or pressEven() functions are triggered by clicking on the buttons, the browser creates a pop-up alert window. The contents of this window will depend on whether the right answer was given, as determined by the value of the isOdd variable. In Figure 23.1, you can see an example of this script in action; you can also try it yourself at http://www.cssin24hours.com/23/demo-23.1.html.

FIGURE 23.1

Netscape 6 displays the page.

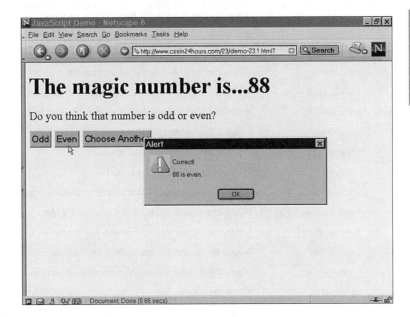

23

HTML Events

A script normally is executed when the browser encounters it; in other words, when the page is being displayed and the browser comes across the script within a <script> tag, it executes. However, you can also set code to execute upon the fulfillment of certain conditions, usually the result of the user's actions. These are called *intrinsic events*. Intrinsic events are defined by the HTML specification and are attributes that can be set on HTML tags. For example, in Listing 23.1, you saw the onclick attribute used as follows:

```
<button onclick="pressOdd()">Odd</button>
<button onclick="pressEven()">Even</button>
<button onclick="document.location.reload()"
        >Choose Another</button></form>
```

The value of an intrinsic event attribute is a small snippet of JavaScript. In the first two examples, the onclick attribute calls a function that is defined earlier in the page. In the third example, the onclick attribute calls a built-in method, document.location.reload(), which reloads the current document. These events happen only when the button is clicked.

A complete list of HTML intrinsic event attributes, and the actions which trigger those events, is shown in Table 23.1.

TABLE 23.1   Intrinsic Events in HTML

Attribute	Triggering Event
onBlur	When the element loses focus (links and form controls only)
onChange	When the current selection changes (<select>, <input>, and <textarea> tags only)
onClick	When the mouse clicks over an element
onDblClick	When the mouse is double-clicked over an element
onFocus	When the element receives focus (links and form controls only)
onKeyDown	When a key is pressed down
onKeyPress	When a key is pressed and released
onKeyUp	When a pressed key is released
onLoad	When the page loads (<body> and <frameset> tags only)
onMouseDown	When the mouse clicks down over an element
onMouseMove	When the mouse pointer moves while over an element
onMouseOut	When the mouse pointer moves off an element
onMouseOver	When the mouse pointer moves over an element
onMouseUp	When the mouse button is released over an element
onSelect	When the user selects text in a text field (<input> and <textarea> tags only)
onSubmit	When a form is submitted (<form> tags only)
onUnLoad	When the page "unloads" (<body> and <frameset> tags only)

For readability's sake, I have capitalized the first letter of words embedded within event attribute names. Because HTML is not case-sensitive, it doesn't matter whether you write onMouseMove or onmousemove.

However, if you are using XHTML, it does matter! XHTML is case sensitive and requires all attributes to be written in lowercase. So for an XHTML document, you could write only onmousemove.

Some of these events should seem familiar to you. The `onMouseOver` event is similar to the `:hover` pseudo-class of CSS, and `onFocus` is like `:focus`. However, each of these events is actually just half of the action; when you move the mouse to hover over an element, two things happen. First, it's now "over" that element, and second, it's no longer where it was before. This is an `onMouseOver` event for the new element, and an `onMouseOut` event for the old location.

How JavaScript Views a Document

In a CSS context, an HTML file consists of a series of nested boxes that have styles applied to them. In JavaScript, HTML elements are referenced as objects. This is because JavaScript is an object-based language. Each object in JavaScript can have associated methods or properties that can be accessed by scripts and can also have other objects under it within a hierarchy. A method is like a predefined function, and a property is a value.

To use a method, property, or subobject, you need to indicate what object you're talking about. This is done by putting the object name before the name of the method, property, or subobject and separating the two with a period (`.`). Here is an example from earlier this hour: the function to reload the current document:

```
document.location.reload()
```

This says to use the `reload()` method, which is associated with the `location` object, which is part of the `document` object. You can think of this as somewhat similar to the way file locations are indicated on a computer's hard drive, such as `C:\My Documents\Word Files\Hour 23.doc`, or even the way Web sites are organized.

To access the properties of a Web document from within a script, you use a method called the *Document Object Model* (DOM). This is a standard way of accessing HTML elements, content, and attributes that was developed by the W3C. Unfortunately, many browsers have their own ways of accessing HTML content from within JavaScript, and most of them fall short of measuring up to the standards of the W3C's DOM. This is one of the reasons that cross-browser HTML can be difficult.

Dynamic HTML

Dynamic HTML is a term you may have heard before, and depending on who is using it, it means different things. In most cases, it means more than just "exciting Web design" and commonly refers to Web pages that move and change interactively, based on the user's actions, without having to go back to the Web server and fetch a new Web page.

In simple terms, dynamic HTML is the interaction of HTML, JavaScript, and CSS properties to produce those interactive effects. An example of dynamic HTML would be a complex mouseover that displays additional information as you move the mouse on the screen, or an animated banner that rolls out to show a list of options from which to choose. These are all the result of combining JavaScript's actions with CSS's presentation.

Using JavaScript with CSS

JavaScript was designed so that it works well with Cascading Style Sheets; a script can set or unset CSS properties. This is accomplished by using the `style` object, part of the DOM that provides access to any HTML object's properties.

The `style` object has properties that generally correspond to CSS properties, although each browser supports a variable set. Most of the basic properties, such as `color`, `background`, and `font`, are well supported. For example, to set the `color` of an object using JavaScript, you'd do the following:

```
object.style.color = blue;
```

CSS properties that are two (or more) words separated by hyphens, such as `background-image`, are written in JavaScript as the first word in lowercase, no hyphen, and then the second word with an uppercase letter—for example, `backgroundImage`.

There are several ways in JavaScript to identify the exact object you want to work with; the easiest method is to employ the `document.getElementById()` method. This selects the object corresponding to a given `id` value, so you can use it only with HTML tags that have `id` attributes. For example, if you want to change the color of an `<h1>` tag with an `id` of `main`, you can use the following line in your JavaScript:

```
document.getElementById("main").style.color = blue;
```

This isn't the only way to use JavaScript to manipulate styles, but it is rather simple and yet powerful. Several of the examples that follow use this straightforward method to set CSS property values. All of the following examples can be accessed on the Web at `http://www.cssin24hours.com/23/`.

JavaScript and Dynamic Styles

The first example of using JavaScript with CSS can be seen in Listing 23.2, which allows the user to select a theme, and then displays text using that theme. A theme is simply a collection of styles.

LISTING 23.2   A Theme Picker in JavaScript

```
<!-- picker-23.2.html -->
<html>
  <head>
    <title>Theme Picker</title>
    <style type="text/css">
      #eg { width: 500px; min-height: 200px;
            border: 2px solid black; padding: 20px;
            margin: 25px auto 0px auto; }
    </style>
    <script type="text/javascript" language="JavaScript">
    function chooseOne() {
        i = document.pick.chooser.selectedIndex;
        newTheme = document.pick.chooser.options[i].value;
        switch(newTheme) {
          case "default" :
            document.getElementById("eg").style.color = "black";
            document.getElementById("eg").style.background = "white";
            document.getElementById("eg").style.font = "12pt serif";
            break;
          case "neon" :
            document.getElementById("eg").style.color = "#00ffff";
            document.getElementById("eg").style.background = "black";
            document.getElementById("eg").style.font = "16pt Verdana";
            break;
          case "inverse" :
            document.getElementById("eg").style.color = "white";
            document.getElementById("eg").style.background = "black";
            document.getElementById("eg").style.font = "12pt serif";
            break;
          case "typewriter" :
            document.getElementById("eg").style.color = "black";
            document.getElementById("eg").style.background = "white";
            document.getElementById("eg").style.font = "12pt monospace";
            break;
          case "microscriptic" :
            document.getElementById("eg").style.color = "white";
            document.getElementById("eg").style.background = "black";
            document.getElementById("eg").style.font = "8pt cursive";
            break;
          case "huge" :
            document.getElementById("eg").style.color = "black";
            document.getElementById("eg").style.background = "white";
            document.getElementById("eg").style.font = "xx-large Verdana";
            break;
          case "kynn" :
            document.getElementById("eg").style.color = "white";
            document.getElementById("eg").style.background =
              "#CCA580 url('kynnbg.jpg') no-repeat";
            document.getElementById("eg").style.font = "18pt Garamond";
```

continues

LISTING 23.2 Continued

```
              break; }
        }
      </script>
    </head>
    <body onload="chooseOne()">
      <h1>Theme Picker</h1>
      <form name="pick" id="pick">
        <label for="chooser">Choose a theme from this list, and it
          will be shown in the box below.</label>
        <select name="chooser" id="chooser" onchange="chooseOne()">
          <option value="default">Default</option>
          <option value="inverse">Inverse</option>
          <option value="typewriter">Typewriter</option>
          <option value="neon">Neon</option>
          <option value="microscriptic">Microscriptic</option>
          <option value="huge">HUGE</option>
          <option value="kynn">Kynn.com</option></select>
      </form>
      <div id="eg">
        <h2>Darned Foxes</h2>
        <p>The quick brown fox jumped over the lazy dog. The
          little dog laughed to see such a sight.</p>
      </div>
    </body>
  </html>
```

This JavaScript uses the <select> tag to create a pull-down menu. When a new selection is made, the onchange attribute of the <select> tag triggers the chooseOne() function. The current value of the pull-down menu is read in these lines, which use the DOM to access the value:

```
i = document.pick.chooser.selectedIndex;
newTheme = document.pick.chooser.options[i].value;
```

That value is then used in a switch, a conditional statement that chooses among several options based on the specified value. Each of the case sections within the switch sets a different group of style values, determined by the chosen theme. These styles are set on the <div> with the id of eg (for example). You can see this in action in Figure 23.2 or by accessing the page via the Web at http://www.cssin24hours.com/23/picker-23.2.html.

FIGURE 23.2

Choosing a theme changes the page dynamically in Netscape 6.

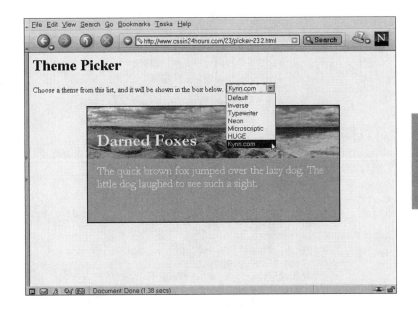

23

JavaScript and Visibility

In Hour 13, "Borders and Boxes," you learned about the `visibility` property, which lets you designate certain CSS boxes as visible or hidden. This isn't all that useful by itself, but when combined with JavaScript it comes into its own. JavaScript enables you to turn off and on the visibility of a display box so you can dynamically hide or show parts of the page.

Listing 23.3 is an example of visibility under JavaScript control.

LISTING 23.3   An HTML Page That Displays Different Panels Using JavaScript

```
<!-- dogs-23.3.html -->
<html>
  <head>
    <title>Dynamic Dogs</title>
    <style type="text/css">
      body { font-family: verdana; }
      #menu { position: absolute;
              width: 140px; height: 290px;
              top: 10px; left: 10px;
              background-color: silver; padding: 5px; }
      #menu a:link, #menu a:visited {
              display: block; font-size: large;
              color: blue; font-weight: bold;
              text-decoration: none;
              cursor: default; margin-top: 0.3em; }
```

continues

LISTING 23.3   Continued

```
        #data { position: absolute;
                width: 300px; height: 300px;
                top: 10px; left: 170px;
                background-color: gray; }
        #data div { position: absolute;
                    top: 10px; left: 10px;
                    width: 260px; height: 260px;
                    visibility: hidden; overflow: hidden;
                    background-color: white; padding: 10px; }
        #data #blank { visibility: visible; }
        #blank:before { content:
            "Mouseover (or tab to) each name to read about our dogs.";
            }
        .dogpic { float: right; margin: 0px 15px 0px 5px; }
      </style>
      <script type="text/javascript" language="JavaScript">
        function showDog(dog) {
          var dogElement = document.getElementById(dog);
          dogElement.style.visibility = "visible";
          document.getElementById("blank") = "hidden";
        }
        function hideDog(dog) {
          var dogElement = document.getElementById(dog);
          dogElement.style.visibility = "hidden";
          document.getElementById("blank") = "visible";
        }
      </script>
    </head>
    <body>
      <div id="menu">
        <h2>Our Dogs</h2>
        <a href="#kim"
           onmouseover="showDog('kim')"
           onmouseout="hideDog('kim')"
           onfocus="showDog('kim')"
           onblur="hideDog('kim')">Kim</a>
        <a href="#angie"
           onmouseover="showDog('angie')"
           onmouseout="hideDog('angie')"
           onfocus="showDog('angie')"
           onblur="hideDog('angie')">Angie</a>
        <a href="#nying"
           onmouseover="showDog('nying')"
           onmouseout="hideDog('nying')"
           onfocus="showDog('nying')"
           onblur="hideDog('nying')">Nying</a>
      </div>
      <div id="data">
```

LISTING 23.3   Continued

```
            <div id="blank">
            </div>
            <div id="kim">
              <img src="kim.jpg" alt="[Kim Picture]" class="dogpic">
              <h2>Kim</h2>
              <p>Kim is the largest of our dogs and is very cute.
                 He is lazy but lovable, and loves to eat.</p>
            </div>
            <div id="angie">
              <img src="angie.jpg" alt="[Angie Picture]" class="dogpic">
              <h2>Angie</h2>
              <p>Angie was born first and is very smart. She loves
                 to explore and bark.</p>
            </div>
            <div id="nying">
              <img src="nying.jpg" alt="[Nying Picture]" class="dogpic">
              <h2>Nying</h2>
              <p>Nying was the runt of the litter and is a little
                 bit crazy. She loves to sleep under Daddy's desk
                 chair.</p>
            </div>
          </div>
        </body>
      </html>
```

This page consists of an embedded style sheet with positioning CSS and generated content, an embedded script, multiple event triggers, and overlapping <div> elements, so it's fairly complex. But what it does is quite cool.

If you look carefully, you'll notice that the <div> elements within the <div id="data"> element, including the blank <div>, all have the same location and dimensions specified in the style sheet. Normally these would overlap, and their order would be determined by the z-index property. However, they are also set to visibility: hidden, which means none of them appear on the page except the <div id="blank"> element. The blank <div> is empty, but content generation will add a short instruction blurb. You can see how this all looks in Figure 23.3.

FIGURE 23.3

The initial list of dogs, with instructions added via content generation.

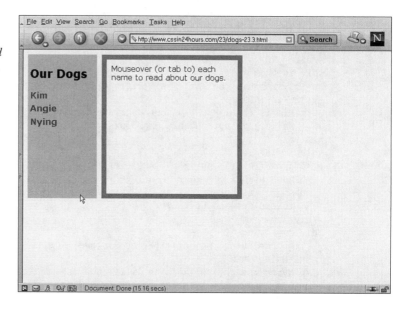

When you move the mouse over one of the links on the left—for example, the name Angie—the `onmouseover` event triggers the `showDog()` function and gives it the value `angie`. That value is used to select the correct `id` and sets that `<div>` to `visibility: visible` while setting the blank `<div>` to `hidden`. This is shown in Figure 23.4.

FIGURE 23.4

Mousing over the name Angie displays the information on that dog.

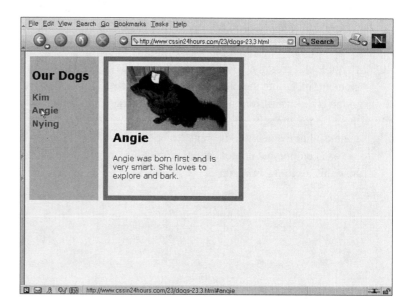

When the mouse is moved off the link, the `hideDog()` function is triggered by the `onmouseoff` event, and that reverses the `showDog()` function by hiding the dog and making the blank `<div>` visible once more. You can use this effect to make complex mouseovers that progressively reveal more information, including helpful tips about a link or additional content.

JavaScript and Positioning

The `style` object also allows you access to the position of an object via the positioning CSS properties. This can be used to create a wide variety of effects, from objects that reposition themselves automatically to those that can be controlled by the user. For example, you could reset the top and left properties to move a text banner across the screen.

A longer example is shown in Listing 23.4; this page moves a picture of a dog around the screen based on what the user types on the keyboard.

LISTING 23.4 A Page That Uses JavaScript to Make a Dog Fly around the Page

```
<!-- flying-23.4.html -->
<html>
  <head>
    <title>The Flying Dog</title>
    <style type="text/css">
      body { font-family: Verdana, sans-serif; }
      #outer { position: relative; overflow: hidden;
               height: 300px; width: 600px;
               background-color: silver; color: gray;
               font-size: 300px; line-height: 300px; }
      #kim { position: absolute; top: 0px; left: 0px; }
    </style>
    <script type="text/javascript" language="JavaScript">
      dogX = 0; dogY = 0;
      function moveDog(event) {
        switch(String.fromCharCode(event.which)) {
          case "h" : dogX = dogX - 10; break;
          case "k" : dogY = dogY - 10; break;
          case "j" : dogY = dogY + 10; break;
          case "l" : dogX = dogX + 10; break;
          default: window.alert("Valid keys: h/j/k/l"); }
        dogX = ( dogX > 550 ) ? 550 : dogX;
        dogY = ( dogY > 250 ) ? 250 : dogY;
        dogX = ( dogX < -100 ) ? -100 : dogX;
        dogY = ( dogY < -100 ) ? -100 : dogY;
        document.getElementById("kim").style.left = dogX;
        document.getElementById("kim").style.top = dogY; }
      document.onkeypress = moveDog;
    </script>
  </head>
```

continues

LISTING 23.4   Continued

```
<body>
  <h1>Kim the Amazing Flying Dog</h1>
  <div id="outer"> Kim!
    <img id="kim" src="kim.jpg" alt="[Kim]">
  </div>
  <table><tr><th rowspan="3" valign="top">Keys:</th>
          <td></td><td>k</td><td></td></tr>
      <tr><td>h</td><td>+</td><td>l</td></tr>
      <tr><td></td><td>j</td><td></td></tr></table>
</body>
</html>
```

You'll notice there isn't an onkeypress attribute set on any tag in the HTML; instead, the line document.onkeypress sets the moveDog function to activate whenever any key is pressed within the document. The String.fromCharCode(event.which) method tells you which key was pressed, and based on that key, the switch() chooses how to change the dog's coordinates. There are four odd lines that keep the dog within bounds, such as the following:

```
dogX = ( dogX < -100 ) ? -100 : dogX;
```

This is a conditional statement that means, "if the value of dogX is less than -100, then the value equals -100; otherwise, it equals dogX."

To see this script in action, load the Web page at http://www.cssin24hours.com/23/flying-23.4.html. Figure 23.5 shows the kind of result you should be able to see.

FIGURE 23.5

Kim moves around the page under keyboard command.

The table at the bottom tells you which keys you can use to move the dog around. Those keys are h for left, j for down, k for up, and l for right; these are the traditional substitutes for arrow keys used by classic Unix programs.

JavaScript and Alternate Style Sheets

One recurring theme throughout previous hours of this book has been browser irregularities. Several workarounds, including the @import trick, have been presented to deal with those deficiencies. JavaScript allows for a method called *browser detection* (or sometimes browser sniffing).

Browser detection uses the navigator object, which returns information about the current browser, to determine which instructions to execute. Listing 23.5 is an example of such a script, which looks for Netscape 4 and, if it finds it, provides an alternate stylesheet. If not, the primary style sheet is used. This listing also demonstrates the types of information available through the navigator object, ranging from the name of the application to the platform.

LISTING 23.5 An HTML Page with JavaScript to Detect Netscape 4

```
<!-- alternate-23.5.html -->
<html>
  <head>
    <title>Alternate Style Sheets</title>
    <script type="text/javascript" language="JavaScript">
      document.write('<link type="text/css" rel="stylesheet" ');
      if (navigator.appName == "Netscape" &&
          parseFloat(navigator.appVersion) < 5 )
      { document.writeln(' href="alternate-23.7.css">'); }
      else
      { document.writeln(' href="primary-23.6.css">'); }
    </script>
  </head>
  <body>
    <h1>Browser Details</h1>
    <p>Your browser has provided the following information via
       the <b>navigator</b> class in JavaScript.</p>
    <script type="text/javascript" language="JavaScript">
      document.writeln("<table>");
      document.writeln("<tr><th>appCodeName:</th><td>" +
                  navigator.appCodeName + "</td></tr>");
      document.writeln("<tr><th>appName:</th><td>" +
                  navigator.appName + "</td></tr>");
      document.writeln("<tr><th>appVersion:</th><td>" +
                  navigator.appVersion + "</td></tr>");
      document.writeln("<tr><th>language:</th><td>" +
                  navigator.language + "</td></tr>");
```

continues

LISTING 23.5 Continued

```
        document.writeln("<tr><th>platform:</th><td>" +
                    navigator.platform + "</td></tr>");
        document.writeln("<tr><th>userAgent:</th><td>" +
                    navigator.userAgent + "</td></tr>");
        document.writeln("</table>");
      </script>
      <noscript>
        <p>...I'm sorry, I couldn't determine anything about your
          browser using JavaScript.</p>
      </noscript>
    </body>
</html>
```

The default style sheet is a gray background with white text, surrounded by a border and written in Verdana font, as shown in Listing 23.6.

LISTING 23.6 The Default Style Sheet for the Page

```
/* primary-23.6.css */

body { background-color: gray; color: white;
      font-family: Verdana, sans-serif;
      margin: 2em; border: 2px solid black; padding: 1em;}
h1   { border-bottom: 1px solid white; width: 50%; }
th   { text-align: left; }
```

The alternate style sheet for Netscape 4 is black text on a white background in Courier font. This style sheet is listed in Listing 23.7. These specific styles were chosen just to be visually distinct for purposes of illustration. If you were using browser detection on a real site, you'd put styles in primary-23.6.css that cause problems in Netscape 4, and alternate-23.7.css would contain only those properties that are considered "safe" in Netscape 4.

LISTING 23.7 The Style Sheet Designed for Netscape 4

```
/* alternate-23.7.css */

body, td, th { background-color: white; color: black;
               font-family: "Courier New", monospace; }
th            { text-align: left; }
```

When a Web browser loads the page, it executes the JavaScript in the `<head>` and creates a `<link>` to load the right style sheet. The rest of the page displays the properties you can access via the `navigator` object. An example of this script in action is shown in Figure 23.6; because Internet Explorer 6 is not Netscape 4, the default style sheet is applied, and the page is gray.

FIGURE 23.6

Internet Explorer 6 uses the default style sheet.

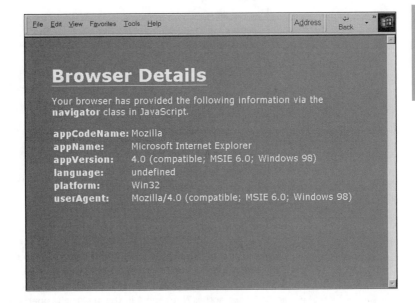

To determine if the browser is Netscape 4, the script uses this conditional statement:

```
if (navigator.appName == "Netscape" &&
    parseFloat(navigator.appVersion) < 5 )
```

This is a compound statement—the && is read as "and"—that checks first to see whether the appName is Netscape and then uses the `parseFloat()` function to see whether the browser version is less than 5. In other words, it looks for Netscape 4 (or less). If you load the page in Netscape 4, you'll get the effect shown in Figure 23.7; because it's a white page with Courier text, it's using the alternate style sheet.

FIGURE 23.7

Netscape 4 receives the alternate style sheet.

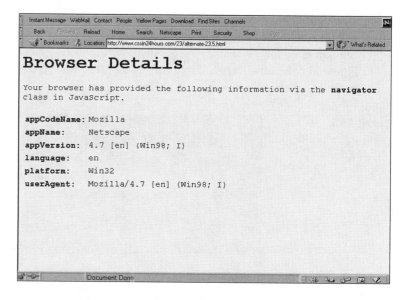

Browsers don't actually have to tell the truth about what they are. In fact, nearly every browser claims to be Mozilla in the `navigator.appCodeName` property, as shown in Figure 23.6. This is because Web developers wrote early browser detection scripts that prevented content from being served to Internet Explorer users, so Internet Explorer masquerades as Mozilla in the `appCodeName` and as Netscape 4 in the `appName` property. The Opera browser lets you choose which of several other browsers it will masquerade as. This means that you can't necessarily rely on browser detection. Check your scripts carefully in all browsers, just as you would with CSS styles.

Summary

JavaScript is a programming language understood by most Web browsers. JavaScript adds actions to the structure of HTML and the presentation of CSS. Together, they can be used as dynamic HTML.

JavaScript can be embedded in the <head> or <body> sections of an HTML file, and it executes when the browser reaches that part of the page. JavaScript can also be set to execute when a certain condition, called an intrinsic event, happens, as determined by HTML attributes. Examples include onClick, onLoad, and onMouseOut.

In addition to JavaScript's other capabilities, such as validating form data and creating interactive scripts, JavaScript can be used to manipulate CSS properties. The JavaScript `style` object is used for this purpose and is part of the Document Object Model (DOM). Content can be styled dynamically, positioned, hidden, or revealed using the `style` object.

Another JavaScript object that is quite useful in conjunction with CSS is the `navigator` object. The `navigator` object provides information on the user's browser, which can then tailor the presentation to that browser's quirks in a process known as browser detection. Browser detection should be used carefully, though, because it is not always reliable.

Browser Support Report Card

CSS Feature	Grade	Notes
JavaScript with CSS	A to F	See following

Any given script can range from a grade of A to F, depending on which objects, methods, and properties are used, and on how they are used. It's safest to not rely on JavaScript for any essential site content, such as navigation, if you can. Test your scripts by disabling JavaScript in your browser's preferences and then trying to use the page.

Q&A

Q **I can use one external style sheet on multiple pages with the `<link>` tag. Can I do the same with JavaScript?**

A Yes, indeed. Instead of making the `<script>` tag a container, you can leave it empty and use the `src` attribute to reference a file name. Your file should end with the `.js` extension. For example:

```
<script type="text/javascript" language="JavaScript" src="runThis.js">
```

Q **What happens if a browser doesn't understand JavaScript?**

A This is always a possibility. JavaScript support doesn't exist in older or limited browsers, such as Lynx, and some assistive technologies used by people with disabilities don't understand JavaScript. Also, users are able to disable JavaScript in their browser preferences. When JavaScript is not available, the `<script>` contents don't execute. Browsers will instead display the contents of any `<noscript>` tags, such as the one shown in Listing 23.5.

Q **Is JavaScript the only way to do browser detection?**

A No; you can also do server-side browser detection by using a program running on the Web server. This can be done using a Perl CGI script, server-side includes, ASP, PHP, or any other server programming technologies. You can learn more about these languages in the rest of the Sams Teach Yourself library.

23

Workshop

The workshop contains quiz questions and activities to help reinforce what you've learned in this hour. If you get stuck, the answers to the quiz can be found after the questions.

Quiz

1. JavaScript can be used for which of the following functions?

   (a.) Animation

   (b.) Validating form input

   (c.) Choosing an alternate style sheet based on browser detection

   (d.) Hiding parts of a page until triggered by an event

2. What is the intrinsic event that triggers when an HTML tag loses the focus?

3. Which property of the `navigator` object contains the name of the browser, unless the browser is masquerading as something else?

   (a.) `navigator.browserName`

   (b.) `navigator.appCodeName`

   (c.) `navigator.appName`

   (d.) `navigator.browser`

Answers

1. Trick question: the answer is "all of these."

2. The `onBlur` event is triggered when an element is no longer the focus.

3. The correct answer is (c.), `navigator.appName`. The `navigator.appCodeName` property will almost always be `Mozilla`, and the other properties don't exist.

Activity

Although you may not be ready to go out and start writing your own JavaScript applications after this hour, hopefully this has whetted your appetite for dynamic HTML and scripting. Download and modify these scripts for your own use, or follow up by reading *Sams Teach Yourself JavaScript in 24 Hours* as your next book.

Hour 24

CSS and XML

Extensible Markup Language (XML) has become one of the buzzwords of
the late 1990s and early 21st Century. Hailed as the next step in the evolution of the Web, XML promises to shake up the way we think about the
design of access to information. The knowledge you've gained about using
CSS with HTML will serve you well if you go on to write XML documents
because CSS and XML complement each other.

In this hour, you'll learn

- What XML is and how it is used
- How an XML-based language is defined
- How Cascading Style Sheets can be used to style an XML document
- Which styles are most useful in creating the presentation style for an
  XML document
- What XHTML is and how Cascading Style Sheets are used with XHTML
- How other XML-based languages, such as Scalable Vector Graphics
  (SVG), use CSS

What Is XML?

If you're not sure what Extensible Markup Language is, that's okay; it's been described as anything from the replacement for HTML to a universal data format, so it's no wonder that there's uncertainty. This hour won't teach you everything you need to know about XML, but it will help you understand enough to know how it works with CSS.

 To learn more about XML, check out *Sams Teach Yourself XML in 24 Hours*, written by Michael Morrison, ISBN 0-672-32213-7.

XML is actually not a markup language per se; instead, it's a set of rules and concepts that can be used to create markup languages. Some people call this a meta-language. Another meta-language is Standard Generalized Markup Language (SGML); SGML rules were used to build the HTML language that you're familiar with.

Using XML, you can construct any number of markup languages, either formally defined or ad hoc; all that matters is that a document follows the rules laid down by the W3C's XML specification. If one does, it's an XML document.

The primary advantage of XML is that it can be used as a common lingua franca for computers and programmers; because everything is defined in a specific format, a program that understands XML can be used with any XML-based language or document. This leads to interoperability, which is a fancy way of saying that computer applications are able to share data and output in an efficient manner.

Basic XML Concepts and Syntax

XML is purposely designed to be simple and easy to use. This is as much for the benefit of the computer applications as for the programmer because programs as well as programmers can more quickly understand a simple language with strict rules.

An XML document is written like an HTML document, with content marked up with tags denoted by less-than (<) and greater-than (>) angle brackets. Attributes, comments, and even character entities, such as < and >, are pretty much the same in XML as in HTML.

The biggest difference between XML and HTML is that XML doesn't define any specific tags that can be used for markup. If you are creating an XML document (or an XML-based language), you can make up any tag name you want. You can name a tag `<thisIsReallyImportant>` or `<Fred>` or `<yrewqjrfjasdfieh>`.

One restriction on XML documents is that they must be *well formed*. A well-formed document is one where the opening and closing tags match up properly; one that is not well formed has tags that are mismatched because they're not closed in the correct order. Here is an example of mismatched tags:

```
<em>This is <a href="link.html">a link</em></a>
```

As you can see, the `<em>` is closed before the `<a>` tag, even though the `<a>` was opened more recently. Nearly any HTML Web browser will display this properly, but it would still be incorrect in XML. (It's technically incorrect in HTML, too, but current browsers are forgiving.) The proper way to write this is

```
<em>This is <a href="link.html">a link</a></em>
```

XML requires that all attribute values be quoted. In HTML, you could get away with typing some values without the quotes around them, but XML is stricter in that regard.

Another important rule in XML is that all elements must have a closing tag of some sort. If a tag is empty, meaning it has no content—such as the HTML tags `<br>`, `<img>`, and `<hr>`—it is closed by writing a final slash as part of the opening tag or by using a closing tag, like in these examples:

```
<empty note="This element is empty" />
<empty note="This is too"></empty>
```

Both of the `<empty>` elements shown above have the same meaning; they are properly closed according to the XML rules.

XML tags are case sensitive. This means that the exact characters and case of those characters matter when closing a tag. In HTML, you can close a `<blockquote>` element with `</BLOCKQUOTE>`, `</BlockQuote>`, `</bLoCkQuOtE>`, or `</blockquote>`. In XML, the case has to match exactly—only `</blockquote>` would be valid in an XML document because the starting tag was named `<blockquote>`.

In Listing 24.1, I give you an example of a simple XML document, which describes a Web accessibility tip in markup.

LISTING 24.1 A Sample XML Document

```
<?xml version="1.0"?>
<tippage revision="2002-06-13" xml:lang="en">
  <accesstip>
    <headline>
      Accessibility Tip:
      Identify Language Changes
    </headline>
```

continues

24

LISTING 24.1 Continued

```
<author>
  <name>Kynn Bartlett</name>
  <email>&lt;kynn@idyllmtn.com&gt;</email>
</author>
<tipbody>
  <para>
    When a blind user accesses a Web page using a
    screenreader, the screenreader uses a specific
    language dictionary to know how words should be
    pronounced, based on the language of the page.
    If the wrong dictionary is used, the speech
    will be very difficult to understand.
  </para>
  <para>
    If the language changes in the middle of the Web
    page, you need to mark that change with the
    <code>lang</code> attribute, which can be set
    on any HTML tag but is usually set on the
    <code>&lt;span&gt;</code> element. This will let
    the screenreader know which language dictionary
    to use when synthesizing speech.
  </para>
  <para paratype="note">
    The XML equivalent of the <code>lang</code>
    attribute is <code>xml:lang</code>.
  </para>
</tipbody>
<tipexample>
  &lt;p&gt;
    &lt;span lang="de"&gt;
      Ich bin Berliner.
    &lt;/span&gt;
    (I am a resident of Berlin)
  &lt;/p&gt;
</tipexample>
</accesstip>
</tippage>
```

Notice that in the listing, the `<tipexample>` element contains HTML code, but the angle brackets have been converted to character entities using `&lt;` and `&gt;`.

Also notice that this document says absolutely nothing about how to display the content; it just defines the information and leaves it at that. This is one of the primary uses of XML—completely separating presentation from content. Later this hour you'll see how CSS can be used to define that presentation.

DTDs and Schemas

To make the jump from an XML document to an XML-based language, you need to have a formal definition for a language. An XML document is not required to be part of an XML-based language, though! An XML document without a formal definition basically creates an ad hoc language as it goes along, and by the rules of XML, that's perfectly valid.

However, if you're writing an application that you mean for others to use, you may need to have the syntax of your XML document written down. There are two primary ways to do this: XML Document Type Definitions (DTDs) and XML Schemas.

DTDs are the original way to define an XML-based language and are based on the way SGML languages are defined. Schemas are a newer development and allow for types of values to be defined in a broader fashion than DTDs allow. Schema support is still under development, however, and DTDs are currently more widely used.

A DTD's purpose is to define exactly what types of elements and attributes can be used in a document and in which combination and structure they may be arranged. A DTD file looks somewhat similar to an XML or HTML file, but technically speaking, it's not XML because it doesn't follow the rules for XML; schemas, on the other hand, do follow the XML rules because XML Schema Language is also an XML-based language.

An example of an XML DTD for our simple accessibility tip language is shown in Listing 24.2. You probably won't be able to understand everything unless you've worked with XML DTDs before, but the effect of this file is to determine what is allowable within the context of our XML-based language.

LISTING 24.2 A Simple DTD for Our XML-based Language

```
<!-- DTD for accessibility tip pages -->
<!ELEMENT tippage (accesstip)+>
<!ATTLIST tippage
    revision CDATA #REQUIRED
    xml:lang CDATA #REQUIRED
>
<!ELEMENT accesstip (headline, author, tipbody, tipexample*)>
<!ELEMENT headline (#PCDATA)*>
<!ELEMENT author (name, email?)>
<!ELEMENT name (#PCDATA)*>
<!ELEMENT email (#PCDATA)*>
<!ELEMENT tipbody (para+)>
<!ELEMENT para (#PCDATA | code)*>
<!ATTLIST para
    paratype (normal|note|warning|tip) #IMPLIED
>
<!ELEMENT code (#PCDATA)*>
<!ELEMENT tipexample (#PCDATA)*>
```

What does that mean? Here's some of what you can glean from the DTD about the structure of the document. This DTD defines a `<tippage>` element as consisting of one or more `<accesstip>` elements and requires that the `revision` and `xml:lang` attributes be set on `<tippage>`. Each `<accesstip>` contains a `<headline>`, an `<author>`, a `<tipbody>`, and zero or more `<tipexample>` elements. A `<tipbody>` holds one or more `<para>` tags, which themselves contain either normal text (`#PCDATA` in DTD terminology) or `<code>` elements. A `<para>` tag can optionally have a `paratype` attribute set, which can take one of four values.

XLink

As I noted before, there's no intrinsic meaning to XML tags, which means there's no default presentation or behavior connected with them. In HTML, the `<a>` link means both "use the default presentation, usually blue underlined text" and "when this link is clicked on, go to the address in the `href` attribute." In XML, we'll use CSS to provide the presentation, but the ability to define behaviors isn't part of the CSS language.

To address this need in XML, several additional specifications have been developed that create special tags and attributes, defining specific behavior or meaning in XML. To distinguish these from other tags or attributes you might create in your own language, they are created using namespaces and namespace prefixes. A *namespace* is a unique URL that is associated with the specification, and a *prefix* is associated with that URL and appended on the front of the tag or attribute.

The way to represent hypertext links and other types of document relationships in XML is to use XLink. The XLink specification defines several attributes related to the XLink namespace; these attributes are used to define relationships among data in XML.

We can use XLink to create a navigation bar for our content, allowing us to link to related resources. XLink allows for simple and complex links; in this case, all we need are simple XLinks.

Warning for Internet Explorer (Windows, Macintosh) and Opera

Only Netscape 6 supports the simple XLink language; the other browsers that display XML do not understand XLink at all. This means that you are unable to create hypertext links in XML that function like the HTML `<a>` tag for users of other browsers.

Listing 24.3 is a revision of the previous XML file with a navigator bar added, complete with simple XLink attributes.

LISTING 24.3   An XML Document with XLinks

```
<?xml version="1.0"?>
<tippage xmlns:xlink="http://www.w3.org/1999/xlink"
         revision="2002-06-13" xml:lang="en">
  <accesstip>
    <headline>
      Accessibility Tip:
      Identify Language Changes
    </headline>
    <author>
      <name>Kynn Bartlett</name>
      <email>&lt;kynn@idyllmtn.com&gt;</email>
    </author>
    <tipbody>
      <para>
        When a blind user accesses a Web page using a
        screenreader, the screenreader uses a specific
        language dictionary to know how words should be
        pronounced, based on the language of the page.
        If the wrong dictionary is used, the speech
        will be very difficult to understand.
      </para>
      <para>
        If the language changes in the middle of the Web
        page, you need to mark that change with the
        <code>lang</code> attribute, which can be set
        on any HTML tag but is usually set on the
        <code>&lt;span&gt;</code> element. This will let
        the screenreader know which language dictionary
        to use when synthesizing speech.
      </para>
      <para paratype="note">
        The XML equivalent of the <code>lang</code>
        attribute is <code>xml:lang</code>.
      </para>
    </tipbody>
    <tipexample>
      &lt;p&gt;
        &lt;span lang="de"&gt;
          Ich bin Berliner.
        &lt;/span&gt;
        (I am a resident of Berlin.)
      &lt;/p&gt;
    </tipexample>
  </accesstip>
  <navbar>
    <navlink xlink:type="simple" xlink:href="http://kynn.com">
      Kynn's Home Page
    </navlink>
```

continues

LISTING 24.3   Continued

```
      <navlink xlink:type="simple"
               xlink:href="http://cssin24hours.com">
        CSS in 24 Hours
      </navlink>
      <navlink xlink:type="simple"
               xlink:href="http://www.w3.org/WAI/">
        Web Accessibility Initiative
      </navlink>
      <navlink xlink:type="simple"
               xlink:href="http://www.webaim.org">
        WebAIM
      </navlink>
    </navbar>
  </tippage>
```

The effect of the xlink:type attribute is to declare the <navlink> elements to be part of a relationship link. In this case, they are a simple link that goes from the <navlink> to an external resource indicated by an xlink:href attribute. The end result is a link that is functionally the same as an <a href> link in HTML. Browsers that understand XLink should treat a <navlink> the same as an <a> link. Styles can be added to display this link in various ways, as well.

Displaying XML

XML is quite useful for direct computer-to-computer communication. Using an agreed-upon common data format, a corporate Web site can communicate automatically with a partner company's site to exchange information. Instant messages can be marked up in an XML-based language for interoperability among messaging systems.

However, all of those aren't really of interest to us when we're talking about XML and CSS. More relevant to this book is the ability of Cascading Style Sheets to provide XML with the presentation layer that it lacks. HTML tags have built-in meaning and presentation styles, but XML tags don't, and that's where CSS styles come in handy.

Default Browser Display

If a browser understands the XML format, it will display an XML page as it displays an HTML page, except that it has no idea what the tags are, so the content alone is shown. Figure 24.1 shows how Netscape 6 displays the XML file from Listing 24.1.

FIGURE 24.1

An XML file displayed by Netscape 6.

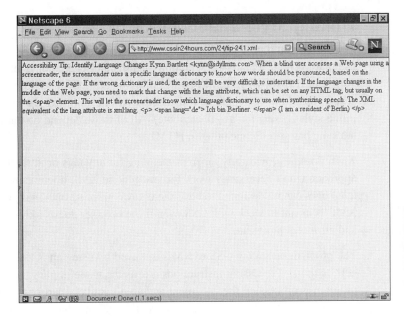

Internet Explorer does something a little more clever with default XML display. Recognizing that XML documents describe a hierarchical tree, Internet Explorer shows unstyled XML files in a clickable tree structure. This is shown in Figure 24.2. You can click on a minus to close one branch of the tree or on a plus to open it up again.

FIGURE 24.2

An XML file displayed by Internet Explorer.

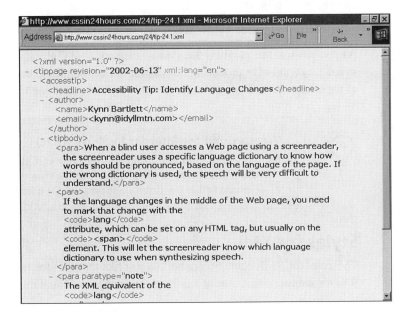

Linking Style Sheets in XML

Now, what you'd probably like to be able to do is apply a style sheet to the XML file and use that to create a better presentation than the Netscape 6 or Internet Explorer default views. In HTML, we have three ways of associating CSS styles with content: linked style sheets (using the `<link>` tag), embedded style sheets (using the `<style>` element), and inline styles (using the `style` attribute). All of those depend on the fact that a tag or attribute has specific meaning in HTML.

XML doesn't provide any inherent meaning for any tags or attributes, so the HTML approach won't necessarily work for any generic XML document. Specific XML-based languages can be designed to have the equivalent of `<link>`, `<style>`, or `style`, but XML is meant to work with CSS even if the browser doesn't know what the specific tags and attributes represent.

The problem of linking CSS to XML is solved by using an XML *processing instruction* (PI for short). Processing instructions are, as the name implies, instructions to whatever program is processing the document and aren't actually part of the content itself. A processing instruction looks similar to an XML tag, but it has question marks directly inside the angle brackets. Processing instructions are not tags, which means that they don't ever have closing tags, although they have something similar to attributes to provide additional parameters.

The processing instruction for linking an external style sheet is called `xml-stylesheet`, and you write it like this:

```
<?xml-stylesheet type="text/css" href="filename"?>
```

As you can see, this parallels the `<link>` element of HTML in syntax and function. The `<?xml-stylesheet?>` processing instruction should be placed before your first element of the document, and you can have multiple style sheets if needed.

Workaround for Internet Explorer (Mac)

Internet Explorer for Mac recognizes only one style sheet per document. Therefore, you will need to use either a single style sheet for each file or an `@import` rule within the first style sheet to apply additional style sheets.

Styles for XML

CSS rules for XML elements are written just like the rules for HTML elements. The selector indicates what part of the file the rule applies to, and the declarations give values to properties.

Selectors for XML are the same as selectors for HTML; element names, attribute values, pseudo-classes, and relationship selectors can all be used in an XML rule. Property values, likewise, are the same as for HTML; you just have to remember that there are no default values already assigned to them. As an example, if you want a <notice> element to be styled as bold, red text in a block box, you simply write a rule like this:

```
notice { display: block;
         font-weight: bold;
         color: red; }
```

Although any CSS property and value can be used with XML, there are a number of properties that are especially useful when designing style sheets for XML display, and later in this hour, we'll discuss how to use them most effectively.

A longer example of styles for XML is shown in Listing 24.4, which is a style sheet for displaying the simple version of the accessibility tip XML document from Listing 24.1 (without XLinks).

24

LISTING 24.4   A Style Sheet for Our Accessibility Tips

```
/* tip-24.4.css */
tippage    { display: block;          font-size: medium;
             background-color: white;  color: navy;
             font-family: sans-serif; }
accesstip  { display: block;          margin: 1em;
             padding: 1em;            border: 2px solid black;
             background-color: #CCCCFF; }
headline   { display: block;          margin-bottom: 0.75em;
             font-size: x-large;      font-weight: bold;
             font-family: Verdana, sans-serif; }
author     { display: block;          margin-bottom: 0.75em;
             font-size: large;        font-weight: bold; }
name       { display: inline;         margin-right: 0.5em; }
email      { display: inline;         margin-right: 0.5em; }
tipbody    { display: block;          border: 2px solid white;
             padding: 0.5em;          margin-bottom: 0.75em; }
para       { display: block;          margin-bottom: 0.65em;
             margin-top: 0.65em; }
para[paratype="note"]
           { border: 1px solid black; padding: 1em; }
code       { display: inline;         font-family: monospace;
             color: black;            font-weight: bold; }
tipexample { display: block;          padding: 0.5em;
             border: 2px solid white;  margin-bottom: 0.75em;
             font-family: monospace;   white-space: pre; }
```

To use this style sheet with the XML file in Listing 24.1, we simply need to add the following line before the `<tippage>` tag:

```
<?xml-stylesheet type="text/css" href="tip-24.4.css"?>
```

To see how the browser shows this file, look at Figure 24.3; it's come a long way from the plain inline look of Figure 24.1!

FIGURE 24.3

An XML file with a style sheet, displayed by Netscape 6.

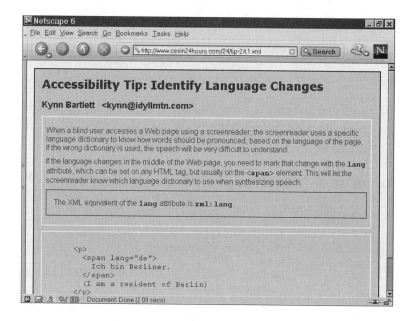

Using `display` to Control Presentation

The `display` property is your biggest friend when using Cascading Style Sheets with XML because it's how you create `block` boxes. As a default, all elements are displayed as `inline` boxes, and they flow together into a mess, as seen in Figure 24.1. Using `display`, you can change these to the `block` value.

You can also use the `display` property to create lists, as covered in Hour 14, "Lists," by using the `display: list-item` value. This allows the list style properties to be applied to those elements.

Data tables can be displayed as HTML tables by using the `display` values for tables, as discussed in Hour 15, "Styling Tables." This allows you the full range of columnar presentation supported by CSS in HTML.

> You'll want to use only table `display` values for actual data tables, though; for layout, you should use positioning CSS, covered in Hours 16, "Page Layout in CSS," and 17, "Advanced CSS Layout."

Generating Content for XML Display

Because the raw content represented by XML files is often lacking in basic user interface clues, the ability to generate content is crucial when applying CSS directly to XML. The `:before` and `:after` pseudo-selectors and the `content` property—all introduced in Hour 22, "User Interface and Generated Content"—are extremely useful when working with XML.

Listing 24.5 is an additional style sheet to be added to the one in Listing 24.4 and applied to the accessibility tip XML document. The easiest way to do this is simply by adding a second processing instruction after the first, as follows:

```
<?xml-stylesheet type="text/css" href="tip-24.5.css"?>
```

Alternately, an `@import` rule could be added to the beginning of the `tip-24.4.css` style sheet.

LISTING 24.5   Additional Style Sheet with Generated Content

```
/* tip-24.5.css */
author:before        { content: "Written by "; }
tipbody:before       { content: "Tip: ";
                         font-family: Verdana, sans-serif;
                         font-size: large; }
tipexample:before    { content: "Example: ";
                         font-family: Verdana, sans-serif;
                         font-size: large; }
para[paratype="note"]
                     { content: "Note: ";
                         font-weight: bold; }
```

These will add various bits of text content to the XML, so that the presentation makes a little more sense. Compare Figure 24.4 with Figure 24.3; it's much clearer, in respect to the generated content, what each section is meant to represent.

FIGURE 24.4

Netscape 6 applies the updated style sheet to the XML.

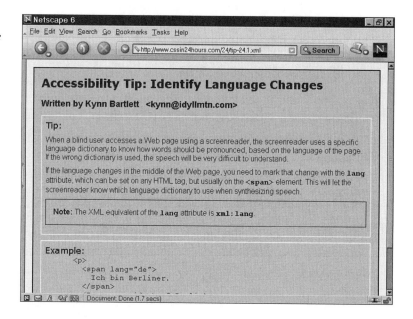

Styling XLink Links

When you style a normal HTML link, you use a selector on the `<a>` element that is modified by a pseudo-class selector, such as `:link`, `:visited`, `:active`, `:hover`, or `:focus`. When styling an XLink, the approach is much the same. A browser that understands XLink will set the appropriate pseudo-class states on XLinks. This lets us write style rules with selectors such as `navlink:link` or `navlink:active`.

Listing 24.6 is a style sheet that is designed to be applied to the extended version of our accessibility tip XML, along with the `tip-24.4.css` and `tip-24.5.css` style sheets. To use these, we'll add three processing instruction lines to the XML document shown in Listing 24.3, which is the longer tip file with the navigation bar. Those lines are:

```
<?xml-stylesheet type="text/css" href="tip-24.4.css"?>
<?xml-stylesheet type="text/css" href="tip-24.5.css"?>
<?xml-stylesheet type="text/css" href="tip-24.6.css"?>
```

LISTING 24.6   Style Sheet for XLink Navigation Bar

```
/* tip-24.6.css */
accesstip        { position: absolute;      left: 200px;
                   top: 0px; }
navbar           { display: block;          position: absolute;
                   left: 0px;               top: 0px;
                   width: 150px;            margin: 1em;
                   border: 2px solid black; padding: 0.5em;
                   background-color: #FFFFCC; }
```

LISTING 24.6   Continued

```
navbar:before    { font-size: large;      content: "Links: ";
                   font-weight: bold;
                   font-family: Verdana, sans-serif; }
navlink           { display: block;        font-size: small;
                   font-weight: bold;       text-align: center;
                   margin: 0em 0.4em;
                   font-family: Verdana, sans-serif; }
navlink:link      { color: blue; }
navlink:visited   { color: purple; }
navlink:hover     { color: red; }
navlink:active    { color: red; }
```

The navigation bar is created by using absolute positioning to place both the
`<accesstip>` element and the `<navbar>` element in their appropriate locations. Link
effects are set using pseudo-classes, and a little extra content is generated at the start of
the navigation bar. The full effect is shown in Figure 24.5.

24

FIGURE 24.5

Netscape 6 displays the XLinks and CSS.

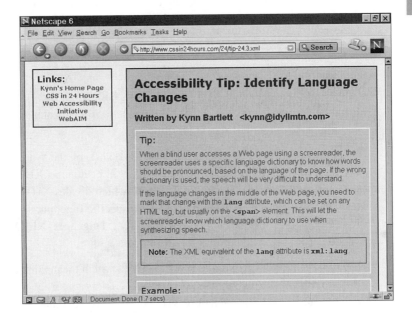

XML-based Languages and CSS

The previous part of this hour described how you can apply Cascading Style Sheets to
generic XML pages—those that are not necessarily part of a language known by the
browser but which nevertheless conform to the rules of XML. The `<?xml-stylesheet?>`
processing instruction is a universal method for applying CSS to any XML file.

However, if you are dealing with an XML-based language where the semantics are known—meaning that the authors of the document and the browser (or other software) both understand what the tags mean—the rules could be very different, depending on how the language has decided to use CSS.

In this section, you'll survey some of the XML-based languages that use Cascading Style Sheets and see what role CSS plays in those languages.

XHTML

Extensible Hypertext Markup Language 1.0 (XHTML) is simply HTML 4.01 written in accordance with the rules for XML. All tags are the same case (lowercase), all attributes are quoted, and all tags are explicitly closed. Like HTML 4.01, XHTML 1.0 comes in three flavors—Strict, Transitional, and Frameset.

> If you want to convert from HTML to XHTML, a good utility is the HTML Tidy program available from the W3C. This can perform a number of functions, from cleaning up your HTML code to changing to the proper XHTML syntax. You can download the program for free from `http://www.w3.org/People/ Raggett/tidy/`.

The primary advantage of XHTML is that it's both XML and HTML at the same time, meaning that you can use it with XML applications for greater interoperability, and you can also use it with existing HTML browsers.

In addition, further development on "non-X" HTML by the World Wide Web Consortium has been stopped; all future work on HTML will be done as XHTML. One example of this work is the *modularization* of XHTML, which divides XHTML tags and attributes into sets called modules. Each module has a specific function, and groups of modules can be combined together to build new XHTML languages. XHTML 1.1 is the newest version of HTML, built from XHTML modules.

XHTML version 1.1 is based on Strict HTML, which means that there are no presentation attributes or elements; instead, XHTML 1.1 relies entirely on CSS for presentation effects. Future versions, including XHTML 2.0, will continue this trend, making knowledge of CSS essential for future XHTML development.

In all versions of XHTML, you can apply CSS as you do in HTML; the <link> and <style> tags and the style attribute are defined as in HTML.

SVG

The Scalable Vector Graphics (SVG) language is an XML-based format for creating vector graphics. Vector graphics, unlike bitmapped graphical formats such as GIF or JPEG, can be scaled up and down in size without loss of resolution, and they are often much smaller than an equivalent bitmap. SVG is a W3C specification developed by the graphics working group.

SVG files use Cascading Style Sheets properties to define color, text effects, fonts, and other presentation qualities. Like HTML, SVG has predefined semantics for linking and embedding style sheets, as well as for inline styles.

XUL

XML-based User Interface Language (XUL) is a language developed by the Mozilla project for use with the Mozilla and Netscape 6 Web browsers. Rather than being a content language, XUL describes the user interface of a program, including the appearance and colors, the menus, and the buttons. Using XUL, browser users can create skins that customize the function and look of their user interfaces. XUL uses Cascading Style Sheets extensively to provide formatting effects on user interface components and is an example of CSS used for something besides simply styling of Web content.

24

XSL

Extensible Style Sheet Language (XSL) is a broad term that actually covers two related technologies, XSL Formatting Objects (XSL-FO) and XSL Transformations (XSLT).

The XSL-FO language describes the end appearance of a document in an XML-based syntax. This is quite useful for a fixed layout, such as on the printed page, but is not as useful on the screen. Formatting objects are XML elements describing specific areas of the printed page and the content contained by them; the formatting objects dictate the ultimate appearance of the document. XSL-FO elements and attributes are based on Cascading Style Sheets properties, and so the transition from CSS to XSL-FO is not particularly hard once you learn the XML-based syntax.

The XSLT language was written to transform an arbitrary XML document, such as our accessibility tip, into XSL-FO. XSLT has evolved beyond this single purpose, however, and can be used for any kind of transformation where you want to convert from one XML-based language to another. For example, you could write an XSL Transformation to change the accessibility tip XML file into an XHTML page, with CSS rules for the presentation effects. Although XSLT does not use style sheets directly, you can easily use CSS and XSLT together to produce custom presentation effects.

Summary

Extensible Markup Language (XML) is not a replacement for HTML; instead, it is a meta-language for creating new languages that can be used on the Web and in computer applications. XML is defined by a strict set of rules, including "tags must nest properly" and "each tag must have a matching closing tag." A document that conforms to these rules is considered proper XML.

XML languages are markup languages that conform to the rules of XML. A language can be formally defined by using an XML DTD or Schema to specify which tags and attributes can be used, but such formal definition is optional. The tags of an XML language don't necessarily have any inherent presentational styles associated with them, and a browser will often display an XML file as plain text content or as a structured tree.

CSS can be used with XML just as it is used with HTML; the properties are the same, as is the way selectors are used. Applying CSS to XML builds a presentation style that can make the structure of the XML content easier to understand. CSS properties for positioning, display, and generated content are especially useful with XML.

XML-based languages, such as Extensible Hypertext Markup Language (XHTML), Scalable Vector Graphics (SVG), XML-based User Interface Language (XUL), and Extensible Style Sheet Language (XSL), were created to work with Cascading Style Sheets. As the technology of Web design continues to evolve along the path of XML, the CSS knowledge you've gained from this book will continue to serve you well!

Browser Support Report Card

CSS Feature	Grade	Notes
Styling XML	B	Not supported by Netscape 4
Multiple style sheets in XML	A-	Workaround required for IE (Mac)
Styling XLinks	D	Supported only by Netscape 6

Q&A

Q I read the CSS Level 2 specification and it says to use `<?XML:STYLESHEET?>` not `<?xml-stylesheet?>`. What's up with that?

A The CSS Level 2 specification was written before the method of associating style sheets with XML documents was formalized. That part of the CSS2 recommendation has been superseded by later specifications that specifically address the relationship between XML and CSS.

Q Do current Web browsers support XHTML?

A Yes and no. Few of them were coded specifically for XHTML, but if you write your XHTML in accordance with backward-compatibility rules, HTML browsers will be able to understand it. The XHTML backward-compatibility rules are listed in the HTML 1.0 specification at `http://www.w3.org/TR/xhtml1`.

Q You said that all XHTML tags are lowercase, but I write my HTML tags as uppercase. Why do I have to write XHTML in lowercase?

A Because XML is case sensitive—unlike HTML—XHTML tags have to match and must be written consistently with respect to the case of the characters. When XHTML was created, the decision was made to use lowercase letters instead of uppercase. Why? It nearly came down to a coin-toss, and effectively it was an arbitrary decision. Either way, half of the people would be disappointed! So lowercase letters were chosen, and that's what we use for writing XHTML. If you use lowercase letters already, you're in luck. If not, you'll just have to get used to it. . .

Q What does XSLT let me do that CSS does not?

A Using XSLT, you can affect the structure of the document, not just the appearance, as you can with CSS. For example, you can write an XSLT transformation that extracts specific content and repurposes it in a completely new manner, such as creating a summary of the hypertext links on a page. If you then apply CSS to the resulting XML (or XHTML), you can make dynamic custom interfaces.

Workshop

The workshop contains quiz questions and activities to help reinforce what you've learned in this hour. If you get stuck, the answers to the quiz can be found after the questions.

Quiz

1. Each of the following is invalid according to the rules of XML. What rule does each one violate?

    (a.) `<author><name>Kynn Bartlett</author></name>`

    (b.) `<catalog code=r343>CSS in 24 Hours</catalog>`

    (c.) `<animation src="glow.mov">`

    (d.) `<timestamp>24-Jun-2002</TimeStamp>`

2. Consider the following very simple XML file:

```
<?xml version="1.0">
<friends>
  <person>
    <name>Russ Smith</name>
    <age>33</age>
  </person>
  <person>
    <name>Nick Mamatas</name>
    <age>30</age>
  </person>
</friends>
```

How would you write a style sheet that displays this as a simple table?

3. Which XML-based language uses CSS to define the colors and text properties of graphics?

   (a.) XUL

   (b.) SVG

   (c.) XHTML

   (d.) XSL-FO

Answers

1. All of these break at least one rule of XML. In (a.), the tags aren't nested properly. In (b.), the attribute value is not enclosed in quotes. There is no closing tag in (c.), and the closing tag doesn't match the case of the opening tag in (d.)

2. You'll need to use the table-related `display` values to do this effectively. Here is a simple style sheet that does that:

```
friends    { display: table;
             border: 3px inset black; }
person     { display: table-row; }
name, age  { display: table-cell;
             padding: 0.5em;
             border: 2px inset gray; }
age:after  { content: " years old"; }
```

3. The correct answer is (b.), Scalable Vector Graphics.

Activity

A number of new technologies were introduced in this hour that are beyond the scope of this book to follow up on. If you're interested in learning more, here are some resources to get you started:

- Learn more about XML by visiting the W3C's XML pages at http://www.w3.org/XML/ or by reading *Sams Teach Yourself XML in 24 Hours.*

- XHTML is covered in *Sams Teach Yourself HTML and XHTML in 24 Hours,* or you can learn more from the W3C's XHTML page at http://www.w3.org/Markup/. Be sure to check out the free HTML Tidy program!

- A good site for Scalable Vector Graphics is http://www.w3.org/Graphics/SVG/, and you can also read about them in *Sams Teach Yourself SVG in 24 Hours.*

- The definitive source for XUL information is the Mozilla Web site at http://www.mozilla.org/.

- Information on XSL, XSL-FO, and XSLT can be found at http://www.xslinfo.com/ as well as on the W3C's site.

24

PART V

Appendices

APPENDIX A

How to Read W3C Recommendations

To fully understand how Cascading Style Sheets work and interact with other Web standards, you'll need to refer to the W3C's recommendations from time to time. These technical specifications cover most of the entire range of Web development, especially when it comes to markup languages; HTML, CSS, XML, HTTP, XHTML, XSLT, SMIL, XSL-FO, SVG, RDF, CC/PP, and many other seemingly random jumbles of letters are all W3C recommendations that are shaping the future of the Web.

This appendix is a trail map to help you find your way through the labyrinthine jungles of the W3C's specifications, especially those that have the greatest effect on Cascading Style Sheets. W3C recommendations may seem daunting at first if you aren't used to this type of writing; hopefully this guide will help you find the references you need.

Anatomy of a W3C Recommendation

A W3C recommendation is different from most other types of technical writing. Most technical works you're familiar with, from user manuals to books like this one, are written as documentation. Documentation is a user resource, something that helps you understand how to use a program or language. Tutorials, reference works, and textbooks are all written with that goal.

Standards, including the de facto standards of W3C recommendations, are written differently. The purpose of a standards document is to be definitive. A specification explicitly defines what is contained within a given set of technology. The key to comprehending a spec is not only understanding how it is organized but also understanding the intended audience and use of the specification.

In nearly all cases, the intended audience of a W3C specification is not you. It's not Web developers, even though the languages defined by these specs are written for use by Web developers. As a Web developer, you'll definitely be able to gain useful knowledge from the W3C's recommendations, but that's just an ancillary effect.

The real audience for W3C recommendations is the software developers who create programs that use the protocols and languages in the specs. The CSS Level Two specification, for example, was written primarily for implementers at Microsoft, Netscape (Mozilla), Opera, and other software companies producing Web-related software.

When you read through a recommendation, you'll find many references to implementation requirements, choices left up to the user agent, and notions of required features. None of these are meant for you, the Web developer, unless you've decided to write your own browser on the side. They're still useful to you because they can give you some hints as to what the browsers are required to support, but even then a requirement means less than you'd think. If you look through the browser report cards for each hour, you'll see that compliance with published standards has not been a major priority for most browser development teams.

So how are Web developers supposed to learn about CSS, if not through the specification? The idea is that there will be intermediaries—translators, if you will—to convert the technical definitions of the language (or "technology") into something that can be used to learn that language. Web tutorials, instructor-led classes, reference works, and books such as this one are the intermediaries by which the masses are meant to make sense of the W3C's arcane lore.

This is similar to learning a foreign language; nobody sits down with only a grammar book and a dictionary to learn a new tongue; those contain the formal definitions of the language, but they don't provide the context you need to understand it. Dictionaries, like Web standards, are useful only to those who already understand the concepts! Like dictionaries, the W3C's specifications are quite useful once you have grasped the basic concepts.

One consequence of being written for those already in the know is that the W3C specifications aren't written linearly but circularly. To make sense of what's written in section two, you'll need to have read not only section one, but also sections three, four, and five, plus the appendix and about a half dozen related specifications. For a definitive work, that's actually quite appropriate; you can't read a dictionary straight through either, and all terms in a dictionary are defined by using other dictionary terms. W3C recommendations are written in the same manner, so you'll probably have to read through several times—following hyperlinks instead of just proceeding linearly—to fully grasp everything.

To approach a W3C recommendation, first discern the structure of the document. Nearly all of them are written with the same general outline. Skim the table of contents and determine the major sections of the recommendation you're reading.

The first part of the structure looks like a bit of legalistic fluff, but is actually quite important; it identifies when the document was written and what status it holds in the W3C's hierarchy of technical recommendations. The W3C Process is a procedure for moving a working group's documents from draft to officially approved recommendation, and there are a number of steps along the way. The status of the document will be stated at the very beginning.

A short introduction usually follows, which states the purpose of the recommendation. A glossary of terms might be provided at the front, but most commonly it is at the end; read it before the main content so you'll recognize the terms, even if they don't make sense until you've read more. Also at the end you'll find a list of references; W3C documents don't usually link directly to other sources but instead link to their reference lists. These references include the links out to other materials you can find on the Web, many of which will be essential to making sense of what you're reading.

The main content is in the middle, of course, and is usually divided into sensible categories (although beware the hyperlinks forward as well as backward). The best W3C recommendations have small menu bars at the top that allow you to page between sections or, more usefully, to jump directly to an alphabetized table listing all elements, attributes, or properties. The index at the back of a long recommendation will also prove invaluable when navigating the structure of the W3C specification.

A

Reading the W3C Specs

The rest of this appendix is a brief listing of the most important specifications you'll want to be aware of as you create CSS-based Web designs. This is by no means an exhaustive list, but it covers the essentials and tells you why these W3C recommendations affect your CSS work.

CSS Level 1

The CSS Level 1 recommendation created the first official version of the Cascading Style Sheets language. This laid out the basic principles for CSS syntax, for the cascade, and for the relationships between HTML and CSS. The URL for this recommendation is `http://www.w3.org/TR/CSS`.

Because CSS Level 2 completely updates and restates the content of the CSS Level 1 recommendation, you'll actually have very little reason to refer to CSS Level 1 other than historical curiosity. It may be interesting to examine the changes between Level 1 and Level 2 to see how ideas on style changed in the years between the two recommendations. For example, in CSS Level 1, an author's `!important` rules took priority over the user's; CSS Level 2 reversed this, granting ultimate sovereignty to the end user. This resulted from a growing acknowledgment that the user's needs have to be respected.

CSS Level 2

The Level 2 specification for Cascading Style Sheets is the defining document for CSS development and will prove to be one of your key resources as you do CSS work, in addition to up-to-date browser support tables, your suite of test browsers, and this book. The URL for CSS Level 2 is `http://www.w3.org/TR/CSS2`, and I suggest downloading a copy to your hard drive for reference.

In CSS Level 2 you'll find the definitions for all the core CSS you'll use, as well as complex formulae for a number of things you may not ever have to touch, such as the `@font` characteristics. CSS Level 2 can sometimes seem like a bewildering mishmash of widely supported and useful features thrown together randomly with a lot of theoretical functions for which there's no support. Generated content, downloadable fonts, CSS positioning, and aural style sheets fall into the latter category of good ideas lacking solid usefulness.

This situation pointed out a gap in the W3C's process for creating Web specifications, which it has since attempted to address. Specifically, all new W3C recommendations need to pass through a Candidate Recommendation state, and to get past that, there need to be two interoperable implementations of the specification. By this standard, something like aural CSS would not have been approved as a formal recommendation, as

EmacSpeak is currently the only program that supports those properties. Such a restriction does slow down the issuance of Web standards, but it ensures that those that receive approval will meet at least a minimum standard of support, hopefully with more to come.

Particularly useful in the CSS Level 2 specification is the property index, a large table listing all CSS Level 2 properties in alphabetical order. The possible values for each property, default values, applicable media types and elements, and inheritance are all shown, with hyperlinks directly to other parts of the specification for further explanation. Also useful is the specification's Appendix A, a default style sheet for HTML 4 that tells how browsers should display default styles for HTML elements.

CSS Level 3

The next stage of development for the Cascading Style Sheets is embodied in the CSS Level 3 project. Rather than simply adding additional properties to expand the language, the CSS working groups have split the specification into a number of modules, in a process called modularization. (The same process has been applied to XHTML as well, as discussed in Hour 24, "CSS and XML.") This lets each module of CSS be developed separately and allows for profiles to be created for specific device types, such as mobile devices. Assembled from sets of modules, these profiles describe appropriate styling support for device types.

Examples of modules being developed include Cascading, Selectors, Box Model, Ruby, Columns, Tables, Lists, and more. A roadmap explaining the current status and relationships of each module is posted at `http://www.w3.org/Style/CSS/current-work`.

As of the first half of 2002, the CSS Level 3 modules and profiles are still under development by the W3C. Few have progressed beyond the working draft stage, as development is still ongoing. As an experienced Web developer and user of CSS (as you should be at the end of this book!), your opinion should be heard on the development of Web standards; in fact the W3C welcomes public comment as part of the W3C process. Check the CSS Level 3 roadmap to see whether there are any calls for comment on current drafts.

HTML and XHTML

Because nearly all Web work is currently done using HTML, the HTML specification is the second most useful W3C recommendation for CSS developers. The current version, HTML 4.01, defines several flavors of HTML, as discussed in Hour 4, "Using CSS with HTML": HTML Strict, which relies on CSS for presentation; HTML Transitional, which allows both CSS and HTML attributes for presentational effects; and HTML Frameset, which sets up frame presentations. The URL for the HTML 4.01 specification is `http://www.w3.org/TR/html`.

A

Like the CSS Level 2 specification, the HTML 4 recommendation is best navigated through an alphabetized table; in fact, it offers two—one for elements and one for properties. Something to be careful about when reading the HTML specification is the distinction between HTML Strict and HTML Transitional. Telling which attributes or elements are deprecated or not used in HTML Strict may require you to follow hyperlinks or learn SGML's DTD language; simply reading the text is often not enough.

The specification for XHTML may be useful to you as well, if you're working with XHTML or XML; as discussed in Hour 24, XHTML is HTML written according to XML rules. The XHTML specification, which refers back to the HTML recommendation for definitions of various elements, can be found at `http://www.w3.org/TR/xhtml1`.

XML

If you are going to use Cascading Style Sheets for displaying generic XML, as described in Hour 24, you're going to need to be aware of the entire family of XML documents. A large number of XML specifications exists, but the core of XML was defined in the Extensible Markup Language 1.0 recommendation, located on the Web at `http://www.w3.org/TR/REC-xml`. More information on XML-related specifications can be found on the W3C's Web site at `http://www.w3.org/XML`.

Web Content Accessibility Guidelines

To ensure the accessibility of the Web to all users regardless of disability, the W3C created a number of guidelines for eliminating access barriers. These are listed in the Web Content Accessibility Guidelines at `http://www.w3.org/TR/WCAG`. The WCAG guidelines strongly urge the use of Cascading Style Sheets and encourage appropriate use of color, font, layout, and other design characteristics.

In addition to the WCAG list, which contains broad guidelines and specific checkpoints, the W3C publishes a set of techniques that can be used to achieve compliance with those checkpoints. The techniques applicable to CSS development are listed at `http://www.w3.org/TR/WCAG10-CSS-TECHS/`. An overview of the accessibility benefits of using Cascading Style Sheets can be found at `http://www.w3.org/TR/CSS-access/`.

APPENDIX B

Replacing Presentational HTML with CSS

One of the goals of the Cascading Style Sheets language is to move presentational effects out of the HTML markup, achieving a separation of content from presentation. Such a separation has many benefits, especially for users with special needs, as discussed in Hour 21, "Accessibility and Internationalization."

The HTML 4.01 specification defines three varieties of HTML—Strict, Transitional, and Frameset—as detailed in Hour 4, "Using CSS with HTML." Within this framework, specific HTML tags and attributes have been designated as deprecated. Deprecated tags are considered obsolete and are intended to be removed from future versions of the HTML language. Strict HTML disallows the use of these tags and attributes, instead relying on CSS rules for the same effects.

Table B.1 provides a list of deprecated tags and attributes, along with CSS equivalents for that HTML; also shown are cross-references to the hours of this book that discuss those CSS properties. You should use the CSS versions when designing Web pages, especially if you are using Strict HTML.

TABLE B.1 Obsolete (Deprecated) HTML Tags and Attributes

Deprecated HTML	CSS Equivalent	Hour
`<basefont>`	`body { font-family }`	Hour 8
`<body alink>`	`a:active { color }`	Hour 11
`<body link>`	`a:link { color }`	Hour 11
`<body text>`	`body { color }`	Hour 2
`<body vlink>`	`a:visited { color }`	Hour 11
`<center>`	`text-align: center`	Hour 12
`<font>`	`font`	Hour 8
`<li type>`	`list-style-type`	Hour 14
`<s>`	`text-decoration: line-through`	Hour 9
`<strike>`	`text-decoration: line-through`	Hour 9
`<u>`	`text-decoration: underline`	Hour 9
`align` attribute	`text-align` or `margin: auto`	Hour 12
`background` attribute	`background-image`	Hour 10
`bgcolor` attribute	`background-color`	Hour 10
`border` attribute	`border`	Hour 6
`clear` attribute	`clear`	Hour 16
`color` attribute	`color`	Hour 2
`height` attribute	`height`	Hour 17
`hspace` attribute	`padding`	Hour 6
`nowrap` attribute	`white-space: nowrap`	Hour 12
`valign` attribute	`vertical-align`	Hour 12
`vspace` attribute	`padding`	Hour 6
`width` attribute	`width`	Hour 17

In addition to deprecated elements, HTML 4.01 also includes a number of presentational elements and attributes that are not considered obsolete but which are redundant with CSS properties. These HTML tags and attributes are allowed with Transitional HTML, but should be avoided with Strict HTML. Equivalent CSS rules are shown in Table B.2.

TABLE B.2   Using CSS Instead of Presentational HTML

Presentational HTML	CSS Equivalent	Hour
`<b>`	`font-weight: bold`	Hour 8
`<big>`	`font-size: larger`	Hour 8
`<hr>`	`border-top` or `border-bottom`	Hour 13
`<i>`	`font-style: italic`	Hour 8
`<pre>`	`white-space: pre; font-family: monospace`	Hour 12
`<small>`	`font-size: smaller`	Hour 8
`<sub>`	`vertical-align: sub; font-size: small`	Hour 12
`<sup>`	`vertical-align: super; font-size: small`	Hour 12
`<table cellpadding>`	`padding`	Hour 6
`<table cellspacing>`	`border-spacing`	Hour 15
`<table frame>`	`border`	Hour 15
`<table rules>`	`border`	Hour 15
`<tt>`	`font-family: monospace`	Hour 8
`char` attribute	`text-align`	Hour 15
`charoff` attribute	`text-align`	Hour 15
`frameborder` attribute	`border`	Hour 6
`marginheight` attribute	`margin`	Hour 6
`marginwidth` attribute	`margin`	Hour 6

B

Often, Web developers will use a valid HTML tag in a way that it wasn't intended to be used in order to get a certain presentational effect, such as using `<blockquote>` to set right or left margins, even when the content is not actually a quote. With CSS allowing much more control over the presentation, there's no longer a need to resort to such tricks. HTML tags should be used only to represent the actual meaning of each tag, and CSS styles can be applied to change the formatting.

Examples of tags that are often misused are listed in Table B.3, and the CSS properties that can replace these tags are shown as well. Remember that these apply only to tags that aren't used for their intended meaning. The `<blockquote>` tag should still be used whenever a block of quoted text is provided; don't just blindly replace it with a `margin` rule in all cases. Ask yourself whether or not the original meaning of the HTML tag is appropriate or not.

TABLE B.3   Frequently Misused HTML Tags

Misused HTML	CSS Equivalent	Hour
`<blockquote>` for margins	`margin`	Hour 6
`<dl>` for margins	`margin`	Hour 6
`<h1>` for large text	`font-size`	Hour 8
`<img>` for list bullets	`list-style-image`	Hour 14
`<ol>` for margins	margin	Hour 6
`<table>` for layouts	Positioning properties	Hour 16
`<textarea>` for scroll box	`overflow: scroll`	Hour 17
`<ul>` for margins	`margin`	Hour 6

The first key to using CSS effectively is to use your markup properly. A solid foundation of valid, properly used HTML will allow you to make the most of your style sheet designs. For more on HTML tags, see the HTML specification at `http://www.w3.org/TR/HTML4`.

APPENDIX C

GLOSSARY

Accessibility   The process of making Web content available to all users, regardless of disabilities. By using CSS, you can make your Web sites accessible to a broad spectrum of users.

Attribute   A quality set on an HTML element in the opening tag, consisting of an attribute name and an attribute value. For example, in the HTML tag `<h2 align="left">`, the attribute name is `align` and the value is `left`.

Aural CSS (ACSS)   The group of CSS properties that dictate how a page should sound when read aloud by a screenreader or a talking browser.

Block Element   An element that is styled as a separate block; it is self-contained and starts and ends with new lines, such as the HTML `<p>` tag. *See also* Inline Element.

Box Model   The way in which CSS browsers display elements—element content, surrounded by padding, a border, and a margin. Not all elements will have these properties, but all displayed elements are presented as boxes, either inline or block.

Browser   A program that displays content of the type usually found on the Web—HTML documents, graphics, multimedia, and style sheets. Browsers are the most common type of user agent.

Calculated Value   A property value that is calculated when it is applied; the actual value is inherited by child elements, rather than a relative keyword.

Cascade   The method by which CSS determines which of several conflicting property values should take precedence. The more specific a rule, the higher the priority granted to it.

Cascading Style Sheets (CSS)   A language created by the World Wide Web Consortium to describe presentation effects for HTML and XML documents.

Child Element   An element contained within another element. For example, within the HTML markup `<div> <img src="kynn.gif" alt="Kynn"> </div>`, the `<img>` element is a child of the `<div>` element.

Class Selector   A selector based on the HTML `class` attribute. A class selector can be used to assign styles to a specific set of elements, which are defined in the markup.

Comment   Text within a CSS or HTML file that is not displayed to the user but instead serves as notes or reminders to the Web developer. In CSS, comments are indicated by `/* slashes and asterisks */`.

Containing Box   The box that contains an element and from which certain properties may be inherited. For example, in the HTML markup `<div> <img src="kynn.gif" alt="Kynn"> </div>`, the `<div>` element is the containing box around the `<img>` element.

Content   Generically, any information that is prepared for display on the Web. In the case of HTML or XML, this is the text and any child elements between the opening and closing tags of an element. Content is usually meant to be presented to the user in some way.

Declaration   The part of the CSS rule that specifies one or more styles to be applied. A declaration consists of pairs of property names and property values and is enclosed within `{ curly braces }`.

Deprecated Markup   HTML tags that have been removed from the official language specification. Older versions may have included these obsolete items, but their functions have been replaced by newer elements or by CSS properties.

Display Box   A box, either visible or not, corresponding to an element in the markup. Boxes can be either inline or block and can contain text content or other boxes. Everything in CSS is conceptualized and displayed as a box according to the CSS box model.

Document Object Model (DOM)   A standard way of using programming languages to access parts of a Web page. JavaScript can be used to manipulate the DOM and create dynamic HTML applications.

Dynamic HTML (DHTML)   The combination of HTML, CSS, and JavaScript to create presentations that change appearance as the user interacts with the content.

ECMAScript   The standardized version of JavaScript, a scripting language available in most browsers.

Element   The basic component of a markup language such as HTML or XML. An element contains content, which can be text or child elements, between opening and closing tags, and elements can have attributes with values set in the opening tag. Elements are represented as display boxes in CSS browsers.

Embedded Style Sheet   A style sheet that is contained within a Web page. An embedded style sheet is enclosed within a `<style>` element in the `<head>` section of the HTML.

Extensible Hypertext Markup Language (XHTML)   The HTML language rewritten to conform to the rules of XML. Like HTML, XHTML 1.0 is available in three versions: Strict, Transitional, and Frameset.

Extensible Markup Language (XML)   A meta-language for creating other markup languages. XML is a set of rules for how languages or documents are constructed, and those rules promote interoperability between programs by defining a common format for information.

Extensible Stylesheet Language (XSL)   An XML-based style language. XSL is composed of XSL Transformations (XSLT), a language for describing transformations between and within XML languages, and XSL Formatting Objects (XSL-FO), a language for rich page formatting.

Font   A group of typefaces that share the same general appearance. CSS allows you to select a specific font family and then choose typefaces by specifying desired qualities, such as size, weight, and type.

Frameset HTML   The version of HTML 4.01 that allows sets of frames to be declared. CSS can be used with Frameset HTML to set the appearance of frames.

Generated Content   Text or other content inserted by style rules. Generated content does not appear in the HTML markup but is added when the style sheet is applied.

Generic Font Families   The set of five font families that are browser defined and can be used as default values. The CSS generic font families are serif, sans-serif, cursive, fantasy, and monospace.

Hexadecimal   A base-16 counting system using the digits 0 through 9 and A to F. Hexadecimal notation is used to write RGB color values in HTML and CSS.

Hypertext Markup Language (HTML)   A markup language for creating Web pages. The current version of HTML is 4.01 and comes in three "flavors," Strict HTML, Transitional HTML, and Frameset HTML. CSS can be used with all flavors of HTML to set the appearance of the page.

id Selector   A selector based on the HTML id attribute. An id selector uniquely identifies one specific element because all id values must be unique within a Web page.

Importing   The process of loading style rules from an outside file. The @import rule in CSS allows for style sheets to be imported.

Inheritance   The method by which elements take on the property values of their containing boxes. Properties in CSS are of two types: those that are inherited and those that are not. The inherit property value can be used with most CSS properties to force a value to be inherited from the containing box.

Inline Element   A markup element that appears within the flow of text across the page, rather than within a separate block box as block elements do. One example of an inline element is the HTML <img> tag.

Inline Style Rule   A CSS rule set by using the HTML style attribute on any element. The inline style rule has only a declaration section; the selector is the element with the style attribute.

Internationalization (I18N)   The process of making Web content available to a broad audience of people who speak a variety of languages. CSS has support for different language types and other features that enhance internationalization. The abbreviation I18N means the letter "i," "eighteen other letters," and the letter "n."

Interoperability   The capability of different technologies to work together seamlessly. Interoperability is the primary goal of the World Wide Web Consortium and is possible only when all parties involved agree to implement the same standards.

JavaScript   A scripting language found in most Web browsers. JavaScript allows manipulation of the DOM and styling properties to create dynamic HTML. The standardized version of JavaScript is known as ECMAScript.

Layout   The way that information is spatially presented on a two-dimensional canvas, either onscreen or in printed material. CSS positioning properties allow for pages to be laid out without resorting to HTML <table> elements.

Linked Style Sheet   A file that contains style rules to be applied to a Web page. The style sheet is external to the HTML file and is linked via the <link> tag in the <head>

section of the page. A linked style sheet can be used by many Web pages, and any given page can link to multiple style sheets.

List   A markup element designed to be displayed as a series of list elements, possibly with markers or counters. CSS allows you to change the appearance of HTML lists with the list item properties.

Markup   Content consisting of normal text with tags added to define the meaning or presentation of the text. HTML and XML are the foremost examples of markup languages.

Measurement   A property value that designates a linear distance or size. Measurements in CSS can be expressed in pixels, points, picas, ems, exes, inches, centimeters, or millimeters.

Media Types   The broad categories of devices that may display a document styled with CSS. Different media categories have different characteristics, based on the output and input capabilities of the device. The most common media categories are screen, print, and aural.

MIME Type   A two-part code identifying the format of a specific file. The MIME type for a CSS file is `text/css`; for an HTML file, `text/html`; and for a JPEG file, `image/jpeg`.

Positioning (CSS-P)   A subset of CSS properties that allows display boxes to be specifically placed in the layout of a page.

Pseudo-class Selector   A type of selector that is based on the state of the Web page but that functions as a class selector.

Pseudo-element Selector   A type of selector that identifies a virtual subelement, one that is not actually present in the markup but can be used to set style rules.

Presentation   The appearance of content, independent of the actual information contained within that content. For example, the content of this glossary is the set of term and definition pairs; the presentation is the formatted, printed representation you hold in your hands, which we call a "book." CSS allows for the separation of presentation from content, increasing the accessibility of Web designs.

Property   One of the qualities that can be applied to style an element using CSS. Properties have property names and property values; the values are set in the declaration portion of a CSS rule.

Recommendation   The official term for a W3C specification. The Cascading Style Sheets Level 1 recommendation created the CSS language; CSS Level 2 is the current

C

recommendation. A W3C recommendation is a specification that has been approved by the Consortium members and is considered a standard of the Web.

RGB Red-Green-Blue; a designation for colors as used on the Web. Three numbers constitute an RGB triple. The first refers to the amount of red, the second to the amount of green, and the third to the amount of blue. Zero is the lowest value, and 255 (FF in hexadecimal) is the highest. In RGB notation, `#FFFFFF` is white, and `#000000` is black.

Rule A complete styling instruction in CSS, consisting of one or more selectors to identify the elements to which the rule applies and of one or more declarations to set property values.

Selector The portion of the CSS rule that identifies markup elements that receive the styling described by the rule's declarations. The selector comes before the curly braces that surround the declaration.

Strict HTML The version of HTML 4.01 that relies upon Cascading Style Sheets for presentational information. Strict HTML disallows elements and attributes that are intended only for presentation.

Structure The internal order and logic of a file's content, as expressed through the markup. For example, if a document is divided into three sections with `<div>`, and each has an `<h2>` tag at the start of each section, that defines a very clear structure within the file. The CSS styles should be written to enhance and to supplement the structure in order to best convey the meaning of the content.

Style The qualities of display that collectively make up presentation. CSS is a style language, which means it is used to define how software should display Web content.

Style Sheet A collection of CSS rules. A style sheet can be external and can be linked via the HTML `<link>` tag or embedded within an HTML file inside a `<style>` element.

Style Sheet Editor A program specifically created for the creation of style sheets. Style sheet editors provide a visual interface for editing style rules and for tracking selectors.

Tables HTML markup elements that display information as cells arranged in rows and columns. Tables are used for two purposes: displaying columns of data or laying out a Web page. CSS rules can be used to enhance the appearance of tables or to replace layout tables entirely.

Tag In a markup language such as HTML or XML, the text that identifies the beginning and end of an element, as well as the attributes set on that element. A tag is distinguished from other text by <angle braces>, and closing tags have a slash before the element name.

Text Editor   A program that provides simple text editing capabilities. As HTML and CSS files are plain text, a text editor can be used for no-frills creation and maintenance of Web pages and style sheets.

Transitional HTML   The variety of HTML 4.01 that allows presentation information to be included in HTML attributes and elements. Cascading Style Sheets can be applied to Transitional HTML pages, and if the CSS properties are not understood, the HTML presentation is available as a backup.

Type Selector   A selector that chooses all elements of a given type; for example, all <h1> elements or all <p> elements. Type selectors are very common in CSS and are often combined with other kinds of selectors.

User Agent   Any software that retrieves a Web document and does something with the information therein. The most common example of a user agent is the humble Web browser, but indexing spiders, robots, intelligent agents, and proxies also fall into this category.

User-defined Style Sheet   A style sheet that resides on the user's hard drive and defines the user's preferences for viewing Web content. A user-defined style sheet can override the author's styles, presenting the content in the method that is most accessible to the end user.

User Interface CSS   The set of properties that interact with the user's environment. CSS allows access to system colors and fonts, and also provides the capability to change the cursor type.

Web Content Accessibility Guidelines (WCAG)   A set of recommendations from the W3C for making Web pages more accessible. Strategies for using Cascading Style Sheets to improve accessibility are detailed in the WCAG Techniques for CSS.

Whitespace   Characters that are considered equal to a space character by a Web browser; this includes actual spaces, carriage returns, linefeeds, and tabs.

World Wide Web Consortium (W3C)   The international industry consortium that creates Web specifications that promote interoperability. CSS, HTML, XML, and many more languages have been developed by the W3C and issued as W3C Recommendations. The W3C's Web site is http://www.w3.org/.

INDEX